McGRAW-HILL PUBLICATIONS IN INDUSTRIAL EDUCATION

CHRIS H. GRONEMAN, Consulting Editor

BOOKS IN SERIES

i

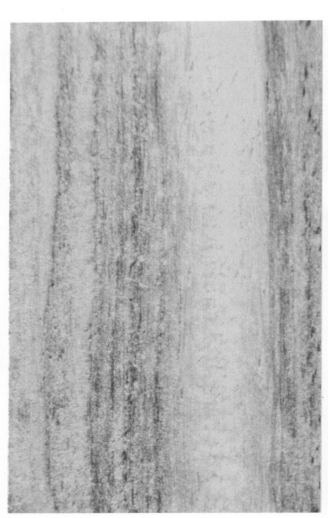

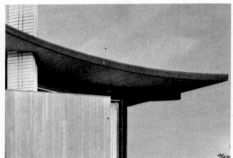

FOURTH EDITION

GENERAL WOODWORKING

CHRIS H. GRONEMAN

McGRAW-HILL BOOK COMPANY

NEW YORK ST. LOUIS SAN FRANCISCO DALLAS
DUSSELDORF LONDON MEXICO PANAMA SYDNEY TORONTO

GENERAL WOODWORKING

ISBN 07-024952-0

ABOUT THE AUTHOR

Chris H. Groneman has a strong, basic background in the practical application of woodworking as it relates both to industry and education. His career includes practical work in the building construction industry, and educational experiences as an industrial arts teacher and coach in junior and senior high schools, junior college, teacher's colleges, and state universities. At present he is Professor of Industrial Arts and Technology at the Fresno California State College. Prior to this he served as Coordinator of Industrial Arts Education at the University of Hawaii. For many years he was Head of the Department of Industrial Education, and Coordinator for the Council on Teacher Education at Texas A&M University.

He is Consulting Editor for the McGraw-Hill Publications in Industrial Education. His own GENERAL WOODWORKING and TECHNICAL WOODWORKING are two of the texts in this popular series. He has also done research for, and contributed to, Encyclopaedia Americanna, and the Eothen Films, Ltd., Boreham Wood, Hertfordshire, England.

His education includes the B.S. and M.S. degrees from Kansas State College, Pittsburg, Kansas, and the Doctorate degree from Pennsylvania State University. He was honored by his Alma Mater with the Meritorious Achievement Citation, the highest recognition which Kansas State College can confer upon one of its graduates.

As a craftsman of high caliber, he won international acclaim for the design and construction of a myrtlewood credenza in an Albert Constantine-sponsored competition. In tribute to his leadership, Dr. Groneman was cited as Man of the Year by *The Ship* at the American Industrial Arts Association annual convention in Toronto, Canada.

PREFACE

This is the fourth edition of GENERAL WOODWORKING, a text that has proved to be one of the most popular and widely-used for the first year course in woodworking. The text is the first to present an innovative experimental research approach, and to provide an opportunity for experimentation in materials relating to the woods industries. An entire new section, consisting of fourteen new units in experimental research, opens challenging vistas for individual activity.

In response to educational trends and consumer inquiry, for the first time a comprehensive Study Guide for students is available as a companion educational instructional aid to supplement and implement GENERAL WOODWORKING 4/e. The study guide makes provision for over 1,500 possible learning responses.

This profusely-illustrated edition helps the student and the teacher to understand and appreciate the vast manufacturing complex of woodworking. It offers many processes involving materials, tools, machines, and manufacturing procedures of fabrication. There are over 1,000 figures, complete with second color, emphasizing procedural direction.

Section One is an introduction into the fascinating field of wood technology, giving information on basic design, reading a working drawing, figuring broad feet, problem solving through orderly planning of procedures, and stressing observation of necessary safety rules. These are some of the fundamentals the student needs before starting activities relating to the never-ending supply of wood products.

Section Two has added many types of new tools and processes. Newer methods of the fabrication of plywood, and the application of plastic laminates are explained in detail.

Section Three gives attention to a much wider use of portable electric power tools for the school and home workshop. The student is given specific instruction toward taking advantage of the full potential of the most modern approach for individual use of the portable type electric hand tools.

Section Four takes up the more widely-used power machines and their processes. The rotary jointer-surfacer, a new machine recently introduced to the industrial and school market, is included to acquaint the student with the latest in modern machine applications.

Section Five presents accepted methods of applying a variety of finishes. These include the popular new wipe-on and bleached effects, applied with either brush or spray gun. Methods of removing a finish efficiently are discussed, not only for the benefit of the student, but for the home craftsman as well.

Section Six contains simple upholstery procedures for slip and spring seats. New illustrations are provided which assist the novice to understand this normally intricate phase of the manufacturing industry.

Section Seven gives technological information and perspective concerning several of the popular wood products, woods industries, automation, numerical control, manufacture and use of hardboard and particleboard, and plastic laminates, as well as an informative and well-planned unit on careers in forest industries.

Section Eight contains new units dealing with research and experimentation. The student is given the opportunity and privilege of personal investigation in the exciting realm of individual participation and discovery.

Section Nine offers suggestions for numerous activities and projects in wood. These vary from the simplest, requiring only a few basic hand-tool skills, to the more complex which call for a high degree of skill in machine-tool operation equating the performances of industrial application. An illustration of the completed project and a working drawing, complete with dimensions, are provided for most projects and activities.

CHRIS H. GRONEMAN

CONTENTS

CONTENTS

ACKNOWLEDGMENTS

Acknowledgment is sincerely given to the following agencies, companies, and individuals who provided helpful suggestions, data, photographs, illustrations, and other assistance in the preparation of this revision: Adjustable Clamp Company; American Forest Products Industries; American Hardboard Association; American Institute of Timber Construction; American Plywood Association; American Wood Working Company; *Archaeology and Society*, J. G. D. Clark; Atkins Saw Company; Baker Furniture Company; Binks Manufacturing Company; The Black & Decker Manufacturing Company; Brodhead-Garrett Company; Buck Brothers, Incorporated; Harry Burton; California Redwood Association; J. I. Case Company; Caterpillar Tractor Company; Clark Equipment Company; The Cleveland Twist Drill Company; Colonial Williamsburg; Conn-Valley Manufacturing Company; Culname-Fattori Associates, Limited; Dowl-it Company; Drexel Furniture Company; Fastener Corporation; Fine Hardwoods Association; Ford Motor Company-Aeronutronic Division-Philco Corporation; Formica Corporation; Georgia-Pacific Corporation; Greenlee Brothers & Company; Greenlee Tool Company; Hamilton Manufacturing Company; Henry L. Hanson Company; Homelite Company; Hyer Hardware Manufacturing Company; *Industrial Woodworking* Magazine; Interiors Import Company, Incorporated; Joerns Brothers Furniture Company; Kittinger Company, Incorporated; R. G. LeTourneau, Incorporated; Long Bell Lumber Company; Magna American Corporation; Mahogany Association, Incorporated; Masonite Corporation; Mattison Machine Works; The Metropolitan Museum of Art, Rogers Fund; Millers Falls Company; Mount Airy Furniture Company; National Lumber Manufacturers Association; National Particleboard Association; National Safety Council; National Starch and Chemical Company; Nicholson File Company; Norton Manufacturing Company; Paxton Lumber Company; Permali, Incorporated; H. K. Porter Company, Incorporated, Disston Division; Rockwell Manufacturing Company, Power Tool Division; Scholtz Homes, Incorporated; Simonds Saw and Steel Company; Southern Pine Association; Stanley Tool Company; Systi-Matic Company; Temple Industries; *The Timberman* Magazine, Timber Structures, Incorporated; TowMotor Corporation; U.S. Forest Service; United States Plywood Corporation; U.S. Forest Products Laboratory; Vega Enterprises, Incorporated; Watco-Dennis Company; Western Wood Products Association; Westinghouse Electric Corporation, Micarta Division; Wetzler Clamp

Company; Weyerhaeuser Company; Wilson Sporting Goods Company; Wilton Tool Manufacturing Company; Wisconsin Knife Works, Incorporated; Wiss, J. & Sons, Company; and *Woodworking Digest* Magazine.

Special mention is accorded Mrs. Betty Fisk Baily, Drexel Furniture Company; J. G. D. Clark, *Archaeology and Society* Magazine; J. C. Glidewell, photographer, Bryan, Texas; Dr. L. V. Hawkins, collector of antique tools, Texas A&M University; Professor Jay Helsel, Unit 3 Design, and Section Nine, Drawings for Suggested Projects, California Pennsylvania State College; Frank Krug, student experiment assistant, Sacramento, California; Dr. Robert Magowan, Section Eight, Memphis Tennessee State University; Mr. Bluford W. Muir, photographer, U.S. Forest Service; Dr. Darrell Smith, line drawings, California Pennsylvania State College; and Dr. Calvin Zabcik, experimental assistance, Arkansas A&M College. The following are sincerely acknowledged for photographs of tools, processes, and machines: Robert Campbell, Stanley Company; Dan Irvin, Rockwell Manufacturing Company-Power Tool Division; Carlton F. Moe, Jr., The Black & Decker Company; and F. J. Roberts, Millers Falls Company. A most special mention is to may wife, Virginia, for her constant inspiration and assistance.

CHRIS H. GRONEMAN

FOREWORD

It is now over twenty years since the first volumes of the McGraw-Hill Publications in Industrial Education were planned, written, and published. Planned or published books in the series cover all industrial arts areas, and wide acceptance of the published volumes demonstrates their functional and practical value for classroom, laboratory, and shop use.

Before beginning the last edition of GENERAL WOODWORKING, the author talked with numerous teachers using the previous editions in their classes, asking for recommendations for changes, additions, and modifications they felt should be made in the new edition. Profiting by their suggestions, and adding information on new materials and equipment in the field, the author has rewritten most of the book.

This edition contains many suggestions by users, including several new units. These are primarily concerned with the new wood products which have resulted from technological advances. A new design unit has also been added.

Color is used throughout this edition in both illustrations and text as a teaching aid. All safety rules are emphasized by the use of color.

Today in the United States more students are enrolled in woodworking than in any other materials area. Although industrial arts woodworking is a form of nonvocational education, it may lead the student into a number of different career interests and opportunities; and since woodworking is a popular homecraft activity, it may provide the student with gratifying avocational benefits during his adult life.

GENERAL WOODWORKING helps the teacher to achieve the objectives of a well-planned industrial arts program. It is planned and written as a guide for one or more years of industrial arts woodworking and for the home craftsman. The book is organized so that the teacher may readily select those units that are the most appropriate to the student's rate of learning and that best fit into the course. Where practicable, the illustrations show the procedures as the student would view them over the shoulder of the instructor.

In GENERAL WOODWORKING teachers and students discover interesting topics not often included in similar books, namely, machine tools, upholstery, plywood construction, historical development, design trends in furniture, and related topics in wood technology. The text provides reference material on trees, forest products, automation and industrial production stories, and careers in the wood and wood-products industries.

THE PUBLISHERS

unit

1

Introduction to woodworking

During this space age when men orbit the earth and walk on the moon and probe even further, we might wonder whether a traditional material such as wood can still be important (Fig. 1–1). But new techniques of processing and use, imaginative design, and inherently desirable characteristics combine to make it one of the best raw materials. The consumption of wood is greater today than ever before.

About half the land area of the earth was once covered by forests (Figs. 1–2 and 1–3). Today only about one-third of the land surface is forested, but there is a possibility that planning and forest conservation will make a never-ending supply of wood available.

Use of wood is traditional, but the variety of uses of lumber in modern times would amaze our Colonial forefathers. As an illustration, the scientific development, processing, and improvement of plywood (Figs. 1–4 and 1–5) indicates the intensive research conducted today. Another valuable process is the lamination of timbers (Figs. 1–6 through 1–8), which resulted from recently developed glues and adhesives.

Since lumber is the oldest manufacturing industry, the use of wood has developed into a strong material technology. The photographs in this unit give evidence of the vision of scientists (Fig. 1–9), engineers, architects,

Fig. 1–1. Because of its low-weight strength and stiffness, Sitka spruce plywood was selected for the nose fairing of a Polaris missile. *(U. S. Forest Products Laboratory.)*

Fig. 1–3. These Douglas firs were old trees when Europeans first settled the forest areas of the Northwest. Today they are ready for market to make way for new forests that will spring up when these trees are removed. *(American Forest Products Industries.)*

Fig. 1–2. Forests such as these now cover approximately one-third of the land surface of the earth. This spectacular view shows Mt. Hood and the forest surrounding it in Oregon, the leading lumber-producing state in the United States. *(U. S. Forest Service.)*

Fig. 1–4. Plywood can be formed into many shapes. *(American Forest Products Industries.)*

Fig. 1–5. Brazilian rosewood, one of the most sumptuous woods in the world, is used lavishly in the plywood panels which line the walls and conceal the built-in closet areas in this executive office. *(United States Plywood Corporation.)*

and contractors. Through the application of new techniques of frabrication and of artistry in design, wood is used in all its forms (Fig. 1–10).

The increasing demand for wood products will probably quicken the current trend of better and more intensive utilization of what was formerly considered unavoidable waste in the forests and at processing plants. Your experiences with this warm, interesting, and versatile material will give you an insight into the vast scientific potential of industrial and consumer uses.

Industrial arts woodworking prepares you in four ways for your future. *First*, it provides an opportunity for study of the vast field of lumber and wood products as related to manufacturing industries. *Second*, in the event you plan to attend college or university, industrial arts gives you an excellent introduction into the study of industry and how technology affects our economy. *Third*, if you decide to prepare yourself for

a vocation or a trade, industrial arts enables you to acquire many practical skills dealing with many materials. You also have the opportunity to study vocational occupations. In doing so, you may make a wise choice of trade or vocational studies in the remainder of your high school career, or in a technical school immediately after high school graduation. *Fourth*, the information and the training you acquire will provide you some saleable skills.

Industrial woodworking laboratory activity must have organized and clear-cut objectives. The following suggestions should help you develop a clear concept of wood technology.

1. Acquaint yourself with the occupational and professional opportunities in careers relating to lumber, research, and wood-products manufacturing.

Fig. 1–6. Engineering and technology open new vistas as wood takes previously undreamed-of shapes and forms. Arches, beams, and trusses can support heavy roof loads in complete safety without a single supporting post. *(Weyerhaeuser Company.)*

Fig. 1–7. This imaginative, dynamic, cliff-hanging house has won many awards for the wood products industries because of the ingenuity in the use of laminated supporting structures, and the interesting use of wood throughout the house. *(American Plywood Association.)*

Fig. 1–9. Scientific investigation of the chemical composition of wood is responsible for many new industrial products. *(Western Wood Products Association.)*

Fig. 1–8. The interior of this home is made most interesting because of the laminated ceiling and roof supports, and the beautiful wood ceiling and wall treatment. *(Weyerhaeuser Company.)*

2. Develop an avocational interest in woodworking.

3. Learn to appreciate the high standards of workmanship in superior products made of wood or wood-oriented materials.

4. Practice the correct and efficient way to handle tools and machines in woodworking.

5. Cultivate a sense of pride in your ability to do useful things well. The skills developed can lead to increased interest in additional woodworking activities.

6. Develop a creative and scientific attitude through involvement in technical experimentation with wood and wood products.

7. Develop an analytical ability through planning and observance of orderly procedure for any activity, project, or experiment undertaken.

8. Study and understand working drawings so that you can make both useful and well designed projects.

9. Understand and appreciate lumber and wood products as one of the major manufacturing technologies.

10. Always use safe working practices with tools, machines, and materials, after learning what these practices are.

11. Take an active interest in individual technology and the problems relating to the production of wood products.

12. Appreciate the importance of lumber and wood products in national as well as world economy.

13. Understand the importance of conservation of our vast timber resources.

Fig. 1–10. The appealing design of this commercial building uses laminated structures to solve a technical engineering problem. *(Southern Pine Association.)*

unit

2

Understanding a working drawing

Craftsmen, engineers, architects, and designers must know how to read and understand a working drawing (Fig. 2–1). This kind of drawing uses a language of its own. It gives the dimensions, or sizes, of the parts of a project, and shows how the project is to be put together. When you study a working drawing or a sketch, you will follow exactly the same steps that a craftsman and an engineer do. They study a working drawing, as you will, before attempting to build any part of a project.

In industry, special classes are often held for workers to teach them how to read blueprints and/or make working drawings (Fig. 2–2). Blueprints are duplicates, or copies, of tracings or original drawings. They are made by chemical action which gives them their color and their name. Industrial workers therefore often read white lines on a blue background. You will read black lines on a white background in most of your work. You will learn to read many types of lines on working drawings. You will also need to know how to explain the views shown.

Fig. 2-1. Details and dimensions of the original piece are carefully measured and checked for industrial production. *(Baker Furniture Company.)*

LINE SYMBOLS

The line symbols in Fig. 2–3 and the description of each will help you to read drawings. Apply what you learn from Fig. 2–3 in your study of a drawing (Fig. 2–4). The photograph in Fig. 2–5 shows the finished project. It will help you understand the views shown in Fig. 2–4.

Border lines are the heaviest of all. They are used only for making a neat border around a drawing.

Object lines are fairly heavy and very distinct. They show the visible portion of an object. They are very important to the craftsman.

Hidden, or *invisible*, *lines* are short dashes which make up a broken line. They show that part of an object which needs to be shown but which is not visible in the particular view drawn.

Extension lines are thin lines. They extend from the edges of a view so that dimension lines may be placed between them. These lines should never connect with solid or object lines.

Center lines are light long and short dashes. They indicate, or mark, the center of any symmetrical figure or object. Every major arc (part of a circle) or circle should have intersecting, or crossing, center lines.

Dimension lines are light lines which include measurements. All dimensions are indicated by this type of line. When you read a working drawing, you should assume that the dimension is the distance between the point of the arrow on one end of the line to the point of the arrow on the other end.

A working drawing usually shows the object in a size smaller than it will really be made. The drawing has to be smaller in order to get it on one sheet of drawing paper. To make the drawing smaller, a draftsman draws the object *to scale*. He makes a scale, or reduced, drawing of the object. This means that he draws the lines only a fraction of their actual length. For example, the lines may be ½, ¼, or ⅛ as long; but the draftsman puts the dimensions of the actual object on them. A working drawing reduced to ¼ scale means that ¼ inch on the drawings equals 1 inch of actual size. A line 2 inches long on this drawing equals 8 inches of real size ($4 \times 2 = 8$). It is labeled with an "8." All dimensions given on a scale drawing are those of the actual size of the completed object.

VIEWS ON A WORKING DRAWING

The working drawing in Fig. 2–4 has two views, front and top. Two views are shown

Fig. 2–2. Architects and structural engineers combine talents and resources to develop drawings and specifications for the use of wood in construction. *(American Institute of Timber Construction.)*

in order to include all the measurements and details of construction. Often only two views (front and top, or front and one end) are needed to give complete measurements and construction details.

Fig. 2–3. Line symbols for drafting.

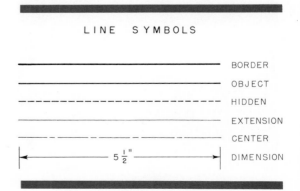

LINE SYMBOLS

BORDER
OBJECT
HIDDEN
EXTENSION
CENTER
5 ½" DIMENSION

7

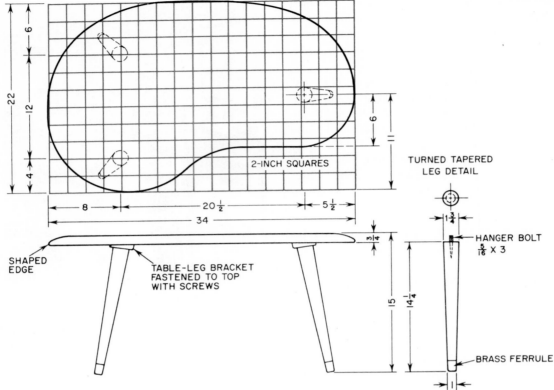

22
12
6
4
8
20½
5½
34

2-INCH SQUARES

6
11

TURNED TAPERED
LEG DETAIL

1¾

HANGER BOLT
5/16 X 3

¾

15
14¼

SHAPED
EDGE

TABLE-LEG BRACKET
FASTENED TO TOP
WITH SCREWS

BRASS FERRULE

1

Fig. 2–4. Working drawing for novelty coffee table.

Fig. 2–5. Coffee table.

It is seldom necessary to show more than three views, such as front, top, and one end. Detailed drawings of construction sometimes require as many as six views: front, top, rear, underside, right end, and left end. Working drawings like the one shown in Fig. 2–4 are called multiview, or orthographic, drawings.

A working drawing is frequently shown as a pictorial sketch with the dimensions added. This kind of drawing is very easy to read and understand because it looks like the actual object.

The method of figuring the amount of lumber used to make a project is discussed and illustrated in Unit 4.

1. What are the overall length, height, and width of the coffee table?
2. What is the thickness of the top?
3. How long is the top?
4. What does the widest part of the top measure?
5. How large is each square in the graph for the top?
6. How many legs are there?
7. How long are the legs?
8. How can you tell whether the legs are round or square?
9. How are the legs fastened to the top?
10. How is the table-leg bracket fastened to the top?
11. Give the size and name of the bolt which fastens the leg to the bracket.
12. What is the diameter of the leg at the top? At the foot?
13. What is fastened to the foot of each leg?

unit

3

Designing in wood

Before the Industrial Revolution, the average person had to make most of the things he needed. Inventive minds and skilled hands joined to create furniture, clothes, homes, and other products necessary to daily living. Ideas, tools, materials, and craftsmanship were the basic ingredients in the design and construction of each of the products and objects. Although intervening years have taken design and manufacturing processes out of the home, design procedure and elements have remained essentially the same.

WHAT IS DESIGN?

Design is creative planning used to solve a problem. The key words of this definition are *creative*, *planning*, and *problem*. These three words are discussed in the following paragraphs to help develop a better understanding of the word "design."

Creative: A person who is creative uses his intelligence, skills, and past experiences to help solve a problem. A good designer will not try to create or solve a design problem by trying to use skills and concepts he has not yet mastered. If he has had no experience with woodworking machines, it would not be practical for him to try to design a complex piece of furniture or cabinetwork involving intricate machine operations. Figures 3–1 and 3–2 are examples of beginning design problems that involve simple woodworking activities.

Planning requires evaluation of the problem to organize thoughts and procedures. To

Fig. 3–1. Freeform shapes usually require simple hand tools for construction.

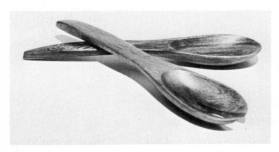

Fig. 3–2. Salad fork and spoon. The jig saw and some hand tools are required for their construction.

solve a design problem in the best possible way, you must first study (analyze) each part, searching for a proper approach to the solution.

The most efficient approach to a design problem is to study it carefully with an inquiring mind. You must use imagination in search of new uses for materials and tools. Since no two people are alike or think alike, no two people will design in the same manner. Figure 3–3 shows two solutions to the same design problem. Although it was the same assignment in each case, there is a great deal of difference between the two end products in function and appearance.

The pair of bookends and the book rack are shown holding the same number of books (Fig. 3–4). However, the bookends are more pleasing in appearance and do a better job of holding books in an upright position.

Figure 3–5 shows another example of two solutions to the same design problem. Here the results are very similar in appearance.

Problems in design begin with a need. The need for man to shelter himself from the weather led to design of homes. His need to clothe himself ultimately led to the design

Fig. 3–3. Two solutions to the same design problem.

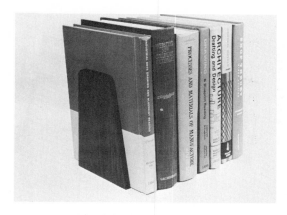

Fig. 3–4. The bookends are more functional and more aesthetically pleasing than the book rack.

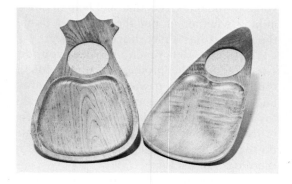

Fig. 3–5. Both serving trays in this design problem are functional and aesthetically pleasing.

of today's styles. To travel great distances, he designed the airplane. The problems with which the designer works invariably stem from human needs of one kind or another.

MAJOR DESIGN ELEMENTS

Three major elements that guide the design process are the function, the material/technical aspect, and the appearance.

The *function* of the finished product or object must be considered carefully. The product must work properly; it must efficiently fulfill the need for which it was designed. It must solve the original problem. If it does not function properly, it is of no value, and hence is poorly designed.

The *material/technical* aspect includes selection of materials as an essential part of good design. Understanding the properties of various kinds of wood and other materials is important. It would be impractical to select white pine to make a baseball bat, or walnut for the frame of a chair that is to be completely upholstered. Cost, as well as the strength of the material, must be considered in each design experience.

It is necessary sometimes to use a variety of materials to solve a problem in design. Figures 3–6 and 3–7 are examples. Stainless steel and ceramic materials were used to make these projects more functional.

Material/technical considerations require development of safe and skillful use of tools before designing a product to be made with them. If you have had experience only in the understanding and use of hand tools, it is difficult to design properly a product requiring the use of complicated woodworking machinery.

If you are to use hand tools to construct the product designed, you should not plan a complex piece of furniture involving a large amount of lumber. Design a product around skills and understandings already acquired. Plan ahead for those closely related skills

11

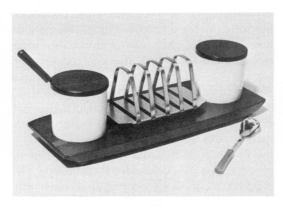

Fig 3–6. Wood, metal, and ceramic are combined in the toast and jam server.

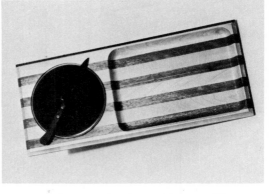

Fig. 3–7. Two kinds of wood are used in combination with the ceramic plate to make the cutting board.

you hope to learn. This means that new processes and concepts may be introduced, provided you have a basic understanding of what is involved in those operations.

The most creative and practical design idea will add little to a product that is crudely constructed. If joints are loose, surfaces not sanded properly, and the drawers not fitted properly, you have not constructed a high-quality product. Sharp tools, skilled hands, and a creative mind go far in complementing a good idea.

Appearance is the third element of a well designed product. The term generally used to describe the appearance, or beauty, of an object or product, is "aesthetics." If the aesthetic qualities of a particular product are valid, it is pleasing to the eye and has an attractive appearance.

A well designed product requires more than a good finish and fancy surface decorations. The form (shape), relationship of lines, color, balance, and other factors all are important considerations in the design process.

Thus, one realizes that the three elements of design, the *function*, the *material/technical* aspect, and the *appearance*, are equally important. If one element is weak, the design

of the completed product will be weak. Figure 3–8 shows examples of well designed pieces of work.

RECOGNIZING GOOD DESIGN

Recognizing the factors that constitute good design helps create a well designed product. When you go to a store to buy furniture, you look for certain characteristics. One of the first is *pleasing appearance*. Does the piece of furniture have a graceful or pleasing shape? Is the color suitable? Will it fit well with other furniture in the room? These are some of the questions that will help in determining whether or not the customer thinks the product has a pleasing appearance.

You consider *function* when you decide whether the product or object fulfills the role for which it was originally planned and designed. If the design problem calls for a bookcase to hold fifty books, and there is room for only thirty, the product will not do the job for which it was intended, and is therefore not useful.

High-quality craftsmanship is essential to good design. No one wants to buy a piece of poorly constructed furniture. Tight joints, smooth finish, and precise cutting and fitting

Fig. 3–8. Examples of well designed products.

of parts are a few of the important considerations in selecting a well designed and well constructed product.

Practical use of materials is another consideration. If a piece of furniture is to be painted, it should not be made from expensive cabinet-quality lumber such as walnut or mahogany. If a piece of furniture is to have a natural finish, it should not be made from yellow pine, poplar, or other kinds of unattractive wood.

EXAMPLES OF GOOD AND POOR DESIGN

Study Fig. 3–9 before going on to the design process steps. The illustrations in this figure show some examples of good and poor design. Study each one carefully, and try to determine what makes the design either a good or a poor one.

THE DESIGN PROCESS

The complete design process involves eight steps:

1. Select and define the problem.

2. Limit the problem in size and complexity.

3. List or sketch several possible solutions.

4. Select the best solution to your design problem.

5. Make refinements in the design. Construct a model, if necessary.

6. Prepare working drawings, materials list (bill of materials), procedure sheet, and a finishing schedule.

7. Select materials and construct the product.

8. Evaluate the final solution, based on the original problem.

Each of these steps should be completed for every design problem. The following paragraphs describe how each step is accomplished. The example given after the description of each step provides an insight into the designing process.

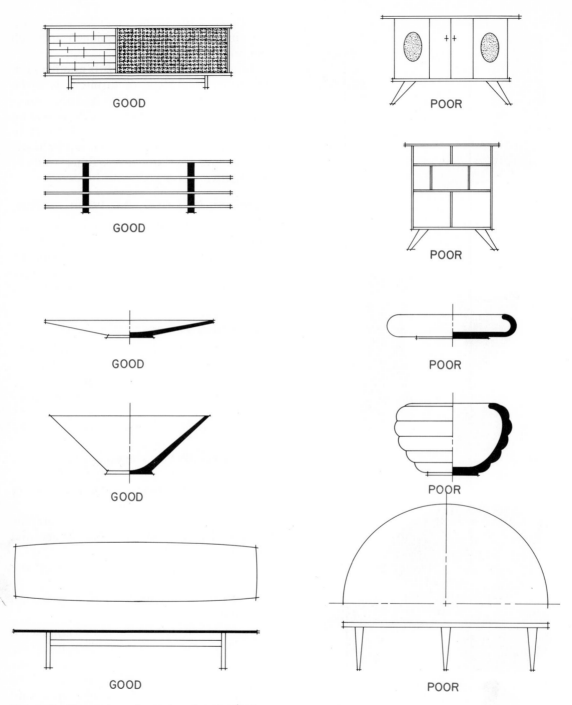

GOOD

POOR

GOOD

POOR

GOOD

POOR

GOOD

POOR

GOOD

POOR

Fig. 3–9. Examples of good and poor design.

14

Select and define the problem. Select a design problem based on a specific need; or you may want to accept one assigned to you. In either case, a clear definition, or description, of the problem should be understood before going to step 2.

Example: Design a desk caddy to fit the following specifications:

1. It must hold 5″ × 8″ note paper.
2. There must be an integral letter holder.
3. There should be a pen holder attached.
4. It should be designed to hold several pencils.
5. It should not scratch the desk top.

Limit the problem in size and complexity. These considerations are based on the amount of time available to construct the object, the amount of material required, and the industrial-laboratory experiences you have had in working with tools and materials. Large objects are difficult to complete in the small amount of time you may have. Therefore, adapt ideas to the guidelines formulated in this unit.

Example:

1. The desk caddy must not involve more than two board feet of lumber.
2. It should not be larger than 4″ × 10″ × 12″ in overall dimensions.
3. Butt, lap, or rabbet joints should be used.
4. Construction should involve hand tools, or simple woodworking machines.

List or sketch several possible solutions. This phase of the design process is sometimes called "brainstorming." At this point you may want to solicit ideas and list several possible solutions in very general terms before you begin to sketch. Freehand sketching is a very valuable part of this phase of the design process. Several pictorial sketches will help visualize your ideas. Figure 3–10 shows some sketches of possible solutions that developed from a brainstorming session for the desk caddy.

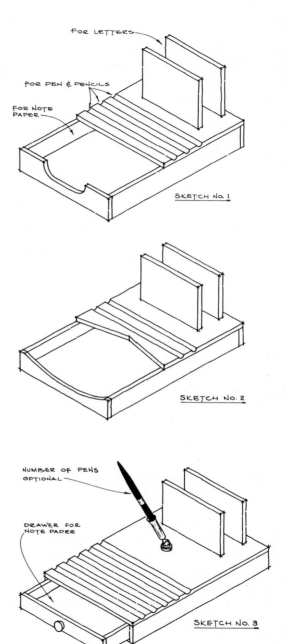

Fig. 3–10. Preliminary sketches of the desk caddy.

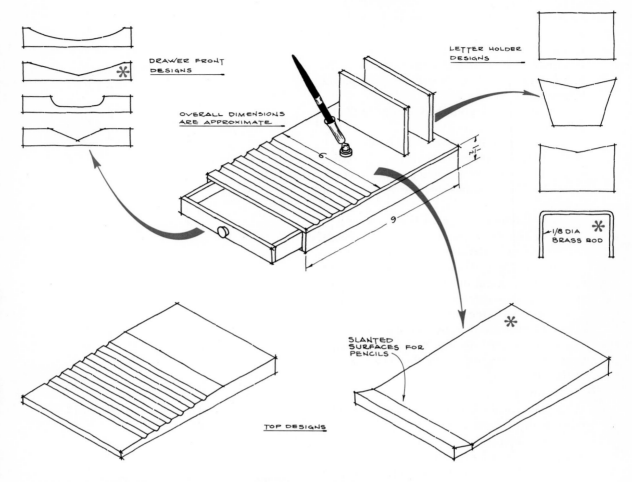

Fig. 3–11. Make refinements while still in the sketching stage of design.

Select the best solution to your design problem. The final solution to your problem should be determined by considering the function (use), and the aesthetics (beauty) of the design. Check back to make sure you have remained within the limitations of size and complexity. Also decide if your design solves the original problem.

Notice that each of the possible solutions shown in Fig. 3–10 will function well, and that about the same amount of material is required for each. However, one of the three might appear more attractive to you than the others.

Make refinements in the design. Construct a model, if necessary. Some refinements can be made while you are still in the preliminary sketching stage, as shown in Fig. 3–11. The stars indicate the selection of parts to be used in the final design. The shape of various parts, as well as the kind and size of materials, may be altered. An accurate pictorial drawing (Fig. 3–12) would ensure pleasing aesthetic qualities.

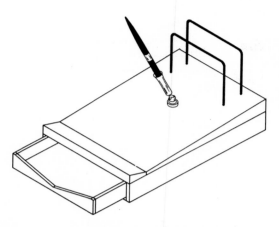

Fig. 3–12. An accurate pictorial drawing will help to ensure good aesthetic qualities.

Sometimes it is desirable to construct a scale model of the proposed product. This technique is generally used when large products of a rather complex nature are being designed.

Prepare working drawings, materials list (bill of materials), procedure sheet, and finishing schedule. The working drawing in Fig. 3–13 is an accurate description of the shape and size of the desk caddy. Do not begin to construct a product unless there is an accurate drawing from which to work. Complete and accurate dimensions are extremely important if all parts are to fit together properly.

The student's plan sheet shown in Fig. 3–14 is also very important. This will include an accurate bill of materials, a list of

Fig. 3–13. Working drawings give accurate size and shape description.

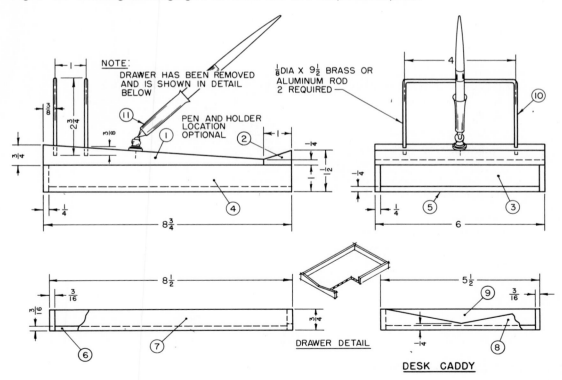

DESK CADDY

Student's Name _TIM JONES_   Class _9-B_

Name of Project _DESK CADDY_   Date Started _MARCH 10_ Date Completed _APRIL 14_

Estimated Time _8 HOURS_   Actual Time _10 HOURS_

Personal Efficiency: Actual Time - Estimated Time = _80_ % Source of Drawing _ORIGINAL_

BILL OF MATERIALS									
PART NO.	PART NAME	NO. OF PIECES	SIZES T	W	L	MATERIAL	UNITS	UNIT COST	EXTENDED COST
1	TOP	1	3/4	6	7 3/4	WALNUT	.33 BD. FT.	$.90/BD. FT.	
2	FRONT RAIL	1	1/2	1	6	"	.02 BD.FT.	"	
3	BACK	1	1/4	1	5 1/2	"	.01 BD.FT.	"	
4	SIDES	2	1/4	1	8 3/4	"	.03 BD.FT.	"	
5	BOTTOM	1	1/4	5 1/2	8 1/2	"	.06 BD.FT.	"	
6	DRAWER BOT.	1	3/16	5 1/8	8 1/8	"	.05 BD.FT.	"	
7	" SIDES	2	3/16	11/16	8 5/16	"	.02 BD.FT.	"	
8	" FRONT	1	3/16	11/16	5 1/2	"	.01 BD.FT.	"	
9	" BACK	1	3/16	11/16	5 1/8	"	.01 BD.FT.	"	
	SUB TOTAL FOR WOOD						.54 BD.FT.	$.90/BD. FT.	$.49
ADD 20% OF COST OF WOOD FOR WASTE AND FINISHING									.10
10	LETTER RACK	2	1/8 DIA		9 5/8	BRASS	19 1/4 IN.	$.01/IN.	.20
11	PEN HOLDER	1	———	STOCK	———			$.50 EACH	.50
								TOTAL COST	$1.29

Tools and Machines Required:

1. HAND SAW   4. TRY SQUARE   7.   10.

2. JACK PLANE   5. BENCH RULE   8.   11.

3. HAND DRILL   6. JIG SAW   9.   12.

Procedure:

1. OBTAIN THE FOLLOWING ROUGH STOCK:

   1 PC 1 X 7 1/2 X 8 (FOR PARTS 1 & 2)

   1 PC 3/8 X 8 1/4 X 9 (FOR PARTS 3, 4, & 5)

   1 PC 1/4 X 3 X 9 (FOR PARTS 7, 8, & 9)

   1 PC 1/4 X 5 1/2 X 8 1/2 (FOR PART 6)

2. PLANE ROUGH STOCK TO FINISHED THICKNESS.
3. RIP STOCK TO OBTAIN INDIVIDUAL PARTS.
4. PLANE PARTS TO CORRECT WIDTH.
5. SQUARE ONE END OF PARTS AND CUT TO CORRECT LENGTH.

6. LAYOUT TAPERS ON PARTS 1 & 2 AND PLANE TO FINISHED SHAPE.
7. CUT "V" SHAPE ON DRAWER FRONT. (JIG SAW)
8. PRE-SAND ALL PARTS BEFORE ASSEMBLY.
9. ASSEMBLE MAIN BODY OF CADDY.
10. ASSEMBLE DRAWER.
11. BEND BRASS RODS AND DRILL HOLES FOR ASSEMBLING LETTER HOLDER.
12. LOCATE POSITION OF PEN HOLDER AND DRILL HOLE FOR ASSEMBLY.
13. ASSEMBLE LETTER HOLDER AND PEN HOLDER AFTER FINISH HAS BEEN APPLIED.
14. SMOOTH WITH 6/0 GARNET PAPER.

Finishing Schedule:

1. SMOOTH WITH 6/0 GARNET PAPER.

2. SELECT A WIPE-ON OIL FINISH AND APPLY ACCORDING TO INSTRUCTIONS ON CONTAINER.

Approved _(J.D.H.)_

Fig. 3–14. A completed student's plan sheet for the desk caddy.

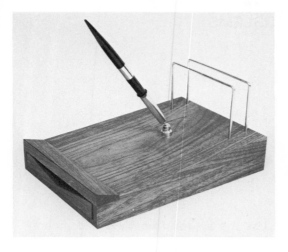

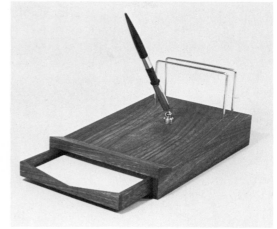

Fig. 3–15. The finished product.

tools and machines required, construction procedure, finishing schedule, and other important information. Study Unit 5 before completing this student's plan sheet.

Select materials and construct the product. The intelligent selection of materials, mentioned earlier, and safe and skillful use of tools are essential factors in good design. The most creative and practical design idea will add little to a product that is crudely constructed from poor materials. Figure 3–15 shows pictures of the finished desk caddy. Notice the effective use of a variety of materials.

Evaluate the final solution, based on the original problem. The following questions help evaluate your work:

1. Is the product functional?

2. Were you able to remain within the design specifications?

3. Is the product pleasing in appearance?

4. Did you select the best possible materials for your specific need?

5. Is the workmanship of high quality?

If you can answer *yes* to all of these questions, you have completed successfully your design problem.

DESIGN PROBLEMS

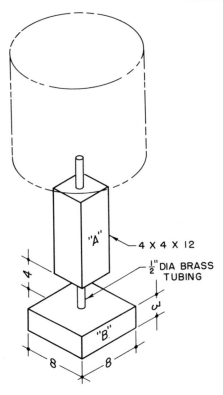

No. 1 Use the approximate sizes and proportions of the lamp shown here. Develop new shapes for blocks *A* and *B* to improve the design of the lamp by making it more pleasing in appearance. Prepare a working drawing and a complete student's plan sheet. Construct the lamp.

"A" — 4 X 4 X 12

½" DIA BRASS TUBING

"B"

4

3

8   8

No. 2 Design and construct a free-form candy dish from a blank of this size. The drawing to the right will give you some suggested free-form ideas. Design the dish to be made using only a band saw, a jig saw, and some basic hand tools.

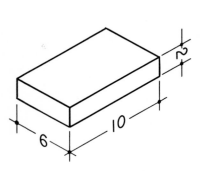

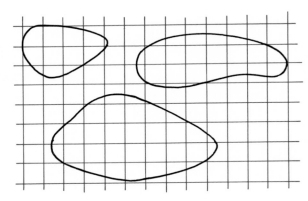

2

10

6

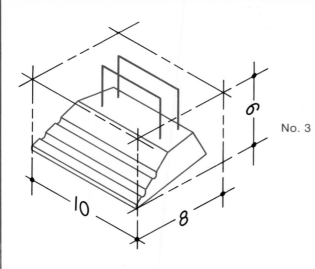

No. 3 Design a combination letter and pencil holder. It should not be larger than the overall dimensions shown here. This drawing shows one solution to this design problem. You may want to include more than one type of material in the finished product.

No. 4 Design a serving tray using wood as the basic material. The surface is to be covered with an interesting mosaic design. The handles may be made from brass rods or may be purchased. You may want the tray to be as small as 8 × 16 inches or as large as 12 × 24 inches. Make refinements in your design during the preliminary sketching stage. Make an accurate pictorial drawing and a complete working drawing. Prepare your student's plan sheet before beginning construction.

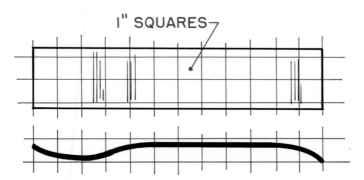

1" SQUARES

No. 5 Complete the top view for the design of a salad fork and spoon using a blank of the size shown here. The blanks are made from five layers of thin veneer. Refer to Unit 22 for information on how to construct the forms for producing the blanks.

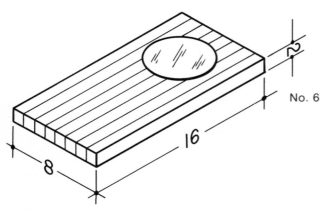

No. 6 Design a cheese cutting and serving tray. Purchase a 6 inch round or square ceramic plate at a hobby shop for the cutting surface. The tray should be made from strips of hardwood glued together. Be sure to make provisions for carrying the tray. Grooves may be cut in the ends or purchased handles may be attached. The drawing will give you an idea from which to begin.

No. 7 Design a turned bowl from a blank similar to the one shown here. Study this unit and Section 9, *Suggested Projects*, for design ideas. Be sure to complete all steps in the design process.

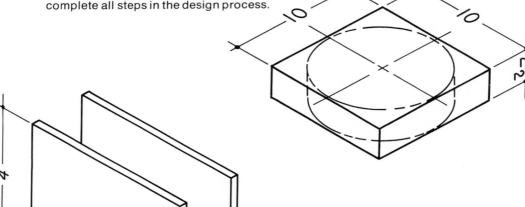

No. 8 Redesign the napkin holder shown here to make it more interesting and more pleasing in appearance. You may want to change the sizes to suit your design ideas. Initials or other designs may be inlaid or overlaid on the sides as desired.

No. 9   Design a barbecue serving tray to hold the following items:

Salt and pepper shakers.

Catsup, mustard, and mayonnaise dispensers.

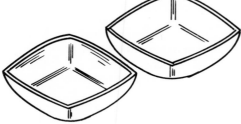

Relish dishes.

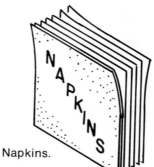

Napkins.

The tray should be designed so that the containers will be held in an upright position and will not be tipped over easily.

No. 10 This drawing shows a silhouette of a gazelle. You will notice that the shape has been streamlined to make it more pleasing in appearance. Some parts are exaggerated to stylize the design. This is sometimes called a characterization.

Use your favorite animal for the subject of this design problem. Find a picture of the animal having clear definition of detail in the outline. A side view of the animal is usually best for this purpose. Sketch the outline of the animal just as it appears in the picture. From this sketch begin to stylize the silhouette by streamlining some parts and exaggerating others. As many as five or six sketches may be necessary to develop a pleasing appearance.

When you have completed your design trace it on ¼ or ⅜ inch thick wood or hardboard and cut it out. If you use an attractive cabinet wood, such as walnut or mahogany, a hand-rubbed oil finish should be used. Harboard should be finished in flat black enamel or lacquer.

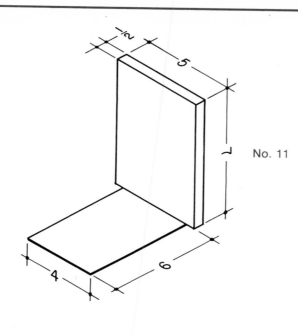

No. 11 Design a pair of bookends using sheet metal as the base, wood as the upright, and mosaics, glass chips, or plastic chips as a surface decoration. The drawing gives some basic sizes from which to start.

No. 12 Obtain a mechanism for a small electric clock. Design a wooden case to house the mechanism. You may want to design and make a new face to complement the design of the case.

No. 13 Design a set of drinking glass coasters and a rack to set them in. The left hand drawing shows one simple solution to the problem. Sheet cork may be used as a pad on which to set the drinking glass. You may wish to begin the design process from the coaster shown in the right-hand drawing.

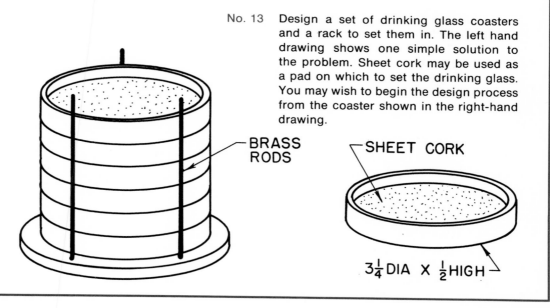

BRASS RODS

SHEET CORK

$3\frac{1}{4}$ DIA X $\frac{1}{2}$ HIGH

unit 4

Purchasing and measuring lumber

You should use a student's plan sheet for planning your project. Figure 5–1 is a good one, unless your teacher has another to suggest for your use. Before you make out the plan sheet, you should know the types of materials needed, how to figure the amount used, and the costs. You will save time and materials if you make an accurate listing of the materials needed before you begin your project.

The words and expressions which you must understand to figure a materials bill successfully are explained in this unit.

PURCHASING INFORMATION

The *board foot* (Fig. 4–1) is the measurement by which most lumber is sold. It represents 144 cubic inches of lumber in its rough state. A piece of wood 1 inch think, 12 inches wide, and 12 inches long contains this amount of lumber. The size is reduced when the wood is prepared for use. It then measures approximately 3/4 to 13/16 inch thick, 11½ to 11⅝ inches wide, and 12 inches long. Wood 2 inches thick by 6 inches wide by 12 inches long also makes a board foot. The reason is that this size also contains 144 cubic inches of unfinished lumber. A board figured as 2 inches thick is actually only 1⅝ inches thick when delivered. The difference between what we figure and what we get is lost in sawing and planing. A board less than 1 inch thick is usually figured as though it were 1 inch thick. Plywood, however, is an exception; it is sold by the square foot. See page 28 for additional information about measuring and figuring board feet.

In a materials bill, the thickness and width of boards are always figured in inches ("). Lengths for long boards are figured in feet ('). Lengths for short pieces are often figured in inches. In estimating amounts of lumber, lengths in feet and in inches require different formulas. You will use both in figuring the problems on page 29.

The lumber industry generally quotes lumber prices by the thousand board feet, as 540/M. This means that one thousand (M) board feet cost $540. One board foot, therefore, would cost 54 cents. The price per board foot is the quotation often given by the teacher. Refer to Table 4–1 for a guide to lumber sizes.

TYPES OF LUMBER

Hardwoods are used for architectural woodwork, furniture, and cabinetmaking. They do not contain resin. *Softwoods* are used in

Fig. 4–1. Three boards which represent a board foot.

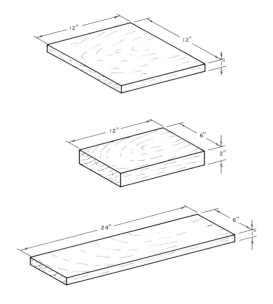

Table 4–1. Guide to Lumber Sizes

NOMINAL SIZE INCHES	ACTUAL SIZE INCHES	BOARD FEET PER FOOT OF LENGTH
1 × 2	$^{25}/_{32} × 1^{5}/_{8}$	$^{1}/_{6}$
1 × 4	$^{25}/_{32} × 3^{5}/_{8}$	$^{1}/_{3}$
1 × 6	$^{25}/_{32} × 5^{5}/_{8}$	$^{1}/_{2}$
1 × 10	$^{25}/_{32} × 9^{1}/_{2}$	$^{5}/_{6}$
1 × 12	$^{25}/_{32} × 11^{1}/_{2}$	1
2 × 4	$1^{5}/_{8} × 3^{5}/_{8}$	$^{2}/_{3}$
2 × 6	$1^{5}/_{8} × 5^{5}/_{8}$	1
2 × 10	$1^{5}/_{8} × 9^{1}/_{2}$	$1^{2}/_{3}$
2 × 12	$1^{5}/_{8} × 11^{1}/_{2}$	2
3 × 6	$2^{5}/_{8} × 5^{5}/_{8}$	$1^{1}/_{2}$
4 × 4	$3^{5}/_{8} × 3^{5}/_{8}$	$1^{1}/_{3}$
4 × 6	$3^{5}/_{8} × 5^{5}/_{8}$	2

building and for construction. For names of some of the common hardwood and softwood trees, see Unit 64, *Common Woods*.

Hardwood lumber is cut in standard thickness and width. Since it is a scarce wood, however, it is cut in any length that can be obtained from the log.

Softwood lumber is generally sawed in even widths, such as 2, 4, 6, or 8 inches, and in even lengths, such as 8, 10, 12, 14, etc., up to 20 feet.

Grading. Hardwood lumber in the United States generally follows the grading, or rating, rules of the National Hardwood Association. The grade of lumber is based upon the amount of usable lumber in the piece. Such timber must have one side *clear* and the reverse side *sound*. This means that it must be free from rot or any other defect which affects the strength of the board.

The term *Firsts* is used for the highest grade of hardwood lumber. *Seconds* is used for the next grade. Firsts and Seconds (FAS) are nearly always combined in one grade. *Selects* form the third grade. Other grades are No. 1 Common, No. 2 Common, Sound Wormy, No. 3A Common, and No. 3B Common. These are only general grades, for there are always exceptions and special rules for certain species, or kinds, of trees.

Softwoods have many more grades than hardwoods do. This is because they are graded by several associations and organizations. Some of these are the California Redwood Association, Southern Cypress Manufacturers Association, Southern Pine Association, West Coast Lumberman's Association, and the Western Pine Association. This makes the grading of softwoods very confused and difficult.

The grading of ponderosa pine will be mentioned briefly here because it is a softwood well known to most woodworkers. Sugar pine is graded in a similar way to ponderosa pine. The Western Pine Association classifies ponderosa pine as *Select*, *Shop*, and *Common*. *Select* grades include B and Better Select (sometimes called No. 1 and No. 2 Clear), C Select, and D Select. *Shop* grades are classified as 3rd Clear (3rd Clear and Factory Select), No. 1 Shop, No. 2 Shop, and No. 3 Shop. *Common* grades are divided into No. 1 Common, No. 2 Common, No. 3 Common, No. 4 Common, and No. 5 Common.

Each association or organization has a similar type of classification, with variations for each kind of timber. *Wood Handbook 72* of the Forest Products Laboratory, U.S. Department of Agriculture, Washington, D.C., gives a very detailed description of lumber grading. Volumes have been written on this subject.

Surfaces. Rough, S2S, and S4S are terms indicating the treatment which lumber has had. *Rough* means that the lumber is in the rough as it came from the mill and has not been planed. *S2S* tells you that it has been planed on the two surfaces, or faces. *S4S* indicates that it has been planed on all four sides, both surfaces and edges. S2S and S4S are common in the treatment of yard lumber.

Methods of Drying Air-dried (AD) means that the lumber has been dried through natural evaporation in the air. The time required varies from weeks to months, depending on the type of lumber and the degree of dryness required. *Kiln-dried* (KD) refers to lumber which has been artificially dried in a kiln. The time required for kiln drying is much shorter.

Methods of Cutting. Plain-sawing and *quarter-sawing* are the principal methods of cutting logs into boards. Quarter-sawing is the more expensive because of the way the cutting has to be done. Refer to Unit 63, *Trees and Forests* for further information and for illustration of these two methods of cutting.

PLYWOOD

Plywood is the result of gluing and pressing thin sheets of wood together. Unit 66, *The Manufacture and Use of Veneer and Plywood*, gives more information on plywood. This product provides more strength by weight than steel does. Panels of plywood are usually made up of three, five, or seven plies, or thicknesses. Plywood is priced by the square foot. The price depends upon the thickness, the kind of veneer, or wood sheet used on the surfaces, and the gluing or bonding agent. Standard-sized plywoods vary in thickness from 1/8 to 3/4 inch. Generally plywood up to 3/8 inch in thickness has three plies; in thicker panels there are five plies, or sometimes seven.

Exterior construction, marine, and aircraft plywoods use a water-resistant phenolic glue or bonding agent which makes them waterproof.

Types and Grades of Plywood. Fir and hardwood are two of the most common types of plywood. The two most common grades of fir plywood are termed *Sound 1 Side* and *Sound 2 Sides.* Fir face veneers are divided into four grades: A, B, C, and D. The A grade is the best. The quality of the fir-plywood panel is expressed by stating the grades of both surface veneers; for example, A–D. This means that the face

veneer is of the best grade or quality (A) and that the back veneer is of the poorest quality. (D). A–A means that both faces are of the best quality.

Fir plywood for exterior use is branded EXT on one end. Ponderosa pine plywood is manufactured under different grading rules, but they are similar to fir-plywood rules. The description is generally the same.

Hardwood plywood is usually graded as *Good 1 Side* (G1S) and *Good 2 Sides* (G2S). These terms refer to the face veneers. G1S indicates that one of the surfaces is of superior quality. G2S indicates that both are superior, G2S plywood panels usually have the same face veneer.

When you buy plywood, you should always indicate the number of pieces; the thickness, width, and length; the number of plies; the kind of wood preferred on the face side; and the grade desired.

BOARD-FOOT MEASURE

After the type of lumber has been selected, you should make an estimate of the amount needed. This will show the rough, or stock, size of the lumber. You will also figure the number of board feet (bd ft) in each piece, in groups of like pieces, and the total number of board feet. You can then estimate the cost of the project by multiplying *the total number of board feet* by *the cost per board foot.*

When the length is given in linear, or running, *feet,* use the following formula:

$$\frac{\text{No. of pcs} \times \text{thickness, in.} \times \text{width, in.} \times \text{length, feet}}{12} = \text{bd ft}$$

or

$$\frac{\text{\# Pcs} \times T'' \times W'' \times L'}{12} = \text{bd ft}$$

Example: To find the board feet in three pieces, $1'' \times 10'' \times 4'$:

$$\frac{\cancel{3} \times 1 \times 10 \times \cancel{4}}{\cancel{12}} = 10 \text{ bd ft}$$

28

When the length is given in linear, or running, inches, use this formula:

$$\frac{\text{No. of pcs} \times \text{thickness, in.} \times \text{width, in.} \times \text{length, in.}}{12 \times 12} = \text{bd ft}$$

Example: To find the board feet in four pieces, $1 \times 8 \times 18$ inches:

$$\frac{\overset{4}{\cancel{4}} \times 1 \times \overset{6}{\cancel{8}} \times \cancel{18}}{\underset{\cancel{3}}{\cancel{12}} \times \underset{\cancel{2}}{\cancel{12}}} = 4 \text{ bd ft}$$

ESTIMATING FINISHES

The different kinds of materials and types of finishes make estimating the cost of finishes a difficult problem. However, many woodworkers figure that the cost of the finishes averages 20 percent of the cost of the lumber.

Section 5 describes and illustrates many of the accepted methods of applying a variety of finishes. Included are the popular wipe-on finishes, as well as numerous finishes which produce modern bleached effects. Brush and spray-gun techniques are described for applying shellac, varnish, lacquer, and enamel. This variety will influence the method of estimating costs.

OTHER COSTS

There will be several additional items to figure in the total cost of a project. These items may include sandpaper, steel wool, nails, screws, other fastenings, and various pieces of special hardware. The cost will depend upon the purchase price and the number used.

Discussion Topics
1. What is a board foot?
2. Explain the meaning of the following lumber terms: (*a*) rough, (*b*) S2S, (*c*) S4S, (*d*) FAS, (*e*) AD, (*f*) KD, (*g*) No. 1 Common, (*h*) A–D, (*i*) hardwood, (*j*) softwood, and (*k*) plywood.
3. Prepare a lumber bill for a project which will list the following information: (*a*) kind of wood, (*b*) number of pieces, (*c*) sizes of pieces, (*d*) grade of lumber, (*e*) surface teatment, and (*f*) condition of lumber.
   Example: Walnut — 6 pcs — $1'' \times 6'' \times 8'$ — FAS — S2S — KD.
4. Describe two methods for drying lumber. how much drying time is required in each of these processes? How are the names of these methods abbreviated?

Practical Problems
Work out these problems in your notebook. Do not write in this book.

No. of pieces	Thickness	Width	Length	Board feet	Kind of wood	Cost per foot, cents	Total cost
1	1″	12″	3′	?	Poplar	45	?
1	1″	6″	12′	?	Walnut	80	?
5	2″	10″	7′4″	?	Honduras mahogany	78	?
4	¼″	48″	96″	?	Fir plywood	24	?
7	2″	2″	30″	?	Red gum	34	?
6	½″	10″	40″	?	Yellow pine	18	?
3	¾″	36″	72″	?	White-oak plywood	55	?
16	2″	4″	14′	?	Yellow pine	22	?

unit
5

Planning your procedure

You should have a carefully-thought-out plan before you build anything. The man who builds a house or business building gives attention to all the details of his construction problems. The proper materials, tools, and equipment must be ready at the right time. He knows that his building will be finished on time only if these things are planned.

The dentist or doctor approaches his problems with a careful analysis of the steps needed to get successful results. By doing this he saves time and effort. He does not always write out his plan of procedure in detail, but during his training it was necessary to plan each step on paper.

The project or experiment which you want to develop is a problem, and every problem requires a solution. Fill out your plan sheet so that you can solve the problem of creating something from wood.

Many types of plan, or order-of-procedure, forms include information which constitutes a set of specifications for doing a job. The information called for on most plan sheets includes: (1) the working drawing, complete with construction details and dimensions, or reference to where such data may be found; (2) a list of the steps, or processes, to be followed in building the object (in construction this is often referred to as the order of procedure); (3) a listing of all of the materials which are necessary to complete the work, including hardware and finishing materials (the figuring of materials was described in Unit 4, *Purchasing and Measuring Lumber*); (4) the tools and machines necessary to perform the numerous steps or operations listed in number 2 above (these tools and machines may be determined by studying the appropriate procedures presented in the units in this text); (5) the sources or references which were used to obtain the specific ideas; and (6) the estimated and the actual time required to complete the activity, which determines your efficiency rating. Your efficiency rating is calculated by dividing the estimated time into the actual time. Such a personal efficiency rating often yields some surprising results. This device can be used to improve your efficiency, both in estimating the time needed and in the actual time spent in the construction processes. Figure 5–1 is one form of a student plan sheet which contains the numerous factors necessary for constructing and finishing a project.

Discussion Topics

1. Make a list of ten professions in which planning a procedure in advance is necessary.
2. Name eight mistakes you might have made in your project or activity if you had not planned it beforehand.
3. Mention at least six factors which you must consider in planning.
4. Prepare a plan sheet for one of the projects shown in Section 9. Use the plan sheet shown in Fig. 5–1, or one suggested by your teacher.

Industrial Arts Woodworking

STUDENT'S PLAN SHEET

Student's Name_____Class_____

Name of Project_____Date Started_____Date Completed_____

Estimated Time_____Actual Time_____

Personal Efficiency: Actual Time ÷ Estimated Time = _____%

Source of the Drawing_____

Materials Required

No. of Pieces	Description of Piece	Sizes	Kind of Wood or Other Materials	Board Feet	Unit Cost	Extended Cost

Total Cost_____

Tools:
1.   5.   9.
2.   6.   10.
3.   7.   11.
4.   8.   12.

Order of Procedure:
1.
2.
3.
4.
5.
6.
7.
8.
9.
10.
11.
12.
13.
14.

Approved_____

Fig. 5–1. Student's plan sheet.

unit

6

Safety

The saying "An ounce of prevention is worth a pound of cure" applies to safety in the school inustrial-arts laboratory, the industrial shop, and the home workshop. Tools and machinery have been developed to save time and do more accurate work. They can be used safely only if they are properly cared for and understood. Whether they are helpful or harmful depends on you.

National Safety Council studies of school-shop accidents show that more happen in the forenoon around ten o'clock than at any other time of day. These studies also show that there are more accidents on Wednesday than on any other day of the week, except those days around vacations.

 **Safety Rules**

The safety rules listed in this unit are generally for the use of hand tools. Safe practices in the use of portable electric tools and power machinery are included in Sections 3 and 4 for reference as you use these machines.

Body Care.

1. Never depend upon your back muscles in lifting something heavy. Get someone to help you, and then lift with your leg and arm muscles.

2. Test the sharpness of tools on wood or paper, not on your hand.

3. Be careful when using your thumb as a guide in crosscutting and ripping.

4. Always cut outward, away from your body, when using a knife.

5. Make sure your hands are not in front of sharp-edged tools that are in use.

6. Use safety goggles or a face shield when doing any operation which might endanger your eyes.

Clothing.

1. Dress properly for work in the laboratory. It may often be desirable to wear an apron or coveralls over your clothing.

2. Tuck in your tie and roll up your sleeves. Get them out of the way, so they will not interfere with your work or get caught in machines.

Tools.

1. Lay tools to be used in a neat arrangement on the bench top. Place the cutting edges *away* from you. Do not let them rub against each other. Be very careful that sharp tools do not extend over the edges of the bench.

2. Keep screwdriver points properly pointed. This will prevent injury to hands and to wood fiber (Fig. 19–5).

3. See that handles are securely fastened on planes, hammers, and mallets.

4. Make certain that all files have handles.

5. *Use tools properly for their intended purpose.* Do not attempt to pry with a file, screwdriver, or wood chisel.

6. Do not carry tools in your pockets.

Materials.

1. Whenever possible, tighten material in a vise before working with it. Hold it securely.

2. Put waste pieces of lumber in the scrap box or in the storage rack.

3. Put the oily rags used for finishing in closed metal containers to prevent possible fires.

Hand tools, such as wood chisels, saws, knives, planes, and files should be used carefully. If these tools are dull, they can slip.

STANDARD STUDENT ACCIDENT REPORT FORM
Part A. Information on ALL Accidents

1. Name: _____ Home Address: _____
2. School: _____ Sex: M ☐; F ☐. Age: _____ Grade or classification: _____
3. Time accident occurred: Hour _____ A.M.; _____ P.M. Date: _____
4. Place of Accident: School Building ☐ School Grounds ☐ To or from School ☐ Home ☐ Elsewhere ☐

5. NATURE OF INJURY

				DESCRIPTION OF THE ACCIDENT
Abrasion	_____	Fracture	_____	How did accident happen? What was student doing? Where was student? List specifically unsafe acts and unsafe conditions existing. Specify any tool, machine or equipment involved. _____
Amputation	_____	Laceration	_____	
Asphyxiation	_____	Poisoning	_____	
Bite	_____	Puncture	_____	
Bruise	_____	Scalds	_____	
Burn	_____	Scratches	_____	
Concussion	_____	Shock (el.)	_____	
Cut	_____	Sprain	_____	
Dislocation	_____			
Other (specify) _____				

PART OF BODY INJURED

Abdomen	_____	Foot	_____
Ankle	_____	Hand	_____
Arm	_____	Head	_____
Back	_____	Knee	_____
Chest	_____	Leg	_____
Ear	_____	Mouth	_____
Elbow	_____	Nose	_____
Eye	_____	Scalp	_____
Face	_____	Tooth	_____
Finger	_____	Wrist	_____
Other (specify) _____			

6. Degree of Injury: Death ☐ Permanent Impairment ☐ Temporary Disability ☐ Nondisabling ☐
7. Total number of days lost from school: _____ (To be filled in when student returns to school)

Part B. Additional Information on School Jurisdiction Accidents

8. Teacher in charge when accident occurred (Enter name): _____
Present at scene of accident: No: _____ Yes: _____

9. IMMEDIATE ACTION TAKEN

First-aid treatment _____ By (Name): _____
Sent to school nurse _____ By (Name): _____
Sent home _____ By (Name): _____
Sent to physician _____ By (Name): _____
Physician's Name: _____
Sent to hospital _____ By (Name): _____
Name of hospital: _____

10. Was a parent or other individual notified? No:___ Yes:___ When: _____ How: _____
Name of individual notified: _____
By whom? (Enter name): _____
11. Witnesses: 1. Name: _____ Address: _____
2. Name: _____ Address: _____

12. LOCATION

Specify Activity		Specify Activity		Remarks
Athletic field	_____	Locker	_____	What recommendations do you have for preventing other accidents of this type? _____
Auditorium	_____	Pool	_____	
Cafeteria	_____	Sch. grounds	_____	
Classroom	_____	_____ shop		
Corridor	_____	Showers	_____	
Dressing room	_____	Stairs	_____	
Gymnasium	_____	Toilets and		
Home Econ.	_____	washrooms	_____	
Laboratories	_____	Other (specify)	_____	

Signed: Principal: _____ Teacher: _____

Fig. 6–1. Report form. *(National Safety Council.)*

Studies show that fewer accidents occur with sharp than with dull tools.

Machine and portable power tools are safe when used properly. Particular caution should be observed when using the jointer, circular saw, wood lathe, grinder, band saw, and drill press.

Report any accident. All shop accidents should be reported on a form. Figure 6–1 shows the standard form prepared by the National Safety Council.

Learn the Safety Rules which are listed on page 32.

SHOP COURTESY

1. Report an accident at once so that first aid can be given.

2. Warn others to stay out of your way when you handle long pieces of lumber.

3. Do not run in the shop, laboratory, or home workshop. It is dangerous.

4. Carry only a few tools at a time.

5. Do not play in the woodworking shop or laboratory. It can be dangerous to you and your classmates.

6. Do not talk and work at the same time. Concentrate on what you are doing.

Discussion Topics

1. Why should we observe safety rules in shops and laboratories?
2. Explain why hand tools cause twice as many injuries as machine tools.
3. Why should reports of accidents be made to school officials and to the National Safety Council?
4. Name at least three advantages in wearing proper clothing or protective covering in the woodworking shop or laboratory.
5. Give three reasons why you should practice shop courtesy.

SECTION 2/PRODUCTION WITH HAND TOOLS

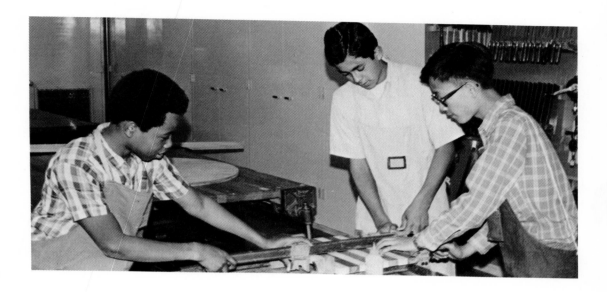

unit

7

Measuring and laying out lumber

Accurate measurement is a skill which must be learned in experimenting and working with wood. The foot (′) and the inch (″) are measurements which are used in most industrial laboratories, shops, and industries. Practically all measuring tools used in woodworking are divided into inches and halves, quarters, eighths, and sixteenths of an inch. Figure 7–1 shows these divisions.

TOOLS

Tools often used to measure and lay out are the wooden or steel bench rule (Fig. 7–2), steel square (7–3), try square (Fig. 7–4), combination square (Fig. 7–5), extension rule (Fig. 7–6), flexible steel tape rule (Fig.

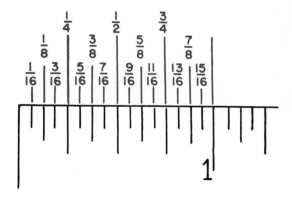

Fig. 7–1. Divisions of an inch.

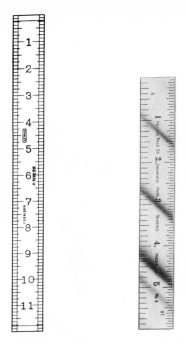

Fig. 7-2. A wooden and a steel bench rule.

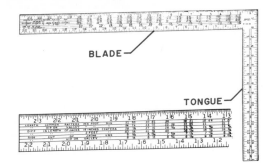

Fig. 7-3. Carpenter's steel square. Notice a section of the roofing table which appears on the blade.

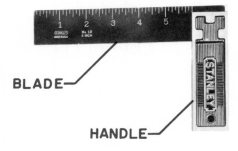

Fig. 7-4. Six-inch try square.

Fig. 7-5. Combination square.

7-7), steel tape (Fig. 7-8), bevel (Fig. 7-9), angle dividers (Fig. 7-10), marking gage (Fig. 7-11), butt gage (Fig. 7-12), level (Fig. 7-13), plumb bob (Fig. 7-14), chalk line reel (Fig. 7-15), marking knife (Fig. 7-16), and scoring tool (Fig. 7-17).

Wooden or Steel Bench Rule. One of the most frequently use tools is the 6-, 12-, or 24-inch wooden or steel bench rule (Fig. 7-2). The front is usually marked in divisions of eighths of an inch; the back in sixteenths.

Steel Square. This square usually has a 24-inch blade and a 16-inch tongue (Fig. 7-3). It is used in bench-, cabinet-, and carpentry-work to measure, to square lines, and to test large surfaces for *wind,** or twist. It also tests for squareness in assembly and in laying out rafters, roof framing, and stairs. There are several mathematical tables on the two arms of the square; these give useful information.

Try Square. The try square (Fig. 7-4) is one of the tools most often used for squaring, testing, and measuring. It is generally made of steel, but sometimes has a handle of wood.

Combination Square. This tool (Fig. 7-5) may be used for marking and checking squareness, 45- and 90- degree angles, and to test vertical and horizontal levelness.

Extension Rule. The extension rule (Fig. 7-6) usually extends to a 6- or 8- foot length.

---

*A glossary of technical terms used in the field of woodworking begins on page 416.

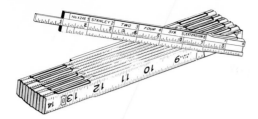

Fig. 7–6. Six-foot extension rule.

Fig. 7–7. Six-foot flexible steel tape rule.

Fig. 7–8. Fifty-foot steel tape.

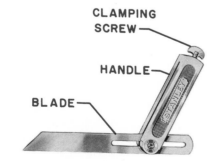

CLAMPING
SCREW

HANDLE

BLADE

Fig. 7–9. Sliding bevel.

It is generally made of wood, but sometimes is of lightweight metal. It is useful for measuring long pieces.

Flexible Steel Tape Rule. A 6-, 8-, or 10-foot flexible steel tape rule (Fig. 7–7) is handy for either outside or inside measuring.

Steel Tape. The steel tape (Fig. 7–8) is available in 50- or 100-foot lengths. It is used to measure long boards and in carpentry.

Bevel. This tool (Fig. 7–9) looks like a try square, but has a movable blade which can be set to lay out any angle. It is also used to check chamfers, bevels, or angles.

Angle Dividers. This is a most useful instrument (Fig. 7–10) for bisecting angles and for fitting molding and inside trim.

Marking Gage. The marking gage (Fig. 7–11) is used to mark a line parallel to a given edge or end. It is made of either wood or metal. The point of the metal spur or pin must be kept sharp at all times.

Butt Gage. The butt gage (Fig. 7–12) is used to mark mortises when hanging doors.

Level. The level in the upper part of Fig. 7–13 may be framed in aluminum or wood. Levels of this type are from 18 to 28 inches long. The lower one shown in this

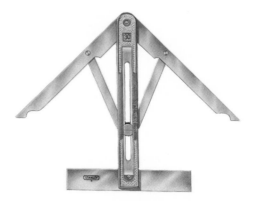

Fig. 7–10. Seven and one-half-inch-length angle dividers.

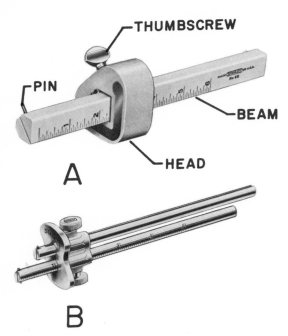

THUMBSCREW

PIN

BEAM

HEAD

A

B

Fig. 7–11. Marking gages: (A) wooden, (B) double-beam steel.

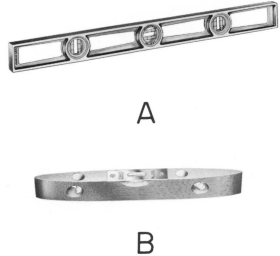

A

B

Fig. 7–13. Levels: (A) 24-inch aluminum, (B) 9-inch torpedo.

Fig. 7–12. Butt gage.

Fig. 7–14. Twelve-ounce plumb bob.

figure is 9 inches long and is called a *torpedo* level because of its design. Both types are especially useful in building cabinetwork or when doing carpentry which must be level and accurate.

Plumb Bob. The plumb bob (Fig. 7–14) is most adaptable for building construction. It is used for *plumbing* (getting true vertical alignment). The size varies from 5 to 12 ounces.

Chalk Line Reel. The type of reel shown in Fig. 7–15 contains 50 to 100 feet of cord. It is used to mark long, straight lines with chalk.

Marking Knife. The marking knife (Fig. 7–16) may be used for very accurate marking across the grain, or fiber, of wood. It also cuts and whittles.

Scoring Tool. The scoring tool in Fig. 7–17 is used to mark and *score* (cut lightly) plastic laminates and composition building materials.

Fig. 7–16. Retractable-blade marking knife.

Fig. 7–17. Scoring tool.

LAYING OUT LENGTHS

1. Select a board which has the fewest checks or cracks (Fig. 7–18).

2. Square a line across the end of the board at a place which will avoid end checks or cracks (Fig. 7–18). Place the blade of the square firmly against the edge of the board. Mark the line against the tongue of the square on the broad surface of the board. The mark will be at a 90-degree angle with the edge (Fig. 7–19).

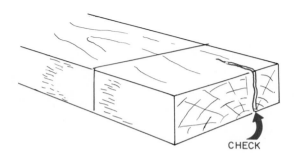

CHECK

Fig. 7–18. Board marked to avoid checks or cracks.

Fig. 7–15. Fifty-foot chalk line reel.

Fig. 7–19. Squaring a line across a board.

Fig. 7–20. Laying out a measurement with the rule on edge.

Fig. 7–21. Laying out a measurement with a flexible rule.

Fig. 7–22. Measuring for width.

3. Lay out the length you want with a suitable measuring rule (Figs. 7–20 and 7–21). Mark it with a sharp pencil or knife. To get a more accurate measurement place the rule on its edge, as in Fig. 7–20.

4. Square the line just marked by following the procedure in step 2.

LAYING OUT WIDTHS

1. Measure and mark the width you want with any of the measuring tools (Figs. 7–20 through 7–22). Divide and mark a board into any number of equal widths. Lay the rule edgewise across the board in a diagonal position, as shown in Fig. 7–23.

2. Mark the width layout on the board by either of the methods shown in Figs. 7–24 and 7–25.

GAGING WIDTH AND THICKNESS

1. Set the marking gage to the distance you want marked.

2. Check the setting against a rule to make certain that it is accurate (Fig. 7–26).

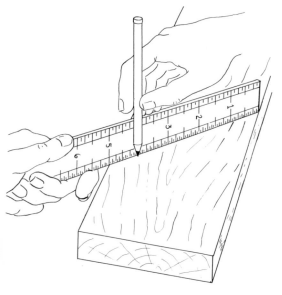

Fig. 7–23. Dividing a board into equal parts.

Fig. 7-24. Rule and pencil used as a marking gage.

3. Push the marking gage forward on the wood to make the marking (Fig. 7–27). Hold the head of the gage firmly against the edge of the board while you scribe, or mark, a light line.

Many craftsmen prefer to gage lines and distances with a sharp-pointed pencil instead of with a marking gage. The objection to the marking gage is that the spur point makes a dent, or groove, in the edge or face of the piece of wood, or tears the fibers of the wood when the marking gage is used across the end of the board.

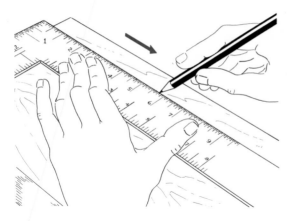

Fig. 7-25. Marking a line along a straightedge.

Fig. 7-27. Pushing the marking gage to scribe a line.

Fig. 7-26. Checking measurement of the marking gage against a rule.

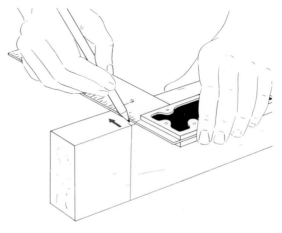

Fig. 7-28. Extending the line along an edge.

LAYING OUT LINES

Mark a line around the edge of the board by continuing the face line (Fig. 7–28). Hold the handle of the try square firmly against the broad side, or face, of the board while you mark along the blade (Fig. 7–28).

LAYING OUT ANGLES

1. Adjust the bevel to the angle you want (Fig. 7–29); then fasten the screw on the handle. This layout tool is especially useful

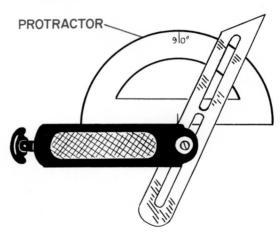

PROTRACTOR

Fig. 7–30. Adjusting the bevel to the desired angle against a protractor.

for any acute angle (less than 90 degrees) or obtuse angle (over 90 degrees). You may set the angle of the bevel by using a protractor (Fig. 7–30).

2. Hold the handle firmly against the face or edge of the board. Mark along the edge of the blade. This is like the method of marking with a try square.

A sharp-pointed pencil will make a suitable marked line.

Fig. 7–29. Adjusting the bevel to the desired angle against a square.

Discussion Topics

1. How many eighths (⅛) are there in 1⅜ inches?
2. Name seven tools used for measuring.
3. What tool is used to lay out angles?
4. Why should you check the measurement of a marking gage against a rule? How is this done?
5. Why do you place a rule on its edge when measuring?
6. Describe at least two methods by which you can divide an 8-inch board in five equal widths.
7. Should the marking gage be pushed away from or pulled toward you? Explain.
8. Explain when and how you would use the following tools; angle dividers, butt gage, level, plumb bob, chalk line reel, and scoring tool.

unit

8

Sawing across or with the grain of the wood

The saw is one of the oldest tools known. The most primitive form dates back to the Stone Age. A stone with ragged edges was used for cutting. The operation of the modern steel saw is very similar to that of the ragged flint one. The steel saw, however, has been developed into a very accurate cutting tool.

TOOLS

Woodworkers' saws are the crosscut saw, the ripsaw, the backsaw, and the dovetail saw. Figure 8–1 shows a typical panel handsaw with the parts identified.

The length of the blade in inches tells the size of the saw. The 24- and 26-inch lengths are the more popular sizes. The number of points per inch, as shown in Figs. 8–2 and 8–3, makes the coarseness or fineness of a saw. This number is usually stamped on the heel of the saw blade near the handle. There is always one more point

per inch than there are teeth. For example, a saw that has eight points per inch will have seven teeth per inch. A coarse saw is better for doing fast work and for cutting green, or undried, lumber. A fine one does smoother, more accurate cutting on seasoned, or dried, wood.

Crosscut Saw. This saw is used to cut across the grain, or fiber, of the wood (Fig. 8–4). The teeth are set, or adjusted, and filed as shown in Fig. 8–5. They cut into the wood to make the *kerf*, or saw cut. See Fig. 8–4.

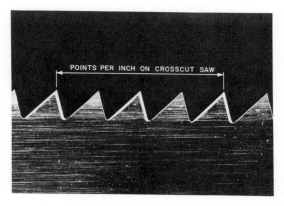

Fig. 8–2. Five points per inch on a crosscut saw.

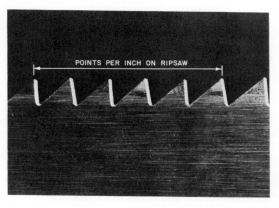

Fig. 8–3. Six points per inch on a ripsaw.

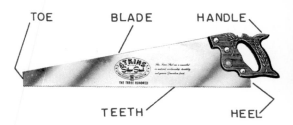

Fig. 8–1. A panel handsaw.

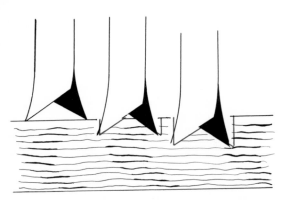

Fig. 8-4. Cutting action of crosscut-saw teeth.

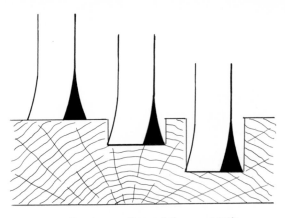

Fig. 8-6. Cutting action of ripsaw teeth.

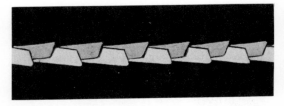

Fig. 8-5. Cutting edges of crosscut-saw teeth.

Fig. 8-7. Cutting edges of ripsaw teeth.

The teeth of a saw are *set*. That is, every other tooth is bent to the right; the alternate teeth are bent to the left. This makes the saw kerf wider than the thickness of the saw blade. It prevents the saw from sticking in the kerf. Saw teeth should always be kept sharp and properly set. Eight to ten points per inch cut easily.

Ripsaw. A ripsaw is used for ripping or cutting with the grain of the wood (Fig. 8-6). The teeth are large, and cut into the wood with short, chisel-like jabs. Figure 8-7 shows how the teeth of a ripsaw are filed and set. Figure 8-6 shows the manner in which this saw cuts into the wood to make the kerf. Five to seven points per inch cut easily.

Backsaw. Figure 8-8 shows a thin crosscut saw with fine teeth. The blade is stiffened by a thick back. A popular length for the backsaw is 14 inches, with thirteen

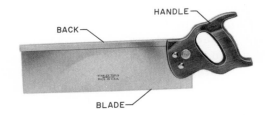

Fig. 8-8. A 14-inch backsaw.

Fig. 8-9. Dovetail saw.

points per inch. This saw is used for very fine work.

Dovetail Saw. This saw (Fig. 8-9) is extremely thin and is used in joint making and fine cabinet work.

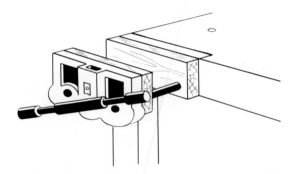

Fig. 8–10. Woodworker's bench vise.

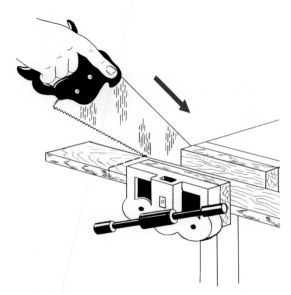

Fig. 8–11. Board held in a woodworker's bench vise for crosscutting.

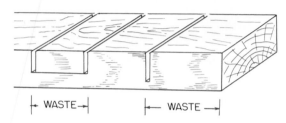

Fig. 8–12. Waste portions of a board.

Vise. A woodworker's bench vise holds lumber to be sawed. Before using this vise, make sure that you understand how it works by looking at Fig. 8–10. Figure 8–11 shows it in use.

CROSSCUTTING

1. Lay out and mark the board to be cut. See Unit 7.

2. Fasten the board in a bench vise if it can be held this way (Fig. 8–11). Wider or longer boards which cannot be firmly held in a vise should be laid across sawhorses (Fig. 8–14).

3. Place the heel (Fig. 8–1) of the crosscut saw near the cutting line on the *waste* side of the wood (Fig. 8–12). Pull it, while you guide it with the left thumb (Fig. 8–13).

4. Make several short strokes. Test these cuts with a try square. Do this to see that the saw blade is cutting at right angles to the surface of the board (Fig. 8–14).

5. Continue cutting. Use long strokes. Cut at about a 45-degree angle to the board (Fig. 8–15). The direction of the cut may be changed by twisting the handle slightly in the direction of the line marked on the board.

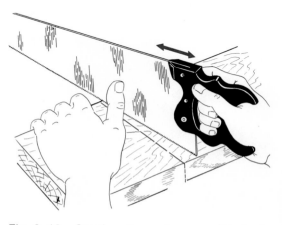

Fig. 8–13. Starting the cut across the grain of the wood.

Fig. 8-14. Testing a saw cut with a try square.

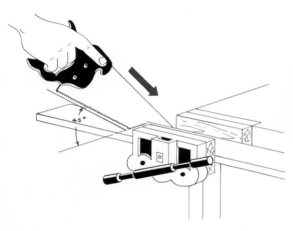

Fig. 8-15. Proper angle of the saw for cross-cutting.

Fig. 8-16. Crosscutting a board held in a bench vise.

Fig. 8-17. Ripping a board on a sawhorse.

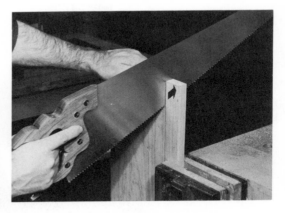

Fig. 8-18. Ripping a board in a vise.

6. Finish sawing. Use short, easy strokes. Hold the end of the lumber to be cut off with your left hand (Fig. 8–16). This keeps the wood from splitting or breaking from its own weight.

RIPPING

1. Mark the lumber to be sawed or ripped. See Unit 7.

2. Hold the board on a sawhorse if possible (Fig. 8–17). Ripping in a vise is also satisfactory (Fig. 8–18).

3. Start ripping in much the same manner as in step 3 under "Crosscutting." Begin the cut by pulling the ripsaw back. Hold the cutting edge at an angle of about 60 degrees to the surface (Fig. 8–17 and 8–18). Be sure that the cut is on the waste side of the board.

4. Continue ripping the board with short, easy strokes.

FINE, OR CABINET, SAWING

1. Lay out and mark the board for cutting.

2. Fasten the board in a vise (Fig. 8–19). You may also hold it firmly against a bench hook (Fig. 8–20).

3. Start cutting with the backsaw the same way you did for crosscutting.

4. Continue cutting with short, easy strokes until the board has been cut. Hold the waste portion with your left hand to keep it from splitting.

Fig. 8–19. Holding a board in a bench vise while cutting with a backsaw.

Fig. 8–20. Cutting a board with the backsaw on a bench hook.

Discussion Topics

1. What are the main differences between the crosscut saw and the ripsaw?
2. What does the number stamped on the heel of the saw mean?
3. Why should the final strokes in sawing be short ones?
4. Why must the teeth of a saw be set? What does this mean?
5. Should the saw be pulled or pushed when starting a cut? Why?
6. How is wood held for cutting with a crosscut saw or a ripsaw?

unit

9

Assembling and adjusting planes

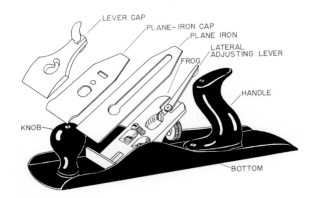

Fig. 9–1. Parts of a plane.

The plane is a very useful tool for the wood-worker. Although there are several types of planes, the assembly, adjustment, and general handling are alike. Common types of planes are the jack, smooth, jointer, block, rabbet, and router. Figure 9–1 shows the main parts of a plane.

Other tools often used to smooth wood are the spokeshave and the several types of scrapers. They are described in Unit 12, *Assembling and Adjusting a Spokeshave* and in Unit 16, *Assembling and Adjusting Scrapers.*

PLANES

The following descriptions and illustrations of planes will help you choose the best one for your working needs.

Jack Plane. This plane (Fig. 9–2) is the most used because of its size and usefulness. It will do the work of the smooth, jointer, and block planes. It is about 14 inches long with a 2-inch cutter blade.

Junior Jack Plane. The junior jack plane (not illustrated) is narrower and shorter than the jack plane, but otherwise is just like it. The bottom is about 10 inches long. It is light in weight and is used by grade and junior high school students.

Smooth Plane. This plane (Fig. 9–3) is exactly like the jack plane except that the bottom is only 9 inches long, with a 2-inch blade. It does fine, or exact, work.

Fig. 9–2. Jack plane.

Fig. 9–3. Smooth plane.

48

Fig. 9–4. Jointer plane.

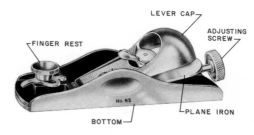

Fig. 9–5. Block plane.

Jointer Plane. The jointer plane (Fig 9–4) looks like the jack plane. The difference is that the bottom is from 18 to 22 inches long with a $2\frac{3}{8}$-inch blade. It is used most often for planing the edges of long boards.

Block Plane. This plane (Fig. 9–5) is made somewhat differently from the jack plane, but is adjusted in the same way. The length is approximately 7 inches with a $1\frac{5}{8}$-inch blade. The blade is at a more acute angle to the plane bottom than the blades in other planes. It is ideal for planing end grain or for easy handling of many small jobs.

Rabbet Plane. The rabbet plane illustrated in Fig. 9–6 is described as "bullnose" because of the way it looks. It is from 4 to 6 inches long. The plane works like the block plane, but is narrower. The 1-inch plane iron is near the front of the bottom to make it easy to plane in close places. The rabbet plane is often used for dressing, or shaping, tenons to fit snugly into mortises, and for dressing other places that are hard to get into. The plane iron extends through both sides of the plane, making it possible to plane along a corner.

Duplex Rabbet Plane. This rabbet plane (Fig. 9–7) has two seats for the cutter; one for regular work, the other for bullnose (close) planing. It is fitted with a spur and a removable depth gage. It also has an adjustable fence which can be used on either side. It is approximately 8 inches in length, with

Fig. 9–6. Rabbet plane.

Fig. 9–7. Duplex rabbet plane.

Fig. 9–8. Side rabbet plane.

49

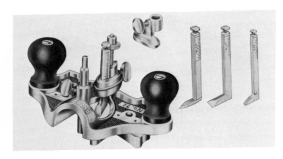

Fig. 9–9. Open-throat router plane.

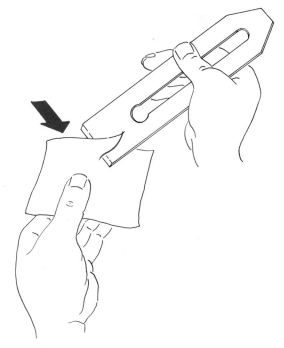

Fig. 9–12. Testing the cutting edge on a piece of paper to determine the sharpness of a plane iron.

Fig. 9–10. Small router plane.

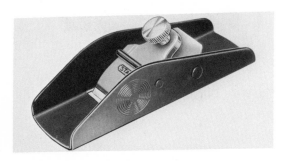

Fig. 9–11. Small trimming plane.

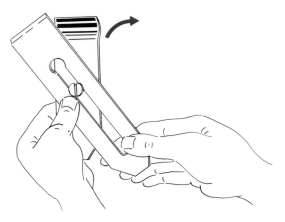

Fig. 9–13. Assembling the plane-iron cap and plane iron.

a 1½-inch cutter blade. Its use is similar to that of the rabbet plane (Fig. 9–6), except it is more versatile because of the many attachments.

Side Rabbet Plane. A plane of this type (Fig. 9–8) is used to trim dadoes, molding, and grooves. It is 5½ inches long; the cutter blade is ½ inch wide.

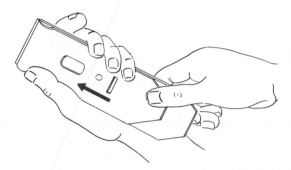

Fig. 9–14. Aligning the plane-iron cap and plane iron.

Fig. 9–15. Assembled plane iron and cap.

Open-Throat Router Plane. Figure 9–9 shows an open throat router plane with three types of cutters which come with it. It is used for surfacing (smoothing) the bottom of grooves or other depressions parallel with the surface of the board.

Small Router Plane. The small router plane (Fig. 9–10) is useful for very narrow work such as inlay and cutting dadoes for shelves. It is only 3 inches long; the cutter blade is ¼ inch wide.

Small Trimming Plane. This small, light plane (Fig. 9–11) is handy for miscellaneous light work and model building. It fits into the palm of the hand. The length is 3½ inches; the cutter blade is 1 inch wide.

ASSEMBLING AND ADJUSTING

Assembling and adjusting a plane are not difficult if you follow the instructions given here. Learn to look at the illustrations and understand what is being shown.

Assembling.

1. Test the plane iron for sharpness (Fig. 9–12). It should cut paper easily with a shearing, or side, cut.

2. Place the plane-iron cap on the flat side of the plane iron with the screw in the slot (Fig. 9–13).

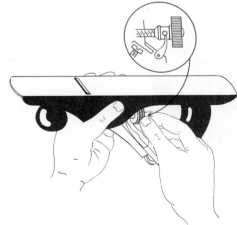

Fig. 9–16. Adjusting the plane iron for cutting depth.

3. Pull the plane-iron cap back and turn it straight with the plane iron (Fig. 9–14).

4. Slide the cap toward the cutting edge of the plane iron. Never push the cap over the edge of the blade (see Fig. 9–14).

5. Adjust and tighten the cap with a screwdriver. The cap should be about 1/16 inch from the cutting edge of the blade (Fig. 9–15).

6. Place the blade and plane-iron cap in the plane. Put the plane iron with its bevel side down on the frog. Be sure that the plane iron is properly placed on the lateral adjusting lever (see Fig. 9–1).

7. Lay the lever cap over the plane-iron assembly so that the screw slides in the slot (see Fig. 9–1).

8. Tighten the lever cap to hold the entire assembly. Figure 9–2 shows the lever cap in its proper position.

Adjusting.

1. Move the plane iron with the lateral adjusting lever until the cutting edge is parallel with the bottom of the plane.

2. Set the cutting depth with the adjustment nut near the handle. Move the nut right or left until you get the correct depth (Fig. 9–16).

Discussion Topics

1. List six parts of a plane. Describe the use of each.
2. What type of plane is the most popular with woodworkers?
3. Name at least five types of planes. Tell how each may be used.
4. Show how to assemble and adjust a jack plane.

---

unit

10

Planing

Planing surfaces, edges, and ends accurately with a hand plane requires skill and a sharp plane iron, or blade. Squaring stock, or lumber, will provide basic experience. A board has been *squared* when all the surfaces are square to each other and are true, or accu-

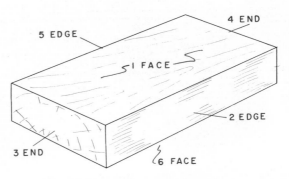

Fig. 10–1. Steps in planing a board.

rate, and smooth. All the pieces in a project will fit together properly if each part has been squared to the dimensions in the drawing. Figure 10–1 shows *by number* a sequence, or order, for the steps to be taken when you square a board.

TOOLS

The tools used in planing and squaring lumber have already been illustrated and described in previous units of this book. They are the jack plane, try square, steel square, marking gage, rule, crosscut saw, ripsaw, and backsaw.

PLANING THE FIRST SURFACE

1. Select the best surface, or face, of the board (see Fig. 10–1). If the board has not been cut to approximate length, refer to Unit 7, *Measuring and Laying Out Lumber* and to Unit 8, *Sawing Across or With the Grain of the Wood.*

2. Place the board on the bench and fasten it between the vise dog and a bench or board stop (Figs. 10–2 and 10–3). Place the board so that you can plane in the direction of the grain, or fiber, of the wood.

3. Adjust the cutting depth of the plane iron so that it will cut evenly and not too deep.

4. Plane the surface until it is clean and smooth (Fig. 10–4).

Fig. 10–3. Bench or board stop.

Fig. 10–4. Planing a surface.

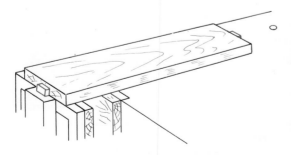

Fig. 10–2. Board fastened on bench against a bench stop, ready for planing.

Fig. 10–5. Testing for flatness.

Fig. 10-6. Testing diagonally for a wind.

5. Test the surface for flatness with the blade of a try square or with the tongue of a framing square (Fig. 10-5). The entire blade should touch the surface throughout the board.

6. Test the surface diagonally across the board to detect a *wind*, or twist (see Fig. 10-6). You may have to use a longer straight-edge such as a framing square.

PLANING THE FIRST EDGE

1. Select the best edge of the board. This will probably be the one requiring the least amount of planing.

2. Fasten the board in a vise with the selected edge up. The direction of the grain should be away from you (Figs. 10-7 and 10-8).

3. Plane the edge until it is square with the *working face*, or planed surface (see Fig. 10-8). Notice where to put pressure on the plane for starting and finishing the stroke.

4. Test the edge with the face for square-ness (Fig. 10-9).

PLANING THE FIRST END

1. Select the best end of the board.

2. Fasten the board in a vise with the selected end up (see Fig. 10-13).

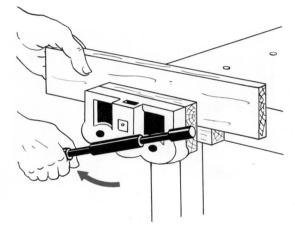

Fig. 10-7. Fastening a board in a vise for edge planing.

Fig. 10-8. Planing an edge.

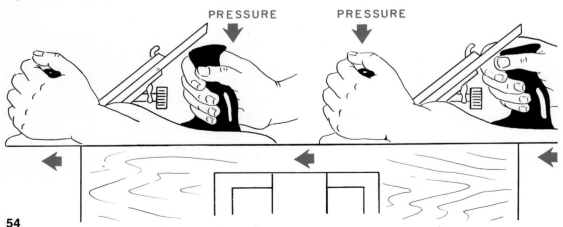

PRESSURE   PRESSURE

Fig. 10–9. Testing an edge for squareness.

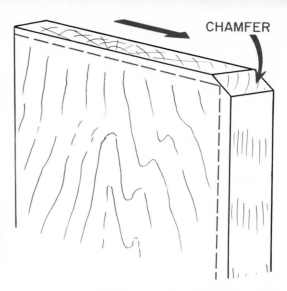

Fig. 10–10. Chamfering an end for end planing.

3. Choose the method you will use in planing the end. Follow one of these three steps, a, b, or c:

    a. Cut the end to make a chamfer as shown in Fig. 10–10. See Unit 11, *Shaping a Chamfer and a Bevel*, for details of a chamfer. This should be cut from the unfinished edge. You may then plane in the direction of the arrow without splitting the edge.

    b. Clamp a narrow piece of scrap wood against the unfinished edge (see Fig. 10–11). Plane in the direction of the arrow. This prevents splintering the outer edge.

    c. Plane two-thirds of the distance across the end from one side, and then reverse the direction. The opposite edge will not split off if the plane is lifted before the blade goes completely across (Fig. 10–12). Use a block plane on very narrow boards.

4. Plane the end until it is square with the planed surface and edge (Fig. 10–13). Hold a wide board in a vise with a hand screw clamp. Fasten it to the board so that the clamp rests flat on the bench top.

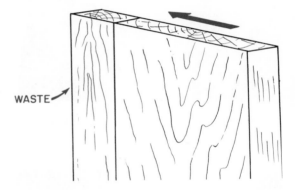

Fig. 10–11. Adding a piece of scrap stock for end planing.

Fig. 10–12. Planing end grain from both directions.

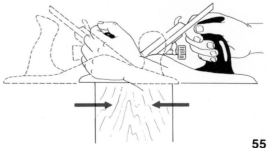

5. Test the end for squareness to the working face (see Fig. 10–14). Test it for squareness to the planed edge (see Figs. 10–15 and 10–16). This may be done with a try square on a narrow board or with a framing square on a wider one.

PLANING THE OPPOSITE END

1. Measure the board for the length needed, and mark it (Fig. 10–17). Allow an extra ¹⁄₁₆ inch for sawing and planing.

Fig. 10–15. Testing squareness of an end with a try square.

Fig. 10–13. Planing the end of a wide board.

Fig. 10–16. Testing squareness of an end with a framing square.

Fig. 10–14. Testing squareness of an end to the surface.

Fig. 10–17. Measuring a board for length.

2. Mark the length square with the planed edge (see Fig. 7–19).

3. Cut off the extra lumber with a cross-cut saw or a backsaw. Figure 10–18 shows how you can make this cut with a backsaw on a bench hook.

4. Plane the cut end to the line so that it will be square with both the planed face and edge. Test for squareness. See the fifth step under "Planing the First End."

PLANING THE OPPOSITE EDGE

1. Measure and mark the board very carefully for width. Refer to the first step under "Planing the Opposite End."

2. Cut off the extra lumber, if necessary, with a ripsaw. Be careful to do this only when the waste is approximately ³⁄₈ inch or more. Remember to allow ¹⁄₁₆ inch for planing to the line.

3. Plane this edge to the line so that it will be square with the working face, or surface, and also square with both ends.

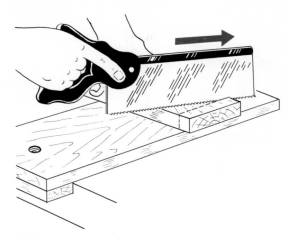

Fig. 10–18. Sawing a board to length with a backsaw on a bench hook.

PLANING THE LAST SURFACE

1. Mark the board for thickness with the marking gage (see Fig. 7–27.) Put the gage line on both edges and ends.

2. Plane this last surface to the gage line. Test it for squareness and smoothness.

Discussion Topics

1. Summarize the six general steps for planing a board. Why should this order be followed?

2. When would the ends of a board not have to be planed?

3. Is it possible to plane a board to the required thickness and still not have the faces true, or accurate? Explain.

4. How would you test a board to make sure that the surface was true?

5. How would you hold a wide board in a vise while planing the end grain?

6. What are three methods of planing the end grain?

7. What is meant by a working face?

8. What is meant by a wind in a board?

9. When you place a plane on a bench, why should it always be placed on its side?

10. What will happen to a planed surface or edge if the plane iron has a nick?

unit

11

Shaping a chamfer and a bevel

A chamfer is a means of decorating an edge. A bevel may be either an edge treatment in itself or a way to fit two boards together at an angle. The chamfer and the bevel look somewhat alike. Figure 11–1 shows the difference. The chamfer is usually planed to a 45-degree angle, while the bevel may be at any angle.

TOOLS

The tools generally used for making either a chamfer or a bevel are the sliding bevel and a jack or a block plane. Each of these has been shown and discussed in earlier units.

LAYING OUT A CHAMFER AND A BEVEL

1. Gage, or mark, the line or lines lightly with the marking gage or sharp pencil to outline the chamfer or bevel. Figure 11–2 shows how to draw a gage line with a pencil. Gaging with a pencil is better because sometimes the spur point of the marking gage cuts and damages the surface grain.

Fig. 11–2. Gaging a line with a pencil.

Fig. 11–3. Planing a chamfer.

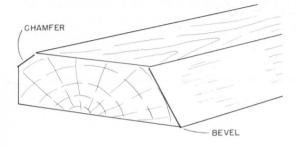

Fig. 11–1. Chamfer and bevel.

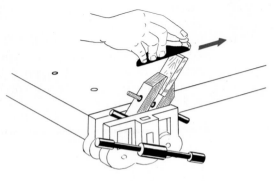

Fig. 11–4. Planing a chamfer on a small block of wood.

Fig. 11–5. Testing the angle of a chamfer with a sliding bevel.

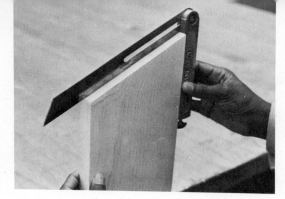

Fig. 11–6. Testing the angle of a bevel with a sliding bevel.

2. Set the bevel to the desired angle and check the outlined chamfer or bevel.

PLANING AND TESTING

1. Fasten the board in a vise (Fig. 11–3).
2. Plane the chamfer or bevel (Fig. 11–3).

If the board or block is small, fasten it in a hand-screw clamp which is held in a vise (Fig. 11–4). It may then be planed with a small block plane.

3. Test the angle of the chamfer or bevel with a sliding bevel (Figs. 11–5 and 11–6).

Discussion Topics

1. Illustrate the difference between a chamfer and a bevel.

2. What tool is used to test the angle of a chamfer? Of a bevel?

---

unit

12

Assembling and adjusting a spokeshave

The spokeshave (Fig. 12–1) is a tool for cutting and shaping. It was used many years ago for making spokes for wheels, hence its name. Today it is used mostly for forming curved edges on boards. Such curved edges are either *concave* (inward) or *convex* (outward). In craft work it is used to make such projects as the bows and hulls of model boats.

The cutting blade of the spokeshave is sharpened like the plane iron. You may either push or pull this tool, whichever is easier.

Follow these steps for assembling and adjusting a spokeshave:

1. Test the blade for sharpness. Refer to Fig. 9–12, since the cutting edge should be as sharp as that of a plane iron.

2. Place the blade carefully into the spokeshave frame; make sure that the slots of the blade will fit on the adjusting nuts.

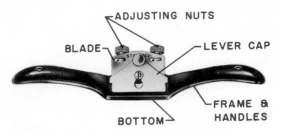

ADJUSTING NUTS

BLADE

LEVER CAP

FRAME & HANDLES

BOTTOM

Fig. 12-1. Adjustable spokeshave.

3. Place the lever cap over the blade. Slide it under the lever-cap screw.

4. Tighten the blade with the thumb-screw.

5. Adjust for the proper cutting depth with the adjusting nuts (Fig. 12-1).

6. Test the cutting depth on a piece of scrap wood.

Discussion Topics

1. How did the spokeshave get its name?
2. Where and why do you use the spoke-shave?
3. How is the spokeshave similar to a plane?
4. Should you push or pull a spokeshave?
5. How is the spokeshave adjusted?

unit

13

Laying out irregular pieces and curves

Pieces that make up a project are often irregular or curved in shape. Because of this, you should know how to enlarge a pattern. Usually working drawings in books are drawn to a scale which fits the page, often to one-fourth of the actual size. The dimensions, however, are given in full size. To make irregular or curved pieces in the full size, you must enlarge the drawing. You should also learn how to draw a hexagon, or six-sided figure, an octagon, or eight-sided figure, and an ellipse, or oval. It is also essential to know how to lay out distances and regular curves with dividers.

TOOLS

The following tools are needed for laying out:

Dividers. This layout tool is used by both wood- and metalworkers (Fig. 13-1). You use it to lay out small circles; for dividing spaces equally; for scribing, or marking, arcs; and for transferring measurements. A compass may be used for the same purpose.

Trammel Points. These are used for laying out large arcs and circles (Fig. 13-2). Another means of scribing a large arc is to tie a piece of string to a pencil, which can serve as a compass.

Rule. This measuring device has been discussed in Unit 7, *Measuring and Laying Out Lumber.*

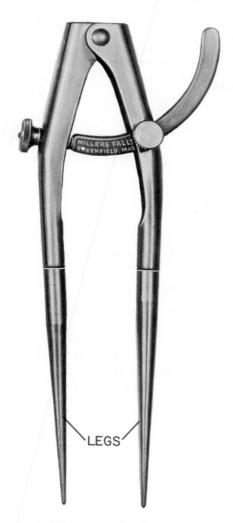

LEGS

Fig. 13–1. Wing dividers.

Fig. 13–2. Trammel points.

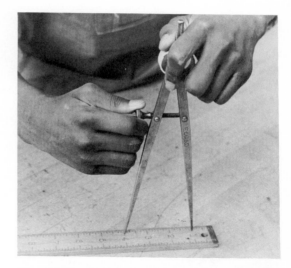

Fig. 13–3. Setting spring dividers for a desired distance. Here they are set for 3 inches.

CURVES, ARCS, AND CIRCLES

1. Set the dividers, compass, or trammel points to the desired radius of the arc, curve, or circle. When dividers are used to set distances, one leg is placed on an inch mark of a rule. The other leg is then placed on a mark far enough away to make the distance desired (see Fig. 13–3). On most dividers, this distance is kept by locking the thumbscrew.

2. Scribe the arc, curve, or circle as shown in Fig. 13–4. Note that a heavy piece of paper or cardboard has been placed under the stationary leg to protect the wood surface.

EQUAL DISTANCES

1. Set the dividers for the distance that is to be duplicated or stepped off.

2. Lay out, or step off, these equal distances as shown in Fig. 13–5.

HEXAGON (SIX-SIDED FIGURE)

1. Decide what length you want for one side of the hexagon.

2. Set a compass or dividers for a radius of the same length as the side in step 1.

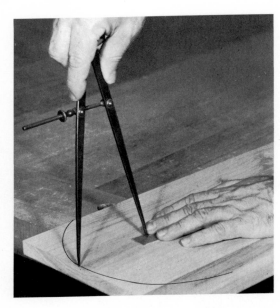

Fig. 13-4. Scribing an arc with dividers. Note the piece of cardboard under the stationary leg to protect the wood grain.

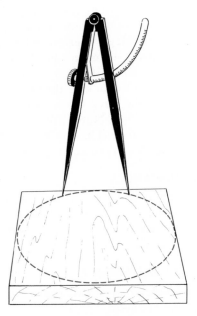

Fig. 13-5. Stepping off equal distances with dividers.

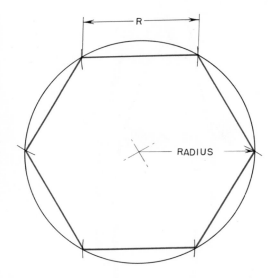

Fig. 13-6. Hexagon (R = radius).

3. Draw a circle, using the radius set in step 2. Do this directly on the wood, or on paper or cardboard. The paper or cardboard may serve as a *template*, or pattern.

4. Step off equal distances with the dividers on the circumference of the circle by using the radius described in step 2 (Fig. 13-6).

5. Connect the intersecting points on the circumference with straight lines (Fig. 13-6). These will make the hexagon.

OCTAGON (EIGHT-SIDED FIGURE)

1. Determine the overall width of the octagon. This will be the distance from one side to the opposite side.

2. Lay out a square this size.

3. Set the dividers or compass for a distance equal to one-half the length of a diagonal of the square. The diagonal is a line extending from opposite corners. In Fig. 13-7, the diagonals are lines AD and BC.

4. Set the points of the dividers on points A and O (Fig. 13-7). Use point A as the center.

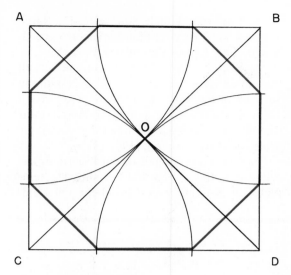

Fig. 13-7. Octagon.

5. Scribe an arc intersecting, or crossing, the sides of the square.

6. Repeat step 5 from the other three corners, *B*, *C*, and *D*.

7. Draw straight lines joining the intersecting points on the sides of the square (Fig. 13-7). This makes the octagon.

ELLIPSE (OVAL)

1. Decide on the desired width and length of the ellipse (Fig. 13-8).

2. Draw a rectangle with sides representing the width and length of the ellipse (Fig. 13-8). Draw this directly on the wood or on a suitable template.

3. Divide the rectangle *through the center* with horizontal line *AB* and vertical line *CD* (Fig. 13-8).

4. Set the dividers to one-half the length of line *AB*. This makes radius *XB* (see Fig. 13-8).

5. Place one point of the dividers on point *D*. Draw an arc which cuts lines *AB* at *E* and *F* (Fig. 13-8).

6. Place brads, thumbtacks, or pins at points *C*, *E*, and *F* (Fig. 13-8).

7. Fasten a string around points *C*, *E*, and *F* to form a triangle, as shown in Fig. 13-8.

8. Remove the brad from point *C*.

9. Place a pencil against the string, starting at point *C*, and draw half of the ellipse *A*, *C*, *B* (Fig. 13-8).

10. Repeat step 9 with the pencil point beginning at *D*. This will complete the ellipse (Fig. 13-8).

11. Remove the brads, thumbtacks, and string. You have formed the ellipse.

Another method of making an ellipse involves the use of a compass and a rule. This method is explained in most of the drawing books.

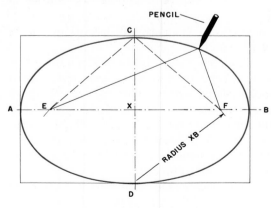

Fig. 13-8. Drawing an ellipse.

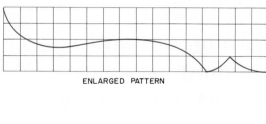

ENLARGED PATTERN

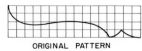

ORIGINAL PATTERN

Fig. 13-9. Enlarging a pattern.

63

ENLARGING AND TRANSFERRING

1. Decide on the portion of the drawing which needs to be drawn full scale (Fig. 13–9).

2. Draw vertical and horizontal lines ¼ inch apart over the section to be enlarged, if the drawing has not already been graphed in this manner. This instruction assumes that the drawing was made to the scale in which ¼ inch equals 1 inch. If the scale is different, draw the graph accordingly (Fig. 13–9).

3. Lay out 1-inch squares on a large sheet of kraft or wrapping paper or on cardboard. This makes the enlarged graph.

4. Sketch on the full-size, enlarged graph the points were the design intersects with the squares in the working drawing (Fig. 13–9).

5. Connect these points freehand until the full-size pattern looks like the reduced, or scale, working drawing (Fig. 13–9).

6. Cut out the paper or cardboard for the full-size pattern. Figure 13–9 shows a template, or pattern, which has been enlarged.

Discussion Topics

1. Why is it desirable to place a piece of cardboard under the stationary leg of the dividers when scribing an arc or circle on a piece of wood?
2. Draw each of the following: (a) a hexagon, (b) an octagon, (c) an ellipse. Which is the easiest?
3. Describe the procedure for enlarging a pattern.
4. List at least three uses for dividers.
5. Give an example where trammel points might be used.
6. Describe: (a) a hexagon, (b) an octagon, (c) an ellipse.

---

unit

14

Cutting out and forming irregular pieces and curves

To cut out and form irregular pieces and curves, you must know what tools to use and how to use them. You should also know which tools will do the best work for each process.

TOOLS

The following tools are essential for cutting and forming irregular pieces:

Coping Saw. The coping saw, shown in Fig. 14–1, is especially useful for cutting small stock, such as thin boards or pieces of plywood.

Compass Saw. Figure 14–2 pictures this saw. There is also a *keyhole saw*, which looks similar and is sometimes considered a fine compass saw. The compass saw is useful for cutting interior curves where a turning saw or a coping saw cannot be used. The cut is usually started by boring a hole near the line to be cut.

Spokeshave. This tool was illustrated and discussed in Unit 12 *Assembling and Adjusting a Spokeshave.*

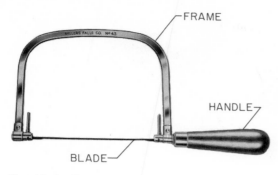

Fig. 14–1. Coping saw.

Fig. 14–2. Compass saw.

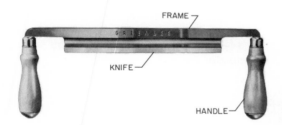

Fig. 14–3. Drawknife.

Drawknife. The drawknife (Fig. 14–3) has a blade approximately 10 to 12 inches long, with a handle on each end.

⬡ *Caution: Handle this tool carefully.*

Skilled workmen use it effectively for removing large amounts of stock rapidly. It is used to trim stock and in building model boats and canoe paddles.

Wood, or Cabinet, Files. The common shapes of files used by the woodworker are flat, half-round, round, and triangular (Fig. 14–4). They come in many lengths, from 4

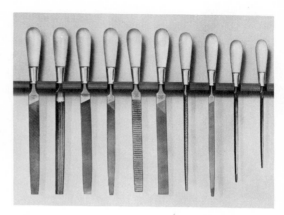

Fig. 14–4. This photograph shows the important practices of placing handles on files and placing the files in the proper rack. From left to right, the names of the files are: flat, half-round, mill, triangular or three-square, half-round wood rasp, hand, round, slim taper, extra-slim taper, double-extra-slim taper. *(Nicholson File Company.)*

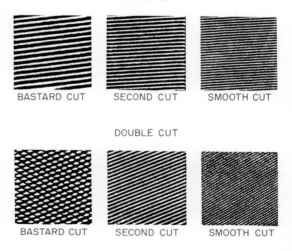

Fig. 14–5. Patterns of teeth on single- and double-cut files.

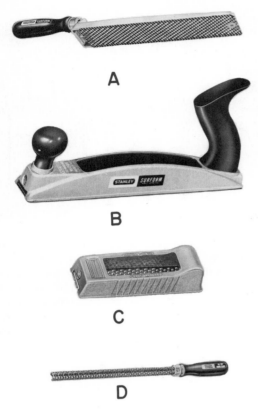

A

B

C

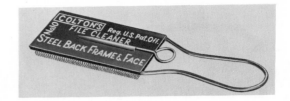

Fig. 14–7. File cleaner.

Fig. 14–8. Tracing a pattern on wood around a template.

D

Fig. 14–6. Surface- and edge-forming tools: (A) file, (B) plane forming tool, (C) block-plane forming tool, and (D) round.

to 14 inches. Files are used for smoothing edges and small curves. The cutting surface consists of rows of teeth which run in parallel lines diagonally across the surface. Figure 14–5 illustrates the patterns of teeth on single- and double-cut files.

Figure 14–6 shows file-type cutting tools. They cut faster than other forming tools.

Pointers on the Use of Files.

1. See that there is a handle on every file.

2. Keep files from rubbing together or against other tools.

Surface- and Edge-forming Tools. The forming tools shown in Fig. 14–6 serve as files or as modifications of planes. The replaceable, inexpensive steel blades will plane,

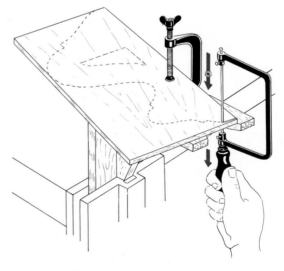

Fig. 14–9. Sawing on a V block.

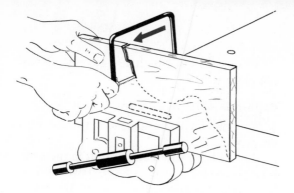

Fig. 14–10. Cutting with a coping saw.

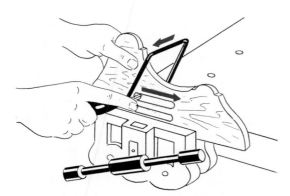

Fig. 14–11. Sawing a pierced design with a coping saw.

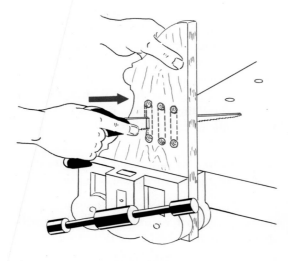

Fig. 14–12. Cutting with a compass saw.

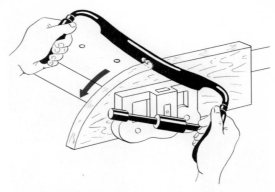

Fig. 14–13. Cutting with a drawknife.

file, and shape wood, soft metals, and plastics. Either tool works fast for fitting, trimming, smoothing, and shaving. The cutting edge of the blade has its own throat through which the cuttings pass.

File Cleaner. The file cleaner, or file card (Fig. 14–7), has steel bristles which are used for cleaning the teeth on a file (see Fig. 14–20).

CUTTING WITH A COPING SAW

1. Lay out the irregular design or pattern. You may make it directly on the wood or trace around a template (Fig. 14–8).

2. Place the wood on a V block or jig, and hold it securely with the hand or with a hand clamp (Fig. 14–9). Hold the V block or jig in a vise, or fasten it directly to a bench top.

Usually the blade of the coping saw is inserted with the teeth pointing toward the handle. This prevents the possibility of buckling, or kinking.

Clamp heavier stock in a bench vise and cut as shown in Fig. 14–10.

3. Grasp the stock securely with the left hand and saw with firm strokes (Fig. 14–10). The first stroke will be a pull.

4. For a pierced, or perforated, design, bore or drill a small hole on the waste part

67

Fig. 14–14. Pushing the spokeshave to smooth a convex edge.

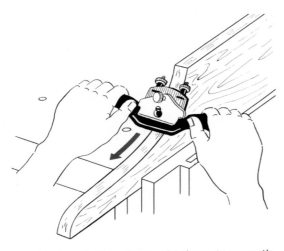

Fig. 14–15. Pulling the spokeshave to smooth concave curves.

of the stock near the line. Remove the blade from the frame, insert it through the hole, and fasten it securely to the frame again before sawing.

5. Saw out the pierced design as shown in Fig. 14–11.

Check the cut which you have made with the pattern.

CUTTING WITH A COMPASS SAW

1. Transfer the design to, or draw it on, the wood.

2. Start the saw kerf, or cut, in the same way you start a crosscut kerf (see Unit 8). Saw slightly outside the line, on the waste portion of the wood. The stock can then be dressed down to exact size.

3. Continue cutting. Use the narrow end of the blade for sharp turns.

4. When cutting inside curves and to irregular lines, bore a hole for starting the cut as shown in Fig. 14–12.

SHAPING WITH A DRAWKNIFE

1. Test the cutting edge of the draw-knife for sharpness. Test it as you test the plane iron (see Fig. 9–12).

2. Fasten the stock securely in a bench vise.

3. Look at the grain of the wood and determine the direction in which you will cut. Always cut in the direction of the grain to avoid splitting the wood.

4. Hold the drawknife firmly with both hands, with the bevel turned down.

5. Carefully cut away the waste portion of the wood with short strokes, pulling toward the body (Fig. 14–13). Adjust the depth of the cut by twisting the wrists. A cleaner cut may be made with a shearing stroke. For this stroke, hold one handle slightly ahead of the other.

CAUTION: Be very careful in using the draw-knife. The sharp edge can be dangerous.

6. Continue cutting until the waste stock has been almost entirely removed. It may then be shaped further with a spokeshave (Fig. 14–14), a file (Fig. 14–16), or a chisel (Fig. 15–9).

Fig. 14–16. Filing a convex curve.

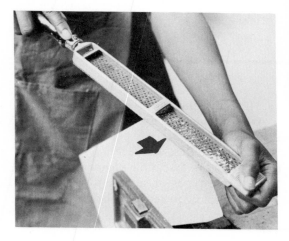

Fig. 14–17. Dressing a convex curve with a forming tool.

Fig. 14–18. Dressing an edge with a plane forming tool.

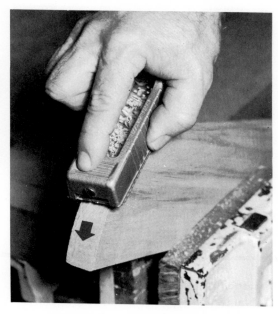

Fig. 14–19. Dressing an edge with a block-plane forming tool.

FORMING WITH THE SPOKESHAVE

1. Adjust the cutting edge of the spokeshave for uniform depth.

2. Clamp stock securely in a bench vise.

3. Smooth the curved edge with the spokeshave to the exact pattern line (Figs. 14–14 and 14–15). This tool is used effectively by either pushing or pulling.

FORMING WITH THE FILE AND SURFACE-FORMING TOOLS

1. Select a medium-coarse wood file of the desired shape for the first smoothing. Use the file for forming only if other tools cannot be used.

2. Fasten the stock securely in a bench vise.

3. Push the file or forming tool across the edge of the wood with a forward and side motion (Figs. 14–16 through 14–19).

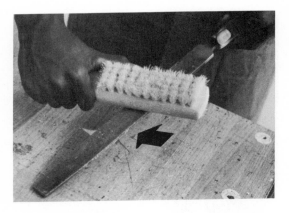

Fig. 14–20. Cleaning the file with a file cleaner.

This gives a shearing cut which prevents splintering of the opposite edge. File the edges of plywood carefully. They break and splinter easily.

4. Continue filing the irregular edge with a medium-coarse file until you get a semi-smooth finish.

5. Finish smoothing the edge curve with a smooth-cut file.

6. Test the irregular edge with a try square for squareness with the surface.

7. Clean the files with a file cleaner (Fig. 14–20). Cleaning files frequently keeps the cutting edges in better condition.

Discussion Topics

1. Name two types of handsaws which can be used for cutting irregular curves.
2. Should the teeth point toward or away from the handle when you use a coping saw?
3. What is the chief purpose of the drawknife?
4. How can the depth of the cut be controlled when using a drawknife?
5. What is the difference between the single- and the double-cut file?
6. Why do you use a file cleaner?
7. List two types of surface-forming tools. Explain how to replace blades.

---

unit

15

Cutting and trimming with a chisel

Accurate cutting, fitting, shaping, and surface decoration are done with sharp and correctly beveled wood chisels. Wood chisels are pictured in Fig. 15–1.

A

B

Fig. 15–1. Wood chisels: (A) tang butt, and (B) socket.

TOOLS

Take the greatest care when you cut and trim with chisels and gouges. Remember that the wood chisel is the cause of more injuries than all other hand tools.

Chisels. Wood chisels are generally classified in two types, socket and tang (Fig. 15–1). The names indicate how the handle is fastened to the blade. Socket chisels are firmer. Both types have a beveled cutting edge. The width of the blade determines the size of the wood chisel. The range is from ⅛ to 1 inch by eighths, and from 1 to 2 inches by fourths.

Gouges. Gouges are chisels used for grooving, for shaping edges, and for model-making. There are two types of gouges. One has the bevel on the inside of the blade (Fig. 15–2); the other has it on the outside (Fig. 15–3). The blades of all gouges are concave (hollowed). They vary from ¼ to 2 inches in width.

Wooden or Fiber Mallet. Use the mallet for additional pressure when you are chiseling (see Fig. 15–4).

HORIZONTAL CHISELING

1. Fasten the wood firmly in a bench vise.

2. Push the chisel with one hand and guide the blade with the other (Fig. 15–5). Use the forefinger and thumb of the guide hand as a brake. Be sure that the bevel of the chisel is turned *up* when it is used in this way. The chisel must be kept very sharp to get a clean cut. Always cut away from you.

3. Continue to make thin cuts, taking care to stop each time before reaching the opposite side. When you are cutting across a board, as in a half-lap joint, you should protect the grain on the opposite side. The three steps to follow are shown in the inset in Fig. 15–5. These will guide you in making a clean cut.

Fig. 15–2. Inside-bevel socket gouge.

Fig. 15–3. Outside-bevel socket gouge.

Fig. 15–4. Soft-face mallet.

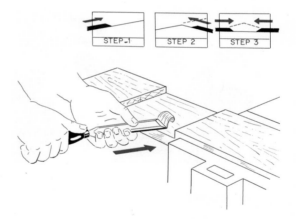

Fig. 15–5. Horizontal chiseling.

VERTICAL CHISELING

1. Fasten the wood securely in a bench vise (Fig. 15–6). You can also hold it firmly on a bench hook.

2. Hold the flat side of the chisel against the wood in a vertical, or upright, position.

3. Hold the chisel with one hand and guide the blade with the other (Fig. 15–6). The guide hand serves as a brake.

71

Fig. 15-6. Vertical chiseling. As you push the chisel with one hand, guide the blade with the other.

Fig. 15-7. Furniture craftsmen handle wood chisels with skill.

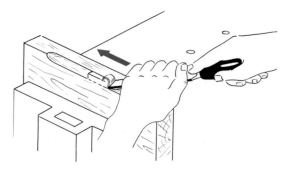

Fig. 15-8. Cutting a stop chamfer with a chisel.

4. Push the chisel and apply a shearing cut as shown in Figs. 15–6 and 15–7.

5. Use a wooden or fiber mallet only when necessary to drive the chisel for cutting out mortises. It takes practice to control a chisel cut when you drive it with a mallet. Make a trial cut on a piece of scrap wood to learn how hard to hit the chisel.

CUTTING STOP CHAMFERS

1. Mark the width and length of the stop chamfer with a pencil on the edge of the board.

2. Fasten the board firmly in a bench vise.

3. Cut or pare by starting at one end of the stop chamfer (Fig. 15–8). Make thin cuts about one-half the length of the chamfer.

4. Continue with light cuts until the pencil line is reached.

5. Reverse the board in the vise, and cut the other half of the chamfer from the opposite end in the same way.

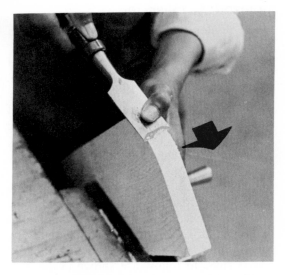

Fig. 15-9. Trimming a convex curve with a chisel. Use a series of short strokes.

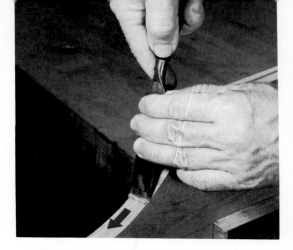

Fig. 15–10. Trimming a concave edge with a chisel. Note the beveled side is against the wood.

Fig. 15–11. Cutting a chamfer on a laminated corbel (weight-supporting member). This piece will form a part of a wooden truss.

Fig. 15–12. Cutting a groove in a surface.

Fig. 15–13. Carving a chair leg.

Fig. 15–14. A carved galloping horse scuptured from walnut. (*Fine Hardwoods Association.*)

CURVED CHISELING

1. Fasten the wood securely in a bench vise.

2. When you cut a round corner, push the chisel in a shearing motion. Use a series of short strokes (Fig. 15–9). Be sure that the bevel edge of the chisel is turned *up*.

3. On a concave edge, trim by holding the bevel side of the chisel against the wood. Push the chisel with the right hand (Figs. 15–10 and 15–11). Use the left hand to hold the chisel against the work. Always cut in the direction of the grain.

GROOVING

Grooves may be cut in boards with a gouge as shown in Fig. 15–12. Internal carving or cutting can also be done with this same tool (Figs. 15–13 and 15–14).

Discussion Topics

1. Name the two general classifications of wood chisels.
2. What is the purpose of a gouge? How should this tool be sharpened?
3. Why should you grind small nicks out of the cutting edges of chisels and gouges?
4. Explain the differences and uses of wood and cold chisels.

---

unit

16

Assembling and adjusting scrapers

Scrapers are used to smooth wood that is difficult to dress with a plane. They are particularly effective on irregular-grained, knotty, and burly lumber. The action of the scraper edge differs from the cut made by a plane or spokeshave. It scrapes by means of a filed or a burred, or turned, edge. See Unit 28, *Caring For and Sharpening Tools*.

TOOLS

The scraping tools described in this unit are simple to adjust. They are equally as easy to use.

Hand Scraper. The two shapes most used in hand scrapers are the rectangular (Fig. 16–1) and the swan neck. Hand scrapers are thin, flexible pieces of high-grade steel. When sharpened properly, they will make thin shavings. They are either pulled or pushed, depending on the job. No assembly is needed since the blade is held in the hands.

Cabinet Scraper. This is a metal frame with two handles which holds a scraper blade (Fig. 16–2). It is perhaps the most common scraper frame. You push it, as illustrated in the following unit, *Smoothing a Surface by Scraping.*

Pull Scraper. The pull scraper, sometimes referred to as the two-edge scraper,

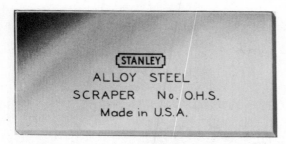

Fig. 16-1. Hand scraper blade.

Fig. 16-2. Cabinet scraper.

is shown in Fig. 16-3. It is pulled rather than pushed on the wood.

Scraper Plane. Perhaps the least used of the three scraper frames described here is the scraper plane. It looks like a smooth plane, except that the blade is held forward for a scraping action.

ASSEMBLING AND ADJUSTING

The following instructions are typical for any of the scraper frames:

1. Test the blade for the proper filed or burred edge. See Unit 28, *Caring For and Sharpening Tools.*

2. Place and tighten the blade in its proper position in the frame (Fig. 16-3).

This position will vary slightly with the different types of scraper frames.

Place the blade so that the filed or the burred edge will produce a shaving. This is a very simple adjustment. It is not necessary to go into detail for each type of frame.

3. Adjust the blade for depth of scraping with the thumbnut or thumbscrew, depending upon the type of scraper you use (Fig. 16-4).

Fig. 16-3. A two-edge, or pull, scraper.

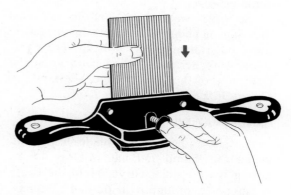

Fig. 16-4. Adjusting a cabinet scraper for depth of scraping action.

Discussion Topics

1. Why and where do you use scrapers?
2. Name two shapes of hand scrapers.
3. Is the scraper blade pulled or pushed?
4. Name three kinds of scraper frames. How did they get their names?
5. What is the most common scraper frame?
6. How do you adjust the blade in a scraper frame?

unit

17

Smoothing a surface by scraping

Surfaces and edges of a wooden board should be scraped if the grain is burly or knotty. The scraper produces a very fine surface. It will remove most irregularities and blemishes that may have been left by the plane. The scraper differs from a chisel or plane in that it does the work with a scraping edge.

Scrapers work very well in the final dressing of cedar. The knots in this wood make hand planing very difficult. The effectiveness of scraping will depend upon the sharpness of the scraper edge. See Unit 28, *Caring For and Sharpening Tools*.

HANDSCRAPING

1. Grasp the scraper blade firmly between the thumb and fingers (Fig. 17–1). Spring it to a slight curve. Hold the blade at an angle of approximately 45 degrees (Fig. 17–2).

2. Pull the scraper blade toward you if it is more convenient (Fig. 17–3).

SMOOTHING WITH A CABINET SCRAPER

1. Assemble and adjust the blade in its proper place in the cabinet-scraper body. See Unit 16, *Assembling and Adjusting Scrapers*, for the correct adjustment. The blade should be sharp.

2. Hold the scraper handles firmly, with the thumbs pressing on the frame behind the blade (Fig. 17–4).

Fig. 17–1. Scraping a surface with a hand scraper.

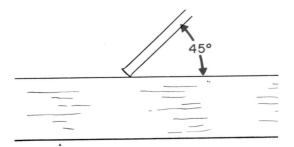

Fig. 17–2. Angle for handscraping.

Fig. 17–3. Pulling a scraper blade.

Fig. 17-4. Smoothing a surface with a cabinet scraper.

Fig. 17-5. Smoothing a surface with a pull scraper.

3. Try the scraper on a piece of wood and adjust it further if necessary. The cabinet scraper should produce a fine, thin, even shaving (Fig. 17-4).

4. Scrape the surface of the wood, being very careful to use long, even strokes. Be sure to work with the grain. Hold the cabinet scraper at a slight angle so that it will produce a shearing cut (Fig. 17-4).

5. Continue scraping until the entire surface has been smoothed evenly.

The pull, or two-edge, scraper, shown in Fig. 17-5, is ideal when you must scrape toward you. The pull scraper is described in Unit 16.

Discussion Topics

1. Why is it often necessary to scrape surfaces of wood?
2. What makes the scraper blade produce fine shavings?
3. At approximately what angle should you hold the hand scraper?
4. What is wrong with the scraper blade when it produces only dust?

unit

18

Boring and drilling holes

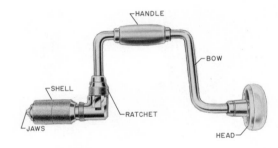

Fig. 18–1. Brace.

Holes are bored or drilled in wood for screws, bolts, dowels, internal sawing, and ornamentation. Types of bits used for boring or drilling include several kinds of auger bits, the twist drill, iron drill, expansive bit, Foerstner bit, door-lock bit, straight-shank drill, and the drill point for the push drill.

A depth gage is a supplementary tool that is useful when you bore holes to a given depth. Study the depth gages which are illustrated and described on pages 80 and 81 before attempting to bore a hole to a specified depth.

TOOLS

The descriptions and illustrations which follow will guide you in the proper selection of bits and other tools.

Brace. The brace (Fig. 18–1) is used with any of the bits which have a square *tang,* or shank (see Fig. 18–5). The corner brace illustrated in Fig. 18–2 is used for boring in corners and against walls and beams.

Hand Drill. The hand drill is used for drilling holes ⅜ inch or less in diameter (Fig. 18–3). The straight-shank drill (Fig. 18–14) should be used with the hand drill.

Push Drill. The push drill (Fig. 18–4) is often used instead of the hand drill.

Auger Bits. The auger bit (Fig. 18–5) varies in length from 7 to 10 inches, with one exception: the dowel auger bit is only

Fig. 18–2. Corner brace.

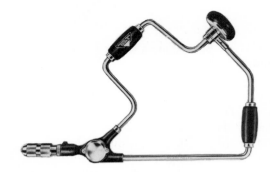

Fig. 18–3. Hand drill.

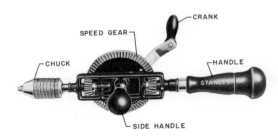

Fig. 18–4. Push drill.

Fig. 18–5. Solid-center auger bit.

5 inches long (Fig. 18–6). Auger bits are sized by sixteenths of an inch. They range from ¼ to 1 inch in diameter. The number stamped on the square tang indicates the bit size in sixteenths of an inch. For example, a bit with "11" stamped on it will cut a hole $^{11}/_{16}$ inch in diameter. One marked "6" will cut a ⅜-inch hole, because it is listed at $^{6}/_{16}$ inch.

A single-thread auger bit is illustrated in Fig. 18–7. It bores a hole in the same manner as the solid-center auger bit in Fig. 18–5. Figure 18–8 is a single-spur auger car bit. It varies in length from 18 to 29 inches, and is used mostly in building-construction work where holes must be bored deeper than can be done with a regular type of auger bit.

Twist Drills. The twist drill (Fig. 18–9) makes holes for screws, nails, and bolts. Twist drills are sized by thirty-seconds and sixty-fourths of an inch, and range from ⅛ to ½ inch in diameter. This drill has a square tang to fit the brace, and may be used instead of a drill bit.

Iron Drill. The iron drill (Fig. 18–10) drills holes in metal as well as in wood. These drills are sized in thirty-seconds of an inch, and range from $^{1}/_{16}$ to ⅝ inch in diameter.

Expansive Bit. The expansive bit (Fig. 18–11) has a scale on the movable spur or cutter. Holes larger than 1 inch in diameter are bored with the adjustable expansive bit. These bits are available with various cutters to bore holes from 1 to 4 inches in diameter.

Foerstner Bit. The Foerstner bit (Fig. 18–12) does many boring operations which the auger bit cannot do. It is made to bore a hole to any depth without breaking through the wood. These bits are available in sizes ranging from ¼ to 2 inches in diameter and are numbered for size in the same way as auger bits.

Fig. 18–6. Solid-center dowel auger bit.

Fig. 18–7. Single-thread point auger bit.

Fig. 18–8. Single-spur auger car bit.

Fig. 18–9. Twist drill.

Fig. 18–10. Iron drill.

Fig. 18–11. Expansive bit with extra cutter.

Fig. 18–12. Foerstner bit.

Fig. 18–13. Door-lock bit.

Fig. 18–14. Straight-shank drill.

Fig. 18–15. Drill point for push drill.

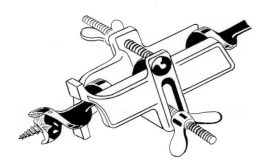

Fig. 18–16. Adjustable metal depth gage.

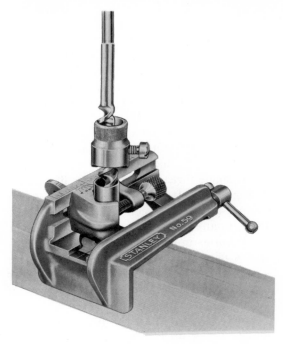

Fig. 18–17. Adjustable depth gage with doweling jig.

Fig. 18–18. Adjustable depth gage.

Door-lock Bit. The door-lock bit (Fig. 18–13) is used mainly by carpenters and cabinet workers to bore holes for tubular door locks and other shallow, large holes. The bit sizes vary from 1⅝ to 2⅛ inches in diameter.

Straight-shank Drill. The straight-shank drill (Fig. 18–14) is gaged for the diameter of the holes to be drilled. It uses any one of three systems: fractional, decimal, or lettered. The fractional is the most common for woodworking and is the most easily read. Fractional-size drills are marked in sixty-fourths of an inch. The smallest size is ¹⁄₁₆ inch. Woodworkers generally have an assortment up to ½ inch.

Drill Point for Push Drill. This type of bit (Fig. 18–15) fits into the automatic drill (Fig. 18–4). It is used for drilling small holes. Sizes vary from ¹⁄₁₆ to ¹¹⁄₆₄ inch.

Depth Gage. The depth gages shown in Figs. 18–16 through 18–18 are necessary when you bore holes to specified depths. You can make a very simple gage by bor-

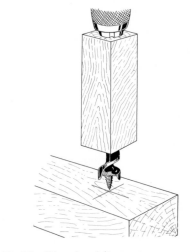

Fig. 18–19. Wooden bit gage.

Fig. 18–20. Scratch awl.

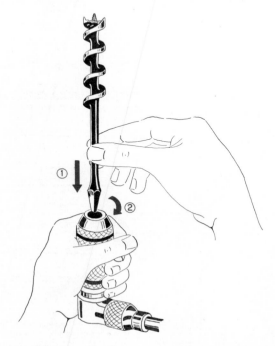

Fig. 18–21. Putting an auger bit into the brace chuck.

Fig. 18–22. Starting the hole with an awl.

ing a hole through a piece of wood lengthwise (Fig. 18–19).

Scratch Awl. Figure 18–20 shows a scratch awl. It is helpful for starting a hole, as shown in Fig. 18–22, so that boring and drilling bits will have a center when beginning a hole.

BORING A HOLE

1. Select the correct size of square-shank auger bit or other bit for boring into wood.

2. Open the chuck by grasping the shell and turning the handle to the left. Keep turning until the jaws are open wide enough to hold the tapered shank of the bit. Place the bit in the chuck of the brace (Fig. 18–21).

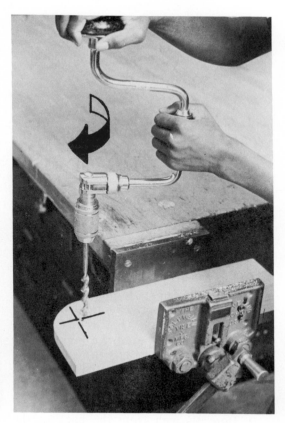

Fig. 18–23. Boring a hole vertically.

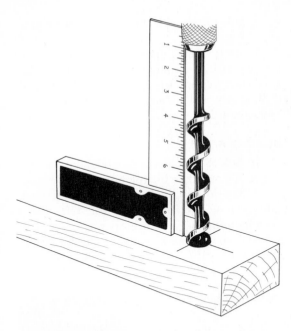

Fig. 18–24. Testing the boring for accuracy.

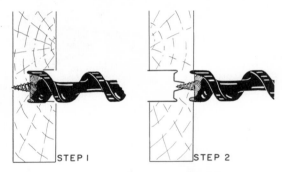

Fig. 18–25. Step 1: Correct procedure in boring a hole. Step 2: Boring a clean-cut hole.

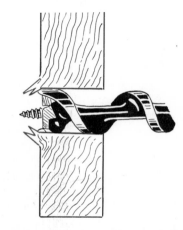

Fig. 18–26. Incorrect boring of a hole.

Fig. 18–27. Boring a hole with the aid of a piece of scrap wood.

3. Fasten the bit firmly in the chuck. Turn the handle to the right until the bit is held securely.

4. Mark the place where the hole is to be bored. Start the hole with an awl to give the feed screw a definite hold (Fig. 18–22).

5. Place the feed screw at the spot marked for the center of the hole. Make a few turns with the brace to start the hole (Fig. 18–23).

6. Place a try square on the wood and against the bit. This is to make certain that the hole is being bored at right angles to the surface of the work (Fig. 18–24).

7. Bore carefully until the point of the feed screw begins to come through on the back of the work (Fig. 18–25, step 1).

8. Remove the bit from the hole by reversing the direction of the boring.

9. Bore through from the back of the work to make the hole clean-cut and with-

out splinters (Fig. 18–25, step 2). Figure 18–26 shows what will happen if the bit goes completely through the wood.

Another method of boring a hole without splintering the back is shown in Fig. 18–27. Holes bored with an expansive bit should be backed up with a piece of scrap wood held behind the board.

When you bore holes for dowel joints, use a regular shortened dowel auger bit with the dowel jig.

BORING TO A SPECIFIED DEPTH

1. Fasten a square-tang bit of the desired diameter in a brace. See steps 2 and 3 of "Boring a Hole," above.

2. Fasten the adjustable metal depth gage (Figs. 18–16 through 18–18) on the bit to regulate the depth of the hole. The wooden depth gage illustrated in Fig. 18–19 can also be used.

3. Check this depth against a rule.

4. Bore the hole until the depth gage stops the boring action.

5. Remove the bit and clear loose wood particles out of the hole.

DRILLING A HOLE

1. Select a straight-shank drill bit of the desired diameter. The push drill can be used instead.

2. Fasten the straight-shank drill bit in the hand-drill chuck. Do this the same way you fasten an auger bit in the brace. The push-drill bit is held in a special chuck. Refer to the instructions which accompany the push drill for fastening it as well as for using it.

3. Locate and mark the hole with an awl.

4. Place the bit on the mark. Hold the drill steady while turning the crank at a moderate, constant speed (Fig. 18–28).

A hole is drilled with a push drill as shown in Fig. 18–29.

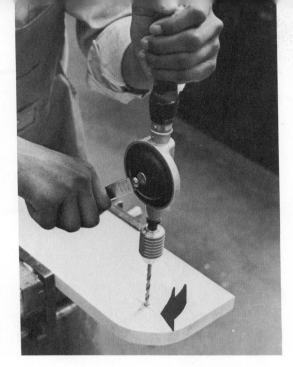

Fig. 18–28. Drilling a hole with a hand drill.

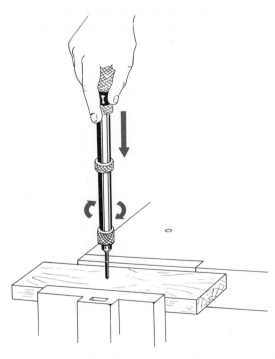

Fig. 18–29. Drilling a hole with a push drill.

1. What is the difference between an auger bit and a drill bit?
2. What does the number stamped on the tang of an auger bit mean? What are the sizes of these bits: 5, 6, and 7?
3. List six other types of bits and give their uses.
4. Describe two ways to bore a hole through a board without splitting the back.
5. How can you make a depth gage?

unit

19

Fastening with screws

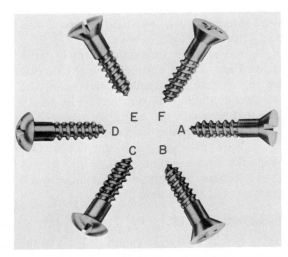

Fig. 19–1. Wood screws: (A) flat-head slotted, (B) flathead Phillips, (C) round-head slotted, (D) round-head Phillips, (E) oval-head slotted, and (F) oval-head Phillips.

Screws are used to fasten boards and assemble projects. A project which has been fastened with screws can be easily taken apart and re-assembled. Screws are superior to nails as wood fasteners because they are more permanent, hold better, and may be tightened easily.

The most common screws for joining wood are shown in Fig. 19–1. These are the *round-head*, *flat-head*, and *oval-head screws*. The first two are used most often in woodworking. Screws with a slotted head have been used for a long time. A more recent type is the *Phillips-head screw*. It gives a neater appearance and has a stronger head. This type also is available with a round, flat, or oval head.

Screws vary in length from ¼ to 6 inches. In gage, or size, they are graded from 0 to 24, according to the diameter of the shank. Most are made of mild steel. Screws are also made of brass for use where humidity is a problem, as in the assembly of boats.

Flat-head screws of mild steel generally have a bright finish. This type is usually abbreviated as FHB (flat head, bright). However, it is sometimes referred to as flat head, steel. Round-head steel screws are often finished in a dull blue. Screws are also available with various plated finishes.

Screws are sold by the dozen in variety stores and hardware stores. They are packaged by the factory in boxes of 100 or one gross (144). The boxes are labeled, as in Fig. 19–2, to show the length, type, material, and quantity (1 gross or 100), and the diameter of the shank. The order and form in which the information is given may, however, vary from the example shown here. Look at several box labels to see if you understand them correctly. Figure 19–3 pictures a variety of other commonly used fasteners and bolts.

TOOLS

The tools used for fastening with screws are the many types of screwdrivers (Figs. 19–4 through 19–11), screwdriver bits (Figs. 19–12 through 19–14), countersink bits

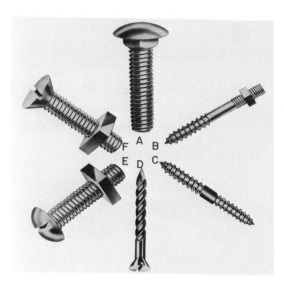

Fig. 19–3. Fasteners and bolts: (A) carriage bolt, (B) hanger bolt, (C) dowel screw, (D) wood drive screw, (E) round-head stove bolt, and (F) flat-head stove bolt.

Fig. 19–2. Factory packages of screws.

Fig. 19–4. Standard-blade screwdriver.

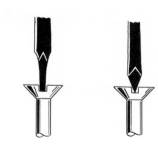

Fig. 19–5. Correctly and incorrectly shaped screwdriver tips.

Fig. 19–6. Screwdriver for Phillips recessed-head screws.

Fig. 19-7. Screwdriver for clutch-head screws.

Fig. 19-8. Spiral-ratchet screwdriver.

Fig. 19-9. Stubby screwdriver with regular tip.

Fig. 19-10. Stubby screwdriver with Phillips-head tip.

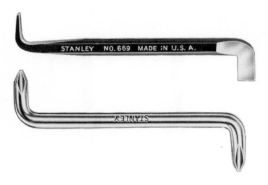

Fig. 19-11. Two types of offset screwdrivers to fit slotted and Phillips-head screws.

Fig. 19-12. Screwdriver bit for straight-slotted screws.

(Figs. 19–15 through 19–17), and combination wood-drill and countersink bits (Figs. 19–18 and 19–19).

Standard-blade Screwdriver. This screwdriver (Fig. 19–4) is available in blade lengths varying from 3 to 12 inches, and is the most commonly used. The tips of the sizes are shaped to fit slots of screws shown in Table 19–1. The tip should always be shaped to fit the slots of the screws. Screwdrivers and bits shown in Figs. 19–4, 19–8, 19–9, the upper view in 19–11, 19–12, and 19–14 have tips pointed as shown on the left in Fig. 19–5.

Screwdriver for Phillips Recessed-head Screws. The screwdriver illustrated in Fig. 19–6 has the tip shaped to fit the several kinds of Phillips recessed-head screws, shown in Fig. 19–1. This screwdriver varies in size, similar to the one described above.

Screwdriver for Clutch-head Screws. Figure 19–7 shows a screwdriver with a special type of point to fit screws used on many electrical appliances, such as refrigerators, deepfreeze units, and other appliances. Its size also varies according to the screw sizes.

Spiral-ratchet Screwdriver. Figure 19–8 depicts an automatic screwdriver with right- and left-handed adjustments. It will drive or draw screws by pushing down on the handle, or it can be set rigid as an ordinary screwdriver. The movement is changed instantly by a simple shifter device. There are usually three bits with varying tip widths which come with it (see Fig. 19–14).

Stubby Screwdriver with Regular Tip. The short screwdriver in Fig. 19–9 comes in lengths from 1 to 1¾ inches. There are different tip sizes obtainable. It is used where space is limited.

Stubby Screwdriver with Phillips-head Tip. This screwdriver (Fig. 19–10) is very similar to the one in Fig. 19–9, except for the tip which is designed to fit Phillips-head screws, as illustrated in Fig. 19–1.

Offset Screwdriver. Figure 19–11 shows two offset screwdrivers. The upper one is designed for regular-slot screws; the lower one has tips to fit Phillips-head screws. This tool has lengths from 3 to 6 inches.

Screwdriver Bit for Straight-slotted Screws. The bit shown in Fig. 19–12 is designed for use with the brace shown in Fig. 18–1. Its overall length is 5 inches. It is available in tip widths varying from 3/16 to 1/2 inch to fit different sizes of slotted screws.

Screwdriver Bit for Phillips-head Screws. This tool (Fig. 19–13) has basically the same specifications as the one in Fig. 19–12. The exception is the tip, which does not vary as greatly in size.

Spiral-ratchet Screwdriver Bit. There are three tip widths of bits (Fig. 19–14) to fit the spiral-ratchet screwdriver shown in Fig. 19–8. These tip widths vary from 7/32 to 9/32 inch. The overall length is approximately 4 inches. This bit is also available to fit the Phillips recessed-head screw.

Countersink Bits. The countersink bit (Fig. 19–15) has a tapered square tang to fit a brace. The cutting edge is capable of countersinking up to 3/4 inch diameter.

Figure 19–16 shows a countersink bit that has a 1/4-inch shank for use either in a hand or an electric drill, or in a drill press. The cutting edge of this bit will countersink to 1/2 inch. The countersink bit illustrated in Fig. 19–17 is designed to fit the spiral-ratchet screwdriver shown in Fig. 19–8.

Combination Wood-drill and Countersink Bits. Figure 19–18 illustrates a combination wood-drill and countersink bit. It cuts holes for the screw thread, screw shank clearance, and countersinks flat-head screws all in one operation. There are many sizes available to accommodate sizes from 3/4-inch No. 6 screws to 2-inch No. 12 length screws.

Figure 19–19 shows a combination tool which performs three operations. It prepares wood for screws without marring the sur-

Fig. 19–13. Screwdriver bit for Phillips-head screws.

Fig. 19–14. Spiral-ratchet screwdriver bit.

Fig. 19–15. Countersink bit to fit a brace.

Fig. 19–16. Countersink bit with a round shank.

Fig. 19–17. Countersink bit to fit a spiral-ratchet screwdriver.

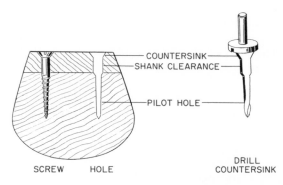

Fig. 19–18. Combination wood-drill and countersink bit.

COUNTERSINK
SHANK CLEARANCE

PILOT HOLE

SCREW HOLE

DRILL COUNTERSINK

Table 19–1. SIZES OF BITS OR DRILLS TO BORE HOLES FOR WOOD SCREWS

NUMBER (GAGE) OF SCREW	APPROXIMATE DIAMETER OF SCREW SHANK	FIRST HOLE (SHANK):		SECOND HOLE (PILOT):	
		Twist-drill size	Auger-bit number	Twist-drill size	Auger-bit number
1	5/64	5/64	—	—	—
2	3/32	3/32	—	1/16	—
3	3/32	7/64	—	1/16	—
4	7/64	7/64	—	5/64	—
5	1/8	1/8	—	5/64	—
6	9/64	9/64	—	3/32	—
7	5/32	5/32	—	7/64	—
8	11/64	11/64	—	7/64	—
9	11/64	3/16	—	1/8	—
10	3/16	3/16	—	1/8	—
12	7/32	7/32	4	9/64	—
14	15/64	1/4	4	5/32	—
16	17/64	17/64	5	3/16	—
18	19/64	19/64	5	13/64	4

face, cuts the shank hole, and also counter-bores ready for a plug or filling compound. Bits shown in Figs. 19–18 and 19–19 have 1/4-inch diameter shanks to fit most power and hand drills.

Table 19–1 gives the neccessary information for the selection of screws, drills, auger bits, and shank and pilot holes.

FASTENING BOARDS WITH SCREWS

1. Mark the location for the screw hole. A mark with an awl makes an excellent beginning for drilling a hole (Fig. 18–22).

2. Select the correct size of bit for drilling or boring the shank hole (Table 19–1). The size of the bit should be large enough to clear the shank of the screw. Where possible, you can get a better alignment when the boards to be fastened are placed in position and the pilot hole (sometimes called the anchor hole) is drilled through both. You can then enlarge one hole to the screw-shank size.

If you plan to use the combination drill and countersink (Figs. 19–18 and 19–19), it will take the place of steps 2, 3, 4, 5, and 6.

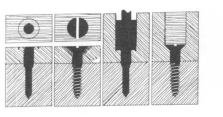

Fig. 19–19. Combination wood-drill, countersink, and counterbore bit.

Fig. 19–20. Shank and pilot holes.

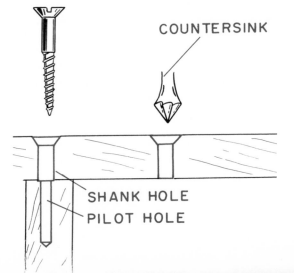

COUNTERSINK

SHANK HOLE
PILOT HOLE

Fig. 19-21. Marking for the pilot hole.

Fig. 19-23. Driving a screw with a screwdriver.

Fig. 19-24. Driving a screw with a screwdriver bit and brace.

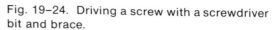

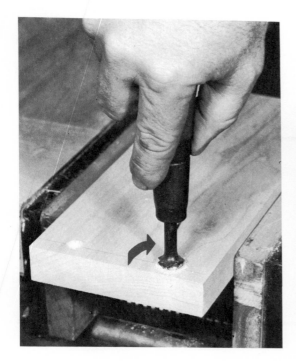

Fig. 19-22. Countersinking for a flat-head screw. Note that the countersink bit is fastened into a file handle.

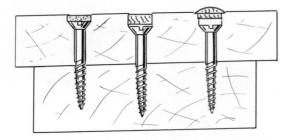

Fig. 19–25. Methods of recessing flat-head screws.

3. Fasten the bit in the brace or the drill in the hand drill. Make the shank hole (Fig. 19–20).

4. Place boards for the joint in position. Mark the location of the pilot hole with an awl (Fig. 19–21).

5. Bore or drill the pilot hole.

6. Countersink the shank hole if a flat- or oval-head screw is to be used (Fig. 19–22). Do not countersink too deep. A countersink bit fitted into a file handle makes a good countersink tool.

7. Select a screwdriver which fits the slot of the screw snugly. The tip should be ground properly (Fig. 19–5).

8. Fasten the screw with a screwdriver (Fig. 19–23), or use a screwdriver bit and brace (Fig. 19–24). Hold the screwdriver firmly and in line with the screw. This will keep it from slipping out of the screw slot. A screw will turn more easily if it is coated with soap, wax, or paraffin.

9. Sometimes the screw is to be hidden with wood plastic or covered with a wooden button or plug. In that case, you must set, or sink, the head in the wood as shown in Fig. 19–25. Standard-size wooden plugs are available commercially, or you can make them.

Discussion Topics

1. What information must you have in order to purchase the correct type and size of screw?

2. Name three of the most common types of slotted screws used in woodworking. Where would each be used?

3. What do the large numbers on the labels in Fig. 19–2 signify?

4. Name two methods of packaging screws.

5. What are two advantages in using Phillips-head screws?

6. What is the purpose of the shank and pilot holes?

7. What tool do you use on the shank hole to make a flat-head screw flush, or even, with the wood?

unit
20
Driving and pulling nails

It takes skill to drive, set, and pull nails correctly. Almost everyone has occasion to drive and pull nails. You should know how to use a hammer and how to select the correct nail. To set a nail, drive the head below the surface with a special tool.

The kinds of nails most often used in woodworking are shown in Fig. 20–1. *Box nails* are relatively thin, have flat heads, and are sometimes cement-coated to increase their holding power. They were first made for nailing together boxes built of wood which was thin and easily split. *Common nails* have heavy, flat heads and are slightly larger in diameter than box nails. *Finishing*

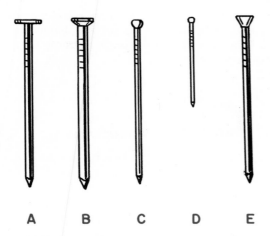

Fig. 20–1. Kinds of nails: (A) box, (B) common, (C) finishing, (D) brad, and (E) casing.

Table 20–1. NAIL CHART

Size (penny)	Length (inches)
2	1
3	$1\frac{1}{4}$
4	$1\frac{1}{2}$
5	$1\frac{3}{4}$
6	2
7	$2\frac{1}{4}$
8	$2\frac{1}{2}$
9	$2\frac{3}{4}$
10	3
12	$3\frac{1}{4}$
16	$3\frac{1}{2}$
20	4
30	$4\frac{1}{2}$
40	5

nails have small heads. They may be set with a nail set and covered with putty or a wood plastic. The *brad* is a small finishing nail. It varies in length from $\frac{1}{4}$ to $1\frac{1}{4}$ inches, and is used to nail thin stock together. *Casing nails* have coneshaped heads. As this shape gives good holding power, the casing nail is used mostly for interior trim and cabinetwork. Resin-coated nails in any of the above types are used extensively because of their holding power.

The size of nails is usually indicated by the term *penny* or its abbreviation, *d*. It is believed that these terms are derived from the weight of a thousand nails. For example, one thousand 10-penny (or 10d) nails weigh 10 pounds, and a thousand 6-penny nails weigh 6 pounds.

The nail chart, Table 20–1, shows the sizes and lengths of nails. A 2-penny, or 2d, nail is 1 inch long. For each additional penny add $\frac{1}{4}$ inch in length up to 3 inches. For example, a 10-penny is 3 inches long. See the chart for the lengths of nails over 3 inches.

Important rules to remember when you nail:

1. Have the length of the nail three times the thickness of the first board the nail goes through.

2. See that the size of the nail is not too large or it may split the wood.

3. Drill a very small pilot hole through the first board when you drive nails through hardwoods such as oak, maple, birch, and others.

4. Do not put nails in your mouth.

TOOLS

The tools used for driving and pulling, or drawing, nails are the nail hammer, half hatchet, nail set, and sometimes the ripping bar.

Nail Hammer. The size of a nail hammer (Fig. 20–2) is determined by the weight of the head. The most popular sizes are the 14- or 16-ounce ones. The one pictured is all steel, having a perforated neoprene-rubber grip handle. This offers a non-slip grip. Other nail hammers have steel heads with white hickory wood handles. The claw may be either curved or straight.

Half Hatchet. The tool illustrated in Fig. 20–3 is all steel with a non-slip neoprene-sleeve handle. It makes a 3 ½-inch cut. Carpenters sometimes prefer the half hatchet for nailing and hammering because it has a cutting end and also a nail-pulling slot.

Nail Set. The nail set (Fig. 20–4) is used to set the head of a finishing or casing nail or brad. The tip of this tool has a slightly concave surface. This keeps it from sliding

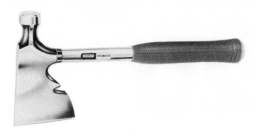

Fig. 20–3. Half hatchet.

Fig. 20–4. Nail set.

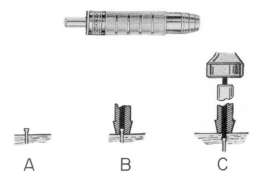

Fig. 20–5. Self-centering nail set, showing sequence of steps for its use: (A) drive nail into wood until head protrudes ⅛ inch, (B) place sleeve of nail set over nail head, and (C) strike plunger with hammer to set nail below the surface of wood. The plunger retracts automatically.

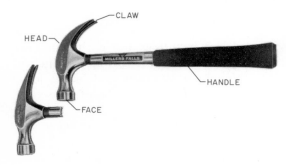

Fig. 20–2. Sixteen-ounce nail hammer, showing curved and straight claws.

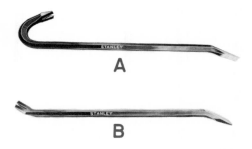

Fig. 20–6. Ripping bars: (A) goose neck and (B) straight.

Fig. 20-7. Ripping chisels.

off the nail head too easily. Nail sets are obtainable in tip sizes from $\frac{1}{32}$ to $\frac{5}{32}$ inch, and are approximately 4 inches long.

Self-centering Nail Set. Figure 20-5 shows a nail set which is self-centering. Its use is illustrated by the sequence steps shown in this figure. A similar tool is available for setting brads.

Ripping Bars. Figure 20-6 shows a gooseneck and a straight ripping bar having a claw with a nail slot. These and other types of ripping bars are sometimes used in construction for pulling or drawing spikes, and for wedging apart nailed boards and planks. They vary in length from 12 to 36 inches.

Ripping Chisels. Either of the ripping chisels shown in Fig. 20-7 is often used by home builders to pry and wedge floor strips while nailing. The cutting edge varies from 1 ½ to 2 inches, and they are approximately 18 inches long.

DRIVING NAILS

1. Select the proper type and size of nail for the job.

2. Hold the nail firmly in place with one hand. Hold the hammer handle firmly near the end, and strike a light first blow (Fig. 20-8).

3. Remove your hand from the nail. Continue to strike the nail directly on the head until it is driven flush, or even, with the wood (Fig. 20-9). Avoid bending the nail. Also, do not dent the wood with the hammer face.

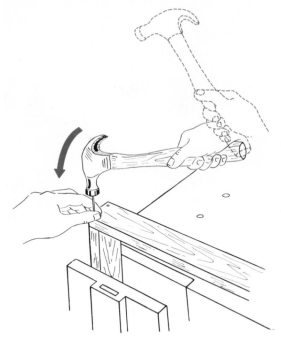

Fig. 20-8. Starting to drive a nail.

Fig. 20-9. Driving a nail.

Fig. 20-10. Setting a nail.

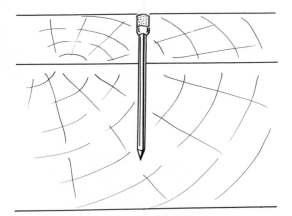

Fig. 20-11. Covering a nailhead.

Fig. 20-12. Toenailing.

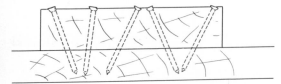

Fig. 20-13. Driving nails at an angle to increase holding power.

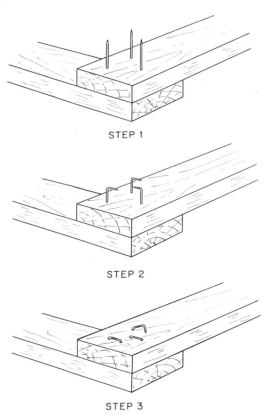

STEP 1

STEP 2

STEP 3

Fig. 20-14. Steps in clinching nails for holding two boards.

Fig. 20–15. Driving a 6d common nail with an industrial type of pneumatic nailer.

Fig. 20–17. Pulling a nail with increased leverage.

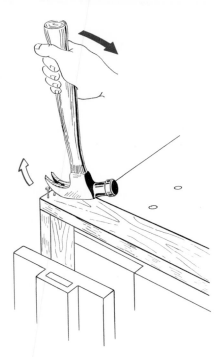

Fig. 20–16. Pulling a nail with a claw hammer.

Keep your eye on the nail. Use a wrist, arm, and shoulder movement as you drive the nail.

4. Where necessary, set the head of the nail about $1/16$ inch below the surface of the wood (Fig. 20–10). This applies especially to the finishing and the casing nails. Use a nail set slightly smaller than the head of the nail.

5. Fill the hole with putty, wood plastic, or wood dough if the nail has been set (Fig. 20–11).

6. Figure 20–12 shows how to drive nails for *toenailing*.

7. You can hold two boards together more securely if you drive nails in at an angle (Fig. 20–13). Nails have greater holding power when driven this way.

8. Figure 20–14 shows the three steps in *clinching* nails to hold two or more boards securely. The nails may be clinched with the grain for a neater appearance. When driving

nails through hardwood, drill a smaller hole first to serve as a pilot hole. Figure 20–15 shows the use of an industrial type pneumatic nailer driving 6d common nails.

PULLING NAILS

1. Slip the claw of the hammer under the head of the nail. Pull the handle until it is at an angle of nearly 90 degrees with the board (Fig. 20–16).

2. Sometimes a nail is too long to come out as suggested in step 1. To pull it, slip a block of wood under the head of the hammer (Fig. 20–17). This increases the leverage and lessens the strain on the hammer handle.

Discussion Topics

1. List the five common types of nails and brads. Explain their uses.
2. What is the purpose of the nail set?
3. What must you know about nails before purchasing them?
4. Give three important nailing rules.
5. What are the two types of heads for the nail hammer?
6. Where might a person use a hatchet in building construction?
7. What would be the advantage in using a self-centering nail set?
8. Name two types of ripping bars. Explain how each might be used.
9. What are ripping chisels used for?

---

unit
21

Joining

A piece of furniture or cabinetwork almost always includes one or more types of joints. There are many kinds of joints. Some of them are variations of the few basic types. All have a definite use which requires layout, cutting, fitting, and assembling. Study the several types and then make the application or adaptation which suits your need.

The joints described here are the butt, dowel, rabbet, dado, lap, mortise and tenon, and miter. These and variations are shown in Figs. 21–1, 21–14, and 21–35. Instructions and illustrations shown in this unit are for making these joints with hand tools. Most of the joints can also be made on the table saw (Unit 36).

TOOLS

You will use a few special tools which have not been discussed in previous units. These are the commercial miter box with stiff-backed saw, a homemade miter box, a doweling jig, and the dowel pointer.

Miter Box. The commercial miter box with stiff-backed saw (Fig. 21–2) is valuable for making joints because of its accuracy. Most miter-box saws have automatic locks at 8, 9, 22 ½, 30, and 45 degrees, right or left. The 0-degree marking is actually 90 degrees, or at right angle to the back fence.

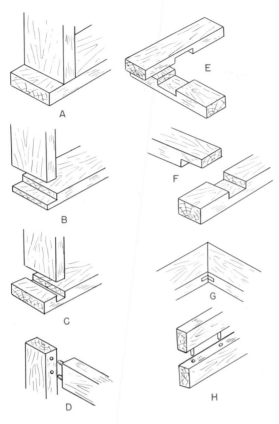

Fig. 21-1. A few of the common joints: (A) butt, (B) rabbet, (C) dado, (D) doweled-butt, (E) cross-lap, (F) middle-lap, (G) splined miter, and (H) doweled-edge.

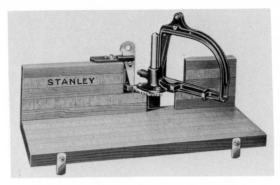

Fig. 21-3. Wood-frame miter box which accomodates panel crosscut or backsaw.

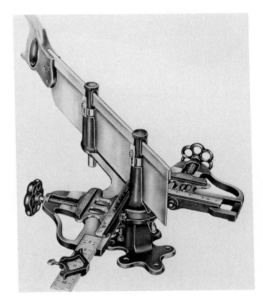

Fig. 21-4. Miter machine with saw.

Fig. 21-2. Miter box with stiff-backed saw.

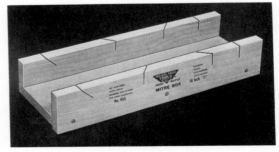

Fig. 21-5. Hardwood miter box.

Fig. 21-6. A motorized miter box.

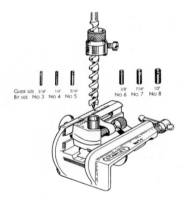

Fig. 21-7. Doweling jig.

Fig. 21-8. Self-centering doweling jig.

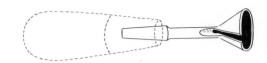

Fig. 21-9. Dowel pointer.

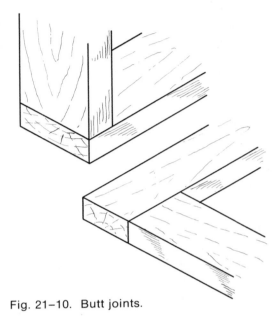

Fig. 21-10. Butt joints.

Most stiff-backed saws to fit the miter box are 4 × 24 inches, or 5 × 30 inches.

The miter box pictured in Fig. 21-3 is a wood-frame tool which accommodates a regular crosscut, or backsaw. It can be set for cutting at several common angles. Figure 21-4 shows a miter machine with saw. Using this machine, any type of mitered joint can be cut, glued, and nailed to make tight, close-fitting corners. It is especially adaptable for fitting molding. A small, wooden miter box may be purchased or made and used when you need only a few set angular cuts (Fig. 21-5). A motorized miter box is shown in Fig. 21-6.

Doweling Jig. The doweling jig (Figs. 21-7 and 21-8) is the best tool for boring and

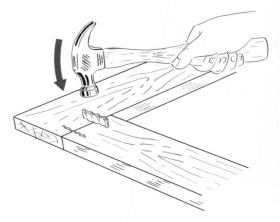

Fig. 21–11. Butt joint held with corrugated fasteners.

aligning holes in dowel joints. The shortened dowel auger bit is often used with either of these jigs. The doweling jig in Fig. 21–7 has several sizes of dowel-guide cylinders. These can be adjusted to locate dowel holes at specified distances on the edge of a board.

The doweling jig in Fig. 21–8 is self-centering. Any hole bored on the edge of a board will be absolutely in the center if this is used. Provision is made for several dowel-and-bit sizes.

Dowel Pointer. The dowel pointer (Fig. 21–9) is a special bit designed to trim points on dowels. A pointed end makes a dowel fit into a hole more easily than a straight end. The bit may be fastened conveniently in a wooden file handle, as shown in Fig. 21–9. This makes the pointer easy to use.

BUTT JOINT

The butt joint (Fig. 21–10) is simple to make but is often weak. It can be held together with nails, screws, or dowels. Use it where the fasteners will not be exposed to view. A variation of the butt joint, held together with corrugated fasteners, is shown in Fig. 21–11. Figures 21–12 and 21–13 show another type of metal fastener for holding butt and miter joints.

Fig. 21–12. Metal fastener holding a butt joint.

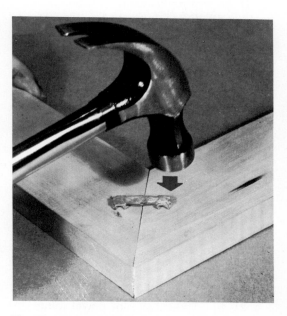

Fig. 21–13. Metal fastener holding a miter joint.

To make a butt joint:

1. Square the end of the board which is to be butted against another piece.

2. Mark the exact location of the joint on the surface that will meet the squared end.

3. Select the type of fastening you will use: nails, screws, dowels, or corrugated fasteners.

4. If you are using nails for the joint, select the most suitable type. Drive the nails so that the points barely go through the first piece.

5. Place the pieces to be joined in their correct positions. Finish driving the nails into the piece which is being butted. Refer to Unit 20, *Driving and Pulling Nails*, for nailing procedure. Check the joint with a try or framing square if you want it to have a right angle (a 90-degree angle). For an angle that is acute (less than 90 degrees) or obtuse (more than 90 degrees), use a sliding bevel.

If the joint is fastened with screws, refer to Unit 19, *Fastening with Screws*.

Fig. 21–15. Two types of dowel pins.

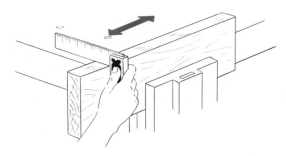

Fig. 21–16. Squaring the edge for a joint.

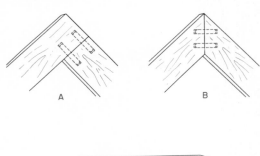

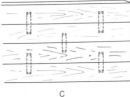

Fig. 21–14. Three types of dowel joints: (A) doweled-butt, (B) doweled-miter, and (C) doweled-edge.

Fig. 21–17. Checking the edge for trueness.

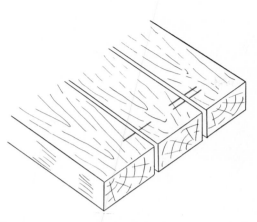

Fig. 21–18. Proper arrangement and marking of boards for edge gluing.

Fig. 21–19. Aligning boards with a straight-edge.

EDGE AND DOWEL JOINTS

Dowels are often used in furniture and cabinet construction. Three types of dowel joints are shown in Fig. 21–14. Sometimes dowels are used in gluing edge, or edge-to-edge, joints. They can be substituted for mortise-and-tenon joints. They can also hold miter joints securely.

The better grades of dowels are made from hardwood, such as birch or maple. They are round pieces of wood available in many lengths and diameters (Fig. 21–15). A grooved dowel pin, as shown in Fig. 21–15, holds glue better than smooth pins.

To make an edge joint without dowels:

1. Plane the edges of the pieces to be glued together. Check to see that these edges are square with the surface (Fig. 21–16). Also, they must be straight and true (Fig. 21–17).

2. Arrange the boards to be joined so that the surface grains run in the same direction. Arrange the end grains alternately, as shown in Fig. 21–18. This tends to relieve warping of the glued-up board.

3. Place the boards as they will join, and mark them as indicated in Fig. 21–18. This prevents interchanging of pieces.

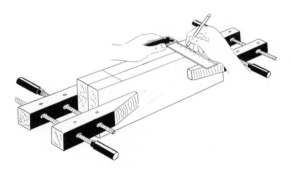

Fig. 21–20. Marking edges for dowels.

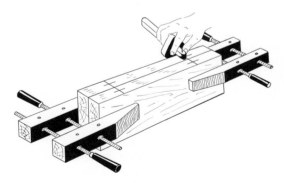

Fig. 21–21. Locating centers for dowels with the marking gage.

4. Assemble the pieces for the joint, and test them for alignment (Fig. 21–19). Glue the edge joint for final assembly. Assemble and clamp as described in Unit 25.

To make an edge joint with dowels:

You will need to perform steps 1 through 4 before continuing with step 5 when using dowels in edge joints.

5. Clamp the boards to be glued.

6. With a try square, mark lines across the edges at intervals of 12 to 18 inches (Fig. 21–20). These lines indicate dowel centers. The end marking should be at least 4 to 6 inches in from the ends.

7. Set the marking gage at half the thickness of each board.

8. Intersect, or mark across, the lines made in step 6 with the marking gage (Fig. 21–21). Keep the head of the gage against the matched working surfaces.

9. Select an auger bit of the same size as the dowel. For most edge joints you will want a bit $5/16$ or $3/8$ inch in diameter.

10. Fasten the bit in the brace, and bore holes to the desired depths for the dowel rods, or pins. You may do this with or without the use of a doweling jig (see Figs. 21–7 and 21–8). Dowels for edge joints are usually 2 to 3 inches long. The hole in each piece should be a little deeper than half the length of the dowel. You can control the depth of boring with the depth gage (see Figs. 18–16 through 18–18).

11. If you use the dowel jig (Fig. 21–22), place the proper size of dowel guide in it. Fasten it into place with the thumbnut.

12. Adjust the sliding piece which holds the guide. Check to see that the centers for all holes are the same distance from the surfaces of the boards. Center this alignment on the marks made in step 8.

13. Place the doweling jig on the edge of the board. The index marking on the jig should be in line with the marks put on in step 6.

Fig. 21–22. Boring dowel holes.

Fig. 21–23. Pointing a dowel pin.

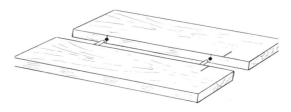

Fig. 21–24. Trial assembly of a doweled-edge joint.

14. Select the proper size of auger bit as indicated in step 9. Fasten it in the brace.

15. Bore all holes to uniform depth. Usually 1¼ to 1¾ inches is sufficient.

16. Cut the dowels to the proper length. This can be ¼ inch shorter, generally, than the overall depth of matched holes.

17. Taper the ends of the dowels with the dowel pointer (Fig. 21–23).

18. Place the dowels in the holes, and make a trial assembly of the joint to see if it fits (Figs. 21–24 and 21–25).

19. Glue the edge joint for final assembly. Put glue in the holes, on the dowels, and on the edges of the boards. Assemble and clamp as described in Unit 25, *Gluing and Clamping*.

RABBET JOINT

The rabbet joint (Figs. 21–1 and 21–26) is similar to the dado joint. The difference is that in the rabbet joint the pieces are joined together at the ends. This joint is ideal for some types of corner construction, and is useful in making drawers and bookcases.

Fig. 21–26. Marking for a rabbet joint.

Fig. 21–27. The first cut in making a rabbet joint.

Fig. 21–25. A craftsman in a furniture plant making a trial assembly of doweled-edge joint.

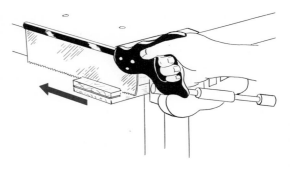

Fig. 21–28. The final cut in a rabbet joint.

103

Fig. 21–29. Assembling a rabbet joint with nails.

To make a rabbet joint:

1. Make and square, to the given dimensions, the pieces that are to be joined.

2. Place the two pieces in their proper positions. Mark the location of the rabbet joint (Fig. 21–26). Mark on the piece to be rabbeted back the thickness of the piece which fits it.

3. Square lines across the surface of the piece to be rabbeted. Use a sharp pencil, or a knife, and the try square.

4. Extend the lines across the edge with the try square.

5. Mark the depth of the rabbet on the end and the edges with the try square and pencil. A marking gage can be used instead of the try square and pencil.

6. Place the piece to be cut in a vise. Saw just on the waste side of the marked line to the planned depth (Fig. 21–27).

7. Cut away the remaining waste stock by making a cut as shown in Fig. 21–28.

8. Fit the two pieces for a trial assembly. If you need to, pare the edge of the rabbet with a wood chisel or a rabbet plane.

9. Assemble the rabbet joint with nails (Fig. 21–29) or screws.

DADO JOINT

The dado joint is one of the strongest when properly made. It is a groove cut across the grain of a piece of wood into which another piece is fitted (Fig. 21–1 and 21–30). Dado joints are used in drawers, shelves, bookcases, and stepladders.

To make a dado joint:

1. Make and square, to the given dimensions, the pieces that are to be joined.

2. Place the two parts of the joint in position. Mark the location (Fig. 21–30).

3. Square lines across the surface of the piece to be dadoed. Use a knife or a sharp pencil and a try square.

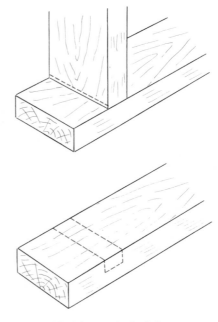

Fig. 21–30. Marking a dado joint.

Fig. 21–31. Guide for hand sawing an accurate dado.

4. Extend the marked lines across both edges. Use a sharp pencil and a try square.

5. Mark the depth of the dado with the marking gage.

6. Saw just on the waste side of the lines to the planned depth. Use a backsaw or dovetail saw.

Figure 21–31 illustrates one procedure in hand sawing the dado joint. This makes the joint fit accurately.

7. Cut out the wood between the saw cuts with a wood chisel (see Fig. 21–34).

8. Fit the two pieces for a trial assembly. If the joint is too tight, pare the edges of the dado carefully with a sharp wood chisel. The pieces should fit snugly, but without having to be driven into place.

9. Make the final assembly with glue and clamps, nails, or screws.

LAP JOINT

There are several kinds of lap and notched joints. One of the most common in furniture making and carpentry is the cross-lap joint (Figs. 21–1 and 21–32).

To make a cross-lap joint:

1. Make and square, to the given dimensions, the pieces that are to be joined.

2. Place the two pieces in their proper positions. Mark the locations of the cross-lap joint.

3. Square lines across the surfaces of both pieces. Use a knife or sharp pencil and a try square.

4. Extend the marked lines on the edges of both pieces.

5. Mark the depth of the notch with the marking gage. The depth should be one-half the thickness of the pieces, because the surfaces are to be flush when joined.

6. Saw just on the waste side of the surfaces of both pieces to the proper depth. Use a backsaw.

7. Make a few extra saw cuts on the waste stock inside the marked lines to ap-

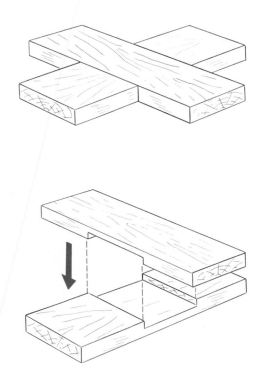

Fig. 21–32. Cross-lap joint.

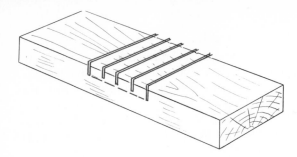

Fig. 21–33. Saw cuts in a cross-lap joint.

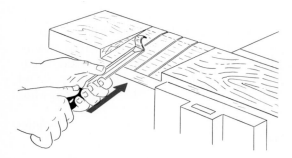

Fig. 21–34. Removing waste stock with a wood chisel.

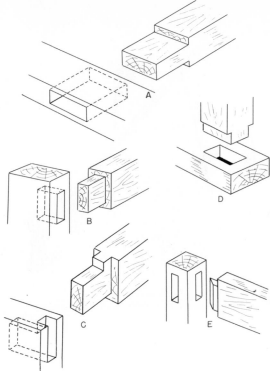

Fig. 21–35. Mortise-and-tenon joints: (A) through mortise-and-tenon, (B) blind mortise-and-tenon, (C) haunched mortise-and-tenon, (D) stub mortise-and-tenon, and (E) mitered mortise-and-tenon.

proximately the same depth (Fig. 21–33). This will make chiseling easier.

8. Cut away the waste stock with a wood chisel (Fig. 21–34). Also refer to Fig. 15–5.

9. Fit the two pieces for trial assembly. If the joint is too tight, pare the edges of the piece carefully with a sharp wood chisel. The pieces should fit snugly, but without being driven.

10. Make the final assembly with glue and clamps, nails, or screws.

MORTISE-AND-TENON JOINT

Mortise-and-tenon joints (Fig. 21–35) are used extensively in furniture and interior cabinetwork. They are used also in doors and window sashes. A few of them are shown in Fig. 21–35. In chairs and stools, the legs and rails are often joined with the blind mortise and tenon. The procedure for making the blind mortise and tenon is de-

Fig. 21–36. Layout for a mortise on a leg. The colored outline shows the part that will be drilled and chiseled out. The dotted center line on the right-hand drawing shows where to place the spur of the auger bit.

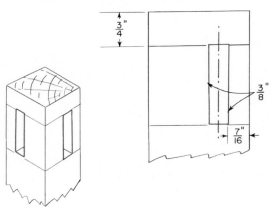

scribed below. Other mortise joints are made in practically the same way.

To make the mortise:

1. Make and square, to the given dimensions, the pieces that are to be joined.

2. Study your working drawing. Determine the thickness and width of the mortise. If the drawing does not give detailed dimensions, the following rules will help:

    a. A mortise and a tenon $\frac{3}{8}$ inch thick are desirable when the rail stock measures $\frac{3}{4}$ or $\frac{13}{16}$ inch in thickness.

    b. In furniture, the face of a rail should be set in at least $\frac{1}{8}$ to $\frac{1}{4}$ inch from the outer face of a leg.

    c. Take advantage of the location of the mortises by having them as deep as possible. The tenons can meet or cross-lap (Fig. 21–39).

3. Lay out the mortise on a leg in a similar way to that shown in Fig. 21–36. Where possible, it is advisable to drop down from the top $\frac{3}{4}$ inch. Allow also a shoulder of $\frac{1}{4}$ inch at the bottom. The layout can be drawn with the try square and a sharp pencil or knife. It can also be drawn with the marking gage.

4. You may need to mark identical mortises, as in marking the legs for a stool or table. Mark all the legs together, as shown in Fig. 21–37. The legs must be perfectly square to do this accurately.

5. Fasten the piece to be mortised on a bench or in a vise.

6. Select an auger bit slightly smaller than the thickness of the mortise, and fasten it in a brace.

7. Bore a series of holes to the depth necessary. Place the feed screw of the auger bit on the center line of the mortise (Fig. 21–38). Use a depth gage to bore holes to a uniform depth.

8. Chisel and pare the sides of the mortise. Carefully cut the ends of the mortise

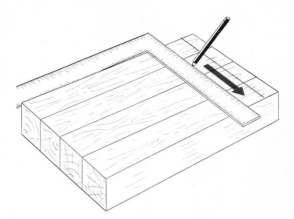

Fig. 21–37. Laying out mortises on four legs at one time.

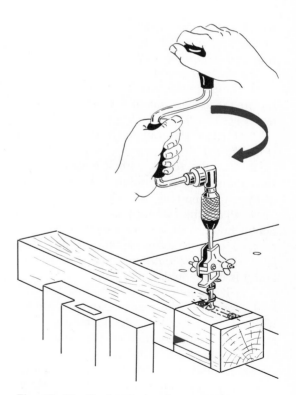

Fig. 21–38. Boring holes for a mortise.

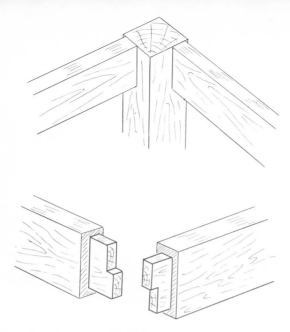

Fig. 21–39. Cross-lap tenon.

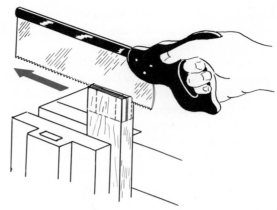

Fig. 21–40. First step in cutting a tenon.

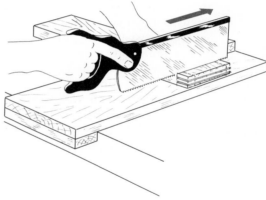

Fig. 21–41. Second step in cutting a tenon.

Fig. 21–42. Cutting a miter joint on molding.

to the gage lines, using a sharp wood chisel of the proper width. Refer to Unit 15, *Cutting and Trimming with a Chisel.*

To make a tenon:

1. Lay out the tenon on the rail according to the dimension of the working drawing (Fig. 21–39).

2. Fasten the rail vertically in a vise (Fig. 21–40).

3. Cut the tenon with a backsaw. The saw line should be barely on the waste side of the gage line (Fig. 21–40).

4. Place the rail horizontally in a vise or bench hook. Cut on the waste side of the marked lines to remove the surplus stock (Fig. 21–41). Continue cutting until the tenon is completed.

5. Fit the mortise-and-tenon pieces for a trial assembly. The pieces should fit snugly without being driven. If necessary, pare the sides of the mortise or the tenon until you get a proper fit (Fig. 21–39).

Make final assembly of the mortise-and-tenon joint by gluing and clamping. Refer to Unit 25, *Gluing and Clamping.*

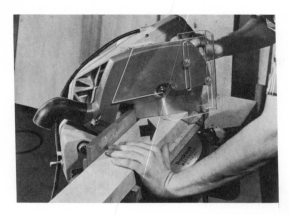

Fig. 21–43. Sawing a miter on the motorized miter box.

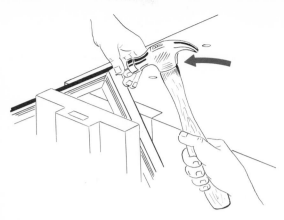

Fig. 21–44. Nailing a miter joint.

MITER JOINT

The miter joint is used where you do not want the end grain to show. Picture frames and door moldings are among the pieces made this way.

Miter joints are most accurately cut on the miter box (Figs. 21–2 through 21–6). The procedures for laying out and cutting are similar in all miter joints. The miter joint described here is for a picture frame.

To make a miter joint:

1. Make or buy a molding which will be suitable for the picture to be framed.

2. Mark the length and the width of the picture along the rabbeted edge of the molding. Mark two pieces for the ends and two for the sides.

3. Place the molding in the miter box with the rabbet face down.

4. Hold the molding firmly to the frame of the box. Lower the saw until it touches the molding on the waste side of the mark.

5. Cut the molding with light, even strokes (Figs. 21–42 and 21–43). Opposite pieces of the picture frame should be exactly the same length.

6. Make a trial assembly to see that all joints fit properly. If necessary, trim all the pieces lightly with a block plane.

Fig. 21–45. Clamping together a mitered joint on plywood.

7. Assemble the mitered joint by one of the following methods:
   a. With brads or nails, as shown in Fig. 21–44.
   b. With a spline (Fig. 21–1).
   c. With the aid of a miter machine (Fig. 21–4).
   d. Clamping with C clamps, as shown in Fig. 21–45. The diagonally split pieces of wood are glued to the boards to be mitered. Note there is a piece of heavy kraft paper in the glue joint so that the glue blocks may be removed easily from the mitered joint. The small amount of paper that adheres can be sanded off.

1. List at least two places where you have seen each of the following types of joints used: butt, dowel, rabbet, dado, cross-lap, mortise-and-tenon, splined miter, and miter.
2. Give at least two reasons for using a dowel in making an edge joint.
3. What advantage does a grooved dowel pin have over a smooth one?
4. List at least two advantages in using a dowel jig.
5. Can a strong edge-to-edge joint be made without dowel pins?
6. Do you prefer to make an edge joint with or without dowels? Give at least two reasons for your preference.
7. List two or more advantages which the mortise-and-tenon joint has over the dowel joint in joining rails and legs.
8. List four methods of assembling a mitered joint.

unit
22

Building up plywood, and veneering

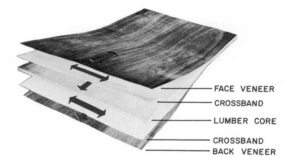

Fig. 22–1. Plywood construction showing the several layers.

The historical development of plywood and veneers and the manufacture of each are discussed in detail in Unit 66, *The Manufacture and Use of Veneer and Plywood*. This unit is concerned with how to prepare lumber and veneer for building up the core, crossbanding, and preparing veneer for the surfaces of both flat and curved sheets (Fig. 22–1).

Clamping facilities must be provided for flat and curved forming. Figure 22–2 shows an excellent shop-made flat clamp, or jig, used to glue up flat sheets of plywood. Curved, or formed, plywood sheets (Fig. 22–3) can be produced by using specially-

Fig. 22–2. Two students operate a shop-built clamp for gluing flat built-up plywood and veneer.

Fig. 22–3. Several laminated pieces made with specially built forms.

Fig. 22–5. Wood form for building a curved plywood panel for a magazine rack. Note that this form uses a piece of tin for exerting even pressure.

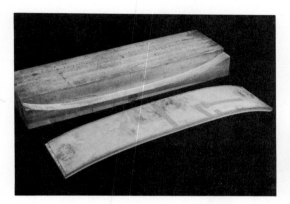

Fig. 22–4. Shop-built forms, made of glued-up lumber. The form is cut on the bandsaw for the curvature required. The glued-up plywood shown in front of the form was designed for use as a drawer front of the credenza shown in Fig. 62–15.

built forms, as shown in Figs. 22–4 and 22–5.

The form in Fig. 22–4 is a wooden, two-part one cut from glued-up stock. Remember to cut out the thickness of material from the form. This is required because of the thickness of the built-up plywood to be formed. This figure pictures the form used to make the veneered front, curved, plywood panel shown standing in front of the form. This form was also used to make the curved

Fig. 22–6. Laminated magazine rack made by using the form shown in Fig. 22–5.

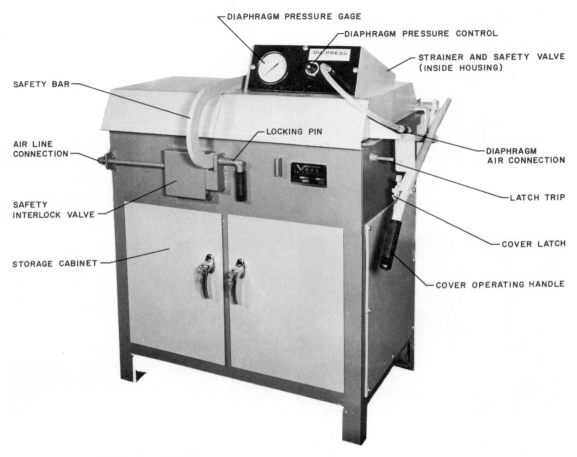

DIAPHRAGM PRESSURE GAGE

DIAPHRAGM PRESSURE CONTROL

STRAINER AND SAFETY VALVE
(INSIDE HOUSING)

SAFETY BAR

LOCKING PIN

AIR LINE
CONNECTION

DIAPHRAGM
AIR CONNECTION

SAFETY
INTERLOCK VALVE

LATCH TRIP

COVER LATCH

STORAGE CABINET

COVER OPERATING HANDLE

Fig. 22–7. A veneering and laminating press designed for school use. *(Vega Enterprises.)*

fronts of the drawers in Fig. 62–15. Pressure used for this form was obtained by a series of 12-inch handscrew clamps, such as shown in Fig. 25–2.

The form in Fig. 22–5 was designed to make a curved plywood panel for a magazine rack shown in Fig. 22–6. Sheet metal makes up the outer wall of this form in order that even pressure can be exerted against the veneer strips.

It is always desirable to use wax-paper sheets between the forms and the glued-up plywood. This keeps the oozing glue from building up on the form and sticking it to the panel.

A commercial veneering and laminating press makes these processes much easier and more uniform. The one illustrated in Fig. 22–7 consists of a strong, shallow box with a hinge cover which may be securely closed to resist internal pressure.

The plies of material to be laminated are glued and positioned inside the box (Fig. 22–8). The rubber diaphragm or bladder is placed over the plies of material (Fig. 22–9), and the cover is closed. Air is then

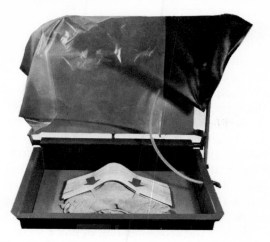

Fig. 22–8. Veneer and plywood build up is taped over a wood mold for proper positioning.

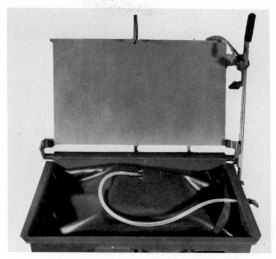

Fig. 22–9. The diaphragm or rubber bladder is placed in position over the glued-up plywood. Note that the diaphragm is laid in such a manner to allow for suitable bag inflation. The inlet air line is placed to function properly, and the press is ready for closing, locking, and pressurizing.

admitted to the bladder. This forces it uniformly against the glued-up plies to make the panel.

This particular press is supported at convenient working height on a cabinet having storage space for molds, materials, and supplies. Air pressure capable of producing 40 lb. per square inch must be available. The limitation of this machine is in the size of the piece it can form. The one shown has an opening of $18 \times 30 \times 6$ inches. A larger size is available. The advantages over shop-made forms are that flat or curved parts can be made by using only one part of the form. The press provides uniform clamping pressure, and eliminates the need for clamps. The operating instructions which come with the equipment must be followed explicitly.

Some of the forms satisfactorily used with this machine are shown in Fig. 22–10. The furniture shown in Fig. 22–11 was made by using some of the forms pictured in Fig. 22–10.

BUILDING UP THE CORE FOR A FLAT SHEET

1. Cut enough boards, approximately 2 to 3 inches wide, to form a core of the required size. These are edge-glued into a

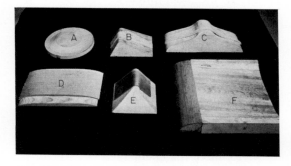

Fig. 22–10. A representative group of simple shop-made molds that have been used with the commercial press: (A) a 12-inch diameter plate mold with a $3/8$-inch drop. By using a male mold, greater compression stresses can be exerted. (B) A 90-degree turn can be used in a male mold of this type to make legs. (C) A coat hanger mold with a piece produced from it. (D) An elliptical curve mold for making trays, chair backs, and stool seats. (E) This book-end mold uses a re-curved corner to allow books to stand without corner interference. (F) One design possibility for a chair seat. On some of the sharp bends, it is recommended that plies be no thicker than $1/32$ inch.

113

Fig. 22–11. These pieces of furniture were made by using some of the forms shown in Fig. 22–10, in the press pictured in Fig. 22–7.

single board to form the core of the plywood. The glued-up core should be slightly larger than the desired overall dimensions of the finished panel.

The thickness of the core stock depends upon the desired thickness of the finished panel. If the final thickness is to be approximately $^{13}/_{16}$ inch, the core stock may be made from inexpensive lumber $^5/_8$ to $^3/_4$ inch thick.

2. Plane the edges of the core boards until all of them fit. Arrange the end grain alternately.

3. Clamp all the boards together carefully with bar clamps for a trial assembly. Be sure the joints fit properly.

4. Remove the clamps.

5. Spread glue on the edges of all the boards. Place them together in position, and clamp them with bar clamps. Refer to Unit 25, *Gluing and Clamping*.

6. Allow the glue to dry thoroughly; then remove the core from the clamps. The time required depends on the type of glue.

7. Plane the core to the required thickness.

CROSS-BANDING

1. Cut the cross-band sheets a little larger than the actual size needed. Cross-band material is available commercially. It

is cut like veneer except that it is cut $^1/_8$ to $^3/_{16}$ inch thick for this purpose.

2. Spread glue on one of the surfaces of the core, but *not* on the cross-band sheet.

3. Place the cross-band material on the glued surface of the core. See that the grain runs at right angles to the grain of the core. Fasten the cross band in place with four thin, $^1/_2$-inch brads, one in each corner. Drive them in about $^1/_4$ inch and cut off the heads with pliers. These brads, or veneer pins, hold the cross-banding in place so that it will not slip under pressure.

4. Place several layers of newspaper over the cross-band surface to keep it from sticking to the press boards. These are usually plywood panels $^{13}/_{16}$ inch thick.

5. Press the plywood press boards until the projecting brads go up into them.

6. Turn the panel and plywood upside down.

7. Spread glue on the outer surface of the core. Place the opposite cross band in position. Secure it as described in steps 3 through 5.

8. Put this glued assembly in a press, or clamp it with handscrew clamps. Allow it to remain until thoroughly dry.

Do these steps quickly. The cross-band veneer will expand if it is allowed to absorb moisture from the glue. This may cause buckling when it is pressed together.

9. Remove the core and cross-band assembly from the press or clamps. Take off the press boards and newspapers. Pull out the veneer pins or brads.

PREPARING VENEER SURFACES

1. Decide on the pattern of matching veneer (Fig. 22–12). Refer to Figs. 22–13 through 22–16. The steps that follow are for the side-to-side match (Fig. 22–13).

2. Select two pieces of veneer having the same pattern. Lay them on top of each other so that the patterns practically match.

Logs must be loaded properly to avoid damage to cellular structure. *(U.S. Forest Service)*

Through proper logging and conservation practices, forests will continue to produce the raw materials needed for wood products industries. *(Thompson Logging Co.)*

Great skill is essential in moving logs from the forest to the mill. *(International Harvester Company)*

The West Coast Forest is characterized by tall, straight conifers like the Douglas fir and, most notably, the redwoods (shown here). Their growth is favored by the abundant moisture that is blown in from the Pacific Ocean. *(St. Regis)*

The Northern Forest covers a region of abundant lakes, river valleys, and hills. Some areas are predominantly coniferous (mainly pine, spruce, balsam, fir, hemlock), some hardwood (mainly maple, birch, beech), and some mixed, as shown here. *(St. Regis)*

The Southern Forest is dominated by southern yellow pines, notably loblolly, slash, and longleaf pine (shown here). However, many hardwoods are found here too, including sweetgum, tupelo, and a large number of oak species. (St. Regis)

The Mountain Forest of the west has less rainfall because moisture from the Pacific is barred by the Cascades and Coast Ranges. Prominent species are ponderosa pine (foreground), western white pine, sugar pine, Englemann spruce, and Douglas fir. *(St. Regis)*

The Tropical Forests of the United States are found only in the southern tip of Florida and a small area in southeastern Texas. Mangrove (shown here in the foreground) and mahogany are the principal trees of our tropical forests. *(St. Regis)*

The Central Forest is characterized by hardwood species. Much of this region was long ago converted to farmland. Important species include oak, hickory, yellow poplar, as well as such conifers as yellow pine and red cedar. *(St. Regis)*

Kiln drying of incense cedar results in an excellent building material. *(Western Wood Products Association)*

The proper stacking and storage of lumber are essential for efficient management of raw materials. *(International Harvester Company)*

Laminated beam structures make possible huge spans for public buildings. *(American Plywood Association)*

House framing techniques have improved greatly, due to better wood products and the use of efficient equipment. *(American Plywood Association)*

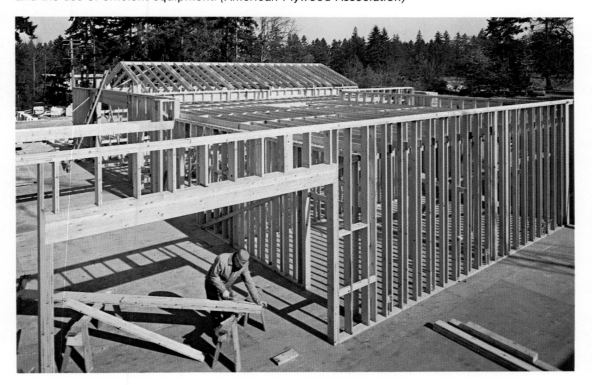

Artistic and well-planned kitchens make use of wood products produced by modern technology. *(International Paper Co.)*

The home construction industry is a major factor in the American economy. *(General Electric Co.)*

The use of laminated beam structures has created an almost entirely new wood products industry. *(American Plywood Association)*

Colorful walls of plastic laminate lend themselves to hygienic maintenance. *(Micarta Div., Westinghouse)*

Plastic laminates are used in increasing quantities because of functionalism and attractiveness. *(Micarta Div., Westinghouse)*

Serviceable plastic laminate surfaces often present beautiful wood grain patterns. *(Micarta Div., Westinghouse)*

Fig. 22-12. The craftsman selects veneers carefully for color and grain figure. *(Baker Furniture.)*

3. Place a steel square or metal straightedge along the matching line. Cut away the surplus with a sharp knife, plane iron, chisel, or veneer saw.

4. Clamp the two pieces of veneer between two boards that have straight edges. See that the edges of the veneer barely project beyond the edges of the boards (Fig. 22-17).

5. Plane the edges to form a perfect joint (Fig. 22-17).

6. Lay the two pieces of veneer on a smooth surface with the jointed edges together. The joint may be fastened with brads on the extreme ends of the veneer.

7. Cut a piece of 1-inch-wide gummed paper tape long enough to cover the joint.

8. Moisten the gummed side of the tape with a wet sponge. Press the tape over the joint (see Fig. 22-18). After it has dried, pull the brads out. The matched veneer is ready to be glued to the cross-band surface.

9. Cut a piece or pieces of veneer for the back. It will not be necessary to match a

Fig. 22-13. Side-to-side match.

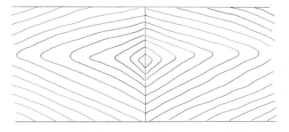

Fig. 22-14. End-to-end match.

115

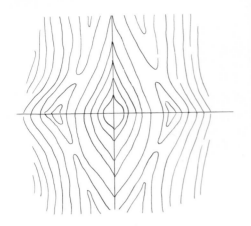

Fig. 22–15. Four-piece match.

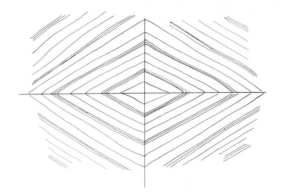

Fig. 22–16. Diamond match.

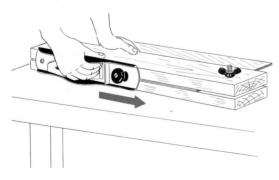

Fig. 22–17. Planing veneer edges for matching.

Fig. 22–18. Pieces of veneer being taped together for final gluing on the surface of plywood.

pattern. This undersurface will probably not be visible. Veneer is needed on the back of the panel to keep it from warping.

GLUING VENEERS

1. Smooth the surface of the cross bands by handscraping and sanding.

2. Spread glue on the surface of the cross band to which the surface veneer is to be glued.

3. Place the veneer on the glued surface. See that the grain runs at right angles to the cross band. Also make certain that the taped side of the veneer is out.

4. Press the veneer by hand and fasten it with four brads, one in each corner. Cut them off near the surface.

5. Turn the board over.

6. Repeat steps 1 through 4 to glue the reverse side.

7. Place sheets of newspaper over each veneered surface. Put the plywood panel between two press boards or panels. Apply pressure with a press or hand clamps.

8. Allow the plywood panel to remain in the press or clamps until thoroughly dry.

9. Remove the built-up panel from the press or clamps. Take off the press boards and newspapers. Pull out the brads or pins.

10. Clean off any newspaper, excess glue, or gummed tape sticking to the sur-

Fig. 22–19. The top of this coffee table is an example of carefully matched veneer pieces.

Fig. 22–20. Strips of two plies of veneering may be glued together to make satisfactory edging on panels.

face of the veneer. The glue and newspaper will handscrape easily. The gummed tape can be removed with a wet sponge.

11. Remove glue stains, if necessary. Sponge the stained surface with a solution of oxalic acid. (Oxalic acid crystals can be bought at a drugstore.) Mix 1 part oxalic acid crystals to 10 parts hot water. Use the solution after it has cooled.

12. Sand the surfaces for final finishing. Use fine-grade sandpaper. Sand only in the direction of the grain.

13. Apply suitable finish (see Fig. 22–19).

FORMING CURVED PLYWOOD

1. Make forms for the desired shape of the panels (see Figs. 22–3, 22–4, and 22–10). It will probably be necessary to glue up several thicknesses of stock to make these forms. Cut them on a band saw to the desired shape.

2. Prepare the stock for making the core. This will usually consist of one, three, or five layers of single-ply poplar veneer 1/8 to 3/16 inch thick. This is the same material that was used for making cross bands in flat panels.

3. Apply glue to the surfaces of the core stock. Place these pieces one on top of the other with the grain at right angles. The

Fig. 22–21. Specially prepared veneer tapes, matched to the surface veneer, are most suitable for edge gluing on the finished plywood panel.

Fig. 22–22. A satisfactory edging may be made to fit a V groove which has been cut on the edge of plywood.

grains of the core and the surface veneers should run at right angles when forming large curved pieces. Magazine racks and chair bottoms and backs are typical pieces of this kind.

4. Spread glue on the outer surfaces of the core stock. Arrange the thin pieces of veneer in their proper positions.

5. Put several layers of newspapers on each side of the plywood panel. Place it in the form. Clamp it securely in a press with clamps, or in a jig.

6. Follow steps 9 through 11 under "Gluing Veneers" for removing the curved plywood from the jig. The shaped piece should then be cleaned and sanded.

FINISHING THE EDGES

Edges of plywood of ½-inch, or greater, thickness should be treated with some type of edging to give a finished appearance. Figures 22–20 and 22–21 show applications of wood-veneer banding. In Fig. 22–20 the edge band is put on with contact cement. Figure 22–21 shows the use of a specially prepared edge banding which is available in almost any type of wood. The adhesive comes applied to the material.

Fig. 22–23. An assortment of wood-grain edge moldings.

Figure 22–22 pictures the use of a piece of solid wood to match the surface veneer. This is cut to fit a V groove in the edge of the plywood. An assortment of wood-grain moldings is illustrated in Fig. 22–23. These are metal or plastic edgings, requiring only a narrow saw kerf on the edge of the panel. The moldings should be mitered at the corners.

Discussion Topics

1. What is the difference between plywood and veneer?
2. Why do plywood panels require an uneven number of pieces?
3. Explain why cross bands in plywood are at right angles to the core stock and to the veneer.
4. When might it be advisable to run the grain of all the plies and the veneer in the same direction? Why?
5. In making a curved form out of wood, why must you remove from the form the same amount of wood as the thickness of the plywood to be formed?
6. List four advantages in using a commercial press over a shop-made form to form plywood as shown in Fig. 22–7.
7. Why is the male part of the form generally used in forming when using the commercial press?
8. List four ways of giving a finished treatment to the edge of plywood.

unit

23

Applying plastic laminates

Plastic laminates are frequently applied to plywood and particle board. Many pieces of furniture are partially, or completely, covered with wood-grained laminate. Plastic laminate is commonly used to cover coffee tables, end tables, and kitchen drainboards. It also has extensive use as counter tops in bathrooms, and on dressing-table areas.

The procedure suggested here is for installing or applying a plastic laminate sheet on a kitchen drainboard or any other flat surface. Each laminate manufacturer recommends a bonding or cementing agent. Contact cement is most often used on the items mentioned above.

Woodworking hand tools, power tools, and machines may be used for sawing, cutting, edge dressing, drilling, routing, and other necessary processes. Two special tools designed for the purpose of working with laminates are a carbide-tipped knife for scoring (marking), described in Unit 7, and a router cutter described in Unit 34. For technical information on laminates, refer to Unit 69, *The Manufacture and Use of Plastic Laminates.*

APPLYING PLASTIC LAMINATES ON EDGES

It is desirable and necessary, frequently, that edges be covered with plastic laminate before the top is put on. If this is the case, follow this suggested procedure:

1. Fill with putty or wood dough all holes in the edges and surfaces of the board or area to be covered.

2. Sand all surfaces and edges smooth for good adhesion (Fig. 23-1).

3. Mark or score the laminate strips a little wider than the edge to be covered (Fig. 23-2).

4. Cut the laminate strips, using a handsaw (Fig. 23-3), or a circular saw. The laminate may also be broken, as shown in Fig.

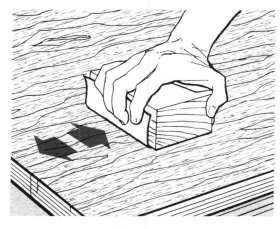

Fig. 23-1. All surfaces and edges should be sandpapered smooth.

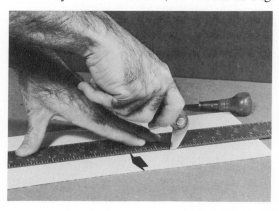

Fig. 23-2. Marking and scoring (cutting) plastic laminate. A carbide-tipped knife will cut through the top and decorative layers.

119

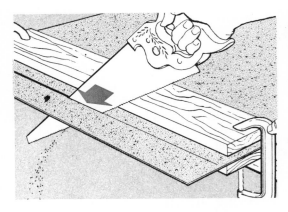

Fig. 23-3. A fine-tooth crosscut saw may be used to cut straight pieces of laminate. The material must be held securely, as shown.

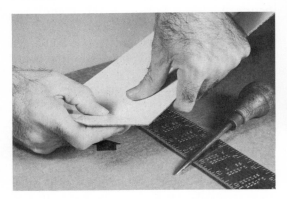

Fig. 23-4. Laminate can be broken after scoring with a scoring tool or an awl. It must be bent toward the decorative surface.

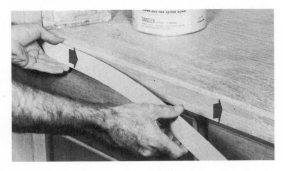

Fig. 23-5. Press the laminate strip firmly against the edge, beginning at one end and following through to the opposite one.

Fig. 23-6. A flat mill file may be used to dress (smooth) the edges.

Fig. 23-7. A special roller-guide and cutter are used in the router to cut edge strips flush with the top.

23-4, if the marking in Fig. 23-2 was scored (cut) through both the top and decorative layers.

5. Apply contact cement to the edge of the wood panel or particle board, and also to the rough side of the laminate strip (see Figs. 23-8 and 23-9).

6. When the cement becomes dry and "tacky," press the laminate strip firmly to the edge (Fig. 23-5). Use a rubber mallet to help set the strip securely in place. Allow a slight overlap or surplus for dressing down.

7. Smooth the laminate edge to the surface of the top with a flat mill file (Fig. 23-6), or a router having a special cutter and roller for this purpose (Fig. 23-7).

Fig. 23-8. A metal spreader with a serrated edge is a good way to spread contact cement evenly.

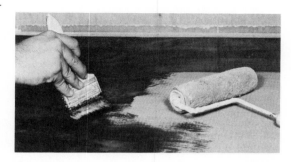

Fig. 23-9. A brush or a roller may also be used to apply cement.

APPLYING PLASTIC LAMINATE TOP SHEETS

1. Follow steps 1 through 4 of the preceding operation for edge dressing. Make sure the piece is cut a little larger than the surface to be covered.

2. Apply contact cement to the entire surface of the board or panel (Figs. 23-8 and 23-9). Also spread contact cement on the rough side of the plastic laminate sheet.

3. Allow the cemented surfaces to dry and become tacky. The time may be 20 minutes or longer, depending upon the type of adhesive used. Follow the manufacturer's directions.

4. Place the laminate sheet in the correct position for final bonding (Figs. 23-10 and 23-11). Position it so it extends over the

Fig. 23-10. Scrap laminate strips prevent the plastic laminate sheet from adhering until accurate alignment. A piece of heavy kraft wrapping paper is satisfactory also.

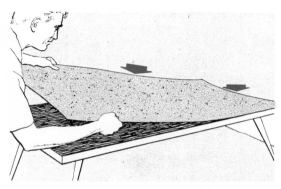

Fig. 23-11. Laying the plastic sheet on the cemented surface.

Fig. 23-12. A rolling pin gives even pressure for bonding the laminate to the surface.

121

edges a bit. In order to ensure perfect positioning, lay some scrap strips of laminate or a sheet of heavy kraft wrapping paper on the top to be covered, as shown in Fig. 23–10. These strips or the paper will not stick, and are pulled out while the laminate sheet is held in correct position. When contact is made, the laminate sheet cannot be moved; therefore every precaution must be taken for proper alignment.

5. Apply pressure over the covered surface to make complete contact (Fig. 23–12). A rolling pin will do this job.

6. Remove the surplus with the router (Fig. 23–13), or a file (see Fig. 23–6).

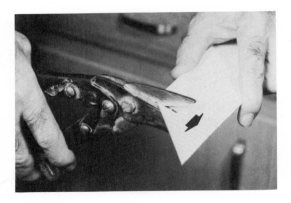

Fig. 23–15. Cutting across a sheet of laminate with a special laminate cutter.

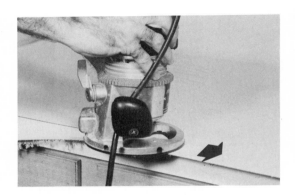

Fig. 23–13. Excess overlap may be smoothed easily and made flush with the edge by using the router and special cutter.

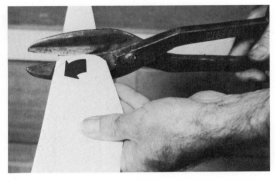

Fig. 23–16. Cutting external curves with a sharp tin snips. Remove only a small amount with each cut to prevent chipping.

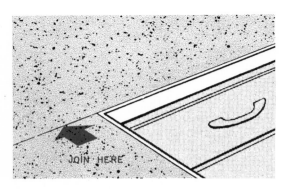

Fig. 23–14. Laminate sheets may be butted together.

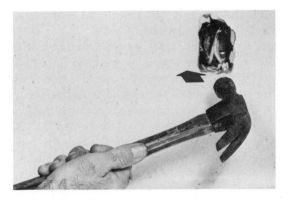

Fig. 23–17. Openings may be made over electrical outlets by tapping with a hammer.

SUPPLEMENTARY PROCEDURES

1. Pieces of plastic laminate may be butt joined, as shown in Fig. 23–14.

2. A special laminate cutter can be used to cut straight across large or small pieces (Fig. 23–15).

3. External curves may be cut with a sharp tin snips (Fig. 23–16).

4. An opening for a wall outlet may be made after the laminate has been fastened, by using a hammer (Fig. 23–17).

5. Cleaning the adhesive from plastic laminate surfaces can be done with the thinner recommended for the cement. The thinner will also clean off the adhesive from the tools used. Laminate can be maintained by cleaning with soap and water.

Discussion Topics

1. Name five processes or operations which can be performed on plastic laminate sheet material.

2. Why must the flat wood or particle board surface be perfectly smooth and clean before the adhesive material is applied to it?

3. What type of bonding agent is usually used to fasten laminate sheets to a flat surface?

4. Why must the plastic laminate sheet be perfectly aligned before pressing it into place?

5. Describe two methods to keep a plastic laminate sheet from adhering to the cemented surface while being aligned.

6. Describe two methods of dressing plastic edges smooth.

7. List three methods of cutting plastic laminate sheets.

unit

24

Furniture and cabinet construction

Furniture and cabinet construction calls for many of the fundamental tool skills discussed and illustrated in previous hand-tool units. Some of the construction details can be accomplished more effectively through using power hand-tool and machine-tool processes. Accepted ways of fastening table tops, making drawers and drawer slides, and building chests of drawers and cabinets are described and illustrated in this unit.

FASTENING A TABLE TOP

1. Decide on the method of fastening the table top to the table. Make this decision before you begin to fasten the rails to the legs.

2. Cut grooves or bore holes, as necessary, in the rails. This will depend upon how you fasten the top (see Fig. 24–1).

3. Fasten the legs to the rails according to the joint being used. Finish sanding for final fastening to the top.

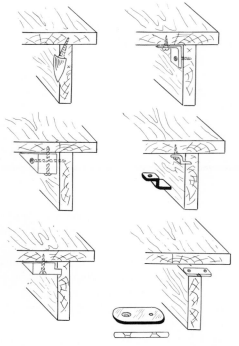

Fig. 24–1. Six methods of fastening table tops to side rails.

4. Place the top and the leg-and-rail assembly upside down on a bench (Fig. 24–2). Sawhorses also make a good platform or support.

5. Locate the leg-and-rail assembly in the proper position. It may be held in place with clamps (see Fig. 24–2).

6. Fasten the rails to the top by the selected method, as shown in Figs. 24–1 and 24–2.

MAKING A DRAWER

1. Study the working drawing to learn the exact overall height, width, and length of a drawer.

2. Use the same kind of wood for the front of the drawer as was used in the rails of the table.

3. Select wood for the sides and backpiece of the drawer.

4. Select material for the drawer bottom. This should be a three-ply panel, $1/4$ inch in thickness, or Presdwood $1/8$ inch thick.

Fig. 24–2. Fastening the top to the table. This illustration shows three types of top fasteners.

5. Cut and square the pieces of wood for the sides and back according to the dimensions. A suitable thickness is approximately ⅝ inch. Use care and accuracy in every step in making a drawer, so it will work easily.

6. Lay out and cut the rabbet joint in the drawer front, as shown in Fig. 24–3. The combination dado-tongue and rabbet joint (Figs. 24–3 and 24–4) is a very sturdy joint.

7. Cut the grooves, or dadoes, in the sides. These should be cut to a depth one-half the thickness of the side stock. They will probably be ⁵⁄₁₆ inch deep.

8. Cut a corresponding groove in the back of the frontpiece to hold the bottom panel.

9. Lay out and cut the backpiece of the drawer.

10. Lay out and cut the dado joints on the inside surfaces of the drawer sides to hold the backpiece. This should be approximately ½ to 1 inch from the rear. The width of the dado should be the thickness of the backpiece. Cut the dado to a depth of one-half the thickness of the sides. The backpiece should fit snugly into the dadoes.

11. Lay out and cut the material for the bottom. Measure it from the insides of the grooves.

12. Make a trial assembly of all parts of the drawer. See that the joints fit snugly and that the drawer is the proper size. Disassemble all parts.

13. Fasten the front of the drawer upright in a vise (Fig. 24–4).

14. Start two or three resin-coated brads into the drawer sides (Fig. 24–4).

15. Apply glue to the joint. Place the drawer side on the frontpiece and drive the brads to hold the joint firmly (Fig. 24–4).

16. Fasten the opposite side to the drawer front in a similar manner.

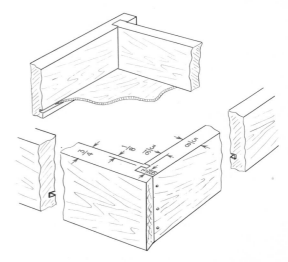

Fig. 24–3. Details of drawer construction.

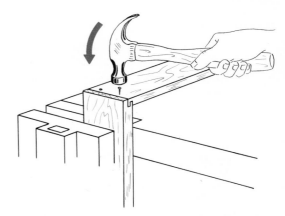

Fig. 24–4. Fastening the side of a drawer to the front.

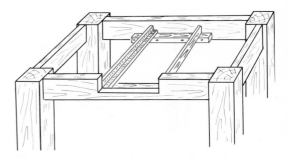

Fig. 24–5. Drawer slides fastened to table rails.

17. Apply glue to the dado joints at the rear of the drawer. Insert the backpiece, and fasten with resin-coated brads.

18. Remove excess glue from all joints.

19. Slide the drawer bottom in place through the grooves from the back of the drawer. Do not glue the bottom in place.

20. Check to see that the drawer is square.

21. Fasten the bottom to the backpiece of the drawer with one or two resin-coated brads. Drive them up from the bottom into the backpiece.

22. Dress all joints smooth with sandpaper.

23. Make a final test to see that the drawer fits easily into the desk or table opening.

MAKING DRAWER SLIDES

1. Select stock from inexpensive lumber to make the slides according to the working drawing. An easy method of making drawer slides is shown in Fig. 24-5.

2. Cut the drawer slides as shown in Fig. 24-5.

3. Make pieces to support the slides. These are pieces of wood about ¾ inch square. They should be long enough to support both drawer slides (Fig. 24-5).

4. Drill or bore the necessary holes for fastening these supporting blocks to the slides and to the rails.

5. Fasten the drawer slides to the supporting blocks with glue and screws or brads. Allow ample space for the drawer to slide.

6. Locate the position on the front and back rails for the slide assembly.

7. Fasten the slide assembly to the rails with screws (Fig. 24-5).

MODERN LEG ASSEMBLY

1. Turn a straight tapered leg according to the dimensions in your drawing.

2. Fit the ferrule, or cap, on the foot of the leg (Fig. 24-7). These are available from many hardware-supply companies.

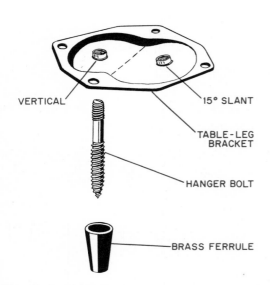

Fig. 24-6. Table-leg bracket, hanger bolt, and brass ferrule.

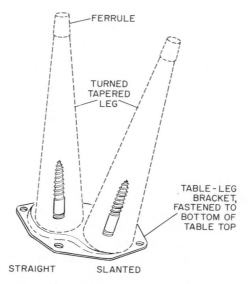

Fig. 24-7. Table-leg assembly showing bracket, leg, and ferrule.

3. Fasten the table-leg brackets with screws on the underside of the table top (Figs. 24–6 and 24–7). Leg brackets are available for mounting legs vertically or at a 15-degree angle. The bracket illustrated in Fig. 24–6 will do either.

4. Drill a pilot hole into the top of the leg for the hanger bolt (Fig. 24–7). The hole should be about the same diameter as the solid body of the bolt under the thread.

5. Screw the hanger bolt into the leg. Leave about ¼ inch extending.

6. Screw the extended part of the hanger bolt, with the leg, into the table-leg bracket (Fig. 24–7).

ASSEMBLING A CHEST OF DRAWERS OR A DRESSING TABLE

Figure 24–8 shows the frame of a chest of drawers. The framework is relatively inexpensive; the exterior is three-ply ¼-inch plywood with a suitable wood-veneer exterior. The two ends are inexpensive wood frames which are doweled together and covered with plywood.

The horizontal drawer dividers and supports are frames held together with triangular ¼-inch plywood corner pieces recessed (set in) in dadoes. The horizontal drawer dividers are fastened to the vertical end frames by means of dowels. This assembly makes for lightweight construction.

Figure 24–9 pictures the completed chest of drawers with the drawers in place. Notice that the wide drawers overlap the vertical end frames, and also the vertical drawer separators. The center drawer fronts may have exquisitely matched veneer facing, as shown, to give the appearance of expensive quality furniture.

Figure 24–10 shows the use of a pneumatic staple-tacker attaching hardboard backing to a chest of drawers. This is done in assembly-line production.

Fig. 24–8. Assembly of framework for chest of drawers. Note the interesting, yet simple, construction details.

Fig. 24–9. The completed chest of drawers.

Fig. 24–10. Attaching the hardboard back on the chest of drawers on an assembly-line production.

1. Describe six methods of fastening a table top to the rails.
2. Which of these methods will allow the top to expand or contract more readily?
3. Why should you not glue the table top directly to the rails?
4. Examine the construction of several drawers in commercially built furniture at home or in an office. How were they built?
5. How were the drawer slides made in the furniture which you inspected in answering question 4?
6. What are the advantages of using the turned tapered leg with the hanger bolt and the table-leg bracket?
7. What features should you look for in a well-built piece of furniture?
8. Describe three other types of drawer construction you have seen.
9. Illustrate and describe the construction of the vertical ends for the chest of drawers shown in Fig. 24–8.
10. Sketch and describe the procedure involved to make the horizontal drawer supports, or dividers, shown in Fig. 24–8.

unit
25.

Gluing and clamping

The fundamental purpose of a wood adhesive is to flow or spread over the areas to be fastened together, penetrate into the wood, and solidify to make a strong joint. Boards are glued together edge-to-edge to make larger surfaces, or face-to-face to increase thickness. When properly made, and when the glue is prepared and applied correctly, glued joints are as strong as the wood. In most cases they are even stronger. Unit 82, *Testing the Strength of Glues and Adhesives*, presents an experiment with wood adhesives.

KINDS OF GLUES

There are many kinds of glues and adhesives for woodworking. They are generally classified as polyvinyl resin, casein, plastic resin, resorcinol resin, epoxy resin, and animal.

Minor classifications include blood albumin, starch, all-purpose cements, and adhesives. These will bind wood to metals, plastics, and glass. Contact cement is a popular bonding agent for cementing decorative laminates to wood.

Glues, adhesives, and cements are listed under many trade names. It is therefore advisable to read the descriptions and directions which come on the packaged product before you make a selection.

Polyvinyl-resin Glue. This is a white, clean liquid, fast-setting, strong, and easy to use. It is best applied by using a plastic squeeze bottle. It is a very popular type of liquid glue, obtainable from practically all variety and hardware stores, supply houses, and lumber yards.

Casein Glue. This is a product made from the curd of milk. It is available in powdered form and is made into a paste by adding water. It is used in furniture and boat construction where humidity is high. Before mixing the powder with water, read the directions carefully.

Plastic-resin Glue. This glue is a urea-formaldehyde powder mixed with water. It is extensively used in gluing plywood for exterior uses on airplanes and boats and for other exposed surfaces.

Resorcinol-resin Glue. This type of glue is made by mixing liquid resin with a catalyst. The two ingredients come packaged in a double container. You must mix them according to the furnished directions. This is an excellent glue for surfaces exposed to weather and for furniture and cabinetwork used in humid places.

Epoxy-resin Glue. This is a relatively recent type of adhesive. Like resorcinol-resin glue, it is obtainable in a two-container package which consists of white epoxy resin and a catalyst. These two ingredients must be mixed according to the manufacturer's directions. The mixture will bond (hold) wood to other materials, such as metals and plastics.

Animal Glue. This type of glue is made from hides, bones, hoofs, and trimmings of animals. These materials are refined and made into the final form of thin sheets, flakes, or powder. Animal glue is usually applied hot and sets very rapidly. It is therefore difficult to use on projects with many joints. It is not waterproof and should not be used in humid regions. This glue also comes commercially in liquid form.

When you apply hot animal glue, have all clamps adjusted properly in advance. This type of glue will set very rapidly upon cooling. Cold liquid animal glue does not require heating. For this reason there is a slight advantage in using it.

Contact Cement. Contact cement is transparent, odorless when dry, nonstaining, resists heat after it has aged, and is water- and moisture-resistant. Most types withstand oxidation, oils, grease, and nearly all chemicals.

Contact cement bonds, or sticks, immediately and permanently without clamps or presses. It is ideal for bonding Formica, Micarta, and other similar decorative laminates on such jobs as sink, counter, and table tops.

Manufacturers provide instructions for their specific brand of contact cement. You should read these detailed instructions carefully and follow them closely.

KINDS OF CLAMPS

The clamps most used in cabinetwork and furniture making are the *cabinet,* or *bar clamp*, the *handscrew clamp*, the *C clamp*, the *lightweight bar clamp*, and the *band clamp*. Each type works by a handscrew adjustment, and each has a particular use. You should always have plenty of clamps available for a job. Set them in advance so that they clamp on the project with a minimum of additional adjustment. This is especially advisable when you use hot animal glue.

Steel Bar Clamp. This clamp (Fig. 25–1) is generally of all-steel construction. It is used to clamp boards edge-to-edge to obtain increased width. The clamp shown has a multiple-disk clutch so that it may be set at any position on the bar. Steel bar clamps are available with maximum opening capacities of from 2 to 8 feet.

Fig. 25–1. Steel bar clamp.

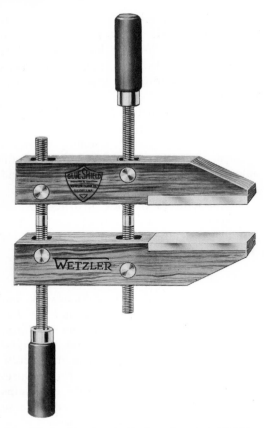

Fig. 25–2. Steel spindle hand-screw clamp.

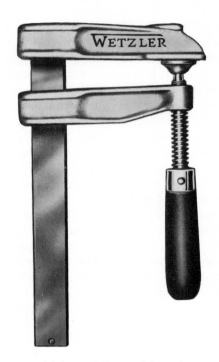

Fig. 25–4. Light-weight steel bar clamp.

Fig. 25–5. Band clamp.

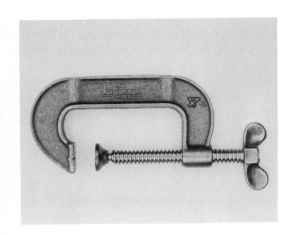

Fig. 25–3. C clamp.

Steel Spindle Handscrew Clamp. Figure 25–2 shows a handscrew clamp with metal-reinforced wooden jaws. The metal inserts serve as a glue shield when clamping up boards for thickness. The maximum opening between jaws of this type of clamp varies from 2 to 17 inches.

C Clamp. C clamps (Fig. 25–3) are of many designs; however all of them have the same general appearance. The maximum opening for this type of clamp ranges from 2½ to 12 inches. It is often used instead of the handscrew clamp.

Lightweight Steel Bar Clamp. This lightweight clamp (Fig. 25–4) has a maximum opening capacity variation of from 6 to 30 inches, depending on the size. It is also often used to replace the handscrew clamp.

Band Clamp. Figure 25–5 pictures a band clamp with a canvas or web band. Some use a steel band. This type clamp is available with a band of up to 30 feet in length. It is often used for clamping circular glued pieces or chairs.

GLUING AND CLAMPING

1. Mix or prepare cold or hot glue in accordance with the manufacturer's directions.

2. Adjust the clamps to fit your job.

3. Make protective blocks for the bar clamps. Have pieces of wood for alignment across the ends of the boards, if necessary (see Fig. 25–7).

4. Make a trial assembly, without glue, of the pieces. This checks the proper fit of all surfaces, edges, or joints. Then take the pieces apart to apply the glue.

5. Have available, or set up, jigs or a clamp donkey to hold the bar clamps.

6. Spread glue rapidly and evenly on the pieces (Fig. 25–6). Use a brush for best results.

7. Assemble the parts of the joint properly, and fasten the clamps as shown in

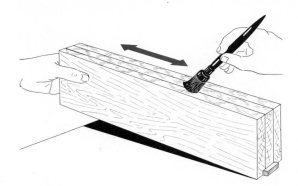

Fig. 25–6. Applying glue on edges.

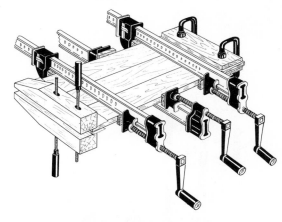

Fig. 25–7. Arrangement of clamps for edge gluing.

Fig. 25–8. Boards glued and clamped, resting on sawhorses.

Fig. 25–9. Instant high-frequency gluing with an electronic gluing machine.

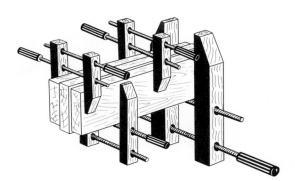

Fig. 25–10. Arrangement of hand-screw clamps for gluing boards to increase thickness.

Fig. 25–11. Incorrect and correct methods of clamping boards, using hand-screw clamps.

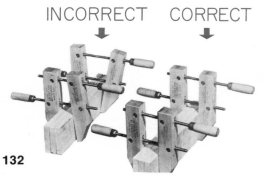

INCORRECT   CORRECT

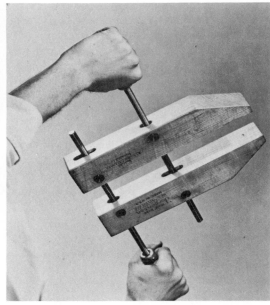

Fig. 25–12. The proper way to operate a hand-screw clamp.

Fig. 25–13. Clamping boards in steel bar clamps in an industrial assembly line.

Figs. 25–7 through 25–11. When you clamp boards, as shown in Figs. 25–6 and 25–7, place bar clamps from 12 to 15 inches apart. You may wish to use scrap blocks to protect the edges of the wood. Note how to operate the handscrew clamp, as shown in Fig. 25–12.

In all clamping operations, it is highly desirable that you have someone to help you. If the boards tend to buckle, keep them in alignment with handscrew and C clamps (see left and right ends of Fig. 25–7). Use a piece of paper between the clamps and the boards. This keeps the clamps from sticking to the glued joints. Use plenty of handscrew clamps in gluing boards to get additional thickness (Fig. 25–10). Fig. 25–13 shows an industrial version of steel bar clamps used for mass production.

8. Remove the surplus glue before it hardens. Use a scraper blade, wood chisel, old plane iron, piece of wood, or damp rag.

9. Wipe the joint thoroughly with a damp or wet rag. You can often clean all traces of glue in this way and avoid the unnecessary work of scraping it off later. All glue must be removed from exposed surfaces before finish is put on.

Discussion Topics

1. Name and give the uses for six types of glue.
2. Name and describe the five kinds of clamps which are helpful in gluing.
3. Why is it desirable to have all clamps set before gluing?
4. Give at least two uses for handscrew clamps.
5. Why should you remove all surplus glue from the joint before it hardens?
6. Explain the purpose of using scrap blocks between the wood and the cabinet or bar clamps, as shown in Fig. 25–7.
7. How long should stock be clamped before it is removed?

---

unit

26

Fastening hinges and other cabinet hardware

Hardware is a part of the final trim in many pieces of furniture. Its use is also a part of cabinetwork. You must be very accurate in fastening hinges and cabinet hardware. Always look for instructions on the packet or container.

Some of the more common pieces of hardware for the woodworker are hinges, drawer pulls, cabinet catches and hasps, locks, and furniture glides. Figure 26–5 pictures and identifies a few of the better-known types of hinges.

TOOLS

Adjustable End Wrench. An adjustable end wrench, as shown in Fig. 26–1, is a convenient tool for assembling certain types of hardware to cabinets and furniture. The one pictured is 8 inches long, and has a maximum opening capacity of 1 inch.

Fig. 26–1. Adjustable end wrench.

Fig. 26–2. Slip-joint pliers.

Fig. 26–3. Pump-type pliers.

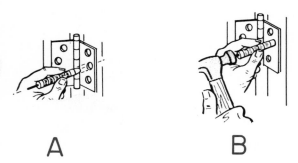

A   B

Fig. 26–4. Self-centering screw-hole punch: (A) position the hinge and fit the tapered head of the punch in the countersunk hole; (B) strike the plunger with a hammer to make the screw-starting hole quickly and accurately; the plunger retracts automatically.

Pliers. Figure 26–2 shows an indispensable tool for fastening. This is called a pair of slip-joint pliers because of its construction.

Pump-type Pliers. This type of pliers (Fig. 26–3) has become very popular because of its easily adjusted opening.

Self-centering Screw-hole Punch. Figure 26–4 pictures a very convenient tool used to locate and start screw-hole centers for hinges. Use of this tool is illustrated in the sequence of steps under the figure.

HINGES

The *butt hinge* (Fig. 26–5) is popular. It requires detailed fitting and *gaining*, or chiseling out, of the cabinet or frame. Some butt hinges are swaged, while others are not (Fig. 26–5). This will determine the depth of the gain (see Fig. 26–16). You can obtain butt hinges with loose or with stationary pins. If the pin is loose, install the hinge with the head of the pin up. Then the pin will not fall out. A variation of this hinge is the concealed wraparound type, shown in Fig. 26–6.

The *surface hinge* (Fig. 26–5) is one of the easiest to install. It is fastened to the surface and is entirely visible. Its patterns vary from ornate shapes to the crude metal strap used on barn doors. Figure 26–7 shows the installation of one type of ornamental surface hinge.

Not shown is the *half-surface hinge,* used in cabinetwork. It is installed so that half of it is visible. The other half is gained to the cabinet or into the frame in which it is fitted. The gained portion is fitted like the butt hinge.

The *chest hinge* (Fig. 26–5) supports chest lids. The *combination hinge* may also be used. This hinge pulls the lid away from the wall as it is opened. It serves as both hinge and lid support.

Cabinet hinges are made for use on flush doors and on overlapping doors (Fig. 26–5).

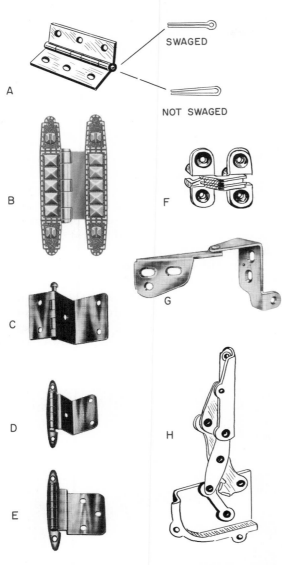

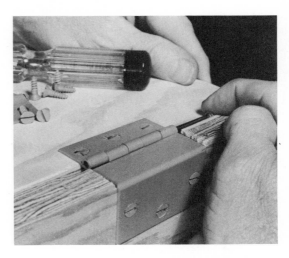

Fig. 26–6. A concealed wrap-around hinge fastened on a cabinet door.

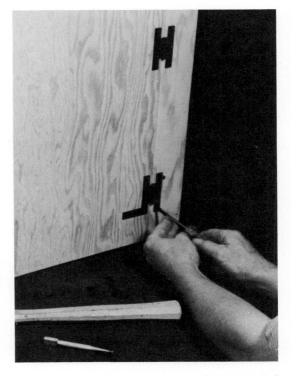

Fig. 26–7. Installing one type of ornamental surface hinge.

Fig. 26–5. A few commonly used hinges: (A) butt, (B) surface, (C) chest, (D) cabinet flush, (E) cabinet overlapping, (F) invisible, (G) concealed pivot pin, and (H) chest-and-lid support.

Fig. 26-8. A semi-concealed hinge being installed on a cabinet door having a lip.

Fig. 26-9. Concealed pivot pin hinges are very popular for cabinet doors.

Figure 26-8 shows how to install a hinge on an overlapping, or lip, door.

Invisible hinges are used in fine furniture, such as writing desks (see Fig. 26-5). Manufacturers supply drawings and directions for the installation of this type of hinge.

The *pivot pin hinge* is a very popular hinge used on cabinet and furniture doors (see Figs. 26-5 and 26-9).

DRAWER PULLS AND KNOBS

Drawer pulls and knobs come in a great variety of materials, patterns, and sizes. They are made from wood, plastic, composition materials, and metals. You are limited only by your personal preference. Figure 26-10 shows seven typical commercial drawer pulls and knobs.

They are supplied complete with screws for fastening. The single-post, or screw, knobs are easy to install. Mark the location and drill a hole of the proper size. More elaborate pulls and knobs have two posts or screws. These holes must be properly centered for correct fit.

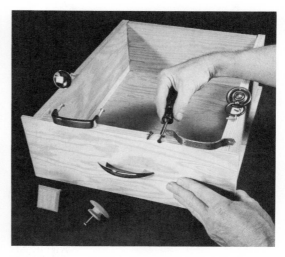

Fig. 26-10. Seven common types of drawer pulls and knobs.

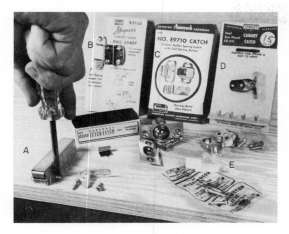

Fig. 26–11. Types of cabinet catches: (A) touch latch, (B) magnetic, (C) rubber roller spring, (D) friction, and (E) double rubber roller spring.

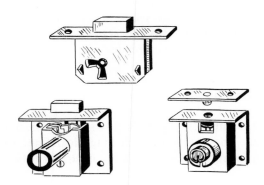

Fig. 26–12. Cabinet and chest locks.

OTHER HARDWARE

Hasps, door and *cabinet catches,* Fig. 26–11, and *furniture glides* are some other types of hardware that are relatively easy to install. For successful installation of the cabinet and chest locks pictured in Fig. 26–12, study the manufacturer's directions carefully. The variety in size and construction of such hardware makes it impractical to outline a uniform procedure for all types.

INSTALLING A BUTT HINGE

1. Select the proper size and kind of butt hinge. The size of the hinge is determined by its length.

2. Place the door in the frame or cabinet. Place wedges below and above to regulate the opening.

3. Locate the hinges according to the working drawing. Mark the location on both the door and the frame or cabinet.

4. Mark the width and depth of the gain (a notch or a mortise). Use a marking gage (Fig. 26–13).

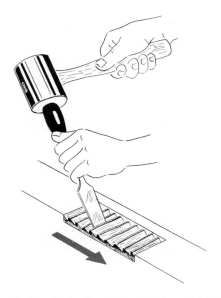

Fig. 26–13. Marking the gain for a hinge.

Fig. 26–14. Chiseling the gain for a hinge.

137

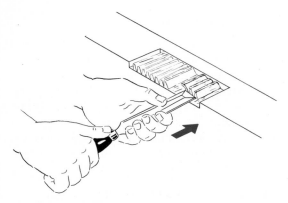

Fig. 26–15. Paring the bottom of a hinge gain.

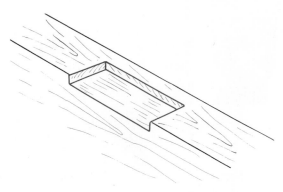

Fig. 26–16. Gain for a hinge completed.

5. Place a chisel in a vertical position on the marked line which locates the ends of the hinge. Drive the chisel lightly with a mallet (Fig. 26–14).

6. Repeat the chisel cut on the line which goes in the direction of the grain. Be careful not to split the wood (Fig. 26–14).

7. Make a series of chisel cuts as shown in Fig. 26–14.

8. Pare the bottom of the gain with a wide wood chisel, as shown in Fig. 26–15.

9. Make a trial fitting of the hinge in the gain. Pare to make a snug fit (Fig. 26–16).

10. Place the hinge in its proper setting. Mark the holes for the screws with a pencil.

11. Drill pilot holes into the wood or drive the hole with a self-centering screw-hole punch (see Fig. 26–4). See Unit 19.

12. Drive the screws with a screwdriver to fasten the hinge securely. Soap the screw threads when driving screws into hardwood. This helps prevent the screw from twisting off.

13. Cut the remaining gains for the hinges in the door or frame and cabinet.

14. Fasten the door in its proper position with screws. It is advisable to fasten only one screw in each hinge leaf first. In this way you can determine if further fitting is needed.

Discussion Topics

1. Name and describe six common types of hinges. Tell where each is used.
2. Name four of the materials from which drawer pulls and knobs may be made.
3. List ten places where you have seen different types of hinges used.
4. What is a gain?
5. What tools are used in making a gain?
6. Why do you soap screw threads?
7. Make a list of ten pieces of cabinet hardware other than hinges. Explain their uses.

unit

27

Hand sanding

You should sand your project thoroughly before applying any finishing materials. Sometimes you might sand your project after final assembly, but often the parts can conveniently be sanded before they are put together. Thorough sanding dresses the planed or scraped surface and edges for successful finishing. This is a most important step toward getting a good final finish (Fig. 27–1).

TOOLS

The abrasive material generally used on wood is called sandpaper. Its name is derived from the resemblance of its abrasive substance to sand. It is in reality crushed flint of grayish-tan color. Flint sandpaper is the least durable, but also the least expensive abrasive. Garnet paper and emery cloth are satisfactory to use. Garnet paper is more durable than flint sandpaper. It is reddish in color. Emery cloth or paper, which is tough and black in color, is used most often in polishing metal.

All three types of abrasive papers and cloth are graded from *fine* to *coarse*. There is some variation, as shown in Table 27–1. You will also note the equivalent number grading of each abrasive. Grit classification by number is the older method. These are natural abrasives. Manufactured abrasives are aluminum oxide and silicon carbide. They are used by some craftsmen. Table 27–1 also gives the grading for the manufactured abrasives.

Fig. 27–1. Proper and thorough sanding is the secret to a good finish. *(Drexel Furniture Company.)*

Fig. 27–2. Melting stick shellac to fill a wood defect.

Fig. 27–3. Pressing in plastic wood, or wood dough, to fill a defect.

Table 27–1. ABRASIVE GRADING CHART
Comparison of Mesh and Grit Numbers

CLASSIFICATION AND USE	ARTIFICIAL	NATURAL		
	Silicon Carbide Aluminum Oxide	Garnet	Flint (Quartz)	Emery
EXTRA COARSE (Sanding coarse wood texture)	12 16 20	16(4) 20(3½)		
VERY COARSE (Second stage in sanding wood texture)	24 30 36	24(3) 30(2½) 36(2)	Extra Coarse	Very Coarse
COARSE (Third stage in sanding wood texture)	40 50	40(1½) 50(1) (Coarse)	Coarse	
MEDIUM (Removing rough sanding texture)	60 80 100	60(½) 80(0) 100(2/0)	Medium	Coarse Medium
FINE (First stage in sanding before applying finish)	120 150 180	120(3/0) 150(4/0) 180(5/0)	Fine	Fine
VERY FINE (Second stage in sanding before applying finish)	220 240 280	220(6/0) 240(7/0) 280(8/0)	Extra Fine	
EXTRA FINE (Rubbing between finish coats)	320 360 400 500 600	320(9/0) 400(10/0)		

PREPARING THE SURFACE

1. Inspect all surfaces to see that mill marks have been removed with the plane or scraper.

2. Remove all traces of glue on surfaces, especially around joints.

3. Raise dents in the wood by moistening the dented areas with water. Steaming with a soldering iron and damp cloth is another way to raise dents. Grain cannot be raised if the fiber has been broken.

4. Fill small knots, holes, checks, or other open defects by melting in colored stick shellac (Fig. 27–2). You can also press in a colored wood plastic or wood dough (Fig. 27–3). Select the color that will match the finished wood.

5. Dress the hardened shellac or wood plastic smooth to the wood surface with abrasive paper.

PREPARING SANDPAPER

1. Tear a piece of sandpaper into four equal parts (Fig. 27–4).

2. Use a commercial rubber sanding block or else a block of wood for holding

Fig. 27-4. Tearing sandpaper on a metal edge.

Fig. 27-5. Sanding a surface with the grain.

the sandpaper. Such a block should measure approximately ¾ by 2½ by 6 inches.

3. Fold the quarter sheet of sandpaper carefully around the block so that you will be able to hold it securely with your hand (Fig. 27-5).

SANDING

1. Fasten the board to be sanded securely on the bench, or place the project so that it can be held while sanding.

2. Sand all flat surfaces *with the grain*, using an even pressure (Fig. 27-5). Avoid sanding across grain or in a circular motion. This will injure the wood fibers. Do the first sanding with medium-grade sandpaper. Finish sanding with fine and extra fine. See Table 27-1.

3. Sand edges and ends (Fig. 27-6) as in steps 1 and 2.

4. To sand concave, irregular, and molded or shaped edges, wrap the sandpaper around a piece of wood that is formed to work in the particular outline.

5. Sand rounded edges by cupping the sandpaper in your hand (Fig. 27-7).

6. Inspect all visible surfaces, edges, and ends. Make sure they have been properly sanded for applying the finish.

Fig. 27-6. Sanding an edge.

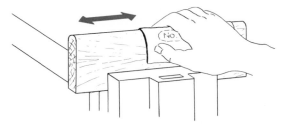

Fig. 27-7. Sanding a rounded edge.

For a fine finish, the surfaces should be lightly sponged with water to raise any loose fibers. When dry, sand with very fine sandpaper.

The properly scraped and sandpapered project is now ready for final finishing. Study Section 5 to determine the finish you want to put on your project.

Study Section 5 to determine the finish you want to put on your project.

Discussion Topics

1. Is sandpaper considered a tool? Explain.
2. Name three natural abrasive materials. Which is the most commonly used? Why?
3. Sandpaper is often sold by the quire. How many sheets make a quire?
4. List the grades of grit for sandpaper, garnet paper, and emery cloth.
5. Why should abrasive paper be held around a block for most sanding?
6. Why should you always sand in the direction of the grain?
7. Why should sanded surfaces be water-sponged before applying the final finish?
8. Name two commercially manufactured abrasives.

---

unit

28

Caring for and sharpening tools

Excellent workmanship in woodworking depends to a great extent upon sharp tools. A dull tool calls for unnecessary extra pressure, which often makes the tool slip. Every tool used must have the sharpest possible edge. The beginner can develop the skill of sharpening tools satisfactorily. You probably will not begin by sharpening such tools as auger bits and saws. You will need to sharpen plane irons, chisels, pocketknives, spokeshave blades, and scraper blades. A plane iron or chisel does not cut properly when it leaves slight ridges in the wood. This is an indication that the cutting edge needs to be sharpened on the grinder, the oilstone, or perhaps both. Check the cutting edges of your tools before starting to work.

TOOLS

Some of the easier tools to sharpen are plane irons, spokeshave blades, chisels, drawknives, pocketknives, and sloyd, or woodcarving, knives. Equipment and tools used to sharpen these include the *grinder* (Fig. 28–1), a slow-speed oil grinder built especially for grinding edge tools in woodworking, and the *oilstone* (Fig. 28–2).

Sharpening scraper-blade edges requires a *single-cut, smooth mill file*, the *oilstone*, and the *burnisher* for turning edges (Fig. 28–3).

The setting and sharpening of handsaw teeth require a special *clamp* (Fig. 28–4), a *saw set* (Fig. 28–5), a *mill file*, and a *triangular, slim taper file* (Fig. 28–6).

Fig. 28–1. Pedestal-type seven-inch grinder.

Labels on Fig. 28–1:
TWIN-LITE SAFETY SHIELD
MOTOR
GRINDING WHEEL
WATER POT
ADJUSTABLE TOOL REST
SWITCH
SPARK DEFLECTOR
WHEEL GUARD
PLANE BLADE GRINDING ATTACHMENT
DUST CHUTE
PEDESTAL

Fig. 28–2. Oilstone.

Fig. 28–3. Burnisher.

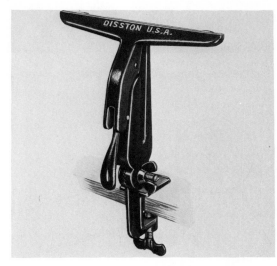

Fig. 28–4. Saw clamp for handsaws.

Fig. 28–5. Saw set. Note the shape of the anvils in the detail for setting the saw teeth.

Auger bits can be sharpened with *triangular*, *slim taper files* or with *special auger-bit files*.

SHARPENING EDGE TOOLS

1. Remove the plane iron from the plane (Fig. 9–1) or the spokeshave blade from the spokeshave frame (Fig. 12–1). For assembling or taking apart these tools, refer to Unit 9, *Assembling and Adjusting Planes*, and Unit 12, *Assembling and Adjusting a Spokeshave.*

2. Fasten the plane iron in the holder on the grinder (Fig. 28–7). The sharpening steps which follow are for grinding either a spokeshave blade or woodcutting chisels. Grind the plane iron, chisel, or blade only if the cutting edge is nicked or if it has been incorrectly ground.

3. Turn on the grinder switch and move the blade or chisel from side to side while the grinding wheel is in motion (Fig. 28–7).

4. Continue to grind until all the nicks are removed. Use a lubricant on the abra-

Fig. 28-6. Triangular, slim taper file.

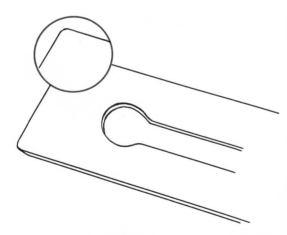

Fig. 28-7. Sharpening a plane iron with a grinder guide.

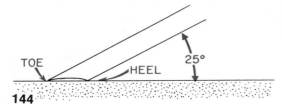

Fig. 28-8. The proper way to round the edges of a plane iron.

Fig. 28-9. Angle for grinding a plane iron.

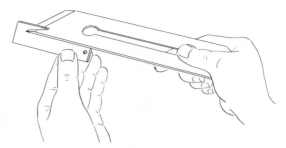

Fig. 28-10. Testing the angle of a plane iron.

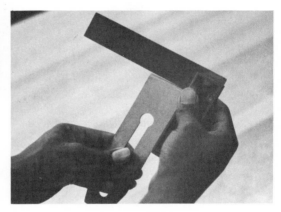

Fig. 28-11. Testing the cutting edge of a plane iron for squareness.

Fig. 28-12. Whetting the cutting edge of a plane iron on an oilstone.

TOE HEEL 25°

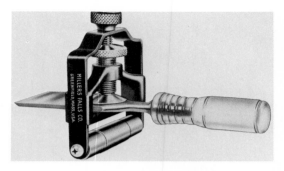

Fig. 28–13. Plane iron and chisel-sharpening holder. An adjustment is provided for the bevel angle.

Fig. 28–14. Whetting the back of a plane iron.

Fig. 28–15. Removing the burr edge from a plane iron.

sive wheel to carry away metal particles and to keep the tool cool. If the grinder does not have a cooling lubricant, be sure to dip the ground edge of the blade in water from time to time to cool it so it will not lose its temper, or hardness. Steel used in tools has been heat-treated to the correct degree of hardness. Any further heating through undue pressure in grinding will destroy the temper, making the tool useless.

Figure 28–8 shows how the edges of a plane iron may be rounded so that it will not leave ridges in planing. This method does not apply to the chisel or the spokeshave blade. Figure 28–9 shows the correct angle for grinding a plane iron.

5. Test the cutting edge for the correct grinding angle (Fig. 28–10). A jig, or tool for testing the correct angles, is often available from tool manufacturers. One may also be easily made in the shop or laboratory.

6. Test the cutting edge for squareness (Fig. 28–11).

7. *Whet*, or *hone*, the plane iron. Do this by placing the bevel side down on an oilstone (Fig. 28–12). Hold the plane iron, chisel, or spokeshave blade so that both toe and heel ride on the oilstone. Then move it in a circular motion. Keep oil on the stone to remove steel particles. Figure 28–13 illus-

Fig. 28–16. Whetting a knife on an oilstone.

trates a tool for holding the plane iron or chisel at the correct angle for whetting and honing.

8. Turn the plane iron, chisel, or spokeshave blade on the back, or flat, side. Move it back and forth gently on the oilstone (Fig. 28–14).

9. Remove the burr, or wiry edge. Carefully pull the sharpened edge tool across a piece of wood (Fig. 28–15). If the burr is not completely removed, repeat steps 7 and 8.

This step is essential. If it is not done correctly, the planed surfaces and the edges and ends will show rough marks.

10. If you desire a very fine, sharp edge, finish whetting with a few pulling strokes on a piece of oily leather.

11. Sharpen a drawknife as you do the plane iron or other edge tools. The drawknife *must* be held against the grinding wheel with both hands.

12. A pocketknife or sloyd knife is sharpened in the same way as a drawknife. Figure 28–16 shows how to get a keen edge on a knife by whetting it on an oilstone.

SHARPENING A HAND SCRAPER BLADE

1. Fasten the hand-scraper blade in a vise.

2. Drawfile the edge at a 90-degree angle with a single-cut mill file. (Fig. 28–17).

3. Whet the filed edge by moving the scraper blade back and forth on an oilstone (Fig. 28–18). Move the blade at *right angles* to the stone.

Fig. 28–17. Drawfiling the edge of a scraper blade.

Fig. 28–18. Whetting a scraper blade on an oilstone.

Fig. 28–19. Removing a filed burr on an oilstone.

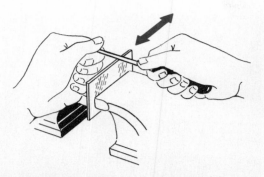

Fig. 28–20. Burnishing a scraper-blade edge.

Fig. 28–21. Filing a bevel edge on the cabinet scraper blade.

4. Place the scraper blade *flat* on an oilstone and move it back and forth to remove the burr (Fig. 28–19). Turn the blade over and remove the filed burr from the opposite side. Some craftsmen like to use the scraper blade as it is now sharpened, without making a turned, or burnished, edge as described in step 5 and shown in Fig. 28–20. You might try it this way.

5. Place the scraper blade in a vise, and turn the edge slightly with the burnisher (Fig. 28–20). The edge should be turned on both sides. This makes an edge which will produce shavings when handled as described in Unit 17, *Smoothing a Surface by Scraping*. An edge of this kind is often called a burred edge.

SHARPENING A CABINET SCRAPER BLADE

1. Remove the blade from the scraper frame.

2. Remove the old burr from the flat side of the blade with a flat mill file.

3. Place the blade in a vise.

4. File a bevel at 45 degrees with a single-cut, flat mill file (Fig. 28–21). Push the file forward and to the side to make a shearing cut.

5. Whet the beveled edge on the oilstone. This is like whetting the plane iron (Fig. 28–12).

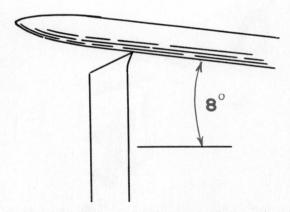

Fig. 28–22. Burnishing an edge of the cabinet scraper blade.

Fig. 28–23. Pulling the burnished edge clean.

Fig. 28–24. Jointing the teeth of a handsaw with a file.

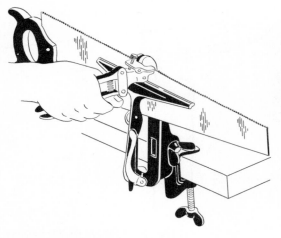

Fig. 28–25. Setting saw teeth.

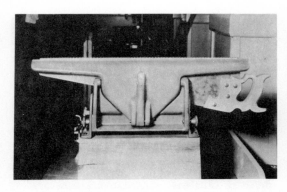

Fig. 28–26. The correct way to hold a handsaw in the saw clamp.

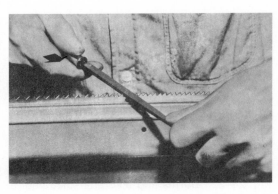

Fig. 28–27. Filing crosscut teeth on the handsaw.

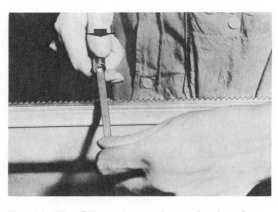

Fig. 28–28. Filing rip teeth on the handsaw.

Fig. 28–29. Sharpening crosscut teeth on a circular saw blade.

6. Whet the back of the blade flat on an oilstone. This also resembles whetting the back of the plane iron (Fig. 28–14).

7. Fasten the scraper blade in a vise and turn the edge with a burnisher (Figs. 28–20 and 28–22).

8. Pull the burnished edge back slightly with the point of the burnisher (Fig. 28–23).

SETTING HANDSAW TEETH

1. Carefully inspect the teeth of the ripsaw or crosscut saw to see if they have been previously set and filed uniformly. This can be done by sighting down the blade from the handle end.

2. If the teeth are uneven in length, *joint* them. Push a flat mill file the full length of the saw blade until all the teeth have been touched (Fig. 28–24). In jointing, hold the saw between two pieces of wood in a vise or saw clamp.

3. Adjust the saw set so that it will *set* the teeth of the handsaw properly. Each manufacturer of a saw set provides instructions for adjusting his product. Read them.

4. Set the teeth, starting from the heel of the saw. Bend the points of *every other one* in the same direction. Be sure to bend them the same way they were originally bent (Fig. 28–25). Teeth must be set so that the cut, or kerf, will be wide enough to keep the blade from binding, or sticking, in the kerf.

5. Turn the saw around in the clamp. Set the alternate teeth in the opposite direction.

SHARPENING SAW TEETH

1. Fasten the saw clamp to the bench top.

2. Fasten the saw in the clamp with the teeth pointing up (Fig. 28–26).

3. File the teeth with a triangular, slim taper file. Start at the heel of the saw. The angle at which you file depends on whether the teeth are crosscutting (Fig. 28–27) or ripping (Fig. 28–28). Unit 8, *Sawing Across or With the Grain of the Wood*, gives this information. Put even pressure on the forward stroke of the file; raise the file on the backward stroke.

4. File all teeth at the proper angle until the points are sharp (Figs. 28–27 and 28–28). Saw sharpening requires much practice before you get the best results.

Figures 28–29 and 28–30 show the process of sharpening crosscut and rip teeth on a circular saw blade. A special saw-filing clamp, as pictured, is required to hold circular saw blades such as are used on the table saw and the radial arm saw.

Fig. 28–30. Sharpening rip teeth on a circular saw blade. A flat, single-cut mill file is used on large rip teeth.

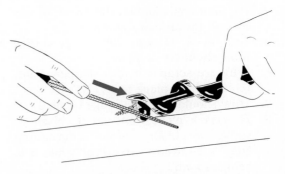

Fig. 28–31. Filing the upper side of the lips of an auger bit.

Fig. 28–32. Filing the inside surfaces of the nibs of an auger bit.

Fig. 28–33. Final dressing (sharpening) on the edge of an axe.

SHARPENING AUGER BITS

1. Hold the auger bit as shown in Fig. 28–31. It should rest on a piece of wood.

2. File the upper side of the auger-bit *cutting lip* until a sharp cutting edge is made (Fig. 28–31). Use a triangular, slim taper file or a small, flat auger-bit file.

3. File the inside surface of the *nibs* of the auger bit until a sharp cutting edge is made (Fig. 28–32). Use a small triangular auger or a flat file. Hold the auger bit against a bench top as shown.

SHARPENING HATCHET AND AXE BLADES

A hatchet or axe edge may be sharpened first on the grinder, and then dressed to a fine edge with a flat mill file (Fig. 28–33).

Discussion Topics

1. Explain the uses of the grinder and the oilstone in sharpening tools.
2. Why do plane irons and wood chisels have a bevel on one side only?
3. Describe the steps for sharpening the plane iron, spokeshave blade, and draw-knife.
4. At what angle should the plane iron be ground for ordinary cutting?
5. List three reasons why edge-cutting tools should be kept sharp.
6. Why are scraper blades sharpened differently from plane irons?
7. How should a scraper edge be filed?
8. How is a plane iron, wood chisel, or spokeshave blade damaged if the cutting edge is allowed to overheat while it is being ground?
9. What is the purpose of a lubricant on a grinder wheel or oilstone?
10. What is the name of the tool used to turn the edges of scraper blades?
11. What is the purpose of jointing the teeth of a saw blade?
12. Illustrate the difference between crosscut and rip teeth. Explain the purpose of each (see Unit 8).
13. Why do the teeth of the saw need to be set?
14. What two essential parts of an auger bit are sharpened?
15. What precautions should be taken to prevent tools from rusting when they are stored or are not used over a long period of time?

unit

29

Sawing with the portable electric handsaw

The portable electric handsaw (Fig. 29–1) is popular in the building trade school and in the home workshop. It is useful for crosscutting, ripping, beveling, and rabbeting and for cutting grooves, dadoes, and miters. Its great advantage is that it can be taken directly to a job.

This tool, fitted with proper blades or abrasive disks, can be used for cutting many materials. It can slice ceramics, slate, marble, tile, nonferrous metals, transite, corrugated galvanized sheets, and almost any kind of building material. Woodcutting blades range in size from 4 to 12 inches. The most popular blade is 6 to 8 inches in diameter. The saw teeth point upward instead of down to keep the saw from crawling. The combination saw blade is the type most commonly used for all-purpose sawing (see Fig. 36–5). It will serve equally well for crosscutting or ripping.

See Fig. 29–1 for the essential parts. The saws are light in weight, ranging from 6 to 12 pounds. Practically all of them have safety guards. Some have a special clutch arrangement to eliminate kickback. A ripping guide (Fig. 29–2) is a regular attachment and should always be used when ripping.

151

Fig. 29-1. Portable electric handsaw.

Fig. 29-2. A ripping guide attached to a portable electric handsaw.

Fig. 29-3. Attaching the proper blade. Note that the operator holds his finger on the button which locks the mechanism while tightening the saw blade.

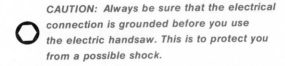

CAUTION: *Always be sure that the electrical connection is grounded before you use the electric handsaw. This is to protect you from a possible shock.*

SAWING

1. Lay out or mark the board to be cut.

2. Make certain the correct blade is attached to the saw (Fig. 29-3).

3. Adjust the blade to the proper depth. The teeth of the blade should extend about $1/2$ inch below the board being cut.

4. Plug the cord into an electric outlet.

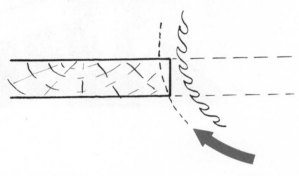

Fig. 29-4. Teeth cut upward.

Fig. 29-5. Starting to make a pocket cut. The front of the shoe is placed firmly on the board, after which the saw is started and allowed to drop gradually into the pocket as it makes the cut. The saw must be held with a firm grip.

Fig. 29–6. Crosscutting with the portable electric handsaw.

Fig. 29–7. Ripping, using a guide.

Fig. 29–8. A straightedge clamped to a board serves as a guide for ripping.

5. Put the front of the base plate on the edge or end of the board. Line up the blade with the cutting line (see Fig. 29–1). Do not allow the teeth to touch the board.

6. Press the trigger switch. Allow the motor to run freely a few seconds before you start to cut. Notice that the teeth cut upward (Fig. 29–4). An exception to starting to saw in this manner is when starting a pocket cut on a board (Fig. 29–5).

7. Guide the saw slowly but steadily on the waste side of the marked line (Fig. 29–6), or use the guide if you are ripping (Fig. 29–7). If the saw stalls, do not release the trigger switch. Back the saw up a little. This will allow the blade to regain full speed.

Fig. 29-9. Cutting a bevel with the aid of a fixed-angle guide.

Fig. 29-10. Cutting a compound bevel with the aid of an adjustable-angle guide.

Crosscutting generally does not require a guide. *Ripping* does (see Fig. 29-7). For ripping beyond the extent of the guide, it is possible to clamp a straightedge on the board which serves to extend the guide (Fig. 29-8). *Bevels* can be cut by regulating the bevel adjustment and by using fixed and adjustable angle guides (Figs. 29-9 and 29-10).

 Safety Rules

1. Always secure your teacher's permission to use this portable tool.

2. Disconnect the plug from the electric-power outlet when the tool is not in use.

3. Check to see that the electrical connection is grounded.

4. Keep blades sharp. Dull blades may cause the saw to stall or bind.

5. Keep the retractable safety guard operating freely. Use it at all times.

6. Always hold the electric saw firmly.

7. Use a guide in ripping.

8. Allow the blade to come to full speed before starting a cut.

9. Protect your clothing.

10. Do not attempt to make adjustments while the saw is in operation.

Discussion Topics

1. Why is the portable electric handsaw so useful?

2. List eight different materials this tool can cut with proper blades or abrasive disks.

3. Name six different woodworking processes this saw can perform. What attachments are necessary to do these additional jobs?

4. List and describe the use of at least six parts of the saw.

5. Mention six safety rules to follow in using the electric handsaw.

6. Why do the teeth of the blade cut upward instead of down?

7. Explain how you can make a ripping guard in case the regular one does not extend far enough.

8. What is a pocket cut? How do you start this cut?

unit

30

Cutting with the portable electric jig (saber) saw

The decorative cutting which is done in Unit 39 on the table-model jig saw could also be done with the portable type. The advantage of the portable electric jig saw is that it can be taken to the place where you are working. This tool is sometimes called a saber saw or a bayonet saw.

The blade works up and down, just as it does on the table model. Blades are available for cutting different types of materials in addition to wood. Some of these are ferrous and nonferrous metals, felt, leather, rubber, plastics, insulating materials, composition board, and linoleum.

The portable jig saw weighs about 3½ pounds. Figure 30–1 shows the various parts.

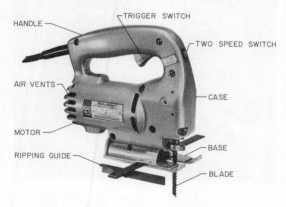

HANDLE
TRIGGER SWITCH
TWO SPEED SWITCH
AIR VENTS
CASE
MOTOR
RIPPING GUIDE
BASE
BLADE

Fig. 30–1. Portable electric jig (saber) saw.

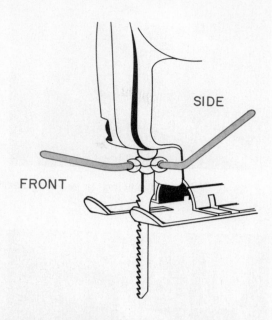

SIDE

FRONT

Fig. 30–2. Fastening a saw blade in the chuck.

Manufacturers have their own recommended methods for inserting and removing blades. Study their instructions.

CAUTION: Before using the portable jig saw, make certain that the electrical connection is grounded. This will protect you from a possible shock.

SAWING

1. Lay out or mark the board to be cut.
2. Disconnect the plug from the electric-power outlet; then insert a blade suitable for your job (see Figs. 30–2 and 30–9 and Table 30–1). Replace the plug in the outlet.
3. Place the forward edge of the base on the edge of the board (see Fig. 30–1).
4. Flip the switch to start the motor. Hold the jig saw firmly as you start cutting. Use a forward and slightly downward pressure (Fig. 30–3).

155

Fig. 30–3. Freehand sawing to an irregular line.

Fig. 30–6. Starting a pocket cut.

Fig. 30–4. Crosscutting heavy lumber.

Fig. 30–7. Continuing the pocket cut.

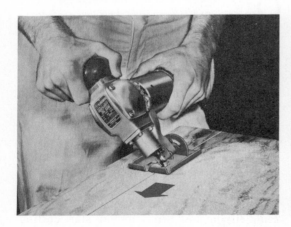

Fig. 30–5. Cutting a bevel with the portable electric jig saw.

Fig. 30–8. Sawing a board with the aid of a ripping guide.

Table 30–1. PORTABLE ELECTRIC JIG (SABER) SAW BLADE CHART

Blade	Type	Length	Use
A	Fine tooth, high speed	4¼″	Fine finish scroll cutting in wood, plywood, hardboard, and plastics
B	Coarse tooth, high speed	4¼″	Fast scroll cutting
C	Coarse tooth, high speed	4¼″	Fast heavy-duty cutting
D	Fine tooth	3″	Medium general duty
E	Medium	3″	Fast smooth scroll and pocket cutting
F	Coarse tooth	3″	Very fast cutting
G	Knife punch blade	1″	Fast scroll cutting of paperboard

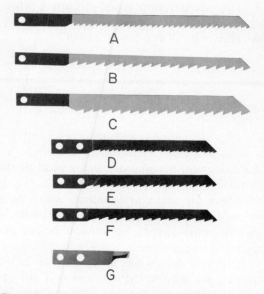

Fig. 30–9. Types of jig saw blades. (See Table 30–1 for the names of these blades.)

Fig. 30–10. Cutting a circle, using the rip fence inverted, and a nail for a guide pin.

5. Use the jig saw effectively for cross-cutting heavy lumber (Fig. 30–4).

6. Adjust the base to any angle desired to make a bevel cut (Fig. 30–5).

7. To make an internal, or pocket, cut, place the front edge of the base on the board with the jig saw tilted forward, as shown in Fig. 30–6.

8. Flip the switch and gradually lower the jig saw (saber saw) into place as you move forward with the cut (Fig. 30–6). Follow step 4 and continue the cut (Fig. 30–7).

9. Attach the ripping guide to make cuts parallel with an edge (Fig. 30–8).

10. Reverse the ripping guide for making true, circular cuts (Fig. 30–10). A nail serves as the center point around which the guide and saw revolve while cutting.

 *Safety Rules*

1. Always secure permission from your teacher to use the portable jig saw.

157

2. Disconnect the plug from the electric-power outlet before you inspect parts, make adjustments, or insert the blade.

3. Check to see that the electrical connection is grounded.

4. Make certain that you have inserted the correct blade.

5. Hold or clamp the board to be cut so that it will not vibrate.

6. Always hold the saw firmly.

7. Allow the blade to come to full speed before starting to cut.

8. Protect your clothing.

9. Concentrate on what you are doing.

Discussion Topics

1. What other names are sometimes applied to the portable jig saw?
2. Why do the teeth of the portable jig saw blade cut upward?
3. With suitable blades, what types of materials does this saw cut?
4. How would you saw to a straight, true line?
5. List six different types of cutting which can be done with the portable jig saw.
6. How may a true circle be cut?

---

unit
31

Sawing with the portable electric heavy-duty saber saw

The portable electric heavy-duty saber saw (Fig. 31-1) is a portable tool used to cut both wood and metal. It is used extensively in building construction, and can perform the same operations as the portable jig saw. Essential parts of this electric hand tool are the aluminum housing or case, motor, depth control shoe, blade, and switch.

There are many attachments which may be used to do specialty cutting. The owner's manual must always be studied before attempting to use them.

The tool shown has a capacity of 2,000 strokes per minute (SPM), and will cut up to 2-inch thickness lumber. This saw weighs approximately 8 pounds, and is only about 15 inches long.

The blade shown in Fig. 31-1 is a general-purpose type used to cut wood and nonferrous metal tubing. Interchangeable blades are available for fast or fine cutting of wood (Table 31-1). A special type cuts through wood, nails, asbestos, and plaster. Other blades used to cut wood are narrow so that small-radius holes and irregular cuts may be easily made. Specially treated blades are available which can be used to cut various gages and different metals and plastics.

Table 31–1. PORTABLE ELECTRIC HEAVY-DUTY SABER SAW BLADE CHART

Blade	Type	Length	Teeth per inch
A	General purpose	6 or 12″	7
B	Fast cutting	6 or 12″	3
C	Flexible-back, wood and composition	6 or 12″	6
D	Down cutting	6″	10
E	Pocket cutting	4 1/8″	6
F	Double edge	4 1/8″	6
G	Fast cutting scroll	3 5/8″	6

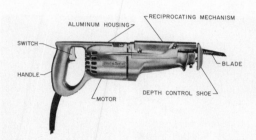

Fig. 31–1. A portable electric heavy-duty saber saw.

 **Safety Rules**

1. Always secure permission from your teacher to use the portable electric heavy-duty saber saw.

2. Tuck in your tie and button or roll up your sleeves.

3. Make all adjustments and see that the correct type of blade is installed before connecting the plug to the electric power outlet.

4. Make certain that the electrical connection is grounded.

5. Hold, clamp, or otherwise secure the board to be cut so that it will not vibrate.

6. Always hold this tool firmly.

7. Allow the blade to come to full speed before you start the cut.

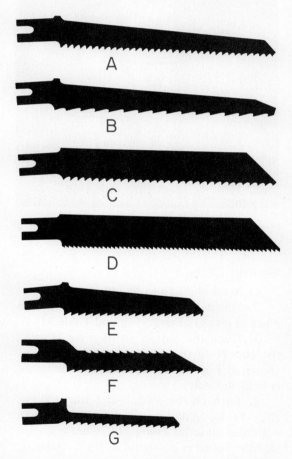

Fig. 31–2. Types of heavy-duty saber saw blades. See Table 31–1 for descriptions.

159

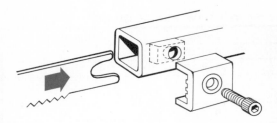

Fig. 31-3. Fastening the saw blade.

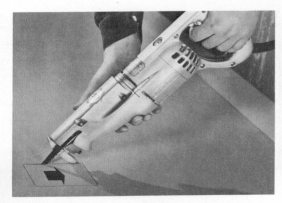

Fig. 31-5. Making a pocket cut.

Fig. 31-4. Making a cut vertically through a piece of plywood.

Fig. 31-6. Sawing flush to a wall.

SAWING

1. Mark the line to be cut.

2. Select and fasten the proper blade in place (Figs. 31-2 and 31-3 and Table 31-1).

3. Place the tool in position for starting the cut. Hold this tool with both hands, as shown in Fig. 31-4. Make certain the board is held securely.

4. Turn on the switch and start the cut (Fig. 31-4). Make sure the saw shoe is flush with the material being cut. Check to see that the board is being cut at right angles.

5. When making a pocket cut, tip the saw backward until the edge of the shoe rests on the work surface (Fig. 31-5). Switch the motor on; permit the blade to obtain maximum speed.

Grip the handle steadily and begin a slow, deliberate upward swing with the handle end of the saw. The blade will begin to feed into the material. Make sure that the blade is completely through the material before you continue to make the pocket cut. Turn off the motor and remove the saw from the completed cut.

Figure 31-6 shows the special attachment on the shoe for making an extremely close cut in a corner edge.

1. What is the principle purpose of the portable electric heavy-duty saber saw?
2. Name four essential parts, and give their functions.
3. About how much does this tool weigh?
4. What types of materials can be cut by using different types of blades with the heavy-duty saber saw?
5. What is the speed of the blade?

unit

32

Drilling holes with the portable electric drill

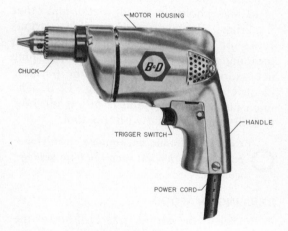

Fig. 32–1. Portable electric drill.

The portable electric drill (Fig. 32–1) made portable tools popular. The ¼-inch drill is a favorite size. It is called this because a drill bit ¼ inch in diameter is the largest the chuck will hold (Fig. 32–2). Larger-sized drills and bits are available, however. Heavy-duty electric drills having chucks with a maximum capacity of ⅜- and ½-inch drill bits are also used extensively. Bits for use with the drill are further shown and discussed in Units 18 and 43.

There are generally two types of chucks available for the smaller electric drill: those which are tightened by hand and the geared-key type (Fig. 32–3), commonly known as Jacob's chuck. The latter is better.

Fig. 32–2. Drill bits for the portable electric drill.

161

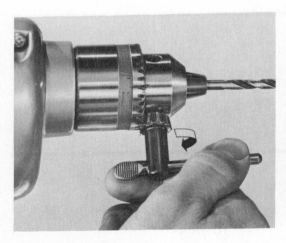

Fig. 32-3. Fastening a drill bit in a chuck, using a key.

Fig. 32-4. Drilling a hole horizontally.

The primary purpose of the electric drill is to make holes in wood, metal, and other materials. However, you can buy various types of drills and bits, a wire wheel, a grinding wheel, and sanding and polishing accessories. Essential parts of the portable electric drill are shown in Fig. 32-1. The main purpose of this unit is to explain how to drill holes in wood with this tool.

CAUTION: Ground the portable electric-drill connection. This will keep you from getting a shock.

DRILLING IN WOOD

1. Select the proper size drill bit for the job.
2. Mark the center point for the hole. Use an awl or a nail. This prevents the bit from wandering and marring the board (Fig. 18-22).
3. Put the point of the bit in this starting hole before you turn on the motor.
4. Turn on the trigger switch and drill the hole (Figs. 32-4 and 32-5). Use a block of wood to back up the materials if you are going to drill through. This is not always

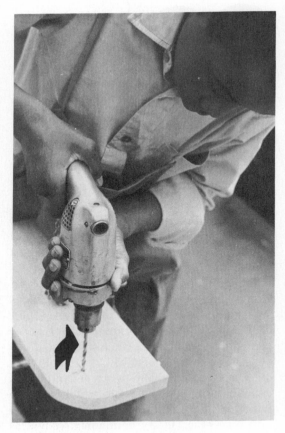

Fig. 32-5. Drilling a hole vertically.

Fig. 32–6. Boring a hole with a heavy-duty drill, using a spade bit.

Fig. 32–7. Boring a hole with the use of a right-angle heavy-duty electric drill.

necessary, especially if the back of the hole will not be seen. Figure 32–6 shows a heavy-duty drill cutting a hole with a spade bit. Figure 32–7 is a right-angle drill boring a large hole on a construction job.

5. Withdraw the bit from the hole with the motor running.

 Safety Rules

1. Secure permission from your teacher to use the portable electric drill.

2. Disconnect the plug from the electric-power outlet before you insert or change drill bits.

3. Check to see that the electrical connection is grounded.

4. Be careful not to use larger bits than those recommended by the manufacturer of your drill.

5. Fasten the bit firmly in the chuck before using it.

6. Keep the air-cooling vents on the drill housing free of dirt.

Discussion Topics

1. What are the advantages of the portable electric drill?
2. How is the size of an electric drill determined?
3. What is the most common size?
4. Why should you start a hole with an awl or nail?
5. Why should you drill a hole in a piece of wood before making an inside cut with a portable jig saw?

---

unit

33

Planing with the portable electric power hand plane

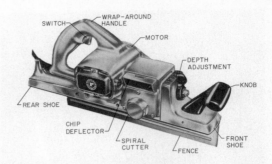

Fig. 33-1. Portable electric power hand plane.

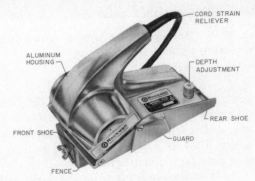

Fig. 33-2. Power block plane.

The portable electric power hand plane (Fig. 33-1) and the power block plane (Fig. 33-2) are used extensively by contractors, carpenters, builders, and cabinetmakers. They plane edges, ends, bevels, and chamfers. The plane shown in Fig. 33-1 can be used to plane a surface by removing the fence.

Both planes, with the fence attached, can be used to produce a square, level, glass-smooth planed surface. The manufacturers claim that either can perform ten times faster than doing the planing by hand. They do the work more accurately, and reduce fatigue.

The cutter blade shown in Fig. 33-3 is spiral in design and is made of specially hardened steel. Often craftsmen prefer to use a carbide-tipped edge spiral blade. It practically eliminates the need of sharpening. Smoothness of cutting with these planes results from the shearing action of the blade at 18,000 to 25,000 RPM (revolution per minute).

The portable electric power hand plane removes up to $3/32$ inch of wood at each stroke. The larger one weighs approximately 10 pounds. The power block plane weighs less than 4 pounds. Each has a depth adjustment which is easily visible. This is the main adjustment to be made, unless the fence needs to be adapted for a bevel or a chamfer cut.

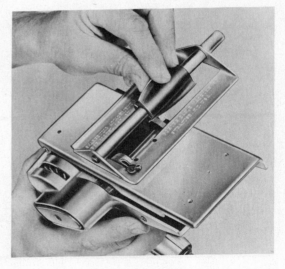

Fig. 33-3. Spiral cutter blade. Also shown is the sharpening accessory which can be attached to the plane.

1. Obtain the instructor's permission to use the portable electric power hand plane or the power block plane.

2. If available, read and study the manufacturer's operating instructions manual.

3. Tuck in your tie, button or roll up your sleeves, and otherwise protect loose clothing from getting caught in the plane.

4. Be sure the switch is in *off* position before you connect the plane to the power source. Make certain the power connection is grounded.

5. When making adjustments, always disconnect the plane from the power source.

6. Place the front shoe of the plane on the edge of the work. Start the motor, and move the plane firmly along the board to start the cut.

7. Maintain constant pressure through the cut.

8. Turn off the motor when the cut has been completed.

9. Do not set the plane down until the motor stops.

PLANING AN EDGE

1. Adjust the depth for making the cut.

2. Make sure the fence is at 90 degrees with the shoe.

3. Plug the electric cord into the electrical outlet.

4. Place the front plane shoe and the fence firmly against the work. Hold the plane with both hands, as shown in Fig. 33–4.

5. Turn on the trigger switch with the right hand.

6. Push the plane forward with pressure on the front shoe. After the rear shoe is on the work, transfer the pressure to the rear shoe (Fig. 33–4).

7. Continue making the cut until the cutter has cleared the work.

Fig. 33–4. Edge planing with the portable electric power hand plane.

Fig. 33–5. Edge planing with the power block plane.

8. Lift the plane.

9. Release the switch trigger.

10. Note that the power block plane can also be used to plane an edge; however only one hand is needed to control this operation (Fig. 33–5).

PLANING A BEVEL OR CHAMFER

1. Repeat steps 1 through 4 in "Planing an Edge," except the fence must be adjusted

165

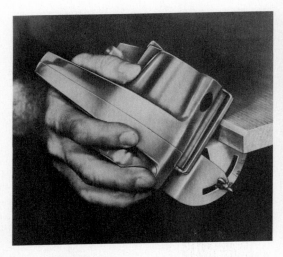

Fig. 33-6. Planing a chamfer with the power block plane.

Fig. 33-7. Planing a surface with the portable electric power hand plane.

to the angle desired for making a bevel or chamfer cut (see Fig. 33-6).

2. Plane the bevel or chamfer (see Fig. 33-6).

3. Follow steps 5 through 9 in "Planing an Edge."

PLANING A SURFACE

1. Remove the fence and bracket assembly from the plane to give the shoe a flat surface.

2. Plane the surface (Fig. 33-7). Follow steps 1 through 9 in "Planing an Edge."

Discussion Topics

1. What are the two most common portable electric power hand planes?
2. List the approximate weights of each.
3. What types of craftsmen would probably be most interested in using these planes?
4. Describe the shape of the cutter.
5. What is the variation of RPM of the two power planes discussed in this unit?
6. Discuss the merits or advantages of using the portable electric power hand plane over the conventional hand plane.
7. How is the depth of cut adjusted?
8. How is the angle of the cut controlled?
9. List five safety rules to observe when using either of these electric hand planes.

unit

34

Shaping and routing with the portable electric router

The router is probably the safest of all portable electric tools, since the cutting edge is never exposed. It is a high-speed machine. It works at rates of from 20,000 to 27,000 revolutions per minute, depending on the model. The router weighs only about 6 pounds, and is easy to handle. The basic parts are illustrated in Fig. 34–1.

This router is rated at one horsepower. It is designed with a flat top, making it easy to stand it on its head to install the router bit. You can also adjust the depth of cut more easily. The base is of non-marring plastic to prevent marking the surfaces being worked on. Most routers of this size accept ¼- and ⅜-inch shank router bits.

The router cuts into and through wood, as well as many other materials, to the desired thickness and depth. Available router accessories make it possible for you to produce intricate joints, decorative cuts, and inlays. You can also use it to shape edges, cut recesses for door hinges, and make beautiful dovetail joints. Figure 34–2 shows a few of the many router bits and the cuts they make.

Accessories to make the router very versatile include the straight and circular guide (Fig. 34–3), the dovetail kit (Fig. 34–4), and the hinge-butt template kit (Fig. 34–5).

 CAUTION: Before using the portable electric router, check to see that the electrical connection is grounded. Failure to do this can result in a shock.

✦ *Safety Rules*

1. Secure permission from your teacher to use the router.
2. Disconnect the motor unit from the electric-power outlet when you change bits or add attachments.
3. Check to see that the electrical connection is grounded.
4. Make sure the bit is inserted at least ½ inch into the chuck. Turn it by hand to make sure it clears the router base.
5. Keep the air vents free of dirt.
6. Be sure the bits and cutters are always sharp.
7. Move the router from left to right when you cut straight edges, counterclockwise when you cut circular or curved edges.

SHAPING AN EDGE

1. Decide on the cutter you will use.
2. Insert the cutter in the chuck at least ½ inch, and tighten it.

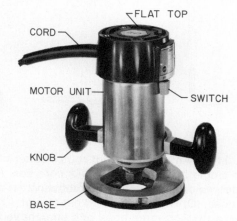

Fig. 34–1. Portable electric router.

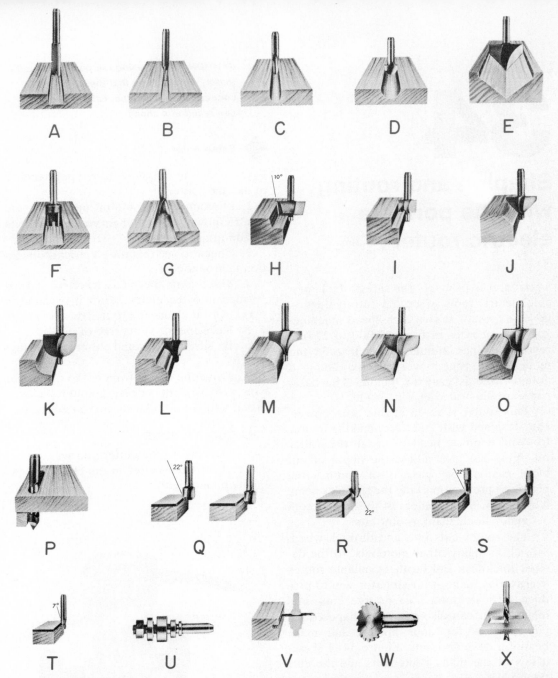

Fig. 34-2. An assortment of router-cutter bits and cuts: (A) straight with two flutes, (B) straight with single flute, (C) veining, (D) core box, (E) V grooving, (F) hinge mortising, (G) dovetail, (H) 10 degree bevel rabbeting, (I) rabbeting, (J) chamfering, (K) cove, (L) beading, (M) corner round, (N) ogee, (O) Roman ogee, (P) panel pilot, (Q) 22 degree combination veneer, (R) 22 degree bevel veneer, (S) 22 degree bevel and straight veneer, (T) 7 degree bevel veneer, (U) veneer trimming arbor, (V) slotting cutter, (W) trimming saw, and (X) aluminum trimming.

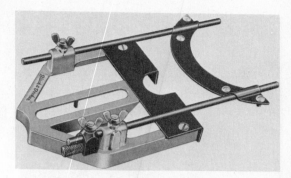

Fig. 34-3. Straight and circular guide.

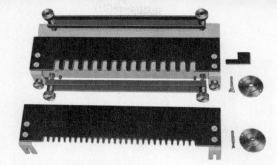

Fig. 34-4. Dovetail kit.

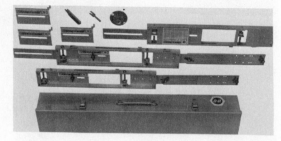

Fig. 34-5. Hinge-butt template kit.

3. Adjust the router for depth of cut. Follow the manufacturer's instructions.

4. Make a test cut on a piece of scrap wood held securely in a vise. Make any necessary adjustments.

5. Fasten the board or the project firmly.

6. Place the router base on the board with the cutter blade over the edge. Move the router with both hands until you get the feel of it.

7. Turn on the switch. Pull the router against the edge of the board until it hits the rub collar. Push it from left to right with both hands. (Fig. 34-6).

8. Cut until the edge has been shaped.

CUTTING GROOVES AND DADOES WITH AN EDGE CUTTER

1. Select the right bit or cutter for the groove you want to cut.

2. Fasten it securely in the chuck.

3. Adjust for the depth of the groove.

4. Attach and adjust the edge guide to the base (see Fig. 34-7).

5. Make a trial cut on a piece of scrap wood. Make any necessary adjustments.

6. Place the router base on the board with the cutter blade over the edge.

7. Turn on the switch and move the router slowly from left to right (Fig. 34-7).

8. Make all the necessary grooves.

Fig. 34-6. Shaping an edge with a router.

Fig. 34-7. Using an edge guide to cut grooves.

Fig. 34–8. Using an edge guide to cut dadoes.

Fig. 34–9. Making circular designs by using a circular guide.

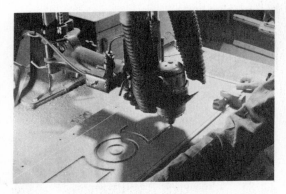

Fig. 34–10. Automated routing of a particle-board decorative door panel insert.

Fig. 34–11. Cutting a sink opening through plastic laminate and ¾-inch thickness ply-wood panel. A cutout piece of hardboard serves as a template.

Follow the same procedure to cut dadoes, but use a different cutter bit (see Figs. 34–2 and 34–8). The number of other cuts and grooves you can make depends upon the bits, cutters, and accessories available to you.

CUTTING CURVES USING A TEMPLATE

The procedure for attaching various types of guides differs slightly with each manufacturer's router. It is advisable to study the manual of each brand for the correct alignment of attachments. Figure 34–9 shows how to make circular designs by using a circular guide.

An industrial application, using a router on particle board, is seen in Fig. 34–10. This is a highly automated process operating from a pantograph.

Figure 34–11 pictures a commercial procedure in using a ½-inch carbide router bit to cut a sink opening through ¾-inch thickness plywood which is covered with laminated plastic. Here a template has been made from hardboard to serve as a guide.

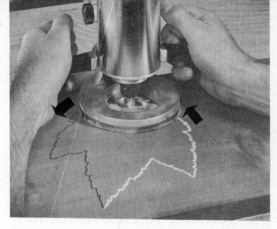

Fig. 34–12. Freehand routing of a penciled design.

Fig. 34–13. Freehand routing through aluminum siding to make a window opening.

Fig. 34–14. Making a dovetail joint for a drawer with the aid of a dovetail template.

Fig. 34–15. Assembled dovetail kit showing the finished corner and drawer joints made by using this accessory.

Fig. 34–16. Cutting a precision mortise for a door hinge, using a hinge-butt template.

Fig. 34–17. Router mortising for a hinge butt on a door jamb.

171

FREEHAND ROUTING

Several routing procedures can be performed freehand. In Fig. 34–12 the design was first penciled on the board. It was then cut freehand with the router, as shown. Straight freehand routing may also be done, as illustrated in Fig. 34–13. In this photograph a craftsman in the mobile home manufacturing industry is cutting a window opening through aluminum. The same procedure would be used to cut through wood.

OTHER ROUTER CUTS

The router with correct cutters is very effective in making dovetail joints (Figs. 34–14 and 34–15). This type of joint is often used in the manufacture of drawers in quality furniture. The manufacturer's manual gives instructions for the correct cutter to use, the setting, and the accessories for this procedure.

Figure 34–16 shows the use of a router to cut a hinge gain on the edge of a door for fitting a butt hinge. Router-mortising for hinge butts on the door jamb done with the aid of a template is shown in Fig. 34–17. This procedure also entails the use of special accessories and a template, as recommended by the manufacturer of the router.

Discussion Topics

1. Why is the router considered the safest portable electric tool?
2. List eight jobs you can do with the router if you have the necessary bits, cutters, and accessories.
3. Define what a router does.
4. Illustrate ten cuts which can be made with router bits and cutters.
5. Explain how to use the router for shaping edges.

unit

35

Sanding with portable electric sanders

Portable electric sanders are used for sanding wood surfaces. The two most common types are the belt sander (Fig. 35–1) and the finishing orbital sander (Fig. 35–2).

Fig. 35–1. Portable electric dustless belt sander.

Fig. 35–2. Portable electric finishing orbital sander.

Fig. 35–3. Adjusting the alignment of an abrasive belt on the portable electric belt sander.

The belt sander has an abrasive belt which runs continuously over pulleys at both ends. The average portable model weighs about 12 pounds. Its size is often designated by the size of the belt; for example, 3 × 21 inches or 4 × 27 inches. Figure 35–1 shows this sander with its parts labeled, including the dust bag.

The orbital sander gets its name from the motion of the base pad. This pad moves back and forth in an orbit, or circle, which permits sanding in any direction. Orbital-sander pads vary in size to take one-fourth to one-half of a sheet of abrasive paper or cloth. Figure 35–2 shows the various parts of an orbital sander. Read and study the manufacturer's manual for each of these sanders to learn the adjustments.

Aluminum oxide and silicon carbide sanding belts are those most suitable for wood. Aluminum oxide, sandpaper, garnet paper, and emery sheets work well on the orbital sander. Most abrasive-belt and abrasive-paper manufacturers use *coarse*, *medium*, and *fine* as grit grades. Sanding guides for both sanders are listed in Table 35–1.

 CAUTION: *Make the necessary ground connection before using the portable electric belt or orbital sander. This is to protect you from a possible shock.*

◆ Safety Rules

1. Secure permission from your teacher to use either of these sanders.

Table 35–1. SANDING GUIDE FOR BELT SANDER AND FINISHING SANDER

	BELT SANDER		FINISHING SANDER	
	Silicon carbide	Aluminum oxide	Aluminum oxide	Garnet paper
Coarse grit	150	40	60	60 (1/2)
Medium grit	280	80	100	100 (2/0)
Fine grit	500	120	150	150 (4/0)

173

2. Disconnect the power supply before changing sanding belts or abrasive paper.

3. Check to see that the electrical connection is grounded.

4. Always pick up a portable electric sander before you plug in the cord.

5. Hold the sander off the wood when you turn on the switch. You may then lower it to the work. Also lift it before you turn off the power.

6. Lay the belt sander on its side when it is not in use.

SANDING WITH A BELT SANDER

1. Fasten the board or project firmly so that it will remain stationary.

2. Select a sanding belt of the proper grit.

3. Lay the sander on its left side and pull back the front, or idler, pulley. Use the tension lever or screw.

4. Slip the belt over the rear pulley and then over the idler pulley. Make certain that the arrow on the inside of the abrasive belt is pointing in the right direction.

5. Place the belt so the edge is even with the edge of the pulleys.

6. Release the tension.

7. Connect the plug to the electric-power outlet and start the motor. Adjust the alignment screw (Fig. 35-3) so that the belt runs evenly on the pulleys. Then turn off the motor.

8. Place the sander on the board or project with both hands to get the feel of it.

9. Lift the sander with both hands and turn on the switch trigger.

10. Lower the sander to the wood. Guide the machine over the surface without pressure. Keep it pointed in the direction of the grain (Fig. 35-4).

11. Work the sander back and forth over a fairly wide area. Be careful not to pause in any one spot while you are sanding. It will make the surface uneven.

Fig. 35–4. Sanding with the portable electric belt sander.

Fig. 35–5. Sanding with a finishing orbital sander on a flat surface.

Fig. 35–6. Sanding a cabinet shelf with the finishing orbital sander.

12. Change sanding belts and continue with finer grits until the surface has been smoothed for final finishing.

SANDING WITH AN ORBITAL SANDER

1. Fasten the board or project firmly.
2. Select abrasive paper or cloth of proper grit (see Table 35–1).
3. Attach the abrasive sheet under the clamps at the end of the base pad.
4. Connect the plug to the power outlet.
5. Lift the sander off the board and start the motor.
6. Set the sander on the work evenly and move it back and forth (Figs. 35–5 and 35–6).
7. Guide the sander with the handle. Use both hands until you get the feel of its operation. The normal weight of the machine is sufficient pressure for most sanding.
8. Change the abrasive grit or cloth. Sand with progressively finer grits until the surface is ready for the final finishing.

Discussion Topics

1. Name the two most common portable electric sanders.
2. How does the finishing orbital sander get its name?
3. What determines the size of a belt sander?
4. List the three general grit classifications for sanding belts and abrasive paper used with portable electric sanders.
5. What type of abrasive is most satisfactory for sanding belts used on wood?
6. Mention six safety rules for using portable sanders.
7. How do you fasten abrasive sheets on finishing orbital sanders?
8. Must the orbital sander be moved with the grain of the wood?
9. Why should you lift either sander when starting and stopping?
10. Explain the procedure for changing a sanding belt.
11. Explain the principle on which the finishing orbital sander works.
12. List the grades of abrasive materials you would use in power dressing a piece of hand-planed wood for finishing.

unit

36

Sawing on the circular, or table, saw

The circular, or table, saw is one of the oldest kinds of power machines for woodworking. The modern circular saw (Fig. 36–1) performs a wide variety of processes. It is one of the most useful woodworking machines for school, industry, or the home workshop. The saw pictured in Fig. 36–1 is a typical one. All are operated similarly. The essential parts of a circular, or table, saw are an arbor on which the saw blade is fastened, and a frame, table, ripping fence, cut-off guide, and safety guard. Fig. 36–2 pictures the several adjustments which can be made to keep the saw in alignment.

The circular saw is a versatile machine; therefore it is also called a variety saw. It will perform such advanced operations as tapering, routing, and making cove cuts. It will also make decorative cuts with the aid of molding cutter heads (see Fig. 36–8).

Machine sawing requires many special types of blades for ripping and crosscutting. Four of the more common types of teeth are shown in Figs. 36–3 through 36–6. The *crosscut*, or cut-off, saw blade (Fig. 36–3) is designed to cut across the grain. The teeth are beveled and set, or bent, alternately right and left; that is, one tooth is bent to the right, the next to the left, and so on. The *ripsaw* blade (Fig. 36–4) is used to cut with the

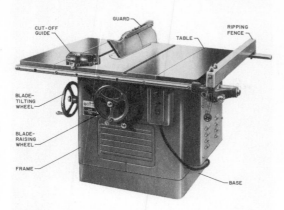

Fig. 36-1. A 12-inch circular, or table saw.

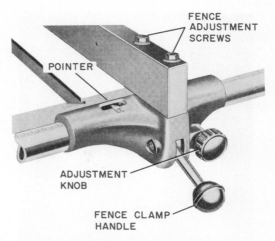

Fig. 36-2. Rip fence control assembly.

grain of the wood. Note that the teeth are filed straight across. The *combination* saw blade (Fig. 36-5) may be used to crosscut, rip, and miter. The smaller, or crosscut, teeth are filed and set alternately right and left, as they are on the crosscut saw; the larger rake, or rip, teeth are filed straight across. This blade is available as a hollow-ground planer blade with the same tooth design, except that the teeth are not set. The hollow-ground blade is thicker on the outer edge (where the teeth are) than it is on the inner edge (near the arbor hole). Because of this the teeth do not need to be set and the kerf (cut) is narrow.

Another very popular type of saw blade is *carbide tipped* (Fig. 36-6). The carbide cutting tips are thicker than the saw blade, and are specially welded to the teeth. This is the most expensive type of blade, but it will outlast the other three types.

A *dado head* (Fig. 36-7) is used for cutting dadoes, or grooves. Figure 36-20 illustrates the outside blade and inside cutter arrangement. Use the correct throat plate.

A *molding head* set of components is shown in Fig. 36-8. Three matching blades are fastened into the molding head and are secured in place with a wrench, as shown. The molding head is placed onto the saw

Fig. 36-3. Circular crosscut, or cutoff, saw blade.

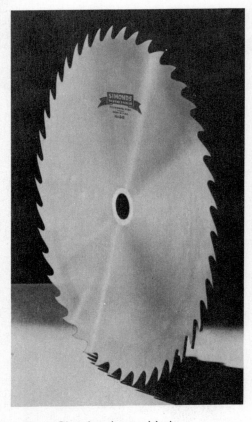

Fig. 36–4. Circular ripsaw blade.

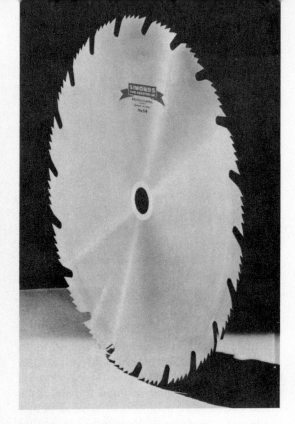

Fig. 36–5. Circular combination, or planer, saw blade.

arbor instead of the saw blade or dado head. The regular throat plate from the saw table top must be replaced with one having an opening large enough to accommodate the molding head, as illustrated in Fig. 36–8.

A special rip fence is required. It must have an opening on the lower side to allow the molding-head blades to operate freely. A thick cutout wood facing can be made and fastened to a regular fence for this purpose.

The table, or circular, saw is an efficient and effective piece of equipment if it is treated properly. Always keep the blade sharp. Protect yourself by using a guard (Fig. 36–9).

Fig. 36–6. Circular carbide-tipped combination saw blade.

Fig. 36–7. Dado-head set. There are two 1/8-inch outside blades, two 1/8-inch thick chipper cutters, one 1/16-inch chipper cutter, and one 1/4-inch chipper cutter. Completely assembled, this dado head will cut a dado 13/16-inch wide.

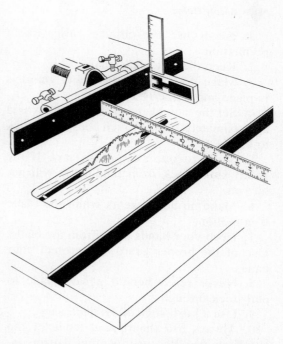

Fig. 36–10. Adjusting the ripping fence to the desired width. It should be at a right angle to the table top.

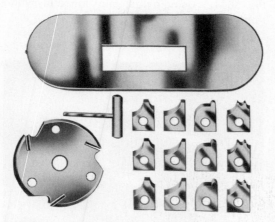

Fig. 36–8. Molding head with four sets of cutter shapes. A wide-opening throat plate is necessary when using the molding head.

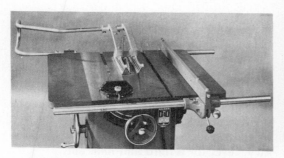

Fig. 36–9. Always protect yourself by using a saw-blade guard.

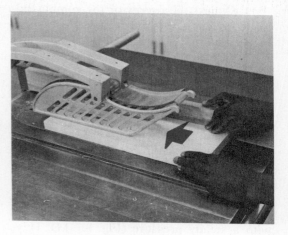

Fig. 36–11. Ripping a board.

1. Never use the circular saw without permission.

2. Keep the saw blade sharp.

3. Make certain that the safety guard is in place and properly adjusted.

4. Set the saw blade so that it will extend approximately $\frac{1}{8}$ to $\frac{1}{4}$ inch above the stock to be cut.

5. Stand to one side of the saw. If the board kicks back from binding, it will not hit you.

6. Make no adjustments while the blade is in motion.

7. Keep your hands away from the blade. Use of the proper guard will protect your hands.

8. Never reach behind a saw blade to pull stock through.

9. Use a push stick when necessary.

10. Always use the ripping fence or the cutoff guide. Because of the danger involved, never saw "freehand."

11. Remove rings and wristwatch when working with any power tool.

RIPPING

1. Adjust the ripsaw or the combination blade to cut approximately $\frac{1}{8}$ to $\frac{1}{4}$ inch higher than the thickness of the stock.

2. Set the ripping fence the desired distance from the saw blade (Fig. 36–10).

3. Fasten the ripping fence in place with the adjusting screws. Remeasure the width for the rip.

4. Make a trial cut on a piece of scrap wood to check accuracy. Cut slightly to the waste side of the marked line to allow for dressing, or planing.

5. Place the board on the table top. Press it firmly against the ripping fence. Push it with a steady pressure (Fig. 36–11). Have the guard in place. Because of the danger

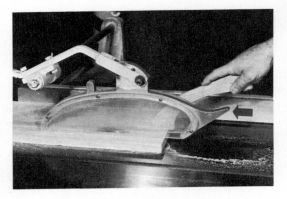

Fig. 36–12. Using a push stick for safety when ripping narrow stock.

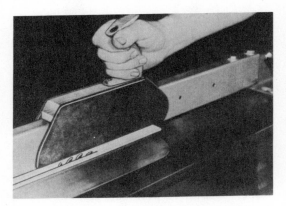

Fig. 36–13. A safe push stick for ripping narrow pieces is one which fits over the ripping fence.

of kickback, do not stand directly behind the board.

6. In ripping stock narrower than 4 inches, be sure to use a push stick for safety (Figs. 36–12 and 36–13). Sometimes, in ripping thick stock, it is wise to set the saw to cut only part of the thickness the first time. Reset it for a deeper cut, and if necessary, reset for a third and final cut.

Figure 36–14 shows how to rip a board to reduce thickness. After making both cuts,

Fig. 36–14. Resawing a board to reduce thickness.

the board can be cut apart with the band saw. This is called resawing.

CROSSCUTTING

1. Place the cutoff guide in the slot, or groove, on the table top. The left groove is the most convenient for crosscutting.

2. Check the guide to see that it is set at the correct angle (90 degrees for a right angle).

3. Mark the board where it is to be cut off.

4. Hold the board on the table top firmly against the cutoff guide. Cut on the waste side of the marked line.

5. Start the saw and let it come to full speed.

6. Push the guide and the board forward (Fig. 36–15) while it is being held firmly against the cutoff guide.

Fig. 36–15. Crosscutting on a circular saw.

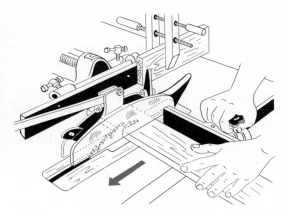

Fig. 36–16. Crosscutting short pieces to the same length. Note the block clamp on the ripping fence.

Fig. 36–17. Crosscutting a bevel by tilting the saw blade.

181

7. Pull back the board and the cutoff guide at the end of the cut.

8. When several short pieces are being cut to the same length, clamp a block on the ripping fence. Do this as shown in Fig. 36–16. This gives sufficient clearance for the boards between the saw blade and the ripping fence.

9. Mark and cut remaining pieces in a similar manner. Miters, bevels, and chamfers can be made by adjusting the saw arbor or table (Fig. 36–17).

RABBETING

1. Square the stock to the given dimensions. This means making the board the required thickness, width, and length.

2. Lay out the size for the rabbet on the end of the piece which is to be cut.

3. Set the saw to the width of the rabbet (Fig. 36–18).

4. Adjust the saw blade for depth (Fig. 36–18).

5. Make a trial cut on a piece of scrap wood.

6. Make the first cut (Fig. 36–18). Cut the other pieces which have the same rabbet.

7. Turn off the saw and re-adjust for the final cut (Fig. 36–19).

8. Make a trial cut on the piece of scrap wood used in step 5.

9. Make the final cut on the piece or pieces (Fig. 36–19). This completes the rabbet.

The procedure outlined in this unit may also be used for cutting across the grain.

CUTTING A DADO OR A GROOVE

1. Assemble a dado, or grooving, head with the blades and cutters as shown in Figs. 36–20 through 36–22. The number of cutters you will need will depend upon the width of the dado (see Figs. 36–20 through 36–22).

2. Replace the regular blade with the dado-head assembly.

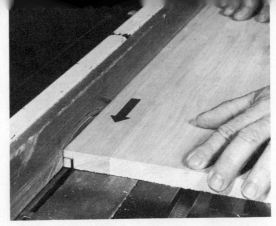

Fig. 36–18. The first cut in making a rabbet.

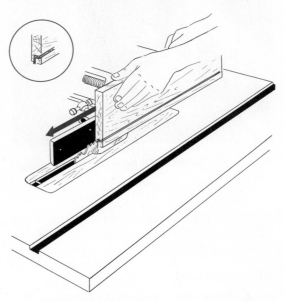

Fig. 36–19. The final cut in making a rabbet. Note the detail in the insert.

Fig. 36–20. Left: arrangement of dado saw blades and cutters. Upper right: overlap of blade and cutter, (A) outside saw blade, and (B) inside cutter. Lower right: outside blades arranged to cut a groove $1/4$-inch.

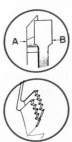

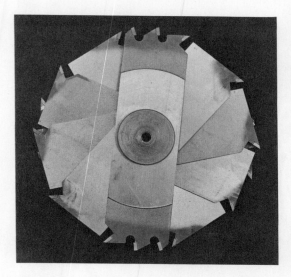

Fig. 36-21. Carbide-tipped dado head assembly.

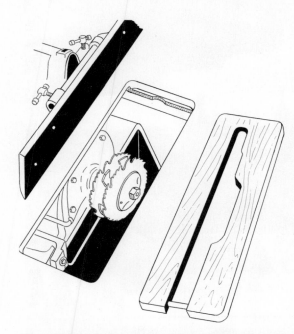

Fig. 36-22. Dado head installed on the saw arbor. Note that the throat panel has been removed for assembly.

3. Replace the plate on the table saw with one which has a wider opening.

4. Check to see that the teeth of the dado-head assembly are pointed in the proper direction. Space the cutters evenly.

5. Lay out and mark the groove, or dado, on the stock.

6. Adjust the ripping fence to the correct distance.

7. Adjust the cutting height of the dado head.

8. Turn on the saw and make a trial cut on a piece of scrap wood.

9. Place the board firmly against the fence. Push it with an even pressure (Fig. 36-23). A dado, or groove, can be made either across or with the grain.

SHAPING

Shaping straight edges and cutting molding may be done satisfactorily with the use of a molding head on the circular saw. The molding head shown in Fig. 36-8 has an assortment of cutter shapes to produce an unlimited variety of cuts.

The molding head is attached on the arbor in a manner similar to the dado head. Figure 36-24 shows how the shaping process may be done safely.

MAKING TENONS

1. Lay out the tenon on the rail or apron. See Unit 21, *Joining.*

2. Adjust the saw blade to cut the length of the tenon.

3. Adjust the ripping fence. Check the fence for squareness with the saw-table top (see Fig. 36-10).

4. Turn on the saw and make a trial cut on a piece of scrap wood. Make any needed adjustments.

5. Hold the face side of the board firmly against the ripping fence. Push it slowly into the saw blade (Fig. 36-25).

6. Repeat this process on other identical tenons to be cut.

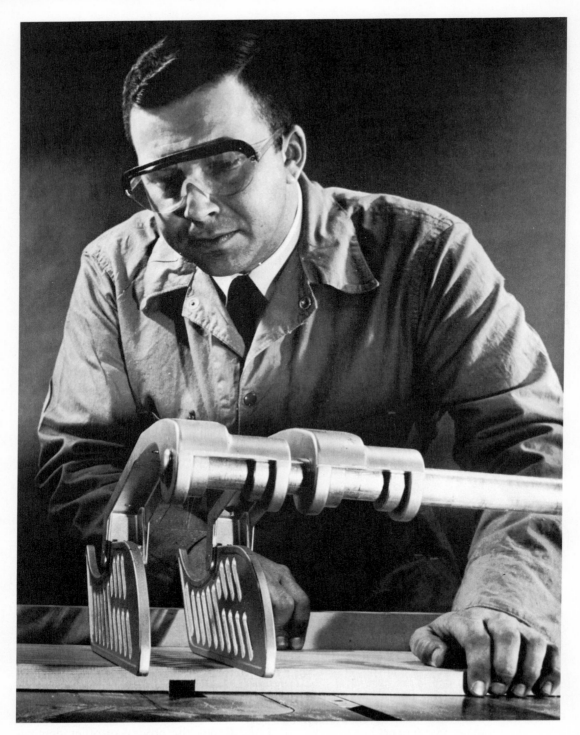

Fig. 36-23. Cutting a dado, or groove.

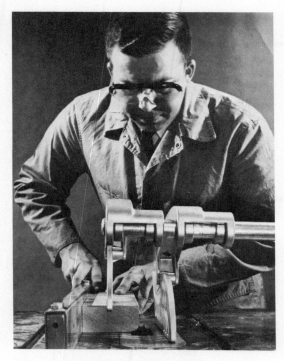

Fig. 36–24. Shaping the edge of a board.

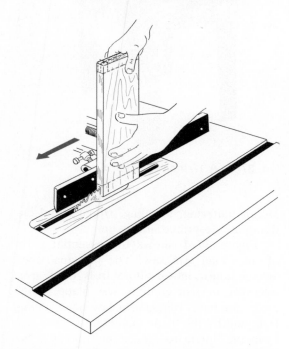

Fig. 36–25. The first cut in making a tenon.

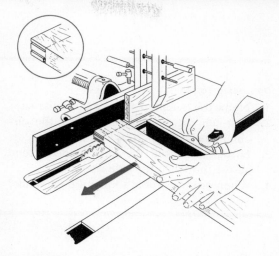

Fig. 36–26. Cutting the shoulder on a tenon. Note the detail in the insert.

7. Stop the machine and adjust the ripping fence to cut the other side of the tenon.

8. Turn the machine on. Make another trial cut on the original piece of scrap wood. Make any necessary adjustments.

9. Again place the tenon piece with the face side against the ripping fence. Cut as in step 5.

10. Reset the ripping fence. Make the remaining cuts across the ends of the tenons.

11. Place the cut-off guide in the left groove of the table top. Adjust it for squareness with the saw blade.

12. Clamp a block on the ripping fence as shown in Fig. 36–26.

13. Adjust the ripping fence for distance.

14. Set the saw blade to the cutting height (Fig. 36–25).

15. Turn on the saw and make a trial cut on the original piece of scrap wood. Make adjustments if needed.

16. Place the tenon piece with the tenon end against the wood block on the ripping fence. Hold it firmly in the cutoff guide, and push it slowly over the saw blade (Fig. 36–26).

17. Use the procedure outlined above to cut the shoulders on the other side of the tenon.

1. Name the essential parts of a circular saw.
2. List ten safety rules for using the circular saw.
3. How far should the saw blade extend above the work for safe operation?
4. When is it desirable to use a push stick?
5. Why should you fasten a block on the ripping fence when crosscutting several pieces to the same length (Fig. 36–16)?
6. What is the dado head? Where is it used?
7. List four operations, other than crosscutting and ripping, of the table saw.

unit

37

Sawing on the radial arm saw

The radial arm saw was developed from the old type of swing saw, in which the saw blade swung back and forth above a worktable. The modern radial arm saw is a precision machine which will perform many operations. This makes it a versatile tool for industry, school, or home workshop. This machine, with its various adjustments and its many accessories, can be used to crosscut, miter, rip, bevel, and compound-bevel. It will rip tapers, make tenons, and plough. It will cut dadoes, rabbets, grooves, and tongues. It will also do molding and router shaping, as well as drilling, sanding, and grinding.

Limited space will not permit detailed discussion and explanation of all of these operations. The more common techniques for crosscutting, cutting pieces to the same

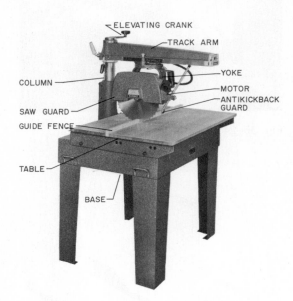

Fig. 37–1. A 12-inch radial arm saw.

length, mitering, beveling, ripping, and dadoing are described in this unit.

Figure 37–1 shows the essential parts of the radial arm saw. The principal ones are the motor, motor-tilt controls, track arm, overarm, upright column, saw blade, guard table, and base. Radial arm saw sizes are determined by the blade diameter. These vary from the 8-inch to the 20-inch models. Information about saw blades and dado heads is given on pages 176 to 182. Also see Figs. 36–3 through 36–8. The combination blade is satisfactory for most jobs. Dadoes may be made by using a dado, or grooving, head just as is done with the circular saw (Figs. 36–20 through 36–22).

 Safety Rules

1. Always get permission to use the radial saw.

2. Check to see that the blade is sharp.

3. Make sure that the teeth of the blade point in the direction shown by the arrow on the guard.

4. Keep the safety guard in place and properly adjusted.

5. Always hold the stock firmly against the table guide strip.

6. Keep your hands away from the path of the blade.

7. In ripping, always use the antikickback guard.

8. In ripping, always feed the stock from the end opposite the antikickback guard.

9. Keep loose clothing out of the way. If sleeves are not rolled up, button the cuffs.

CROSSCUTTING

1. Set the track arm at zero degrees (0°) on the miter scale, and lock it securely.

2. Set the depth of the cut by adjusting the elevating crank. The teeth of the saw blade should barely scratch the top of the table.

3. Place the board on the table top and against the guide fence (see Fig. 37–2).

4. Hold the board securely with one hand.

5. Turn on the power switch.

6. Pull the saw slowly across the board exactly where desired (Fig. 37–2).

7. Return the saw behind the guide fence. *Always do this before removing the board.*

8. Turn off the power switch.

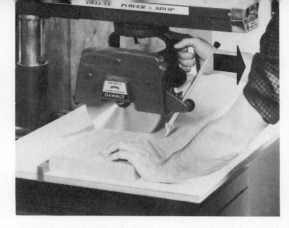

Fig. 37–2. Crosscutting a board. The pressure of the top-side cutting action of the blade helps hold the board safely against the fence.

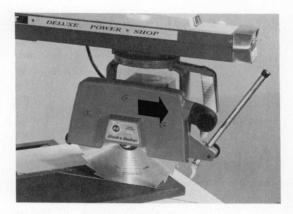

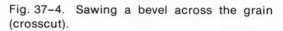

Fig. 37–3. Making a miter cut.

Fig. 37–4. Sawing a bevel across the grain (crosscut).

CUTTING MITERS

1. Swing the track arm to the desired right- or left-hand angle on the miter scale. Lock it securely.

2. Set the depth of the cut by adjusting the elevating crank.

3. Place the board on the table top and against the guide fence (see Fig. 37-3).

4. Turn on the power switch.

5. Pull the saw slowly across the board (Fig. 37-3), just as you do in crosscutting.

6. Return the saw behind the guide fence. Always do this before removing the board.

7. Turn off the power switch.

BEVEL CROSSCUTTING

1. Adjust the track arm and yoke for simple crosscutting, then tilt the blade down to the desired angle. The most common bevel position, of 45 degrees, can be set with the bevel stop. Other angles are set by using the bevel scale.

2. Set the depth of the cut by adjusting the elevating crank.

3. Place the board on the table top against the guide fence (see Fig. 37-4).

4. Turn on the power switch.

5. Pull the saw slowly across the board (Fig. 37-4) just as you do in crosscutting. Figure 37-5 illustrates crosscutting a compound angle. This requires additional adjustment.

6. Return the saw behind the guide fence. Always do this before removing the board.

7. Turn off the power switch.

RIPPING

1. Set the track arm to the crosscutting position.

2. Adjust the yoke so that the blade is parallel to the guide fence.

3. Set the depth of the cut by adjusting the elevating crank.

4. Push the carriage carefully along the track arm to correct position for the ripping

Fig. 37-5. Crosscutting a compound bevel miter.

Fig. 37-6. Ripping on the radial arm saw. The antikickback guard should be in place, as shown.

Fig. 37-7. Wide panels may be ripped on most radial arm saws.

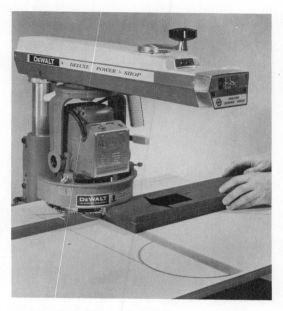

Fig. 37–8. Perfect grooving may be done by placing the board flat on the table against the fence, while feeding it into the horizontally set blade.

Fig. 37–9. A lock joint may be cut by setting the motor vertically. The two pieces of wood are placed on edge on a special jig fixture of 2-inch material. The edges are slit by cutting past the stock at desired increments (spacings).

width desired. Lock the carriage securely by tightening the rip-clamp handle.

5. Place the board on the table top and against the guide fence (see Fig. 37–6).

6. Lower the rear of the safety guard to clear the board, and lock it.

7. Adjust the antikickback guard. Make certain that the points of the antikickback-guard fingers are set 1/8 inch below the surface of the board as shown in Figs. 37–6 and 37–7.

8. Turn on the power switch.

9. Feed the board into the saw slowly. Make sure that it moves against and along the guide fence (Figs. 37–6 and 37–7). Do not feed the material into the antikickback end of the saw guard. Figures 37–8 and 37–9 show the saw set for grooving and for cutting a lock joint.

10. Turn off the power switch.

CUTTING DADOES

1. Lock the track arm at the desired angle for a straight, or right- or left-hand dado. Set the track arm at zero degrees (0°) for a straight dado.

2. Replace the saw blade with the dado head that will make a groove of the desired width. See Figs. 36–20 and 36–21.

3. Adjust the depth for the dado cut with the elevating crank.

4. Place the material on the table against the guide fence (see Fig. 37–10).

5. Hold the board securely against the guide fence with one hand.

6. Turn on the power switch.

7. Pull the cutter head slowly across the board exactly where desired (Fig. 37–10). Successive passes, or cuts, can be made if the dado cut must be wider than the head. Angle dado cuts require adjusting the track arm.

8. Return the saw behind the guide fence. Always do this before removing the board.

9. Turn off the power switch.

Fig. 37–10. Cutting a dado.

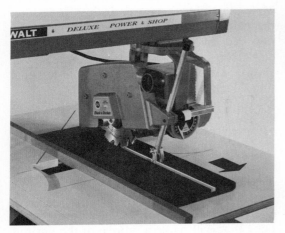

Fig. 37–11. Ploughing, or grooving, with the dado head.

Fig. 37–12. Making a bevel rabbet cut. A straight rabbet cut is shown on the right edge of the board.

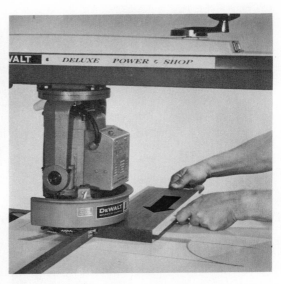

Fig. 37–13. Cutting a groove for a tongue-and-groove joint. The tongue has been cut on the right edge of the board.

Fig. 37–14. Shaping a straight edge by attaching a shaper head on the saw arbor.

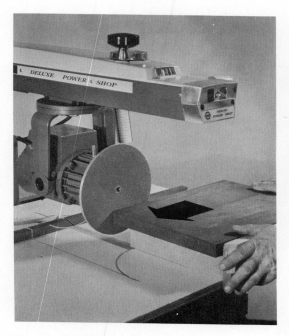

Fig. 37–15. Disk sanding an edge.

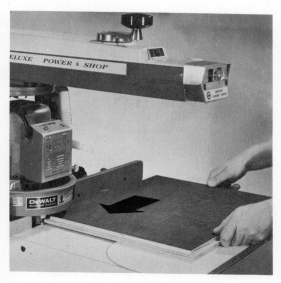

Fig. 37–17. Shaping a cabinet door lip cut.

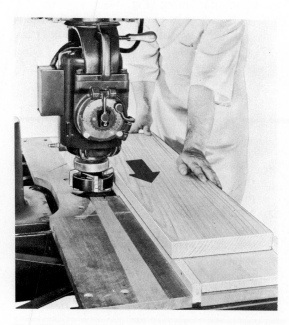

Fig. 37–16. Jointing an edge by using a special cutter head and the table adaptor.

OTHER RADIAL SAW OPERATIONS

A list, and illustrations, of several additional special operations which may be performed on the radial saw are given here. See your teacher, or someone acquainted with the radial saw, or study the manufacturer's manual before you attempt to set the machine attachments.

1. Ploughing or grooving can be done with the dado head while the radial saw is set for ripping (Fig. 37–11).

2. A bevel rabbet can be cut by tilting the motor (Fig. 37–12). The rabbet shown on the right side of the board was cut with the dado head set horizontally.

3. A tongue and groove can be made by using dado inserts with collars of the exact dimensions needed (Fig. 37–13).

4. The radial saw can be converted into a shaper by installing a shaper head on the saw arbor (Figs. 37–14 and 37–17).

5. A special jointer cutter head may be attached to the radial saw to perform jointing operations (Fig. 37–16). (Jointing operations

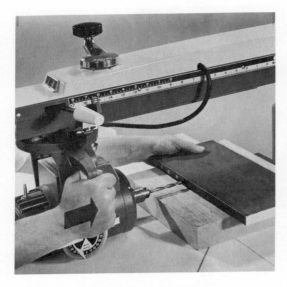

Fig. 37–18. Edge boring for a dowel.

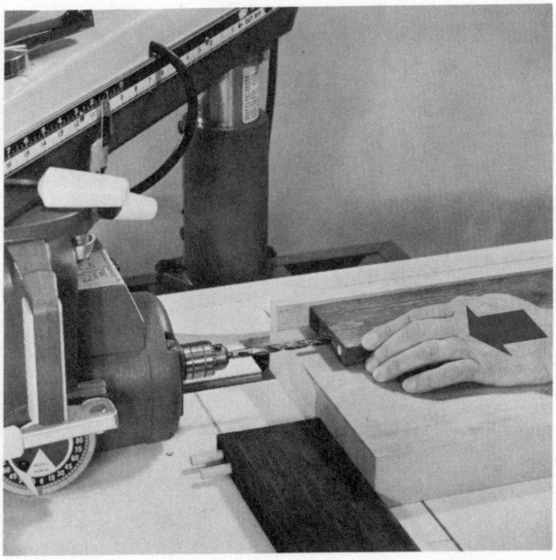

Fig. 37–19. End boring for a dowel.

are machine-planing operations.) Note that a special table has been attached to the regular radial-saw bench top for this process. Generally it is best to plane edges on the jointer.

6. Edges can be sanded by using a drum sanding attachment (Fig. 37–15).

7. Boring jobs can be done on the radial saw with the use of an adaptor chuck (Figs. 37–18 and 37–19).

Discussion Topics

1. Name the essential parts of a radial saw.
2. List fifteen different types of cutting which may be done with the radial saw.
3. List eight safety rules for using the radial saw.
4. List four types of saw blades which might be used on the radial arm saw.
5. What kind of blade may be used for both crosscutting and ripping?
6. How far should the blade extend into the table top for crosscutting and ripping? Why?
7. Name and describe four special adaptors and attachments which can be used with the radial arm saw.
8. What size radial arm saw do you have in the school laboratory or in your home workshop? What indicates the saw size?

unit

38

Sawing on the band saw

The band saw can be used for straight sawing as well as for cutting curved pieces. The essential parts are the frame, with two wheels mounted on it; an adjustable table; two adjustable saw guides, located above and below the table; wheels and levers for making various adjustments; the band-saw blade; and necessary guards (Fig. 38–1). A ripping fence and a cut-off guide are also available. Figures

38–2 and 38–3 show names and details of the upper and lower guide assemblies. These are typical of most band-saw machines. Their adjustments are easy to make.

The size of the band saw is indicated by the diameter of its wheels. The 14- to 30-inch band saw is a convenient size for use in school shops and laboratories. The home-workshop enthusiast will probably use the 12- to 14-inch size. Wheels of smaller diameters tend to crystallize band-saw blades in

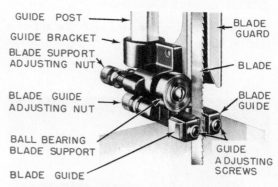

Fig. 38–2. Upper guide assembly details.

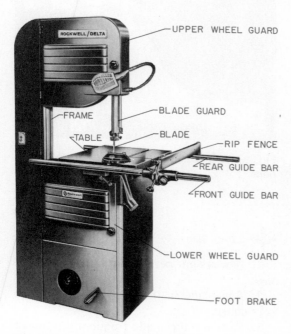

Fig. 38–1. A 24-inch band saw.

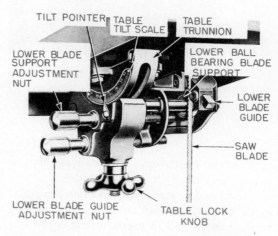

Fig. 38–3. Lower guide and table assembly details.

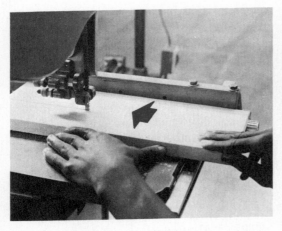

Fig. 38–4. Sawing a board with the aid of a ripping fence.

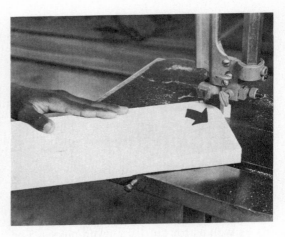

Fig. 38–6. Sawing a sharp corner curve.

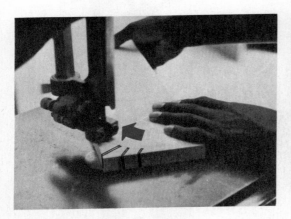

Fig. 38–5. Relief cuts. These are desirable when sawing sharp curves.

Fig. 38–7. Resawing a board to reduce thickness.

a relatively short time. This causes them to break more easily.

The band saw is one of the more popular types of machine-tool equipment to be used in the school and in the home. It is reasonably easy to maintain and does not require very much floor space.

 Safety Rules

1. Always get permission to use the band saw.

2. The blade in the band saw should be kept sharp.

3. Examine the blade frequently to make sure it is in good condition.

194

4. Check tension on the blade with the manufacturer's specifications.

5. Keep the machine well lubricated.

6. Keep safety guards fastened firmly.

7. Feed work into the band-saw blade firmly, but without pushing it too fast.

8. Maintain a well-balanced position on both feet while sawing.

9. Avoid backing out of a cut. It may pull the blade off the wheel.

10. Make cuts on curves gradually. Use relief cuts, as shown in Fig 38–5.

11. Check to see that the upper guide clears the stock by 1/4 inch.

SAWING

1. Surface or plane the stock to the required thickness.

2. Mark the board, make a layout, or transfer the pattern.

3. Adjust the upper guide on the band saw to clear the thickness of the stock by approximately 1/4 inch (Fig. 38–4).

4. Start the saw. Make certain that it is running at full speed before you start to cut.

5. Move the board gently against the saw blade and the rip fence, and start the cut

on the waste side of the line (Fig. 38–4). Allow approximately 1/16-inch surplus for final smoothing.

6. If there are sharp curves, make several *relief cuts* first (see Fig. 38–5). This depends somewhat upon the kind of lumber and the width of the saw blade. A 1/8-inch blade will cut to a radius of approximately 1 inch. A 3/8-inch blade will cut to a radius of 1 1/2 inches.

7. Make the cut on the waste side of the line (Fig. 38–6).

RESAWING

1. Make a *jig*, or guide, from wood like that shown in Fig. 38–7.

2. Raise the upper guide to clear the board and the jig.

3. Fasten the jig to the table top with a hand clamp (Fig. 38–7). Set the distance for resawing when you fasten the guide in place. A rip fence could also be used if the blade cuts true.

4. Start the saw and push the board very slowly into the blade. Make certain that you do not push the board too fast, because this may overheat or crystallize the blade, making it brittle.

Discussion Topics

1. Name the essential parts of the band saw.
2. What are the safety precautions for cutting on the band saw?
3. How do you determine the size of a band saw?

4. What is the purpose in making relief cuts?
5. What other types of sawing can be done on the band saw?
6. When does it become necessary to resaw a board?

---

unit
39

Sawing on the jig, or scroll, saw

The jig saw, often called the scroll saw, is used for cutting either internal or external curves. The main parts are the base, frame, table, upper and lower chucks, tension sleeve, and guides (Figs. 39–1 through 39–3). Many jig saws also have hold-down devices.

The size of a jig saw is determined by the horizontal distance between the saw blade and the arm of the frame. This gives clearance in cutting. Popular and practical sizes measure 18 to 24 inches from blade to arm.

Blades used in jig saws are often manufactured expressly for that purpose (Fig. 39–4). Jewelers' and coping saws may also be used with success. Each machine has certain specifications for blade tension and adjustment. Follow the specifications for these machines when you operate them.

 Safety Rules

1. Always obtain permission before you use the jig saw.
2. Set all adjustments as directed by the manufacturer.
3. Fasten the blade with the teeth pointing down.
4. Maintain the proper tension on the blade at all times.
5. Always adjust the hold-down device so it will barely clear the work.
6. Handle the board being cut with both hands.

196

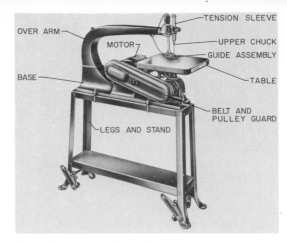

Fig. 39–1. A 24-inch jig, or scroll, saw on a stand.

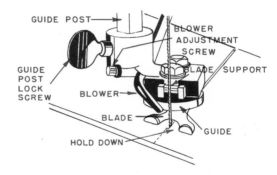

Fig. 39–2. Upper guide assembly for the jig saw.

Fig. 39–3. Lower guide assembly for the jig saw.

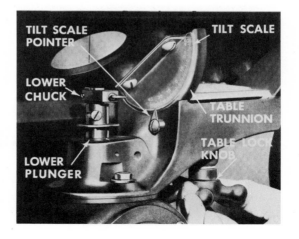

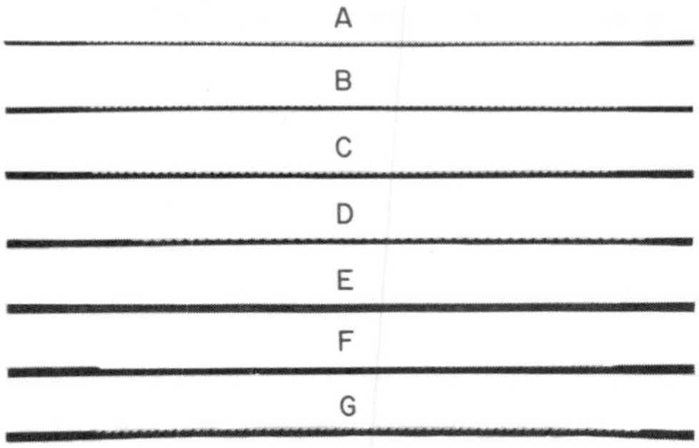

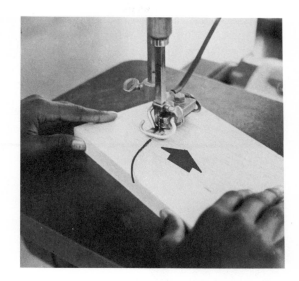

Fig. 39–4. Several common sizes of 5-inch jig saw blades:
(A) .008 thick, .035 wide, 20 teeth per inch
(B) .010 thick, .048 wide, 18 teeth per inch
(C) .010 thick, .055 wide, 16 teeth per inch
(D) .019 thick, .055 wide, 12 teeth per inch
(E) .020 thick, .070 wide, 32 teeth per inch
(F) .020 thick, .070 wide, 20 teeth per inch
(G) .020 thick, .070 wide, 15 teeth per inch

Fig. 39–5. Cutting a curve on a jig saw.

SAWING

1. Mark, lay out, or transfer the design to the board or boards.

2. Fasten the blade in the lower chuck. Be sure the teeth point down.

3. Release the tension for the top chuck, and fasten the top end of the blade in it.

4. Adjust the tension of the blade according to instructions.

5. Place the board on the table top and against the saw blade. Lower and adjust the top guide so that it will barely clear (see Fig. 39–5). Be sure the blade is square with the table top.

6. Turn on the saw. Gently move the stock against the saw blade and start the cut on the waste side of the mark or pattern line to allow for edge dressing (Fig. 39–5).

7. When you cut internal designs (Fig. 39–6), drill or bore a hole in a waste portion of the design. Insert the blade through this hole. See steps 2, 3, and 4.

8. Cut the internal design as explained in step 6.

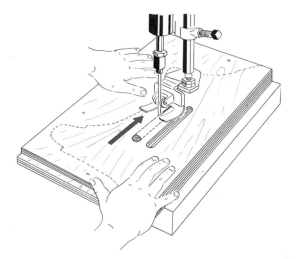

Fig. 39–6. Making an inside cut.

9. Continue sawing. Move the stock with both hands.

10. In sawing duplicate parts on thin stock, fasten them together with brads in the waste portions, and cut both pieces at once to make sure they are identical (Figs. 39–5 and 39–6).

1. What are the essential parts of the jig saw?
2. Name five safety precautions for using the jig saw.
3. How is the size of a jig saw determined?

4. What is another name for the jig saw?
5. What is the procedure for internal sawing?
6. How may duplicate parts be sawed identically?

unit
40
Planing for thickness

The planer, also called the thickness planer, or surfacer (Fig. 40–1), is a woodworking machine for making a smooth, planed surface on a board. It planes the board to an even thickness. Modern planers are either double or single surfacers. The one described here is a single surfacer, the most common for school use. A double surfacer has a cutter head on top and bottom.

Basic parts of the planer are a table, feed mechanism, feed control, elevating handwheel, and cutter head. The planer illustrated is an 18- by 6-inch thickness machine. This means it can plane boards up to 18 inches wide and up to 6 inches thick. Larger planers operate in the same way as this size. Figure 40–2 illustrates the details of a typical planer head.

PLANING

1. Turn the handwheel to bring the table to the desired thickness indicated on the scale. Do not try to remove too much stock

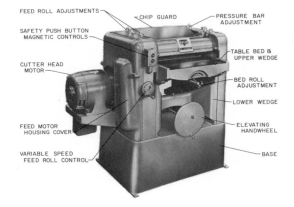

Fig. 40–1. An 18 × 6-inch thickness planer.

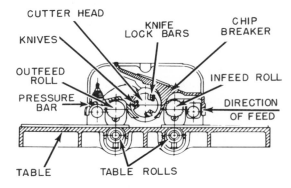

Fig. 40–2. Planer head details.

in one cut. It is suggested that the maximum cut should be ⅛ inch.

2. Check the board or boards for nails, dirt, or knots. These can cause damage to the blade or possible kickback.

Fig. 40-3. Feeding a rough board into the thickness planer.

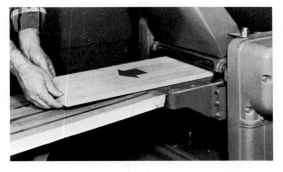

Fig. 40-4. Removing a surfaced board from the planer.

3. Place the board flat on the infeed side of the table. Push it straight forward until the infeed roll pulls the board (Fig. 40-3).

4. Stand to one side in case of kickback.

5. Remove the board after it has been completely planed (Fig. 40-4).

6. Check the thickness of the board to see if you have planed it enough. If not, adjust the handwheel for another cut, and repeat steps 3 through 5.

 Safety Rules

1. Always get permission to use the planer.

2. Inspect wood before planing, and remove any nails, dirt, or other things that will injure the cutting blade.

3. For safety, do not plane a board shorter than 14 inches. The board should be long enough for the outfeed roller to start pulling it before the infeed roller releases it.

4. Never bend over to watch the board being planed. Chips may be thrown in your face. A dust-collection system such as that shown in Figs. 40-3 and 40-4 will prevent this.

5. Plane only one board at a time.

6. Keep loose clothing, such as ties and sleeves, tucked in or rolled up.

7. After the board starts through, remove your hand and stand aside.

Discussion Topics

1. What two other terms are applied to the planer?

2. What is the size of the thickness planer used in your industrial laboratory?

unit
41

Planing on the jointer

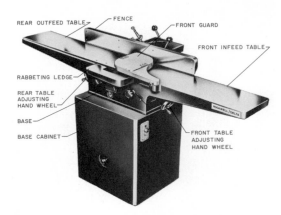

Fig. 41–1. An 8-inch long-bed jointer.

The jointer is an electric-power machine which does the work of a hand plane. It will do many jobs in addition to straight planing. An experienced craftsman will often cut rabbets, tapers, bevels, chamfers, stop chamfers, and molding on it.

The essential parts of a jointer are the base, front and rear tables, the cutter head with blades, the fence, and the safety guard (Fig. 41–1). The cutter head contains three and sometimes four blades (Fig. 41–2). The size of the jointer is determined by the length of the knives or the widest cut it can make. Six- or eight-inch jointers are adequate, but frequently 10- or 12-inch ones are used in the larger school laboratories and in industry. The front table, which is nearest the operator, has an adjustment for the depth of the cut. Some handwheels have a locknut which tightens the depth adjustment.

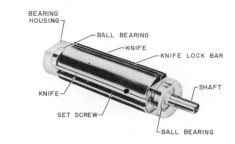

Fig. 41–2. Details of a jointer head with cutter knives.

PLANING

1. Adjust the front table for a cut of approximately $1/32$ inch for surface planing. Cut $1/16$ inch for edge planing. The rear table should be adjusted to line up with the cutting edge or be tangent to the cutting circle. Once it is adjusted, be careful not to disturb it except for special work.

2. Test the fence for squareness to the table surface with a try square (Fig. 41–3). Make the necessary adjustments for an angle of 90 degrees unless a bevel is being cut.

3. Place the safety guard in position over the cutter head, and see that it works

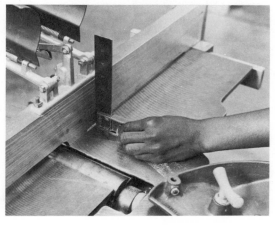

Fig. 41–3. Testing squareness of the fence to the table.

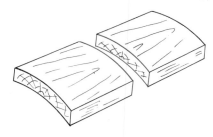

Fig. 41-4. The concave (cupped) face of a board should be planed first.

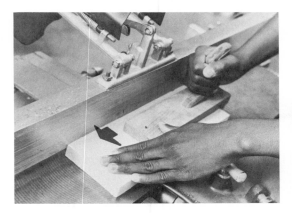

Fig. 41-5. Planing the surface of a board. Note the use of a wood push block for safety.

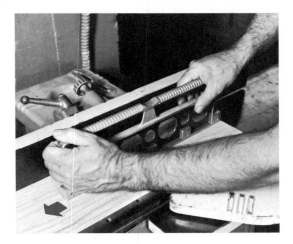

Fig. 41-6. Planing the surface of a board using a commercial grip guard.

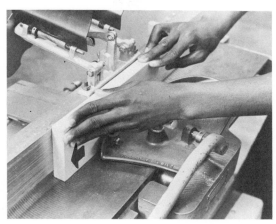

Fig. 41-7. Planing the edge of a board.

Fig. 41-8. Planing a bevel on an edge.

properly. Some guards go up as material is fed through; others spring out.

4. Turn on the jointer. Make a trial cut on a piece of clean scrap stock. Make adjustments for depth, if necessary.

5. Place the board flat on the front table top for planing the surface. If the board is warped, place the concave face down (Fig. 41-4).

6. Feed the board slowly, but firmly, over the rotating cutter head. Push it through until the entire face has been planed. Use a wooden push block (Fig. 41-5) or a com-

mercial grip guard (Fig. 41–6) to protect your hands from the cutters of the jointer.

7. In planing an edge, place the board on its edge on the front table. Hold it firmly against the fence, and feed it slowly over the rotating cutter head (Fig. 41–7).

8. Chamfers and bevels may be cut easily. Adjust the fence to the angle desired with the front table (Fig. 41–8). Follow the process described in step 7.

 Safety Rules

1. Ask permission to use the jointer.

2. Keep the safety guard in place at all times.

3. Plane only boards longer than 12 inches. Shorter ones are unsafe.

4. Use the push block in surfacing, or planing, boards on the jointer.

5. Always hold the board firmly against the fence or on the table of the jointer.

6. Surface the concave side of a warped board first.

7. Make certain the jointer blades are sharp.

8. Take a firm position to the left of the machine. Never stand at the end of the front table because a board may accidentally kick back.

9. Do not attempt to plane the end grain on narrow boards.

10. Always try to plane with the grain.

11. Never allow your fingers to pass over the revolving blades.

Discussion Topics

1. What are the essential parts of a jointer?
2. List at least eight safety precautions to be observed when you use a jointer.
3. How is the size of a jointer determined?
4. Which table do you adjust to determine the depth of cut?

5. What adjustment must be made for cutting a chamfer or a bevel?
6. How should the rear table be adjusted with respect to the cutting edges of the blades? What will happen if the rear table is set too low?

---

unit

42

Planing on the rotary jointer-surfacer

The rotary jointer-surfacer is a relatively new machine designed for jointing (edge planing), or for surface planing of material up to 6 inches in width or thickness (Fig.

42–1). The cutters are so safely designed and protected that a very small piece of wood may be planed. This machine, which has a trade name of *Uniplane*, will plane, joint, bevel, chamfer, trim, taper, and perform almost any process that can be done on a jointer or saw.

Essential parts are the table, infeed fence, outfeed fence, cutterhead and cutters, cutterhead guard, base, and cabinet. The infeed fence is adjustable for depth of cut since the cutterhead operates vertically. The depth is adjusted by the microset depth control.

The table is adjustable from 90 to 45 degrees for making a bevel or a chamfer cut. It is adjusted with a tilt scale and table lock.

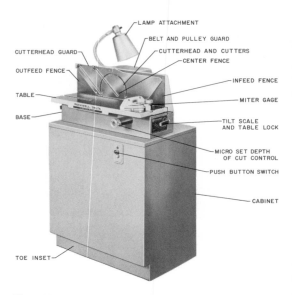

Fig. 42–1. A rotary jointer-surfacer. *(Power Tool Division, Rockwell Manufacturing Company.)*

Fig. 42–2. The cutterhead showing the four roughing (R), and the four finishing (F) cutters. The cutters are fastened securely with set screws. The four roughing and the four finishing cutters are arranged alternately to make a clean cut.

Fig. 42–3. Starting to plane a board, the first stage. Hold the board securely and firmly against the fences. Note the arrows indicating slight pressure.

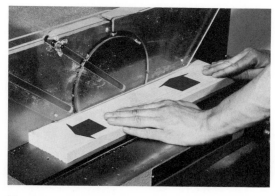

Fig. 42–4. Planing the edge, the second stage. Note the arrows.

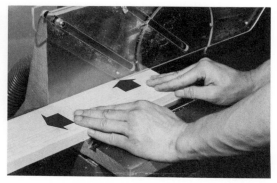

Fig. 42–5. Finishing the edge cut, the final stage. Note the arrows showing slight pressure.

203

Fig. 42–6. Planing the surface of a board.

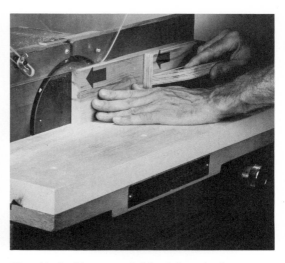

Fig. 42–9. Use a push block for planing a surface on short material.

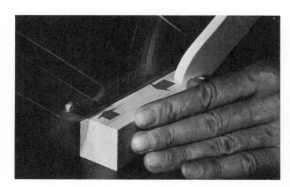

Fig. 42–7. A wooden push block should be used when planing small material.

Fig. 42–8. Use a push block for planing thin material.

Fig. 42–10. Always use two push sticks when cutting small pieces.

Make adjustments only after studying the service manual, or follow the instructions given by your teacher.

The cutterhead operates at a speed of 4,000 RPM, or 32,000 cuts per minute, because there are eight cutters; four for rough cutting, and four for finishing. These are alternately spaced on the cutterhead, making first a rough (R) then a finished (F) cut (Fig. 42–2).

 Safety Rules

1. Secure permission to use the *Uniplane*.
2. Tuck in your tie, and roll up your sleeves.
3. Always disconnect the machine from the power source before making adjustments.
4. Keep the cutterhead free of wood gum and pitch.
5. Make sure cutters are securely held in the cutterhead.
6. Always wear safety glasses or a face shield.
7. Keep safety guards in place and use them all the time.
8. Always hold the work pushed firmly against the fence.
9. Always use a push block or push sticks, expecially when working with small material.
10. Shut off the power when you have completed the cut.

PLANING

1. Adjust the infeed fence to the desired depth of cut.
2. Test the fence for squareness to the table surface. Use a try square. Make the necessary adjustment for a 90 degree angle, unless a bevel is to be cut.
3. Turn on the switch.
4. Make a trial cut on a clean scrap of stock. This is to make certain you get the correct depth of cut.
5. Feed the work piece slowly. A little experience will determine the correct speed.

Fig. 42–11. A miter gage is used when making a compound bevel cut.

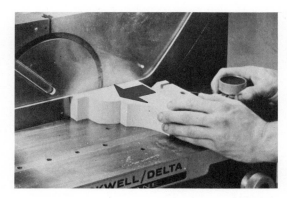

Fig. 42–12. Use a miter gage for planing end grain.

6. Hold the work piece firmly against the infeed fence. Start the cut (Figs. 42–3 through 42–6).
7. Push the board without hesitation against the outfeed fence. Hold it firmly against both fences at all times. Follow the sequence in Figs. 42–3 through 42–5.

Hold and push short or thin stock with the aid of a push block (Figs. 42–7 through 42–9).

Use two push sticks when cutting small pieces (Fig. 42–10).

Use the miter gage when planing bevels (Fig. 42–11), chamfers, or end grain (Fig. 42–12). This involves adjusting either the table or the angle of the miter gage, or both.

1. Name eight essential parts of the rotary jointer-surfacer. Give the purpose of each part.
2. What is a trade name for this machine?
3. List at least eight safety precautions to be observed in using the rotary jointer-surfacer.
4. Which fence should be adjusted for depth of cut?
5. What adjustment should be made for cutting a chamfer or a bevel?
6. Specify at least six operations which may be done on the rotary jointer-surfacer. Give an example of each.

unit

43

Boring and drilling holes with the drill press

The drill press can be used for the basic woodworking operations of boring and drilling holes. It can also be used for many other operations in woodworking, such as mortising, shaping, routing, and sanding. The essential parts are the base, table, vertical column, housing and motor support, spindle, chuck, and adjusting devices. Figure 43–1 shows a variable speed drill press.

The arrangements of pulleys and belts give many speeds on stop-pulley drill presses. Manufacturers furnish charts and tables which give the numerous speeds of the belt and pulley combinations. The lower speeds are for drilling and boring; the higher ones are for mortising, shaping, routing, and sanding.

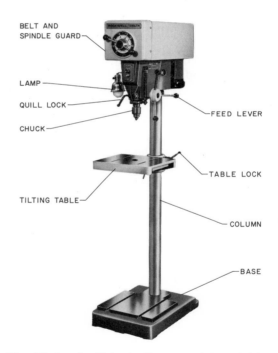

BELT AND SPINDLE GUARD

LAMP

QUILL LOCK

CHUCK

FEED LEVER

TABLE LOCK

TILTING TABLE

COLUMN

BASE

Fig. 43–1. A 17-inch floor model variable-speed drill press.

Fig. 43–2. A machine bit for wood.

TOOLS

Drill Bits. Unit 18, *Boring and Drilling Holes,* gives a description of drill bits and sizes. Bits used in hand drills and portable electric hand drills may also be used in the drill press. The chuck on most drill presses, such as the one shown in Fig. 43–1, will accommodate bits or bit shanks up to ½ inch in diameter.

Machine Bit for Wood. Figure 43–2 pictures a machine drill bit with a reduced shank. These bits have shank diameters of ¼, ⅜, and ½ inch, so that bits with greater diameter than the shank sizes can be used in chucks having limiting capacities. This permits cutting larger holes in wood than the chuck would normally allow.

Spade-type Power Bit. This bit is also called a zip bit (Fig. 43–3). It fits ¼-inch and larger chucks, and cuts holes from ⅜ to 1 inch in diameter.

Power Bore Bit. Figure 43–4 shows a bit which will drill accurate, clean holes without clogging. It fits ¼-inch and larger chucks. It has a brad point and cuts holes ⅜ to 1 inch in diameter.

Large Hole Bit. The large hole bit (Fig. 43–5) cuts holes from 1¾ to 2⅛ inches in diameter. It is designed for boring holes for cylinder lock sets, pipes, and similar-size installations.

Foerstner Bit. This bit, with a round shank, will bore holes just like an auger bit, except it does not have a feed screw (Fig. 43–6). It is sized from ¼ to 2 inches in diameter.

Multi-spur Bit. A bit of this type (Fig. 43–7) is designed for construction purposes. Sizes vary from ⅞ to 2 inches in diameter.

Hole Saw. Figure 43–8 illustrates a series of three sizes of hole saws. The principle of this tool is that the center-cutting bit is followed through by a circular type saw, in order to cut holes from ⅝ to 2½ inches in diameter.

Fig. 43–3. Spade-, or zip-type, power bit.

Fig. 43–4. Power bore bit.

Fig. 43–5. Large hole bit.

Fig. 43–6. Foerstner bit.

Fig. 43–7. Multi-spur bit.

Fig. 43–8. Three sizes of hole saws.

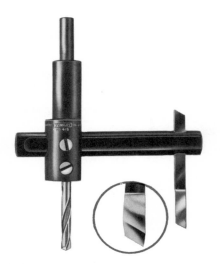

Fig. 43–9. Circle cutter.

Fig. 43–10. Plug cutter.

Fig. 43–11. Countersink bit.

Fig. 43–12. Drum forming tool.

Fig. 43–13. Three sizes of sanding drums.

Circle Cutter. The cutter shown in Fig. 43–9 is designed to cut large holes in wood, plywood, hardboard, particle board, and other laminated materials. It can be set to cut holes from $13/16$ to 5 inches in diameter.

Plug Cutter. This tool (Fig. 43–10) cuts round plugs slightly beveled to permit easy insertion in holes. It is available in sizes of $3/8$, $1/2$, and $5/8$ inch.

Countersink Bit. The countersink bit shown in Fig. 43–11 is used on wood and soft metal. The round shank makes it ideal for use in the drill press, portable electric drill, or hand drill. Maximum cutting edges vary from $1/2$ to $3/4$ inch.

Drum Forming Tool. Shaping, cutting, and forming can be easily done with this 2-inch diameter tool which fits a drill press chuck (Fig. 43–12).

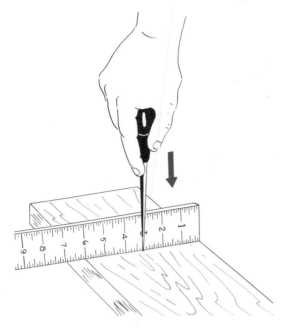

Fig. 43–14. Marking the center with an awl for drilling or boring a hole.

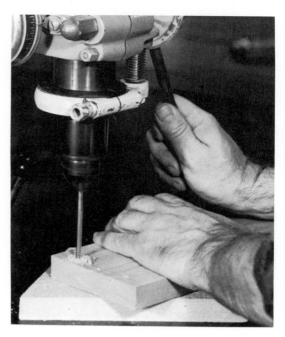

Fig. 43–16. Drilling holes for screws.

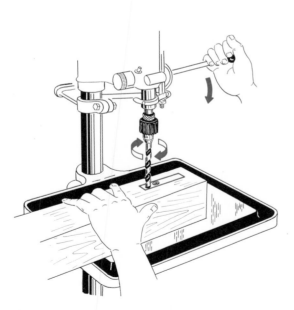

Fig. 43–15. Drilling a series of holes for a mortise.

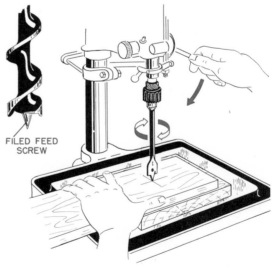

FILED FEED SCREW

Fig. 43–17. Boring a hole with a spade-type wood bit. Note the scrap board that protects the table. On the left is an ordinary auger bit that has been filed for use on the drill press.

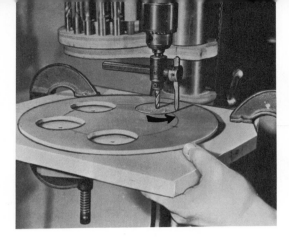

Fig. 43–18. Cutting circles in plywood with the circle cutter.

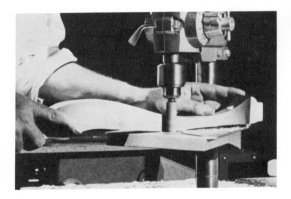

Fig. 43–19. Accurate sanding can be done on the drill press by using a sanding drum.

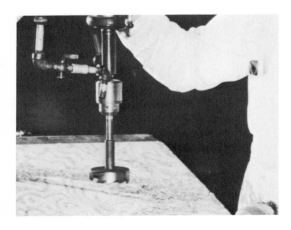

Fig. 43–20. Large holes can be cut with the multi-spur bit.

Fig. 43–21. A sturdy drill press can also serve as a router.

Sanding Drum. Sanding drums are made in various diameters (Fig. 43–13). Manufacturers also supply sanding sleeves in varying grits and sizes to fit the drums. Adapters are available to make these drums fit the chuck of a drill press.

Safety Rules

1. Get permission to use the drill press.
2. Always remove the key from the chuck before starting the drill press.
3. Check the pulley combination to see if the proper speed is set up.
4. Protect loose clothing, such as a necktie and sleeves.
5. Use goggles or a face shield when using the drill press at high speed.
6. Cover the pulleys with a guard to keep clothing and hair out of them.
7. Hold the work firmly so that it will not fly off the table and injure someone. Sometimes it is best to fasten the work securely with clamps.
8. Remove your wristwatch and rings.

BORING AND DRILLING

1. Lay out and mark the center for drilling or boring a hole as shown in Fig. 43–14.

2. Select a drill bit or other tool of the correct size (see Figs. 43–2 through 43–13). Fasten it in the chuck.

3. Place the board on the table of the drill press. Adjust the table to the correct height. Place a piece of scrap wood underneath the board.

4. Turn on the drill press. See that the bit or tool is properly fastened in the chuck and does not wobble.

5. Hold the board securely. Apply even pressure in feeding the bit into the wood slowly. If the wood smokes, release the pressure on the bit. Excessive speed may also cause the wood or bit to burn. Figures 43–15 through 43–21 illustrate the use of the drill and the other tools on wood. At the left in Fig. 43–17 is a specially filed auger bit.

Discussion Topics

1. Name the essential parts of the drill press.
2. List the necessary safety precautions to observe when you use the drill press.
3. How can an auger bit be adapted for use on the drill press? Name two other types of bits for this machine.
4. How is the speed of the drill press changed?
5. Name at least three operations, besides drilling and boring holes, which can be performed on the drill press.

---

unit

44

Shaping on the shaper

The shaper used in woodworking is for making molding and paneling, for grooving on straight or curved edges, and for pattern shaping. It may be used also for fluting furniture legs. The vertical spindle rotates at a speed of from 7,000 to 10,000 RPM. This makes it important that the shaper be used safely.

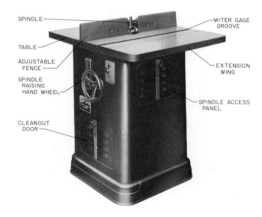

Fig. 44–1. Heavy-duty wood shaper.

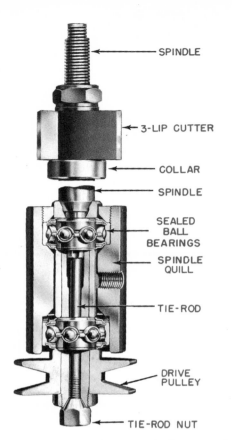

Fig. 44–2. Typical shaper spindle assembly.

SPINDLE

3-LIP CUTTER

COLLAR

SPINDLE

SEALED BALL BEARINGS

SPINDLE QUILL

TIE-ROD

DRIVE PULLEY

TIE-ROD NUT

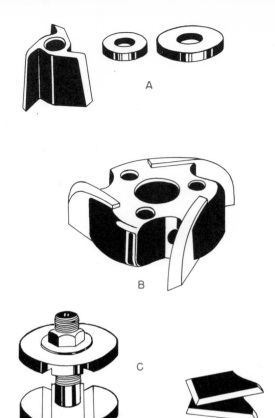

Fig. 44–4. Three common types of shaper cutters: (A) solid three-lip cutter with rub or spacing collars, (B) three-knife safety cutter-head, (C) bevel-edged cutter knives and slotted collars.

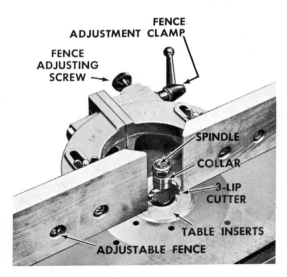

FENCE ADJUSTMENT CLAMP

FENCE ADJUSTING SCREW

SPINDLE

COLLAR

3-LIP CUTTER

TABLE INSERTS

ADJUSTABLE FENCE

Fig. 44–3. Shaper fence assembly details.

Fig. 44–5. Three-lip shaper cutters with rub or spacing collars.

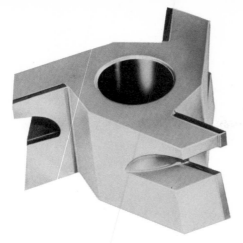

Fig. 44–6. Three-lip shaper cutter with carbide reinforced edges.

The essential parts of the shaper shown in Fig. 44–1 are the frame, vertical spindle cutter head, adjustable fence, adjustable guard, various collars, and cutters. The table adjusts on some machines; on others, the spindle is adjustable. A typical spindle assembly is illustrated in Fig. 44–2. Figure 44–3 shows a shaper fence assembly.

The most common types of available cutters are (A) solid lip, (B) three-knife cutter heads, and (C) open, bevel-edged cutter knives in slotted collars (Fig. 44–4). Solid lip cutters, with various size rub or spacing collars, are the safest (Figs. 44–5 through 44–7).

Fig. 44–7. A selection of popular designs of shaper cutters, showing their cuts:
(A) carbide-tipped slotting   (D) cove   (G) surface bead
(B) straight-face grooving   (E) corner round   (H) corner bead
(C) 45 degree bevel chamfer   (F) carbide-tipped door lip   (I) cove and bead

A

B

C

D

E

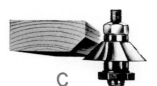

F

G

H

I

Fig. 44–8. Shaping a straight edge. Note the use of pressure guides.

Fig. 44–9. Shaping an irregular edge.

Fig. 44–10. Four-blade molding cutter.

Fig. 44–11. Selection of six-blade molding cutters, showing the cuts made.

Fig. 44–12. Detail of cutterheads in an industrial molding machine.

Fig. 44–13. Mass production shaping in industry is often performed on the automatic molding machine.

SHAPING

1. Select the cutter, or cutters, for edge shaping. The solid three-lip cutter is suggested as safer.

2. Place the cutter, or cutters, on the spindle. Tighten the nut with a wrench.

3. For straight cutting, place the adjustable fence on the table. Fasten it in the desired position. This position is determined by the depth and width of cut to be made on the edge of the board (Figs. 44–3 and 44–8).

4. When shaping curved or irregular edges on a board, leave the fence off. Set up a guide pin for starting your work. Put a rub collar on the spindle to control the depth of the cut (Fig. 44–9).

5. Start the machine.

6. Test the cut on a piece of scrap wood of the same thickness as the piece to be shaped. Examine the edge pattern and make any necessary adjustments.

7. Shape the edge of the board. Hold it firmly against the fence or pin and rub collar. Push it slowly into the cutter (Figs. 44–8 and 44–9). Always push from right to left. Where possible, try to use a guard to protect your hands.

Figures 44–10 through 44–13 show industrial cutters and applications of shaping on a molding machine.

Safety Rules

1. Secure permission to use the shaper.
2. Always keep the cutters sharp.
3. Make certain that the cutter or cutter knives are fastened securely before you use the shaper. Also make certain that all adjustments are tight.
4. Keep all moving parts well lubricated.
5. Keep the safety guards in place at all times.
6. Keep a well-balanced position when operating the shaper.
7. Have plenty of shadow-free illumination on the work.
8. Hold the board firmly against the fence for straight work. Hold it directly against the rub collar on the spindle for curved pieces. Feed the stock slowly into the cutter at an even pressure and speed.
9. Always wear safety goggles.

Discussion Topics

1. Name the essential parts of a shaper.
2. What are the approximate revolutions per minute of the spindle?
3. Why is such a fast speed necessary?
4. How may the depth and height of a cut be controlled?

5. Mention five uses for the shaper.
6. List at least seven safety precautions.
7. Name at least six types of cuts which can be made on the shaper.
8. What type of industrial machine is often used to mass-produce shaper cuts?

unit

45

Wood turning

The wood lathe is one of the oldest types of power equipment known for fashioning wooden objects. Modern lathes enable craftsmen to produce beautifully turned pieces. Basic operations performed on the lathe are turning between spur (live) and cup (dead) centers, and turning on a faceplate.

The size of a lathe is usually determined by two factors: (1) the maximum length of the piece which can be turned between the centers, and (2) the swing of the faceplate, which indicates the maximum diameter of the piece which can be turned. Essential parts (Fig. 45–1) are the headstock, spur center, faceplate, tailstock, cup center, tool rest and holder, the frame which supports the ways on which the tailstock and tool holder move, and several necessary handwheels and adjusting levers (see Figs. 45–2 through 45–6).

On the more elaborate lathes, speed is controlled by a variable-speed motor built in the headstock. On less expensive ones, it is regulated by a combination of pulleys and V belts. A general rule to remember is that the larger the stock to be turned, the slower the speed required.

WOOD-TURNING TOOLS

Special types of chisels or woodturners' tools are used for turning. Some of the more

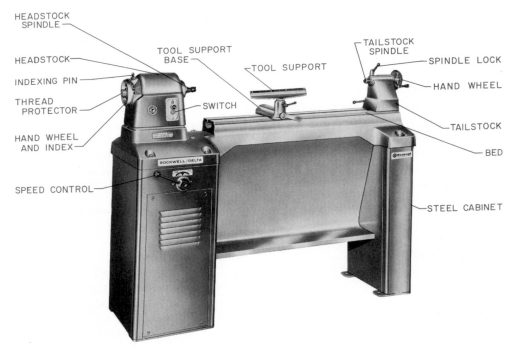

Fig. 45–1. A 12-inch, variable-speed, wood-turning lathe.

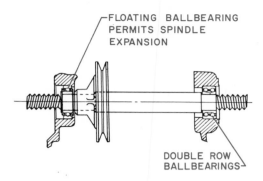

Fig. 45–2. Typical wood lathe headstock spindle assembly.

Fig. 45–3. Spur center.

Fig. 45–4. Cup center.

Fig. 45–5. Screw-center faceplate.

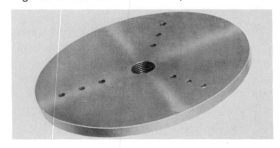

Fig. 45–6. Faceplate.

commonly used ones, shown in Fig. 45–7 are the gouge, skew chisel, parting tool, round-nose chisel, and diamond-point chisel. The last three are used principally for scraping.

The *gouge* (D and H) is generally used for rough turning, particularly in reducing stock between centers. It is available in sizes varying from 1/8 to 2 inches. The smaller ones are used for producing coves and grooves. The 1-inch size is commonly used for roughing.

The *skew chisel* (B and F) is so called because the cutting edge is skewed at an angle to the side. Use it to make a shearing cut after the stock has been reduced to the rough size. The most common size of skew chisel is the 3/4 inch.

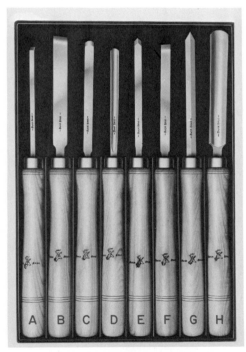

Fig. 45–7. Set of wood-turning chisels:
(A) 1/4-inch square nose
(B) 3/4-inch skew
(C) 1/2-inch round nose
(D) 1/2-inch gouge
(E) 1/2-inch spear
(F) 1/2-inch skew
(G) parting
(H) 3/4-inch gouge

217

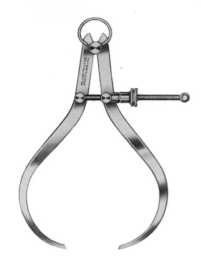

Fig. 45–8. Outside spring caliper.

Fig. 45–9. Inside spring caliper.

Fig. 45–10. Round-edge India oilstone slip stone.

The *parting tool* (G) is used for cutting grooves which have straight sides and square bottoms. This tool cuts by a scraping action. One measuring $3/16$ inch will do.

The *roundnose chisel* (C) is a scraping tool used mostly in rough turning and for forming grooves and coves. You may also use it for faceplate turning.

The *diamond-point spear chisel* (E) is a scraping tool. The $1/2$-inch width is very serviceable.

Additional tools used in wood turning are the caliper and the slip stone. The outside spring caliper (Fig. 45–8) is used to check the outside diameter. The inside spring caliper is used to measure inside measurements on face plateturning (Fig. 45–9). The slip stone (Fig. 45–10) is for whetting turning tools.

 Safety Rules

1. Secure permission to use the wood lathe.

2. Check frequently to see that the locking adjustment on the tailstock assembly does not become loose. If it is not secure, the turning stock will work loose and will be thrown from the lathe.

3. Protect loose clothing. Do not wear a necktie.

4. Wear clear goggles or a face shield.

5. Keep the turning chisels sharp. Dull tools produce inferior work.

6. Have plenty of natural light.

7. Maintain a firm, well-balanced stance on both feet.

8. Adjust the lathe for its slowest speed for all beginning rough turning. Advance the speed as the work smooths out.

9. Lubricate the cup or dead-center end with lubricating oil or beeswax. This prevents burning. Many workers prefer to use a ball-bearing cup center.

10. Always hold the tool firmly in both hands.

11. Revolve the stock by hand before you turn on the power. This prevents it from jamming against the tool rest.

12. Stop the machine when you measure or caliper.

STRAIGHT, OR SPINDLE, TURNING

Stock for turning between centers must be well-centered for balance and even turning.

Preparing Stock for Turning.

1. Select a piece of wood approximately 1 inch longer than the finished size and nearly square in cross section. Allow at least ¼ inch for turning down to the finished diameter.

2. Draw diagonal lines across both ends of the stock (Fig. 45–11). The point of intersection, or crossing, serves as the center.

3. Cut a saw kerf on the diagonal lines on one end about ⅛ inch deep (Fig. 45–12).

4. Place the stock to be turned on a solid surface, or hold it securely in a bench vise.

5. Remove the spur or live center from the headstock of the lathe. Use the pin or rod provided for that purpose.

6. Place the spur center in the saw grooves, or kerfs. Tap it a couple of times firmly with a mallet to drive it in. This seats the prongs in the kerf and the spur point at the point of intersection (Fig. 45–13).

7. Remove the spur center, and place it back in the headstock of the lathe.

8. Make a small hole with an awl at the point of intersection marked on the opposite end of the stock.

9. Put two or three drops of lubricating oil or beeswax on this hole. Soap also works well.

10. Place the wood with the grooved end against the spur center. Hold the stock in position with your left hand.

11. Release the tailstock and draw it up to within 1 inch of the stock. Clamp the tailstock against the bed of the lathe frame.

12. Turn the handwheel on the tailstock so that the spindle will guide the point of the

Fig. 45–11. Drawing diagonal lines to locate a center.

Fig. 45–12. Sawing on diagonal lines to locate a center.

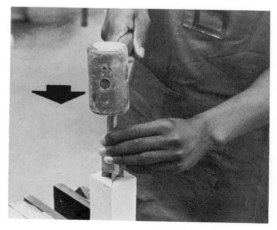

Fig. 45–13. Driving the spur, or live center, in place.

Fig. 45–14. Turning stock fastened between centers.

Fig. 45–15. Rough-cut turning with a gouge.

Fig. 45–16. Setting the caliper to the desired diameter.

Fig. 45–17. Reducing the turning stock to the required diameter.

Fig. 45–18. Cutting the stock to the required diameter.

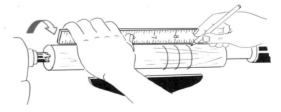

Fig. 45–19. Marking the cutting lines on the turned stock.

cup or dead center into the hole made with the awl. Sometimes a ball-bearing center is used, eliminating the need for a lubricant.

13. Tighten the stock with the handwheel on the tailstock until it feels secure. Lock the handwheel with the adjusting lever. Figure 45–14 shows the stock fastened between centers.

Turning Stock Between Centers.

1. Adjust the tool rest slightly above the center of the piece to be turned. Allow at least 1/8-inch clearance between the stock and the tool rest.

2. Revolve the work by hand to see that there is sufficient clearance.

3. Adjust the lathe to run at a slow speed; then start the motor.

4. Place the gouge (Fig. 45–7) on the tool rest. Hold it in a position like that shown in Fig. 45–15.

5. Start the rough cut by moving the gouge from left to right or right to left on the tool rest (Fig. 45–15). Start the cut from the end. (Some craftsmen prefer rough cutting from the center out. You might try both methods.)

6. Continue rough cutting until the piece of wood is round.

7. Set the caliper to the maximum diameter desired (Fig. 45–16).

8. Cut the stock with the gouge or parting tool until the caliper will barely slip over the work (Figs. 45–17 and 45–21).

9. Dress down the entire length to the diameter turned in step 8 (Fig. 45–18).

10. Turn off the motor, and mark locations for the shoulders on the stock with a pencil and a rule (Fig. 45–19).

11. Revolve the stock by hand or with the handwheel. Finish marking around the cylinder with a pencil, as shown in Fig. 45–19.

12. Trim the ends with a skew chisel (Fig. 45–20).

13. Set the tool rest about 3/16 inch below the center of the work. Set it as close to the work as possible, for safety and for added leverage for the tool handle.

14. Turn on the motor. Place the parting, or cutoff, tool on the tool rest at a place marked for any one of the shoulders.

15. Hold the parting tool firmly on the tool rest. Push it into the wood steadily until the set caliper will barely slip over (Fig. 45–21).

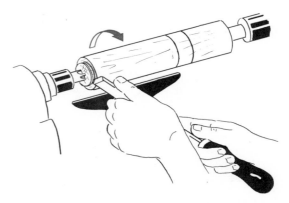

Fig. 45–20. Trimming the ends with a skew chisel.

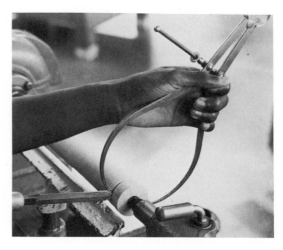

Fig. 45–21. Cutting shoulders to the required diameter with a parting tool.

221

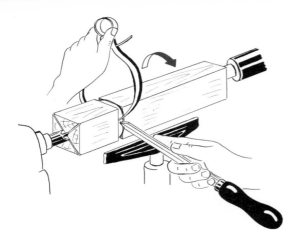

Fig. 45–22. First cut in turning a leg (or any other piece) of which sections are to remain square.

Fig. 45–23. Sanding a turning on the lathe.

Fig. 45–24. Sanding a spindle turning lengthwise on the lathe. This eliminates the circular sanding marks made in the previous step (see Fig. 45–23).

16. Cut to the remaining shoulders with the parting tool in a similar manner. Reset the caliper for each shoulder, if necessary.

17. Turn all concave cuts.

18. Cut the convex parts and beads, or half rounds, with a skew chisel or a scraping chisel.

19. Many designs, such as desk and end-table legs, require the turning of only certain parts of the piece. The rest remains square. In this case, mark the stock and cut a shoulder (Fig. 45–22). Rough down the part to be turned, as shown in Fig. 45–15. The remainder of the turning process is like that described and illustrated above.

Sanding.

1. Tear off a narrow piece of medium or fine sandpaper.

2. Move the tool rest away from the work.

3. Start the lathe at a low speed.

4. Sand all shoulders first, with the folded sandpaper. Make sure to hold the paper so that the shoulders will not get rounded.

5. Sand the other parts of the turning. Hold the sandpaper as shown in Fig. 45–23.

6. Use extra fine sandpaper for finish sanding.

7. Stop the lathe. Sand the turning with the grain to remove cross grain scratches made while the work was revolving (Fig. 45–24).

Figure 45–25 shows an industrial application of spindle turning. The inset illustrates the series of cutters which shape the leg all at once.

FACEPLATE TURNING

Turning on the faceplate involves careful location of stock on the faceplate.

Preparing Stock for Turning.

1. Select the stock for type of wood, thickness, width, and length. When rough-cut, it will resemble the piece in Fig. 45–26. Allow a surplus of approximately ½ inch in width and length and ⅛ inch in thickness.

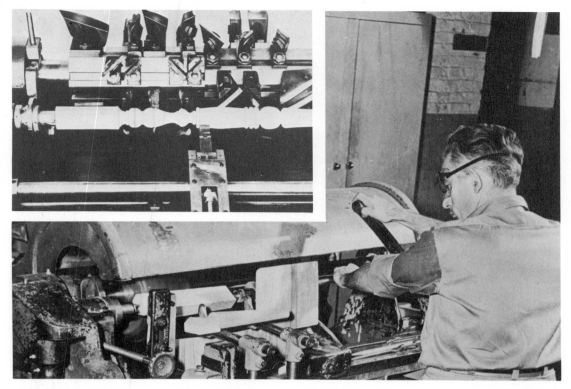

Fig. 45–25. An automatic mass-producing lathe in an industrial plant. The inset shows the various shaped cutters which make duplicate spindle turnings.

2. Plane one face smooth.

3. Lay out the circle by drawing diagonals on the block to locate the center (Fig. 45–26).

4. Cut off the corners, as shown in Fig. 45–27, or cut off waste stock on the band saw.

5. Select a faceplate to fit the block.

6. Glue a ¾-inch-thick piece of scrap wood to heavy wrapping paper. Glue the paper to the stock to be turned as shown in Fig. 45–28. When the turning is completed, the project can be separated or pried from the scrap easily, since paper is glued between the two pieces.

7. Fasten the faceplate to the scrap block with screws (Fig. 45–28). The screws should not be too long.

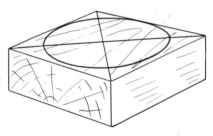

Fig. 45–26. Square stock cut and marked for faceplate turning.

Fig. 45–27. Corners cut for faceplate turning.

223

Fig. 45–30. Smoothing the face with a round-nose chisel.

TURNING

WRAPPING PAPER

FACEPLATE

SCRAP WOOD

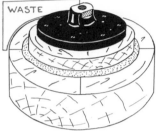

WASTE

Fig. 45–28. Faceplate fastened to the wood.

Fig. 45–31. Truing the edge with a gouge.

Fig. 45–32. Truing the edge with a round-nose chisel.

Fig. 45–29. Smoothing the face with a gouge.

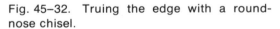

Faceplate Turning.

1. Screw the faceplate assembly on the lathe spindle.

2. Fasten the tool rest parallel to the face of the block. It should be ¼ inch away from the block, and down about ⅛ inch from the center.

3. Turn the lathe to a slow speed.

4. Smooth the face with a gouge (Fig. 45–29) or with a roundnose scraping tool (Fig. 45–30).

5. Reset the tool rest parallel with the ways of the lathe bed. Set it about ¼ inch from the outer edge and down ⅛ inch from the center.

6. Turn the wooden block by hand to see that it does not hit the tool rest.

7. True the edge with a gouge (Fig. 45–31) or with a roundnose tool (Fig. 45–32). There is another way to make this cut: Set the tool rest at right angles to the lathe bed; then cut straight in from the front with a parting tool (Fig. 45–33).

8. Finish turning according to the design or drawing. Use any of the turning chisels which fit. Scraping tools are preferred, since they produce a smoother finish (Figs. 45–30 and 45–32).

9. Sand the turning. See steps 1 through 7 for sanding spindle turning, page 222.

FINISHING ON THE LATHE

Finish is often applied to the lathe project as a final step before removal from the lathe. A shellac-oil finish is not difficult to put on. If stain and filler are needed, put them on at least 24 hours before the final coat is applied.

Follow these steps for finishing on the lathe:

1. Sand with the grain to remove all circular sandpaper scratches.

2. Clean the project and the lathe. This keeps dust from being stirred into the air while the finish is being applied.

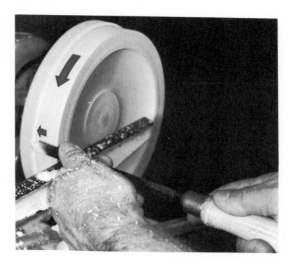

Fig. 45–33. Truing the edge with a parting tool.

Fig. 45–34. Preparing a pad for finishing. The center of the pad is moistened with thin white shellac and a few drops of linseed oil.

Fig. 45–35. Applying a shellac-and-oil finish to the turning on the lathe.

3. Make a pad by folding a piece of clean, soft cotton cloth five or six times (Fig. 45–34).

4. Lay the pad on a flat surface, and moisten the center with thin white shellac; then add a few drops of linseed oil (Fig. 45–34).

5. Start the lathe to the speed used in turning the project.

6. Hold the pad against the revolving surface with an even pressure, as shown in Fig. 45–35. If you hold the pad under the turning, you can see how smoothly the finish is going on.

7. Continue to apply the shellac and linseed oil mixture until you have the desired finish. This finish will require several coats.

Discussion Topics

1. What are the essential parts of a wood lathe?
2. How is the size of a lathe determined?
3. Name and describe five of the basic turning chisels. Tell where each is used.
4. What lubricants are applied if the cup center is used? Why?
5. What are the two general types of turnings which can be made on the lathe?
6. Mention at least two methods of dressing the corners of faceplate work for turning.
7. Are cutting or scraping tools preferred for inside faceplate turning? Why?

---

unit

46

Sanding on sanding machines

Stationary floor-type sanding machines are used extensively both in the wood products industry and in industrial laboratories and shops. The sanders most suitable for school use are the belt table (Fig. 46–1), small belt (Fig. 46–2), sander-grinder (Fig. 46–3), disk (Fig. 46–4), and the oscillating rotary spindle sander (Fig. 46–5). The small belt sander may be operated in any position from vertical to horizontal.

The purpose of each of these types of sanding machines is to sand wood smooth in preparation for applying finishes. A very small amount of material is removed when sanding is done properly.

Essential parts of each of the types mentioned are indicated on each illustration. Adjustments and alignments on each machine are usually set by the instructor, and should be left that way. The abrasive belts and sheets vary in grit size from rough to very fine, as given in Table 46–1.

Table 46-1. ABRASIVE SELECTIONS FOR SANDING MACHINES

WOOD	ROUGH SANDING	MEDIUM-FINE SANDING	VERY FINE SANDING
Hardwoods	Natural 30–40 (2½–1½) Artificial 36–50	Natural 60–80 (1/2–1/0) Artificial 60–100	Natural 100–180 (2/0–5/0) Artificial 120–180
Softwoods	Natural 1½–1	Natural 1/0	Natural 2/0–5/0
Comparison of NATURAL (garnet) grit numbers and ARTIFICIAL (aluminum oxide and silicon carbide) sizes of grits: 3 = 24 grit 2/0 = 100 grit 2½ = 30 grit 3/0 = 120 grit 1½ = 40 grit 4/0 = 150 grit 1 = 50 grit 5/0 = 180 grit 1/2 = 60 grit 6/0 = 220 grit 1/0 = 80 grit 8/0 = 280 grit		

◆ Safety Rules

1. Secure permission before using any of the sanders.

2. Tuck in your tie and roll up or button your sleeves.

3. Work safely by keeping your hands from getting near the moving belts or disks. Abrasive burns on fingertips are very painful.

4. Wear a face shield or goggles to protect your eyes.

5. Make sure all adjustments are correctly made.

6. Move the work (piece of wood) to avoid "burning" either the wood or the abrasive belt or disk.

7. Sand only on the downstroke half of the disk sander to control the sanding.

8. Prepare a jig as a holding device when sanding small pieces.

Fig. 46-1. A school-size belt table sander.

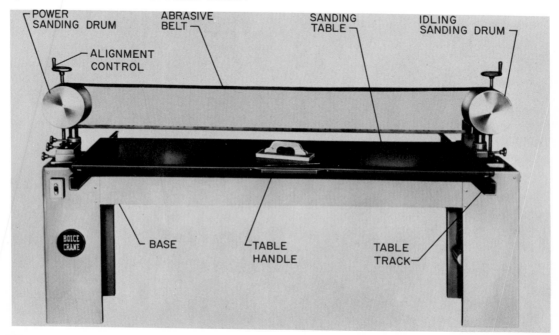

POWER SANDING DRUM   ABRASIVE BELT   SANDING TABLE   IDLING SANDING DRUM

ALIGNMENT CONTROL

BOICE CRANE   BASE   TABLE HANDLE   TABLE TRACK

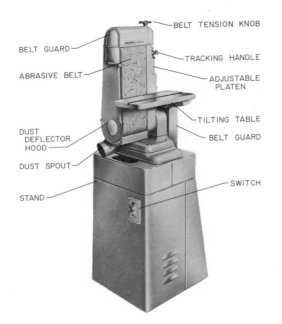

Fig. 46-2. Small, 6-inch abrasive belt finishing machine.

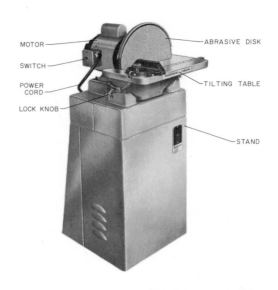

Fig. 46-4. Twelve-inch disk finishing machine.

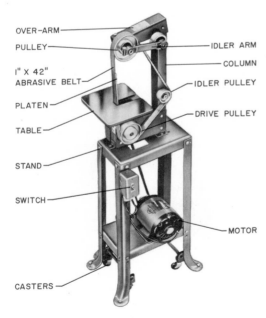

Fig. 46-3. Sander-grinder.

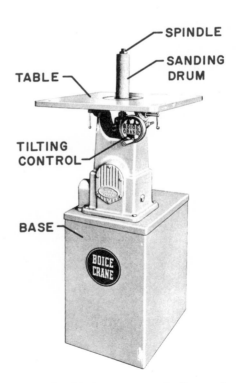

Fig. 46-5. Oscillating rotary spindle sander.

Fig. 46-6. Sanding on the top side of a board.

SANDING ON THE BELT TABLE SANDER

1. Check with your instructor to make certain that the abrasive grit and the belt clearance for doing the work are correct.

2. Place the board on the table, properly positioned, so it will not slip.

3. Turn on the switch.

4. Sand the board. Use a sander block to press down on the inside of the moving sanding belt.

5. Move the sander block back and forth, and lengthwise, until the board is smooth and evenly sanded. Use the table handle (see Fig. 46-1) to pull the board being sanded back and forth. Figure 46-6 shows how to sand on the top side of a board.

6. Turn off the power.

7. Wait for the sanding belt to stop before you remove the board.

SANDING ON THE SMALL BELT SANDER

1. Adjust the tilting table when the sander operates vertically; or the fence when the sander operates horizontally. This adjust-

Fig. 46-7. Rounding the corners of a small cabinet on the small belt finishing machine.

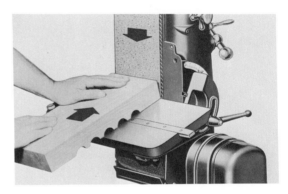

Fig. 46-8. Starting to sand a bevel on the small belt finishing machine.

Fig. 46-9. Sanding a bevel with the small belt finishing machine tilted backward.

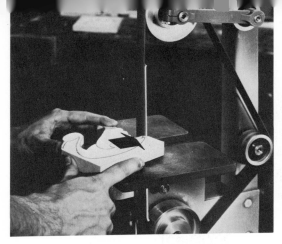

Fig. 46–10. Detail edge sanding on the sander-grinder.

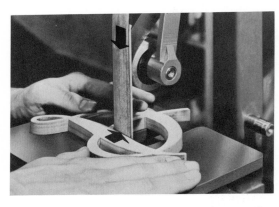

Fig. 46–11. Intricate internal sanding on the sander-grinder.

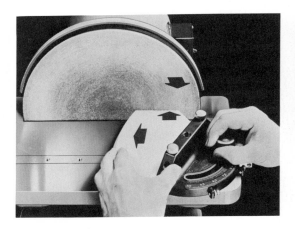

Fig. 46–12. Sanding on the disk sander with the aid of a guide.

Fig. 46–13. Sanding a corner freehand on the disk sander.

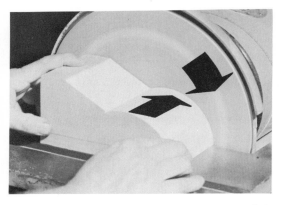

Fig. 46–14. Dressing an edge on the disk sander.

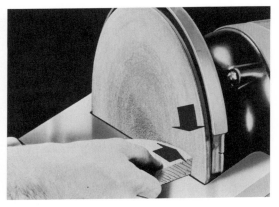

Fig. 46–15. Sanding a bevel freehand on the disk sander. Note the table has been set (adjusted) to the desired angle.

ment should be at 90 degrees to the sanding belt, unless a bevel is being smoothed.

2. Be certain that the belt has the correct grit of abrasive.

3. Move the work slowly on the table or against the fence, to get an even smoothness (Figs. 46–7 through 46–9).

4. Turn off the power when finished.

SANDING ON THE SANDER-GRINDER

1. Adjust the table for the desired angle of sanding.

2. Make certain the belt has the correct grit of abrasive.

3. Move the board slowly on the table against the sanding belt. This machine is especially suitable for intricate and small sanding jobs (Figs. 46–10 and 46–11).

4. Turn off the power.

SANDING ON THE DISK SANDER

1. Adjust the table for the correct angle of sanding.

2. Check that the disk abrasive is of the correct grit.

3. Move the board slowly on the table in making contact with the revolving disk. Feed the board into the disk on the *down* side of the rotation (Figs. 46–12 through 46–15).

4. Turn off the power.

Fig. 46–16. Sanding on the spindle sander.

Fig. 46–17. Sanding a 90-foot laminated beam with a floor sander.

SANDING ON THE OSCILLATING ROTARY SPINDLE SANDER

1. Make certain that the sanding sleeve has the correct grit of abrasive.

2. Move the work slowly on the table and against the spindle (Fig. 46–16).

3. When you have finished, turn off the power.

Figure 46–17 illustrates how sanding is performed on a 90-foot laminated beam with a portable floor sander. This is a view of a modern wood laminating plant.

Discussion Topics

1. Name the five basic types of sanding machines illustrated and described in this unit.

2. List three important parts of each type, and give the uses of each.

3. What is the purpose of the alignment and tracking controls of the belt table sander and the abrasive belt finishing machine?

4. Of what purpose is the idler pulley on the sander-grinder?

5. Which types of floor-model sanding machines are in your school shop or laboratory?

6. List six safety rules to observe when using sanding machines.

7. What is meant by the term "oscillating rotary spindle sander"?

8. List and describe other types of sanding machines used in some of the wood products industries of your community.

SECTION 5/ FINISHING

unit

47

Selecting finishing materials

A fine finish on furniture and cabinetwork improves appearance and increases value. It is therefore important to study the different kinds of finishing materials and woods. Before a finish can be applied, however, all exposed surfaces, edges, and ends of the wood must be smoothly scraped and sandpapered.

EQUIPMENT AND MATERIALS

Equipment and materials used to put on finishes are brushes, spraying equipment, sandpaper, linseed oil, turpentine, alcohol, steel wool, pumice stone, rottenstone, rubbing oil, lacquer thinner, synthetic thinning agents, and wax. Such materials as stains, bleaches, wood filler, shellac, varnish, lacquer, lacquer thinner, sealer, paint, and enamel are described in other units in this section. Spray-gun equipment is described further in Unit 55.

Brushes. Use a good brush to get a high-quality finish. A good brush with bristles set in rubber will hold paint or varnish better than a cheap one.

When brushes are not in use, keep them in a solvent which is a thinner for the finish being applied. Alcohol is a solvent for shellac, turpentine for enamel or varnish, linseed oil for exterior paint, and lacquer thinner for lacquer.

The bristles of a brush should be kept straight. Drill a hole through the handle, put a wire through the hole, and suspend the brush in a can.

When a brush is not to be used for a period of time, clean it in the same solvent or thinner used for the finish you have applied. Solvents such as lacquer thinner, varnish remover, or detergent brush cleaners are helpful in cleaning brushes thoroughly.

Linseed Oil. This is a product of flaxseed. It may be used to bring out the rich color of walnut, mahogany, and cedar. When using it to bring out the color of these woods, mix two-thirds linseed oil with one-third turpentine. Apply it with a cloth, swab, or brush. Linseed oil mixed and applied in this manner will penetrate deep into the wood.

This application may take the place of stain. Make a sampling on a scrap of appropriate wood to find out whether you can get the desired color tone. Linseed oil is also used to bring out the color and grain on gunstocks. Danish oil may also be used to bring out color and grain.

Turpentine. Turpentine comes from the sap of the longleaf pine tree. After much processing it is refined to an inflammable liquid. It is used as a thinner in paints, enamels, and varnishes, and can be used for cleaning the brush.

Alcohol. Alcohol is used principally for thinning shellac. It is made from ethyl and wood alcohol. In addition, you will find it useful for cleaning brushes used in applying shellac.

Steel Wool. Steel wool is available in rolls or pads. Grades vary from No. 3/0

Fig. 47-1. Finishing requires the utmost care in the selection of the correct materials and of suitable color tones.

Fig. 47–2. Finishers in furniture manufacturing plants constantly test finishes for resistance and reaction to the wearing elements encountered in everyday use. This test is referred to as the "garbage test;" it measures resistance to different household products. *(Drexel Furniture Company.)*

(very fine) to No. 3 (coarse). It is sometimes used instead of sandpaper for rubbing down between coats of finish.

Pumice Stone. Pumice stone is a light colored powdered substance made from lava. The most suitable grades for rubbing finishes are No. FF and No. FFF. It is mixed with a rubbing or paraffin oil or with water and then applied.

Rottenstone. This dark gray powdered material is produced from shale. It is a much finer abrasive than pumice stone. Mixed with a rubbing or paraffin oil it produces a smoother final finish than pumice stone.

Rubbing Oil. Rubbing oil, used with pumice or rottenstone, may be either a petroleum or a paraffin oil. The latter is preferred.

Wax. Wax is available in liquid or paste form. The latter makes a heavier, more durable final coating. Both are made from a base of beeswax, carnauba wax, paraffin, and turpentine. A waxed surface must be renewed periodically to be effective.

WOODS AND APPROPRIATE FINISHES

You should select the proper finish for the wood used in your project (Figs. 47–1 through 47–3). Learn the types of finishes recommended for open- and close-grained woods.

Open-grained Woods. These include oak, mahogany, and walnut. The three kinds mentioned are the most common open-grained woods. Their finish may be natural or stained. They require a paste wood filler rubbed in for a smooth-finished surface. Any of these woods can be bleached effectively.

Oak can be finished in more ways than other open-grained woods. It lends itself to the two-toned, limed, or blond finishes.

Mahogany can have a natural finish or be stained to a brown or red tone. Always test a scrap piece for the desired color.

Walnut is one of the most beautiful cabinet woods. It should not be stained darker than its natural color. Apply water stain to the sap, or light, streaks only.

Close-grained Woods. These woods include alder, birch, cherry, fir, gum, maple, pine, and poplar. They do not require a paste wood filler.

Alder is an inexpensive west-coast species which resembles poplar. It works and stains easily.

Birch is a fine wood for cabinet- and furniture-making. It is used in furniture where blond finishes are desired.

Cherry is a hardwood which takes a finish well. It is one of the finest cabinet woods in America.

Fir may be stained with the various oak stains or finished in natural tones. It is also often painted or enameled.

Gumwood may be stained to imitate walnut or mahogany. Red gum is often finished in its beautiful natural tone.

Maple, finished in its natural shade, is a beautiful light gold. It is ideal for blond finishes. Maple can be colored with water stain.

Pine serves as an excellent base for paint and enamel finishes. It is used extensively in general cabinet trim.

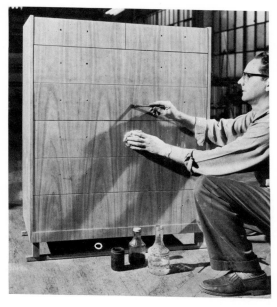

Fig. 47–3. It is necessary to color sap portions of some wood surfaces to obtain uniformly-toned finishes. Expert finishing is a real art, and furniture manufacturers often have men whose research efforts are directed toward producing more pleasing and longer-lasting finishes. *(Baker Furniture Company.)*

Poplar is used in the furniture industry because it can be stained easily to imitate mahogany or walnut. Poplar takes a paint or enamel finish perhaps better than any other wood.

Discussion Topics

1. List three reasons for applying finishes on wood.
2. From what materials are furniture waxes made?
3. From what is linseed oil made?
4. What is the source of turpentine?
5. From what is pumice stone made?
6. What is rottenstone?
7. List four open-grained woods.
8. How might you color walnut sap streaks to match the remainder of the board?
9. List seven close-grained woods.
10. Which woods lend themselves to blond finishes?
11. What woods are especially suitable for paint or enamel finishes?

unit

48

Finishing guides

Procedure guides for applying finishes on various types of woods and for obtaining desired color tones are given in this unit. You can follow these step-by-step suggestions and then refer to specific units for detailed instructions about each finishing process.

VARNISHING WALNUT, MAHOGANY, OAK, OR OTHER OPEN-GRAINED WOODS

1. Sand all surfaces, edges, and ends with fine sand- or garnet paper (Units 27, 35, and 46). Dust the surfaces.

2. Apply stain, if desired (Unit 49). Allow it to dry for 12 hours or overnight. Walnut and mahogany often need only a coat of hot linseed oil cut with turpentine to bring out the color and the grain.

3. Brush on a shellac wash coat (1 part shellac to 7 parts alcohol). See Unit 52. Dry at least 1 hour. This coat serves as a primary filler.

4. Sand with extra fine sand- or garnet paper. Dust.

5. Fill with paste wood filler colored to match the finish (Unit 50). Wipe off clean. Allow to dry 24 to 48 hours.

6. Brush on a coat of cut white shellac (dilute 1 part of Four Pound Cut shellac with 1 part alcohol). See Unit 52. Allow to dry at least 24 hours.

7. Sand smooth with extra fine sand- or garnet paper or with fine steel wool.

8. Brush on the first coat of cabinet rubbing varnish (see Unit 53). Thin this 1 part turpentine to 7 parts varnish. Dry at least 24 hours.

9. Sand with extra fine sand- or garnet paper.

10. Brush on the second coat of varnish as it comes from the can. Dry at least 48 hours.

11. Sand with No. 500, or very fine, waterproof paper and water. Allow it to dry for at least 12 hours.

12. Brush on a third coat of the same varnish. Dry 3 to 4 days.

13. Rub the finish with a pumice stone and water paste.

14. Rub with a paste of rottenstone and water or oil.

15. Wax, if desired.

VARNISHING BIRCH, BEECH, MAPLE, OR OTHER CLOSE-GRAINED WOODS

Follow steps 1 through 4, and 6 through 15 of "Varnishing Walnut, Mahogany, Oak, or Other Open-grained Woods." Wood filler is not applied to close-grained woods; therefore leave out step 5.

LACQUERING WALNUT, MAHOGANY, OAK, OR OTHER OPEN-GRAINED WOODS

1. Follow steps 1 through 5, "Varnishing Walnut, Mahogany, Oak, or Other Open-grained Woods."

2. Spray on one coat of sanding sealer (Unit 55). Dry at least 1 hour.

3. Spray on one coat of clear lacquer. Dry at least 2 hours.

4. Sand lightly with very fine sand- or garnet paper.

5. Spray on a second coat of clear lacquer. Dry at least 4 hours.

6. Sand lightly with very fine sand- or garnet paper.

7. Spray on a third coat of clear gloss, semigloss, or flat lacquer. Allow it to dry overnight.

8. Rub to a satin finish. Lacquer can be rubbed with wet-dry paper and then smoothed with rubbing compound and oil. (Wet-dry paper is a special kind of sandpaper that gives a smoother finish when moistened and used with water.) Clean the surface and then wax.

LACQUERING BIRCH, BEECH, MAPLE, OR OTHER CLOSE-GRAINED WOODS

1. Stain with an oil stain (Unit 49). Dry at least 3 hours.

2. Spray on sanding sealer (Unit 55). Dry at least 1 hour.

3. Sand with very fine sand- or garnet paper.

4. Repeat steps 5 through 8, "Lacquering Walnut, Mahogany, Oak, or Other Open-grained Woods."

PRODUCING A BLEACHED (BLOND) FINISH

1. Bleach the wood (Unit 51). Use any good commercial bleach. Dry overnight.

2. Sand with very fine sand- or garnet paper.

3. Brush or spray on a wash coat of shellac (1 part shellac to 7 parts alcohol). See Unit 52. Dry at least 1 hour.

4. Sand lightly with very fine sand- or garnet paper.

5. Apply natural or white wood filler (Unit 50). Rub in thoroughly. Dry at least 24 hours.

6. Finish with two or more coats of water-white lacquer.

7. Rub to a satin finish.

BRUSHING OR SPRAYING FOR A COLONIAL MAPLE FINISH

1. Stain with antique maple stain (either non-grain-raising or water stain). See Unit 49.

2. Brush on a shellac wash coat (Unit 52). Dry at least 1 hour.

3. Sand smooth with extra fine sand- or garnet paper. Dust.

4. Brush or spray on a coat of cut white shellac (1 part Four Pound Cut shellac with 1 part alcohol). Allow it to dry for at least 24 hours. Sanding sealer may be used instead of shellac.

5. Sand smooth with extra fine sand- or garnet paper.

6. Apply two coats of cabinet varnish or clear lacquer (Units 53 and 55). Sand smooth between coats.

7. Sand with No. 700, or extra fine, waterproof paper, and use rubbing oil or water as a lubricant.

8. Clean the project.

9. Wax very carefully with a brown paste wax.

FINISHING PHILIPPINE MAHOGANY

1. Stain the wood reddish brown or brown, if desired (Unit 49). Philippine mahogany finished without stain is also very attractive. Allow stained wood to dry at least 12 hours.

2. Brush or spray on a wash coat of shellac, lacquer, or sanding sealer (Units 52 and 55). Dry at least 1 hour.

3. Sand with fine sand- or garnet paper.

4. Fill with tinted brown paste filler (Unit 50). Allow to dry for at least 24 hours.

5. Seal with cut white shellac or sanding sealer (1 part shellac to 1 part alcohol, or 1 part sanding sealer to 1 part lacquer thinner). (Units 52 and 55). Allow to dry for at least 2 hours.

6. Brush or spray on mahogany wiping stain. Wipe off, blending the highlights with a soft brush or cloth. Dry at least 4 hours.

7. Brush on two coats of varnish, or spray on three coats of clear lacquer. Rub between coats with extra fine sand- or garnet

paper. Dry (1 hour for lacquer or 24 hours for varnish) between coats.

8. Rub to a satin finish.

DANISH OIL FINISH

1. Sand the raw wood, using very fine sandpaper, to obtain the desired smooth final surface.

2. If you wish to alter the color of the wood by staining, apply an alcohol-base wood stain, using a clean cloth or brush. Let it dry five minutes, then repeat the application for darker shades (Unit 54), if desired.

3. Saturate all wood surfaces with a penetrating coat of Danish oil. Apply it with either a brush, sponge, roller, cloth, or spray gun.

4. Allow the Danish oil to penetrate the surface of the wood for 30 minutes. Wipe off the surplus oil with a clean cloth. Rub with the grain of the wood.

5. Put on second and third coats of Danish oil, if desired, using the same method of application.

6. Allow the final coat of wiped surface to dry at least four hours, or overnight.

7. Rub the dried oil surface vigorously, using a hard-textured cloth to produce a semihardened finish to the wood fiber.

8. Apply two, and preferably more, coats of a good grade carnauba paste furniture wax. Allow each coat to dry 20 or 30 minutes. Rub each coat smooth with a soft cloth. The final finished surface will have a semisatin luster, and will last for years.

unit
49
Staining

Stain is put on wood to produce a desired color effect. Much manufactured furniture is made from inexpensive woods and then stained to resemble walnut or mahogany. Woods such as walnut, mahogany, and cedar have sufficient natural color. They will not need staining. On the contrary, they need only a coat of hot linseed oil cut with turpentine or a coat of Danish oil to bring out the richness of the natural color.

Oil, water, and alcohol are the bases of three widely used stains.

OIL STAIN

Oil stain is easy to apply. It is available in many colors and produces an excellent finish. Generally it will not raise the grain of the wood. A disadvantage is that the colors sometimes tend to fade. When you apply oil stain to end grain, first give the end grain a coat of linseed oil. This prevents it from turning many shades darker than the surface and edges.

To apply oil stain:

1. Select the color of stain desired.

2. Pour some stain into a cup or other open container.

3. To test the color, brush the stain on a scrap of the type of wood you will be staining. If it is too dark, lighten it by adding turpentine.

4. Apply a coat of linseed oil to all exposed end grain. This is important because end grain absorbs more stain. Linseed oil will prevent blackening of the end grain.

Fig. 49-1. Applying stain with a brush.

Fig. 49-2. Wiping off surplus stain.

5. Apply the stain with a medium-size brush to the entire project. Brush with long, even strokes (Fig. 49-1). You can get the same results by using a cloth instead of a brush.

6. Wipe off the surplus stain quickly with a cloth (Fig. 49-2).

7. Allow the stain to dry overnight.

WATER STAIN

Water stain brings out the full beauty of wood. It is made by dissolving a powdered aniline dye in hot water. The chief objection to it is that it raises the grain of the wood. It must therefore be resanded before further finishing can be done. For a more uniform finish, sponge the wood with water, allow it to dry, and sand it before water stain is put on. This reduces the amount of sanding required after staining.

To apply water stain:

1. Sponge the wood lightly with water. Allow it to dry at least 2 hours.

2. Sand the dried area with fine sand- or garnet paper. Sand *with* the grain.

3. Wipe off the dust with a brush or cloth.

4. Mix the color with water in a cup or other open container. Follow the directions given by the manufacturer.

5. Test the color of the stain on a piece of scrap wood. Wait until it dries thoroughly to see its true color.

6. Apply the stain evenly with a medium-size brush to the entire project (Fig. 49-1). Brush it on with long, even strokes. Surplus water stain is not wiped from the surface. All brush marks will show if the stain is not applied evenly. Allow it to dry overnight.

7. Sand lightly with fine sand- or garnet paper to smooth raised grain.

8. After the sanding is completed, the project should be cleaned thoroughly.

ALCOHOL STAIN

Alcohol-base wood stains come in a wide range of colors. One of the newer stains of

Fig. 49–3. Alcohol-base wood stain is easy to apply with a cloth pad.

this type, manufactured by Watco, has been mentioned favorably in wood-products and finishing magazines. It is applied by wiping with a cloth, brushing, spraying, or diping. When the alcohol-base stain is sprayed on, the pressure of the spray gun should be much less than that used for spraying lacquer.

This particular product is a non-grain-raising stain, having even penetration with the clarity of water stain; it has a fast drying time of five minutes. It also possesses high fade resistance. When a final rubbed-oil finished effect is desired on certain woods, it is advisable to stain them first.

To apply alcohol stain:

1. Sand the raw wood to a very fine surface.

2. Select the color of stain desired. Check the color chart recommended by the manufacturer.

3. Shake the container of stain, and then pour some into a cup or other open vessel.

4. Brush or wipe the stain on a scrap piece of the same wood as the object to be stained to check the color.

5. Apply the stain with a medium-size brush or with a cloth (Fig. 49–3). Rub in the direction of the wood grain.

6. Allow 5 minutes for the stain to penetrate and dry. If you wish to darken or intensify the wood tone, recoat the surface with more stain. Allow this application to dry at least 45 minutes before applying further finish.

Discussion Topics

1. What is the purpose of stain?
2. Mention at least three woods on which stain is not necessary.
3. What are the three general types of stain?
4. Why should you sponge wood lightly with water before you apply water stain?
5. Which type of stain must have the surplus wiped off after it is applied?

unit
50

Applying wood filler

Wood filler in liquid or paste form is used to fill the pores of wood to form a smooth surface. Apply the filler after the shellac or lacquer wash coat. Open-grained woods such as ash, mahogany, oak, and walnut must be filled.

Paste wood filler is made from silex, a ground silicon, mixed with linseed oil, japan drier, and turpentine. The filler should be colored to the desired tint of the final finish. Colors in oil should be used to tint it.

Apply the filler with a stiff-bristle brush of medium width. Wipe it off with small pieces of burlap. Use waste cloth or rags for final rubbing.

To apply wood filler:

1. Mix the filler to a thin paste with turpentine or japan drier. This assumes that you are using the commercial product, which is usually very thick.

2. Add the desired color in oil. Stir the paste, making sure that it is thoroughly mixed.

3. Apply the filler on the exposed surfaces of the project with a stiff-bristle brush (Fig. 50–1). Cloth, burlap, or coarse toweling may be used instead of a brush, if you desire. Rub the filler into the wood by brushing or wiping *across* the grain. This forces the filler into the pores.

4. Continue to rub the paste filler into the pores of the wood with the palm of the hand. Work across the grain in a circular motion.

Fig. 50–1. Applying wood filler with a brush.

Fig. 50–2. Rubbing filler into the pores, and wiping off the surplus.

5. When the filler looks dull, wipe the surplus off across the grain with burlap.

6. Wipe the project with the grain, using a clean cotton cloth (Fig. 50–2). This removes cross grain strokes.

7. Clean the filler from corners and grooves with a sharp pointed stick.

8. Allow the filled project to dry 24 to 48 hours before you proceed with further finish.

unit

51

Bleaching

Bleaching is the process of removing the natural color in the wood. Bleaching must be done carefully with the proper materials to avoid injuring the wood fibers. A bleached finish is sometimes referred to as blond, limed, or wheat.

CAUTION: Be careful when you apply bleaching material. Wear rubber gloves, protect your eyes with goggles, and wear a rubber apron.

Bleaches are strong chemicals. If the bleaching liquid gets on your skin, wash it off *immediately* with soap and water.

The most satisfactory bleaches are commercial two-solution liquids. These are most often applied separately. Read thoroughly the directions which come on the containers. Follow them.

Oxalic acid crystals diluted in water form a fairly effective bleaching solution. Try one tablespoon of crystals to one cup of warm water. If the result is not noticeable, mix a stronger solution.

To get a bleached finish:

1. Sand all surfaces smooth with very fine sandpaper.

2. Prepare the bleach according to the directions on the container. If you use a two-solution liquid, study the instructions to know which solution is applied first.

3. Apply bleach to the surfaces by brushing, swabbing, or spraying. Allow to dry at least 2 hours. Swabbing with a cloth wrapped around a stick is satisfactory for small surfaces. If you brush on the bleach, do not use a good brush because the bleaching liquid damages bristles.

4. Sponge the project lightly with water. Allow it to dry overnight.

5. Sand lightly with very fine finishing abrasive paper. Remove all dust. If the bleached surface is not light enough, repeat steps 3 and 4.

6. Brush or spray on a shellac or lacquer wash coat. Use 1 part shellac to 7 parts alcohol or 1 part lacquer to 6 parts thinner. (See Units 52 and 55.) Dry at least 1 hour.

7. Rub in natural or white wood filler (see Unit 50.)

8. Spray on the sanding sealer coat (see Unit 55). The bleached effect can be increased by tinting the sanding sealer lightly with lacquer. Be careful not to put too much in.

9. Brush on varnish, or spray on a clear bleaching lacquer (see Unit 53, pages 245 and 246, and Unit 55, pages 249 to 251).

10. Rub the final finish to a dull, semigloss, or gloss finish. This depends upon the finish you want and the compound used in rubbing.

Discussion Topics

1. What precautions must you take when you work with bleaching liquids?
2. Define bleaching.
3. How long should a bleached surface dry?

4. Why is it necessary to sand the bleached surface lightly?
5. How can bleaching be made more effective when you apply sanding sealer?

---

unit

52

Applying shellac

Shellac, one of the oldest finishing materials, has been used since the sixteenth century. It is the product of an insect found in the East Indies and Asiatic countries. This insect feeds on a resinous material and leaves a secretion on the tree. After several generations, the secretion forms a coating. This is stripped off by hand and separated from impurities such as twigs and other foreign matter. It is then heated, strained, and processed into sheets. These sheets are later further refined and dissolved in denatured alcohol to form the liquid shellac.

Shellac produces a good finish. It is easy to apply, dries rapidly, and rubs out smoothly to make a fairly hard finish. The disadvantage of shellac finish is that it is not waterproof.

Shellac comes in two colors, white and orange. Both are exactly the same except that the white shellac has been bleached and is therefore more expensive. White shellac is used as a sealer and a natural finish. Orange shellac is often used as a primer for painting and for finishing patterns in pattern making.

A good mixture is 4 pounds of shellac to 1 gallon of alcohol. This is labeled *Four Pound Cut.* Alcohol is used with shellac

243

Fig. 52–1. Brushing on shellac.

as a thinner and it is also used for cleaning the brush.

To apply shellac:

1. Dust the surface. Make certain that the stain or linseed oil already applied is completely dry.

2. Pour a small amount of white shellac into an open container, such as a cup.

3. Thin the shellac for a wash coat (1 part shellac to 7 parts alcohol).

4. Brush on wash coat. Dry at least 1 hour.

5. Rub the wash coat with fine steel wool.

6. Apply filler for open-grained woods (Unit 50).

7. Thin some shellac until it is approximately one-half alcohol. Stir the mixture.

8. Brush the thinned shellac on the entire project. Apply it evenly and quickly because it dries rapidly (Fig. 52–1).

9. Allow the shellac coat to dry at least 24 hours.

10. Rub smooth with very fine sand- or garnet paper or with fine steel wool.

11. Wipe the surfaces clean. Use a dry cotton cloth or one that has been made tacky, or sticky, with a few drops of shellac.

12. It you desire a final shellac finish, put on another coat of two-thirds shellac and one-third alcohol. Dry at least 24 hours.

13. Rub smooth with very fine (No.000) steel wool.

14. Put on a coat of good furniture wax. Allow it to dry 20 minutes. Rub it to a luster with a clean cotton cloth. This makes a relatively hard finish.

Discussion Topics

1. What are the principal ingredients of shellac?
2. Explain how shellac is made.
3. What is the purpose of shellac?
4. When should a wash coat of shellac be used?
5. What is the essential difference between white and orange shellac, aside from the color?
6. Why does shellac dry rapidly?
7. What is meant by Four Pound Cut in a shellac mixture?

unit
53

Applying a hand-rubbed varnish finish

Varnish preserves wood surfaces. Apply it either directly to the wood or over a surface that has been filled and sealed with shellac. It can be rubbed either with pumice or rottenstone and combined with either water or oil to give a beautiful luster. Originally all good varnishes were made from imported fossil gum. However, during the last few years, synthetic resins have replaced the original basic material.

Transparent varnish is available commercially. Or varnish may be colored to make varnish stain. Varnish stains are not suitable for fine-finished furniture because the stain blurs the natural-grain effect of the wood.

Spar quick-drying varnish is very popular. It is tough, waterproof, and heat resistant. It dries to a hard, durable, high-gloss finish and can be rubbed satisfactorily.

The quality of a varnish finish depends upon the grade of the varnish used, the evenness of application, and the drying conditions. Varnish should be applied in a room with a temperature of about 70 degrees Fahrenheit. The room should be as free of dust as possible.

APPLYING VARNISH

To apply varnish with a brush:

1. Check the surfaces to be varnished and make certain that they are free from dust. All previous treatment should be thoroughly dry.

2. Pour a small amount of varnish into a cup or other container (Fig. 53–1). Follow directions on the can for thinning the varnish.

3. Thin the first coat of varnish with turpentine if the directions on the container advise it.

4. Put on the first coat of varnish with a good grade of fine, long-bristle brush (see Fig. 52–1). Flow it on evenly with long strokes. Varnish has a tendency to run. Look at your work in a good light and brush out any runs which develop.

5. Allow the first coat to dry at least 24 hours.

6. Rub the varnished surface lightly with very fine wet-dry sand- or garnet paper and water. The rubbed-varnish surface will be a milky color until the next coat is put

Fig. 53–1. Remove excess varnish across the wire in the container.

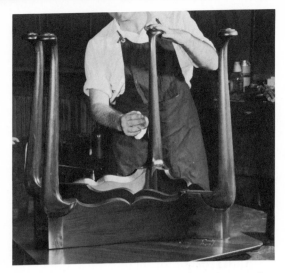

Fig. 53–2. Rubbing a varnished surface, using a cloth pad with a mixture of pumice stone and rubbing oil.

Fig. 53–3. Mechanically rubbing a final finish on the exotic Kevazingo paneling installed at the Lincoln Center Metropolitan Opera House. These panels have a particle board core and are fire-retardant. *(U. S. Plywood Corporation.)*

on. This sanding smooths the varnish for the next coat.

7. Apply two more coats of varnish, or more as necessary, without thinning. Sand all but the last coat as described in step 6. Allow a drying time of 48 hours between additional coats.

FINISHING VARNISHED SURFACES

To rub varnished surfaces:

1. Prepare a thin paste of No. FFF pumice stone and either rubbing oil, paraffin oil, or water.

2. Rub this on the varnished surface, back and forth in the direction of the grain. Use a soft pad (Fig. 53–2). A piece of felt or a blackboard eraser is excellent for rubbing finish. Continue until all traces of brush marks and other blemishes are smoothed.

3. Wipe the surface clean to remove the pumice-stone mixture.

4. Prepare a thin paste of rottenstone and either rubbing oil, paraffin oil, or water.

5. Rub this on the varnished surface as described in step 2. A fine luster and sheen will be the result of hand rubbing. It is also possible to employ a commercial rubbing compound instead of the mixtures described above (Fig. 53–3).

6. Apply a coat of high-grade paste furniture wax. Allow it to dry for fifteen or twenty minutes. Polish with a clean cotton cloth.

Discussion Topics

1. What is the main purpose of varnish?
2. Why is varnish stain not desirable for high-quality finishes?
3. What is used for thinning varnish?
4. Why is spar varnish popular?
5. List ten items on which spar varnish should be used.

6. How long should a varnish coat dry and harden between the first and second applications?
7. Why do you use pumice stone to rub down a varnish finish?
8. What is the purpose of rubbing with rottenstone?

unit
54

Penetrating wood finishes

Penetrating, or wipe-on, wood finishes are very popular because they can be applied with relative ease. They also possess satisfying, lasting qualities. This type finish adds greatly to the beauty of the wood surface, and makes a durable, wear-resistant finish. It is very suitable on interior paneling, trim, and furniture. The three types described are *Danish* penetrating resin-oil, *Deft* sealer, and a *floor-seal* finish.

Watco Danish oil has a resin base which, in one application, seals, primes, preserves, hardens, and finishes. It is available in several shades to give different tones in walnut and mahogany woods. It penetrates deep into the wood before solidifying and becoming a part of it, thereby making the wood 25 percent harder. Several applications of the oil, and a final polishing with paste wax produce a soft luster of deep sheen.

Deft sealer and finish is a clear product which dries dust-free in 30 minutes. It is considered a very excellent semigloss, penetrating, water-repellent finish which also seals the wood pores. It is a synthetic product which may be applied easily to obtain expert results. Brushes can be cleaned with lacquer thinner.

Floor-seal finishes have taken the place of varnish on many types of surfaces, such as gymnasium floors. They are also satisfactory on furniture and cabinets because of the ease of application and long-wearing, scuff-resistant qualities.

TO APPLY A DANISH OIL FINISH

1. Prepare the surface by final sanding, using fine garnet or sandpaper.
2. Stain and/or fill wood surfaces, if desired.
3. Apply Danish oil liberally, flooding and saturating the surface. Use either a brush, spray gun, roller, or cloth pad (Fig. 54–1). Keep the surface wet for 15 or 20 minutes to assure good penetration.
4. Sand the wet surface for 1 or 2 minutes with No. 600 wet or dry silicon carbide paper. This scuff-sanding helps harden the wood surface.
5. Remove all surface oil with a soft, lint-free cloth.
6. Allow the finished surface to dry at least 12 hours.
7. Wipe the finished surface lightly with a rag moistened slightly with Danish oil. Rub it dry.
8. Rub the surface with an open-weave type of cloth to produce a hard finish.

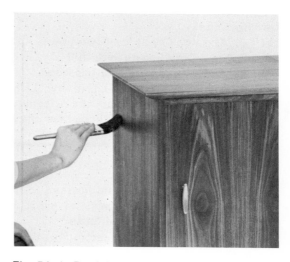

Fig. 54–1. Danish oil finish is easy to apply with either a brush, cloth pad, or roller.

Fig. 54-2. Hand rubbing to a fine finish with 4/0 steel wool.

9. Apply a good grade of paste or liquid carnauba satin wax. Buff (rub) it to a soft luster. The degree of sheen will depend upon the number of successive coats of wax which are applied and rubbed down.

TO APPLY DEFT SEALER AND FINISH

1. Sand the wood smooth with fine garnet or sandpaper.

2. Stain, fill, or use Danish oil on the surface.

3. Stir or shake the contents of the container of finish.

4. Pour a small amount into a small, open receptacle.

5. Apply a full, even coat of the Deft sealer liquid with a brush, cloth pad, roller, or spray gun.

6. Allow to dry at least two hours.

7. Sand lightly with No. 400 abrasive paper. Sand with the grain of the wood.

8. Apply a second coat of the Deft sealer, if desired. Two coats are adequate to produce a fine finish. Successive ones only tend to produce an uneven finish because each coat loosens the previous one.

9. Rub down the final coat with 4/0 steel wool or rubbing compound (Fig. 54-2).

10. Apply one or more coats of wax to give the appearance of a hand-rubbed finish.

TO APPLY A FLOOR-SEAL FINISH

1. Check the surfaces to be finished and make certain that they are free from dust.

2. Pour a small amount of penetrating finish into a cup or other container.

3. Apply the finish liberally to the surface with a cloth.

4. Allow it to dry for about 20 minutes, then wipe the excess from the surfaces with a clean, dry cloth.

5. Allow it to dry for at least 3 hours. Overnight is better.

6. Rub the finish with steel wool until it is smooth (see Fig. 54-2).

7. Apply a second coat in the same manner as the first. If the wood is porous or open-grained, apply paste wood filler before the second coat of penetrating wood finish is put on. See Unit 50, *Applying Wood Filler.* Allow to dry overnight.

8. Put on three more coats at least 3 hours apart. Apply each coat in the same manner as the first, rubbing each smooth with steel wool. Let the final coat dry overnight.

9. Rub the final coat smooth with fine steel wool, and then apply a coat of paste wax.

Discussion Topics

1. Define a penetrating wood finish.
2. What are three advantages in using a penetrating type of wood finish?
3. Name three types of penetrating wood finishes.
4. Why is the Danish oil finish so popular?
5. Describe the procedures for applying Danish oil, Deft synthetic, and floor-seal penetrating finishes.

---

unit

55

Spraying lacquer

Lacquer is ideal for finishing furniture. It dries quickly, so successive coats may be put on within a few hours. It is available clear or in a variety of colors. True lacquer was discovered in China about 3000 B.C. Eastern lacquer is the natural sap of the Asiatic sumac. No other substance, except perhaps a coloring agent, is normally added to the natural juice.

THIN LACQUER BEFORE SPRAYING

Lacquer is thinned with a commercial lacquer thinner. Each manufacturer has a special type of thinner for his product. Lacquer is manufactured, to produce a gloss, semi-gloss, or dull finish. It should be applied with a spray gun for best results (Fig. 55–1). Always read and follow the directions which are on the container.

EQUIPMENT FOR SPRAYING

A spray gun and a stationary or portable compressor make up the special equipment needed (see Figs. 55–1 and 55–2). Applying lacquer with a spray gun requires skill. *Always* clean the nozzle and other parts *before* and *after* using the spray gun. Other types of finishes, such as varnish, shellac, paint, and enamel, can also be put on with a spray gun, but they must be thinned considerably to be sprayed.

CAUTION: Adequate ventilation must be provided when spraying. Remember that lacquer is highly flammable; therefore it should be stored in closed containers.

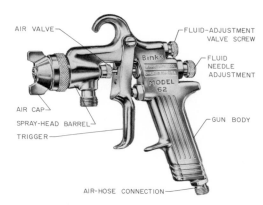

AIR VALVE
FLUID-ADJUSTMENT VALVE SCREW
FLUID NEEDLE ADJUSTMENT
MODEL 62
AIR CAP
SPRAY-HEAD BARREL
TRIGGER
GUN BODY
AIR-HOSE CONNECTION

Fig. 55–2. Parts of the spray gun.

Fig. 55–1. A portable compressor and spray gun.

Fig. 55–3. Straining sanding sealer.

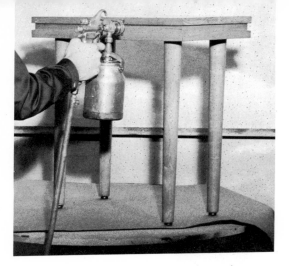

Fig. 55-4. Spraying sanding sealer, or lacquer, horizontally on the rail or apron.

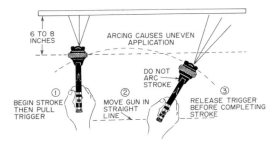

Fig. 55-5. The proper pattern for spraying.

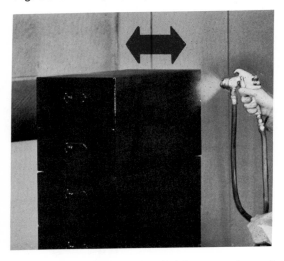

Fig. 55-6. Smooth color finishes may be put on with a spray gun.

APPLY SEALER BEFORE LACQUER

Spray lacquer sealer or sanding sealer on the project before applying the first coat of lacquer. This seals the wood as shellac does for varnish.

SPRAYING LACQUER

To apply lacquer with a spray gun:

1. Dust or clean off the sanding which was done in the previous finishing.

2. Pour and strain sufficient sanding sealer into the spray-gun container (Fig. 55-3). Dilute the sealer with an equal amount of thinner. Stir the mixture.

3. Fasten the container to the spray-gun assembly. Make certain all fittings are secure and gaskets tight. Consult the manufacturer's chart or instructions for the particular spray gun you are using to learn its adjustment.

4. Turn on the compressor and regulate the air pressure between 35 and 45 pounds.

5. Pull the trigger of the spray gun and adjust the nozzle. The lacquer mixture should come out in an even mist.

6. Spray by moving the gun from left to right and back again in an even pattern (Figs. 55-4 through 55-6). In vertical spraying, always move from top to bottom.

Note that the air cap is turned differently for horizontal than for vertical motion. This difference gives the proper spray pattern. Always keep the nozzle of the gun the same distance from the work. Dry at least 1 hour.

7. Pour the sealer from the spray-gun can back into the original container.

8. Spray lacquer thinner through the gun to clean it (Fig. 55-7).

9. Sand the sealed surface lightly with very fine sandpaper or garnet paper.

10. Pour lacquer into the spray-gun container. Fill it only one-third full because thinner is to be added.

11. Add lacquer thinner to make a mixture of 1 part lacquer and 1 part thinner. Stir.

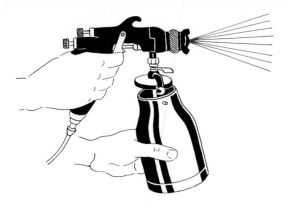

Fig. 55–7. Cleaning a spray gun with lacquer thinner.

Fig. 55–8. The process of touching up and hand rubbing final lacquer finishes requires skill and patience. *(Drexel Furniture Company.)*

12. Fasten the container to the spray gun. Check all connections.

13. Spray one coat of lacquer over the entire project. Follow the same procedure you used in spraying on the sealer (step 6). Allow it to dry for at least 2 hours.

14. Remove the container and pour the remaining lacquer mixture into the original can.

15. Clean the spray gun and the container by spraying lacquer thinner through it (see Fig. 55–7).

16. Sand lightly with very fine sand- or garnet paper.

17. Spray two or more coats of lacquer over the entire project. Thin the lacquer (as in step 11) for each coat. The final coat may be gloss, semigloss, or flat. Since spray coats are thinner than brush coats, more are needed.

18. Allow each coat to dry for at least 4 hours.

19. If desired, rub the final coat with a commercial rubbing compound to a satisfactory smooth finish. This is not necessary in all cases, but will improve the final appearance (Fig. 55–8).

20. Apply a coat of high-grade paste furniture wax. Allow it to dry 20 minutes. Polish with a clean cotton cloth.

Discussion Topics

1. At approximately what date was lacquer first used?
2. What is used as a base to seal wood before you apply a lacquer finish?
3. How is lacquer thinned?
4. What are the essential parts of a spray gun?
5. What should be the approximate air pressure for lacquer spraying?
6. Illustrate and explain the correct way to apply finish with the spray gun.
7. Why are more coats of lacquer needed in spraying to get a smooth finish than when shellac and varnish are brushed on?

unit
56
Painting and enameling

Paint and enamel are protective and decorative coatings for the less expensive woods where a transparent finish may not be desirable. Either paint or enamel can be used satisfactorily as a colorful finish on furniture and cabinets.

Paint is generally applied to exterior surfaces or to projects which are used out of doors. Enamel is suitable for interior trim and projects used in the home. It comes in a gloss, semigloss, or dull (flat) finish.

Enamel usually produces a harder finish than paint because varnish is an ingredient in it. Both paint and enamel are available in many colors. Both can also be bought either in white or tinted with colors ground in oil. The many types of paints and enamels have their own recommended thinners. Read the instructions on the container for the method of thinning and for the manufacturer's suggestions for applying.

To mix and apply paint or enamel:

1. Prepare the surfaces for painting or enameling. They should be properly planed, scraped, and sanded.

2. Read the directions on the container before it is opened. Each manufacturer recommends the correct mixture and method for putting on his paint or enamel. The drying time is also specified.

3. If the directions call for a primer coat, apply it first. Orange shellac also makes a good primer coat.

4. Shake the can thoroughly. Remove the lid and pour off some of the top liquid into another container.

5. Stir the base mixture with a wooden paddle. Add the top liquid to the base mixture a little at a time, and stir until they are thoroughly blended.

6. Add turpentine, linseed oil, or the thinner recommended on the can.

7. Select a suitable brush of high quality with the bristles set in rubber.

8. Dip the brush into the paint so that about three-fourths of the length of the bristles absorbs paint. Press the surplus paint or enamel off on the edge of the can as you remove the brush (Fig. 56–1).

9. Apply the paint or enamel to the surface with long, even strokes (see Fig. 56–2). A little practice determines the proper

Fig. 56–1. Press surplus paint or enamel off on the edge of the container.

Fig. 56–2. Use long, even strokes when applying wood finishes with a brush.

amount to apply to the surface. It should cover smoothly and evenly. Do not allow it to run.

10. Allow the coat to dry thoroughly according to the time given in the directions. Sand smooth with fine sandpaper. Wipe the surface with a clean cloth.

11. Apply a second and a third coat if needed. Do not sand the final coat, because this will dull the finish.

Discussion Topics

1. Where is paint generally used?
2. Where is enamel usually used?
3. What is the purpose of paint? Of enamel?
4. Why does enamel usually produce a harder finish than paint?
5. How would you find the proper thinner to use for either paint or enamel?
6. How are paint and enamel applied?
7. Can paint and enamel be applied with a spray gun?

unit
57

Removing a finish

Protective finishes on furniture and cabinet-work tend to deteriorate (check and crack) with age. Lacquer, shellac, varnish, paint, and enamel finishes, or coatings, can be removed most easily with a commercial remover. The instructions printed on the container should be followed very closely, because they vary according to the manufacturers. The directions given in this unit are of a general nature and apply to most removing solutions.

REMOVING FINISHES

1. Read the instructions on the container carefully.

2. Shake the container thoroughly.

3. Pour a small amount of the liquid or solution into a smaller open container.

Fig. 57-1. Apply paint and varnish remover until the finish begins to swell, bubble, and soften.

254

Fig. 57–2. Scraping off the softened finish.

Fig. 57–3. Wiping off the softened finish with burlap.

4. Apply several coats of remover. Use an inexpensive brush (Fig. 57–1). Put one coat on top of another until the old finish bubbles and gets soft.

5. Remove as much of the finish as possible with a scraper blade (Fig. 57–2).

6. Apply another coat of remover to soften the remaining traces of finish.

7. Rub and wipe off the finish with pieces of burlap and clean rags (Fig. 57–3).

8. After the surface is dry, brush on a thick coat of neutralizing agent, as recommended by the manufacturer of the finish remover. Allow to dry.

9. Scrape and sand the wood surfaces as you would prepare a new project. See Unit 17, *Smoothing a Surface by Scraping*, Unit 27, *Hand Sanding*, Unit 35, *Sanding with Portable Electric Sanders,* and Unit 46, *Sanding on Sanding Machines.*

Discussion Topics

1. Why is it sometimes necessary to refinish furniture?
2. Describe the steps for removing an old finish.
3. Why is it necessary to apply a neutralizer after using some types of paint and varnish removers?
4. Check with your science teacher to find out what chemical reaction takes place when paint and varnish remover is applied.
5. What must be done to cleaned wood surfaces to prepare them for applying a new finish?

unit

58

Materials and tools for upholstering

Basic upholstering information is given in the units of this section. Two types of simple upholstering are described. One is the re-movable slip seat with a webbing base, the other, coil and no-sag springs built in a wooden frame.

MATERIALS

Basic materials used in upholstering are webbing; burlap; various types of stuffing, such as horse, cattle, and hog hair, moss or tow, and foam rubber; cotton; muslin; cambric; sewing twine; spring twine; tacks; steel upholstery springs; and the final upholstering fabric.

Upholstery webbing is made from coarsely woven jute fiber. It comes in various widths and grades; the 3½-inch width is generally satisfactory. Webbing is stretched and tacked across both directions of a slip seat or back to form a flexible base. It is sometimes used across the bottom of a frame for fastening coil springs.

Burlap is a cloth woven from jute yarn. It can be obtained in many widths and weights. The 40-inch width in an 8- to 10½-ounce weight is especially satisfactory for use over springs. This forms a base for the stuffing. It is also used to cover stuffing and rubberized-hair pads.

Stuffing materials made of curled hair from horses, cattle, and hogs are excellent to use in upholstering. These materials are bought by the pound and must be thoroughly separated before use. This is done to remove lumps and foreign matter from the animal hair.

Rubberized hair is available in sheets of different thicknesses, widths, and lengths. Owing to the rubberizing process, these sheets are easily cut and formed to make an excellent base.

Moss is a good stuffing material.

Tow, a fiber of the flax class, is a general-purpose stuffing. It will make a firm pad and is relatively inexpensive.

Foam rubber is a rather expensive material, but makes a very fine base in upholstering. It is available in sheets of almost any thickness and in many sizes. Often thin sheets are used instead of cotton batting. Thick sheets or pads are frequently used in place of the entire spring unit. It can be cut and formed in accordance with the manufacturer's directions, which usually accompany such material. Many upholsterers use a less expensive but satisfactory polyurethane foam plastic padding instead of foam rubber.

Cotton used for upholstering comes in sheets about ¼ inch thick and generally 27 inches wide. It is bought by the roll and is used as padding over the stuffings.

Muslin of the unbleached kind is ideal for the covering underneath the final up-holstery fabric. Standard widths are 36 to 40 inches.

Cambric is a glazed cotton fabric. It is tacked under the bottom of an upholstered seat as a dust cover.

Sewing twine is a thin twine made from flax fiber. It is used for the many sewing operations before the final covering.

Spring twine is used for tying the tops of springs in place. Since all spring work is dependent upon the strength of the twine, it is important that this material be of the best grade. Six-ply Italian hemp should be used for tying furniture coil springs.

Tacks used in upholstering vary according to their purpose. The upholsterer's tack has a smooth, flat head. An 8- to 10-ounce one may be used for tacking spring twine. The 4- to 6-ounce tack fastens down burlap, muslin, and the final covering. The 2- to 3-ounce tack is used to fasten cambric under the seat.

The tack for fastening webbing is the webbing tack. It is similar to the upholsterer's tack except that little points project from the shank. The 12- to 14-ounce tack is desirable.

Gimp tacks have small, round heads and are ideal where tack heads may be visible. Many upholsterers, however, prefer to fasten gimp for final trim with hot animal glue used sparingly to ensure neatness.

Steel upholstery springs are made in a variety of styles and sizes. The coil spring with both ends open is most used for seat work. Each size is available with a wide or a narrow center. Those with wide centers are softer than the narrow, twisted type. The standard sizes vary from No. 00 (4 inches high) to No. 6 (14 inches high), and are generally sold by the pound.

Final coverings may be chosen from a wide selection of many varieties and colors. Mohairs, velours, and tapestries have been standard for many years and are relatively easy to handle. Leathers, leatherettes, and

Fig. 58–1. A 7-ounce magnetic-head upholstering hammer.

Fig. 58–2. Stuffing regulator.

Fig. 58–3. Dual-pointed straight needle.

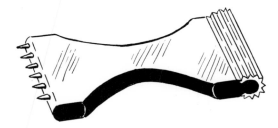

Fig. 58–4. Curved needle.

Fig. 58–5. Webbing stretcher.

Fig. 58–6. Heavy-duty fabric shears.

plastic fabrics are colorful and serviceable, but they are more difficult to manipulate.

TOOLS

The tools used most often in upholstery are the magnetic tack hammer, regulator, double-pointed straight needle, curved needle, webbing stretcher, fabric shears, and tack claw.

The *tack hammer* (Fig. 58–1) is the most important tool. The double-faced type with one face magnetic is preferred.

Regulators (Fig. 58–2) range in size from 6 to 12 inches. They are used to smooth out roughness in stuffing and to shape edges.

The *straight needle* (Fig. 58–3), pointed at both ends, is used for sewing back and forth without turning. One about 8 inches long is suitable.

Curved needles (Fig. 58–4) are pointed at one end and range from 1½ to 10 inches in diameter. The 3-inch curved needle is satisfactory for most purposes. It is used in sewing through flat surfaces where all sewing must be done from one side.

The *webbing stretcher* (Fig. 58–5), measuring approximately 4 by 6 inches, may be made in the laboratory. You should pad the end which does not have teeth.

Shears (Fig. 58–6) should be strong enough to cut twine and coarse fabrics.

A *tack claw* (Fig. 58–7) is used to remove tacks when necessary.

If you do much upholstery work, you should have a few *trestles*, or padded sawhorses, on which to set projects while upholstering.

Fig. 58–7. Tack claw.

1. List six essential tools used in upholstering.
2. What sizes of tacks should you use for fastening the following: (*a*) webbing, (*b*) spring-tying twine, (*c*) burlap, (*d*) final covering, and (*e*) cambric?
3. What are four suitable materials for stuffing?
4. What fabric is fastened underneath a chair to serve as a dust cover?
5. List and describe six types of fabrics which can be used for final covering.

unit

59

Upholstering a slip seat

Fig. 59–1. Slip seat on a vanity stool.

The removable slip seat is the simplest type of upholstering. You often see it on dining-room chairs and stools. Figure 59–1 shows a slip seat on a vanity stool. The materials and tools needed for the work have been discussed in Unit 58.

The covering fabric of a slip seat may be easily removed for cleaning.

MAKING A SLIP SEAT

1. Make a wooden frame which will fit the stool or chair. This can be made from stock ¾ inch thick. The length of the various pieces will depend on the size of the seat to be made. A good joint for this frame is the butt joint with two dowels. See Unit 21, *Joining*.

2. Round the outer edge of the top side of the frame. This removes the sharp edge

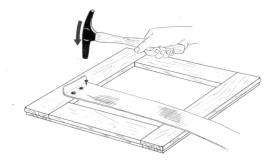

Fig. 59–2. Tacking webbing to a slip-seat frame.

and prevents upholstery materials from wearing through easily. This can be done with the hand plane or on the shaper.

3. Tack one end of the webbing to the frame with No. 12 upholstery tacks (Fig. 59–2). Space the distance between the webbing strips at ½ to 2 inches. Drive three tacks through the first layer. Fold back ¾ inch of webbing, and then drive in two more tacks (Fig. 59–3).

4. Stretch the webbing with a webbing stretcher until it is tight (Fig. 59–3). A little experience in making a few stretches will help you decide when the webbing is sufficiently tight.

5. Make the end of the webbing secure by driving three tacks, as shown in Fig. 59–4.

6. Cut the webbing with the shears about ¾ inch beyond the tacks. Fold it back and drive in two more tacks.

7. Fasten the remaining strips of webbing as shown in Figs. 59–5 and 59–6. The strips should form an interwoven pattern.

8. Cover the webbed section of the frame with a single thickness of close-grained burlap. Fasten it in place with No. 8 tacks (Fig. 59–7).

9. Cut a rubberized-hair pad 1 inch thick to the size of the slip-seat frame. Use an upholsterer's shears, or scissors (see Fig. 59–8).

If you prefer to use stuffing (curled hair, moss, or tow), pull it apart and remove all sticks and foreign matter. Spread it evenly over the burlap to a depth of about 2 inches.

Fig. 59–4. Fastening the stretched webbing.

Fig. 59–5. Fastening burlap webbing with an air tacker, to form the base for a seat frame.

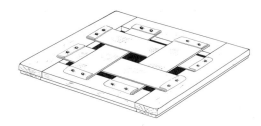

Fig. 59–6. Webbing completed on a slip-frame seat.

Fig. 59–3. Stretching webbing on a frame.

Fig. 59–7. Burlap fastened over webbing.

Fig. 59-8. Rubberized hair pad cut to fit the seat frame.

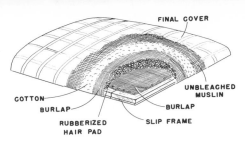

Fig. 59-10. Cross section of an upholstered slip seat.

Fig. 59-9. Regulating the stuffing for smoothness.

Fig. 59-11. Underside of the slip seat, showing a finished corner.

Fig. 59-12. Fastening the slip seat to the stool through a corner brace.

10. Cover the rubberized pad or stuffing with burlap and tack it under the frame. Drive the tacks only about halfway in so that they can be withdrawn, if necessary, to tighten the burlap further. It should be tightly drawn when finished (Fig. 59–9).

11. If you have used loose stuffing, smooth it with a regulator (Fig. 59–9). Cut away the surplus burlap on the corners to eliminate bulkiness.

12. Cover the tightly tacked burlap with a layer of cotton padding or polyurethane foam (Fig. 59–10).

13. Cover the cotton with a piece of unbleached muslin and tack it tightly under the frame.

14. Arrange the final covering fabric in place and tack it under the frame. Fold the corners of the final covering as shown in Fig. 59–11.

15. Cover the underside of the seat with a piece of colored, glazed cambric. This serves as a dust cover.

16. Fasten the slip-seat frame in place with screws from underneath as shown in Fig. 59–12.

***

Discussion Topics

1. What is a slip seat?
2. What is the advantage of using webbing for the foundation of a slip-frame seat, instead of a solid board?
3. What tools are used to make a slip seat?
4. Why do you round the outer top edge of the frame?
5. How is a slip seat held in place?

unit
60
Upholstering springs

Simple spring-seat upholstering, which you can do, includes working with coil springs (Fig. 60–3) and with no-sag springs (Fig. 60–13). You can also learn to build a wire edge on coil springs to give a box effect. Some furniture manufacturers use no-sag springs instead of the coil type. Spring upholstering is used in many pieces of living-room furniture.

Figure 60–1 shows a typical view of an upholstery department in a large furniture manufacturing plant. Note that the skilled upholsterers work independently and use many of the same techniques which you will perform.

The instruction in this unit is very elementary. If you wish to go further, study some of the excellent books on upholstering. Figure 60–2 pictures a spring-upholstered ottoman.

COIL SPRINGS

1. Make, or have ready, a chair frame, ottoman, or other suitable piece of furniture to be upholstered.

2. Fasten the strips of wood in place for the base, or stretch webbing as a spring foundation.

Fig. 60-1. View of a typical upholstering division of a large furniture manufacturing plant. *(Drexel Furniture Company.)*

3. Determine the height of the springs and the number to be placed. This depends entirely on how high the seat is to be built and how hard it is to be. The best way to find this out is to place several springs of various sizes in different positions.

4. Place the selected springs in rows to be fastened to the wood or web base. Figure 60-3 shows a neat spacing.

5. Fasten the coil springs to the base. On a wood base, use staples; on a web base, sewing twine. Cover the board with burlap to serve as a silencer, so the springs will not hit the wood (Fig. 60-3).

6. Drive a No. 10 upholstery tack part way into the edges of the wood frame for each outer spring, as shown in Fig. 60-3.

7. Cut several pieces of spring-tying twine to length. This should be about double the length or width of the frame.

8. Knot one end of the twine around a tack on the edge of the frame, and drive the

Fig. 60-2. Spring-upholstered ottoman.

264

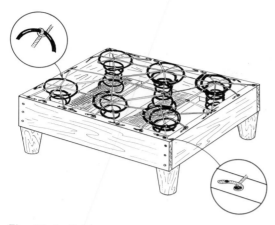

Fig. 60-3. Springs properly tied to an ottoman.

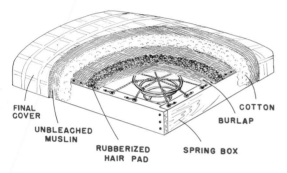

FINAL COVER
UNBLEACHED MUSLIN
RUBBERIZED HAIR PAD
SPRING BOX
COTTON
BURLAP

Fig. 60-4. Cross section of an upholstered spring seat.

Fig. 60-5. Fastening burlap to a frame, using an electric air tacker.

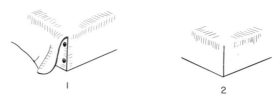

Fig. 60-6. Steps in forming a corner.

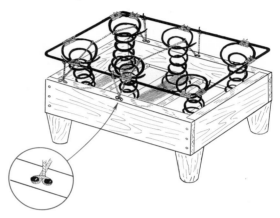

Fig. 60-7. Wire edge fastened to springs, with two rows of springs tied properly.

tack down. This is the first step in tying a row of springs. Leave a ¾-inch surplus as an anchor for the twine and the first tack (Fig. 60-3, right detail).

9. Hold the first spring in position and pull the twine over the top. Tie a spring-tying knot, and proceed across the row of springs (Fig. 60-3, left detail).

10. Fasten the end of the tying twine in the same way you did when starting.

11. Finish tying all the rows of springs until the pattern looks like Fig. 60-3.

12. Tie all springs diagonally, as shown in Fig. 60-3. A cross section of the springs and frame will look like Fig. 60-4.

13. Cover the springs with a single layer of close-grained burlap. Fold the edges and tack them to the frame (Fig. 60-5).

14. Cut a sheet of 1- or 2-inch thick rubberized curled-hair pad to fit over the spring-tied area. If you wish, you may use any of the other types of stuffing. Build this up at least 2 inches.

15. Complete upholstering, beginning with step 10 in Unit 59, *Upholstering a Slip Seat.*

16. Form the corners of the final covering as illustrated in Fig. 60–6.

WIRE-EDGE COIL SPRINGS

1. Follow steps 1 to 5, "Coil Springs."

2. Bend a spring-steel upholstery wire to match the shape of the wooden frame.

3. Tie this wire to the coil springs as shown in Fig. 60–7. Follow the steps shown in Fig. 60–8 for tying.

Figure 60–9 shows the wire edge fastened to coil springs which are attached to a plywood-platform base. Note the triple

Fig. 60–8. Steps in tying a spring-steel wire edge to coil springs.

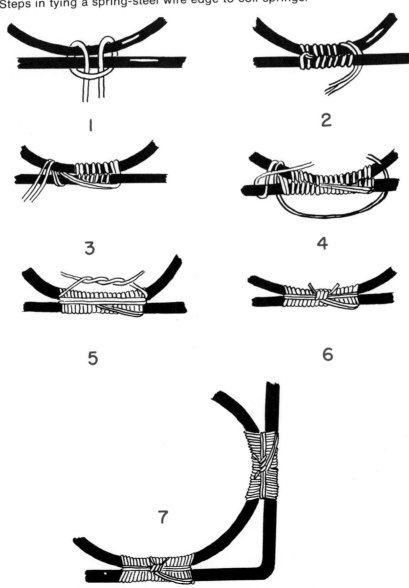

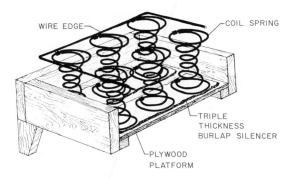

Fig. 60–9. Wire edge fastened to coil springs which are attached to a plywood platform base.

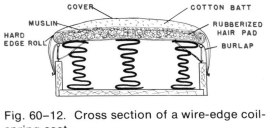

Fig. 60–12. Cross section of a wire-edge coil-spring seat.

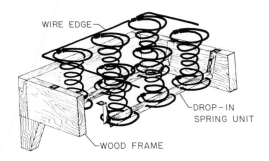

Fig. 60–10. Drop-in spring units fastened to a frame for upholstering.

Fig. 60–13. Ottoman frame with no-sag springs fastened in place, ready for further upholstering.

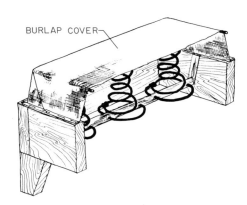

Fig. 60–11. Burlap tacked to the frame over drop-in spring units.

Fig. 60–14. Underneath view of an upholstered chair, showing no-sag springs in place.

Fig. 60-15. Final upholstery fabric being tacked in place on a frame.

Fig. 60-16. Ornamental-head nails give an interesting, contrasting effect on a beautifully upholstered chair.

thickness of burlap which serves as a silencer. Figure 60-10 illustrates how drop-in spring units are fastened to a frame. The wire edge is then attached or fastened to the coil springs. In Fig. 60-11 the burlap cover is attached over the drop-in spring units and tacked or stapled to the frame.

4. Follow steps 5 and 6 in "Coil Springs."

5. Knot one end of the twine around the tack on the edge, being careful to leave a surplus of 5 inches. Drive the tack to hold the twine.

6. Start another tack about ½ inch from the first one. Wrap the surplus end of the cord around it, and fasten the tack (Fig. 60-8).

7. Tie the surplus end of the twine on the wire edge to the desired height (Fig. 60-8).

8. Follow steps 9 through 12 of "Coil Springs."

9. Sew a commercial hard-edge roll to the burlap. Follow the shape of the wire frame (Fig. 60-12).

10. Complete the upholstering by following steps 14 through 16 of "Coil Springs."

NO-SAG SPRINGS

No-sag springs are often used instead of coil springs. The spring stock should be cut to length and fastened in place as shown in Figs. 60-13 and 60-14.

The procedure for upholstering over a no-sag spring base is like that followed in "Coil Springs," pages 263 to 266.

Figure 60-15 shows the final cover or fabric being secured in the upholstery division of a furniture plant. Ornamental rails are being driven in place in Fig. 60-16.

Discussion Topics

1. Inspect several pieces of factory-built furniture to see how the coil or no-sag springs have been fastened to the frame. Note also how they have been tied in place.

2. Why must springs be tied in so many directions?

3. Why must you use the best grade of twine?

4. What tools did you use in your spring-upholstering job?

5. What is the advantage in having a wire edge on coil-spring upholstering? How is it fastened in place?

unit

61

The use of wood through the ages

It is difficult to trace the use of wood by man in prehistoric times because this was the period before written history and because wood is a highly perishable material.

Trees existed all around early man; we may assume therefore that wood was probably used by him in some form as fuel (although it is not known how he learned to make fire), and he later used wood for his crude rafts or boats.

The earliest looms were made from tree branches. Bows and arrow shafts were also made of wood. It has been thought that the American Indians of 20,000 years ago used wood for making utensils and weapons.

Wood does not survive in moist climates very long, and even in dry, desert climates traces of wood items are scarce. Moisture has seeped in through the fissures, or cracks, in the limestone of many ancient tombs and

269

has warped or destroyed a number of the wooden objects left in the tombs.

NEOLITHIC (NEW STONE AGE) CULTURE

The remains of the lake villages of the Alps (in what is now Switzerland) give tangible evidence of the perishable aspect of the material culture of late Neolithic man. It is believed that the wooden houses of these villages were built on platforms raised on piles over the open waters of the lakes, and that the houses were linked by bridges to the shore. Evidence of these structures has survived because they eventually sank into the lake and were gradually buried by the peat moss deposits of the lake beds. Vegetable remains of these Alpine sites which survive include clubs, hammers, handles of all kinds, shuttles, ladles, scoops, wood dishes, bows, and fish-net floats.

THE EARLY BRONZE AGE (ABOUT 3500 B.C.)

Oak coffin burial sites dating from the early Bronze Age in northern Europe reveal coffins made from halves of hollowed-out oak trunks. With the skeletons were found wooden sword scabbards, birchbark pails, cups and bowls of carved wood, and textiles which were used by these Nordic people over 3,000 years ago.

In central Asia a grave pit was discovered which is over 2,000 years old. In the pit were two rectangular wooden chambers. In one chamber was a wooden coffin, and, on the walls, hanging from wooden pegs, was a black felt carpet. Ten horses had been killed

Fig. 61–1. The remains of a Viking ship. *(Archaeology and Society, J. G. D. Clark.)*

Fig. 61–2. Boxwood and acacia chair found in front of the sealed door of the tomb of Rá-mose and Hat-nūfer, probably belonging to Hat-nūfer. *(The Metropolitan Museum of Arts, Rogers Fund, 1936.)*

Acacia, boxwood, and sycamore were types of wood used by the Egyptians for furniture, boxes, and coffins during the XVIII dynasty (about 1580-1322 B.C.). See Fig. 61–2. The craftsmen of ancient Egypt often veneered their wood products with ivory and ebony. The ruins of a dam built on the Nile River about 1800 B.C. show that woodworkers helped to build it, using baulks of timber to reinforce the massive walls. The tomb of Tut-ankh-Amūn, a Pharaoh of the XVIII dynasty, yielded such wooden objects as

Fig. 61–3. A table from the tomb of King Tut-ankh-Amūn, XVIII dynasty. *(The Metropolitan Museum of Art. Photograph by Harry Burton.)*

and thrown in the portion of the grave not occupied by the wooden chambers, and the harness was well-preserved. The body had been borne on an oxcart to the grave, and remains of the cart and yokes were found heaped over the wooden chambers.

Boats have been uncovered in peat bogs in northern Europe (Fig. 61–1); ploughs, sledge runners, all manner of handles, sheaths, scabbards, and other wooden objects have also been found. In very cold climates the permanently frozen soil acts as a giant refrigerator and holds the process of decay in check. Therefore, archaeological investigation among the Eskimos has uncovered many objects, such as wooden arrows, sledge runners, bowls, dippers, drum handles, dolls, and toys.

ANCIENT EGYPT

The ancient Egyptians used timber imported from Lebanon for their ship construction.

Fig. 61–4. A three-legged stool from the tomb of King Tut-ankh-Amūn, XVIII dynasty. *(The Metropolitan Museum of Art. Photograph by Harry Burton.)*

Fig. 61–5. Intricate wood carving in a 14th-century English cathedral.

tables, stools, beds, and gaming boards, and a relief of carved wood which was overlaid with gold and silver (Figs. 61–3 and 61–4).

THE IRON AGE IN EUROPE (ABOUT 800 B.C.)

Some of the timber houses from the early Iron Age have been identified because they burned and were thus carbonized. This made it possible to determine their age by the carbon-14 test (this test is described on page 274).

The culture of the pre-Roman Iron Age in England can be studied in the ancient lake village of Glastonbury. Its site is now meadowland, but at one time this area was a peat bog. The wooden huts which made up the village were surrounded by a palisade of closely set wooden stakes. The woodwork had very accurate turnery and joinery. Dugout canoes, cups, tubs, ladles, handles, parts of looms, and axles have been unearthed.

ANCIENT LIFE IN GREECE

It is known that Greek soldiers were buried in cypress wood coffins as far back as 400 B.C. Early wars spurred the development of tools and weapons. Wood was used for spears, chariots, ships, and the many other weapons, accessories, and implements of warfare.

The most interesting of all early Doric buildings, the Heraeum (temple of Hera) at Olympia, was built hundreds of years before Christ. Some portions of the walls were faced with wood and the columns originally were of wood. Later, during the 2nd century A.D., a temple was built which had two columns of oak.

EARLY DESERT PEOPLES

The Basket-maker culture of the southwestern part of North America left some traces of the use of wood. (This culture existed at the time of Christ and was fully developed by 500 A.D.) Preserved in caves in Arizona were found such things as trays, planting sticks, and trinket boxes.

In the Takla Makan, a desert area in central Asia, the excavation of an ancient settlement disclosed quantities of official memoranda and other documents inscribed on wooden tablets and on leather. This settlement dates from the 3rd century A.D.

EUROPE IN THE 14TH CENTURY

Religious buildings evolved through thousands of years, and, by the 14th century, the cathedral had become a glorious example of art in construction and carving. Figure 61–5 is an interior view of a 14th-century English cathedral.

The people who worked with wood and timber formed guilds. The *carpenter* was one who worked on the frames of buildings. The *joiner* worked on doors and smaller

Fig. 61–7. Eighteenth- and 19th-century wood hand tools. The flat plane on the left is from Saipan. It is designed for pulling rather than pushing, like our American planes. The other two planes, top center, and right, are banding planes. The top center one is for wide banding, and the one on the right is for narrow banding. These were used to cut out the parent wood so that furniture could be inlaid. The saw in the center is a depth saw, used to cut dadoes. The saw at the bottom is an old compass saw. (*The L.V. Hawkins private collection.*)

Fig. 61–6. An early method of ripping timber during the American Colonial period is still practiced today in many parts of the world. (*U. S. Forest Service.*)

Fig. 61–8. Wood craftsmen in Colonial Williamsburg, Virginia demonstrate how cabinet and furniture making were done 200 years ago. (*Colonial Williamsburg.*)

Fig. 61–9. A young apprentice turns the wheel to produce power to operate the wood lathe of Colonial times. *(Colonial Williamsburg.)*

woodwork. The shipworker was called a *shipwright*.

The Fraternity of Carpenters was formed in 1308. Guilds grew as town and industrial life expanded, and the woodworkers' guilds became thriving organizations of craftsmen in 14th-century England.

COLONIAL AMERICA

Wood seemed to be the only raw material which the American colonists had in plentiful supply at first. They sawed lumber and timbers for buildings (Fig. 61–6), and used wood for utensils such as bowls, plates, and buckets. Figure 61–7 shows some old wood tools. They are antiques now, but they were very useful to the wood craftsmen during the 18th and 19th centuries.

A Colonial cabinetmaking shop has been restored, and is once again in operation, in Williamsburg, Virginia. Here skilled craftsmen demonstrate with the tools and methods of two hundred years ago as they reproduce popular articles of their forebearers. Figures 61–8 and 61–9 depict this Colonial craftsmanship.

TWENTIETH CENTURY

Within the past twenty years there has evolved a new and accurate method of determining the age of an object. This method is based upon the atomic disintegration of an elemental isotope called carbon 14. The carbon-14 method, as it is called, takes into consideration the amount of carbon 14, a radioactive carbon, which all living things assimilate, or take in, while they are alive. At death assimilation ceases, and the assimilated radiocarbon begins to discharge particles. As a result, the radiation of the object grows progressively weaker with the passage of time. Since the discharge of radiocarbon takes place at a precise rate, careful measurement of the strength of radioactivity at any given time gives evidence of the number of years which have elapsed, or passed, since death.

Substances which are particularly suitable for dating by means of their radiocarbon content are charcoal, charred organic material, well-preserved wood, grasses, cloth, and peat.

At present, the extent of satisfactory measurement is about 30,000 years. That is, the age of objects older than 30,000 years cannot as yet be satisfactorily determined. However, scientists are working to perfect new methods for dating objects. The reliability of the carbon-14 method is checked by comparing the object in question with items of known age; for example, the radioactivity of an object might be checked against the radioactivity of a portion of a deck board from the funerary boat of Pharaoh Sesostris III, who is known to have lived from 1887 B.C. to 1849 B.C.

Recently it was determined that the sport of skiing is not as new as many think. The carbon-14 test showed that the Rama ski, found on an arctic moor, is well over 2,500 years old. This relic is being preserved in a museum in Norway.

1. List seven general historical periods discussed in this unit. Give the approximate dates for each.
2. Why are traces of ancient wood items difficult to find in moist climates?
3. What were some of the wooden items unearthed in the tomb of Tut-ankh-Amūn?
4. How were wooden objects from the Neolithic culture of the lake villages of Switzerland preserved?
5. Give two examples of the use of wood by the ancient Greeks.
6. How was wood used in the combat arms of ancient wars?
7. What objects have been found at the oak coffin burial sites of the early Bronze Age?
8. How have peat bogs added to our knowledge of history?
9. Where did the ancient Egyptians find the timber they needed?
10. How might the age of some of the timber houses from the early Iron Age in England be determined?
11. What is the most glorious example of the woodworker's art during medieval times?
12. Give the approximate date of the formation of the Fraternity of Carpenters.
13. What is a carpenter? A joiner? A shipwright?
14. When did the woodworkers' guilds thrive in England?
15. What was one of the most plentiful raw materials for the first American colonists? How did they use it?
16. Briefly explain the carbon-14 test. What is it used for?
17. Visit your school or city library. Prepare a report on the use of wood throughout any of the periods listed in this unit. You might begin with books on archaeology and the encyclopedias.

unit

62

Design trends in furniture

A study of the furniture of different historical periods shows many variations in design. This unit deals with a few outstanding periods in furniture design which have proved their worth through the years.

Fig. 62–1. This exciting bedroom has modern adaptations from the Italian Renaissance. *(Drexel Furniture Company.)*

275

Fig. 62–2. Some Mediterranean influences are noticeable in this beautifully decorated, but functional, library room. *(Drexel Furniture Company.)*

Fig. 62–3. A very modern Chinese Chippendale feeling prevails in this bedroom-sitting-room apartment. *(Drexel Furniture Company.)*

Fig. 62–4. Several period designs are blended into a beautiful grouping. See if you can identify some of the outstanding characteristics of each piece. *(Drexel Furniture Company.)*

Features of design found in the several traditional periods of furniture have been used in modern furniture design. For example, styling from the 18th century and earlier periods has been adapted to contemporary design (Figs. 62–1 through 62–4). In these furniture groupings the designers kept the essence of the earlier styles and added the lightness of scale, the convenience, and the functional features which are characteristic of modern design.

QUEEN ANNE

An English furniture style dating from about 1700 to 1714 was named after Queen Anne. It is characterized by the simple lines of the cabriole leg, which was shaped like a bent knee (Fig. 62–5). Typical Queen Anne chairs show an animal claw-and-ball foot, and the solid fiddle-shaped splat in the back.

Fig. 62–5. An authentic reproduction of a Queen Anne hall chest. *(Drexel Furniture Company.)*

Fig. 62–6. The Chippendale chair is characterized by the delicate "ribband" back. *(Drexel Furniture Company.)*

Fig. 62–7. A subtly treated Hepplewhite-style chest with contrasting inlay and pleasing curves. *(Drexel Furniture Company.)*

CHIPPENDALE

Thomas Chippendale was beyond doubt the most fashionable cabinetmaker of London from 1750 to 1775. His early work was a development of the decorated early Georgian style. In chairs the fiddle-shaped splat became the delicate ribbon back (Fig. 62–6).

HEPPLEWHITE

George Hepplewhite was a practical cabinetmaker. He developed in his own way the treatment of the shield-back chair. He always avoided massiveness in design, and is particularly famous for his chairs and sideboards, in which he used curves to advantage (Fig. 62–7).

SHERATON

Thomas Sheraton was a furniture designer in the last half of the 18th century. His style of furniture is essentially feminine in appear-

Fig. 62–8. Sheraton chair. *(Mahogany Association, Inc.)*

Fig. 62–9. Louis XVI-style chairs are simple and graceful. *(Drexel Furniture Company.)*

Fig. 62–11. Duncan Phyfe chair. *(Mahogany Association, Inc.)*

Fig. 62–10. Modern adaptation of French Empire lines on an English Regency chair. *(Drexel Furniture Company.)*

Fig. 62–12. Adaptation of Queen Anne design for a silver chest. *(Drexel Furniture Company.)*

ance, but is structurally strong and sound (Fig. 62–8).

LOUIS XV AND LOUIS XVI

The Louis XV style in furniture is somewhat similar to the French style created during the reign of Louis XIV. Both types were ornate; Louis XV pieces, however, were smaller and are better adapted to small rooms.

Furniture in the Louis XVI style, developed in the latter part of the 18th century, is characterized by delicate scale (Fig. 62–9).

FRENCH EMPIRE

From 1800 to 1814 the designers of furniture were influenced by Napoleon's conquests. This style was carried to England and then to the United States, where it was modified by American craftsmen. Regency is the name under which English furniture of the French Empire period is best known (Fig. 62–10).

AMERICAN COLONIAL

The era of design prior to 1750 in America is often referred to as Colonial; that from 1750 to 1775, as Pre-Revolutionary. Fine furniture was imported from England by the wealthy settlers and planters of Virginia. American Colonial design was greatly influenced by Chippendale.

FEDERAL AMERICAN

The American Revolution produced a new design in furniture, referred to as Federal American or Post-Revolutionary. By 1800 Federal American furniture design was a mixture of Hepplewhite and Sheraton, with some semblance of French Empire, due to the influence of Duncan Phyfe.

DUNCAN PHYFE

Duncan Phyfe was the first outstanding furniture designer in America. During the early part of the 19th century he received patronage from the John Jacob Astor family. In his early work the influence of Hepplewhite and Sheraton predominated. He is best characterized by his use of the lyre, brass ferrules, Pompeiian designs, and graceful outcurved legs for chairs and tables (Fig. 62–11).

OTHER AMERICAN DESIGNERS

During the last half of the 18th century, America had many first-rate cabinetmakers and designers. Among these men were Elijah and Jacob Sanderson and Samuel McIntire, architect, designer, and woodcarver, who was noted for carved modifications of several styles. William Savery was famous for design applications to chests (Fig. 62–12). John Gillingham was noted for chairs with trefoil (clover-leaf-shaped) backs. Thomas Afleck was a leader influenced by Chippendale. John Folwell was a follower of Chippendale design and is credited with making the famous Speaker's Chair in Independence Hall.

NINETEENTH CENTURY

The major contribution to furniture making during the 19th century was the develop-

Fig. 62–13. Nineteenth-century rocker. This is a replica of that used by Abraham Lincoln. *(Mahogany Association, Inc.)*

Fig. 62–14. Outstanding example of Swedish Modern simplicity. *(Drexel Furniture Company.)*

ment of woodworking machinery and the introduction of machine-made furniture.

Americans in the 19th century were generally so concerned with the building of a great nation that attention to art and beauty was neglected. Lincoln's rocking chair (Fig. 62–13) is a typical example of 19th century styling.

TWENTIETH CENTURY

One of the most striking and popular furniture styles which has emerged during the present century is Modern. Early Modern was unsymmetrical and had box-like lines. Later the style acquired the waterfall front, then suffered an overdose of veneer treat-

ment. More recently blond-type finishes have affected the design. Modern styling now has the simplicity of Swedish Modern fashion (Fig. 62–14).

It is difficult to define design because, like most things in life, it is relative. When one plans an original design for a piece of furniture or cabinetwork, he should consider whether the project fits its purpose, shows organization, makes good use of materials, and displays good craftsmanship (Fig. 62–15).

The modern designer uses a minimum of materials. He avoids excess bulk, and tries to keep the proportions in balance. Functionalism with beauty is the essence of good design.

Fig. 62–15. This handsome, rare myrtlewood credenza, designed and hand crafted by the author, Chris H. Groneman, reflects eighteenth-century styling. The brass drawer pulls are also custom-made of subtly tinted metal enamelling by Virginia Groneman.

Fig. 62–17. A grouping of exciting International Modern furniture. *(Fine Hardwoods Association.)*

Fig. 62–16. An oriental influence is noticeable in this furniture grouping. *(Mount Airy Furniture Company.)*

Fig. 62–18. Early American, one of the more popular traditional styles, includes adaptation of Dutch Colonial design. *(Drexel Furniture Company.)*

Fig. 62–19. This traditional piece shows Spanish influence. *(Drexel Furniture Company.)*

TRADITIONAL INFLUENCES

Free line forms, new combinations of textures and materials, and unusual functional ideas keep the subject of design fresh and exciting. Functional furniture serves to enhance the beauty and comfort of traditional design, and both are important in home furnishing and decoration.

Revivals of English Regency, 18th century styling (Fig. 62–15), and French Directoire are currently popular. In modern collections, established styles such as Danish Modern, Oriental Modern (Fig. 62–16), and International Modern (Fig. 62–17) are popular and functional. Early American (Fig. 62–18), French Provincial, and Spanish (Fig. 62–19) are still traditional favorites, but they have a new look.

These illustrations show that pleasing and beautiful lines are achieved by (1) using period designs as they are, (2) altering them to take into consideration modern needs and architecture, (3) following only modern concepts of basic design, or (4) using the elements in both traditional and modern to gain the effect desired. When these basic principles are interchanged to form individual styles in themselves, the results are effective and satisfying.

1. What is meant by period furniture?
2. Name two distinctive characteristics of Queen Anne furniture.
3. How did Chippendale alter the fiddle-shaped splat of the Queen Anne style? How did he alter the cabriole leg?
4. What characterizes the back of a Hepplewhite chair?
5. Give two characteristics of Sheraton furniture.
6. Who was the first outstanding furniture designer in America? List four important characteristics of his design.
7. Name four American furniture designers who worked about 1750. Name one important characteristic of the design of each of them.
8. Why was furniture more easily obtained in the 19th century than before that time?

unit

63

Trees and forests

Trees provide the raw material for many thousands of wood-fabricating industries. They are also the basic material for the woodworking novice or the hobbyist. You should therefore have an understanding of the parts of a tree, the growth, the structure, and how it is cut.

THE TREE

A study of Fig. 63–1 gives interesting information about the tree. It consists of three main parts: crown, trunk, and roots. The leaf buds, root tips, and cambium layer are the growing parts.

The leaves of trees contain a green pigment called chlorophyll. It utilizes the energy of light to combine carbon dioxide (a gas coming from the air) with water absorbed by the roots into a simple food, called carbohydrate. This food is carried by the inner bark to all parts of the tree. Evaporation of water from the internal part of the leaves through the leaf pores is called transpiration.

Figure 63–2 gives a cross section of wood. This shows the porous formation. The complete cross section of a log is shown in Fig. 63–3. Figure 63–4 is an actual photograph of the annular, or yearly, rings of a shortleaf pine log. The outer rings represent the most recent growth and are farther apart than the inner rings. The larger rings indicate a thinning of the forest, completed eight years before the picture was taken. This allowed the tree to grow more rapidly.

A log can be cut into lengths by three methods (Figs. 63–5 through 63–7).

Figure 63–9 is a marked log end to show how forest industries saw a *round log* into *square boards*. Unevenly shaped slabs from around the log's edge are ground into chips for pulp and paper manufacture, or for hardboard and particle board composition. Sawdust is often collected for plant mulch and fertilizer. Planer dust usually goes into wood-

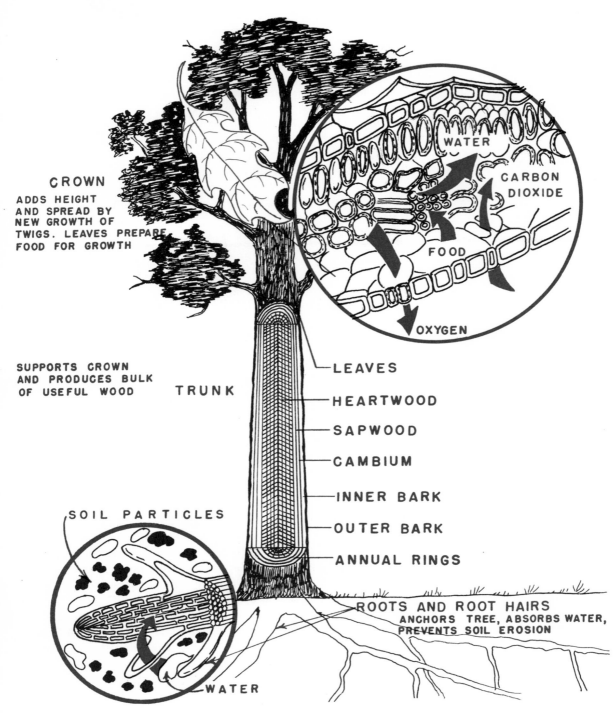

CROWN
ADDS HEIGHT
AND SPREAD BY
NEW GROWTH OF
TWIGS. LEAVES PREPARE
FOOD FOR GROWTH

WATER

CARBON
DIOXIDE

FOOD

OXYGEN

SUPPORTS CROWN
AND PRODUCES BULK
OF USEFUL WOOD

TRUNK

LEAVES

HEARTWOOD

SAPWOOD

CAMBIUM

INNER BARK

OUTER BARK

ANNUAL RINGS

SOIL PARTICLES

ROOTS AND ROOT HAIRS
ANCHORS TREE, ABSORBS WATER,
PREVENTS SOIL EROSION

WATER

Fig. 63–1. The growth of a tree. *(American Forest Products Industries.)*

284

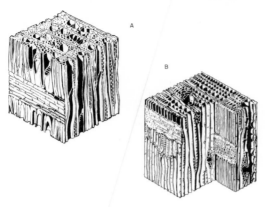

Fig. 63-2. Enlarged cell structures: (A) hardwood, and (B) softwood. *(American Forest Products Industries.)*

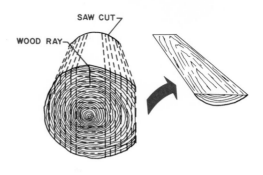

PLAIN SAWED

Fig. 63-5. Plain-sawing of a log. Boards are cut tangent to annular rings.

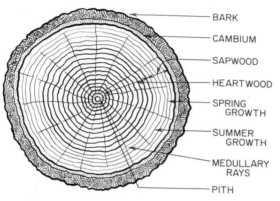

BARK
CAMBIUM
SAPWOOD
HEARTWOOD
SPRING GROWTH
SUMMER GROWTH
MEDULLARY RAYS
PITH

Fig. 63-3. Cross section of a log.

Fig. 63-4. Annular rings of a shortleaf pine. *(American Forest Products Industries.)*

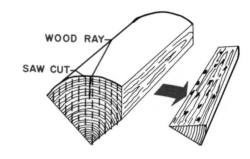

WOOD RAY
SAW CUT

QUARTER SAWED

Fig. 63-6. Quarter-sawing of a log. Boards are cut to show figure grain.

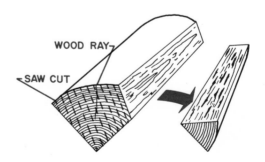

WOOD RAY
SAW CUT

RIFT SAWED

Fig. 63-7. Rift-sawing of a log. Boards are cut to show pencil-line grain.

flour products. Researchers are working on various uses for bark.

FORESTS

There are ten principal forests in the United States which produce timber-harvested crops (Fig. 63–8). Alaska and Hawaii are included in this discussion.

The *West Coast Forest* (Fig. 63–10) extends along the moist western slopes of Washington, Oregon, and northern California. Most of the timber in Washington and Oregon is Douglas fir. There are also hemlock, Sitka spruce, and western red cedar. The redwood is the characteristic tree of northern California. The West Coast Forest

Fig. 63–8. Forest regions of the United States. *(American Forest Products Industries.)*

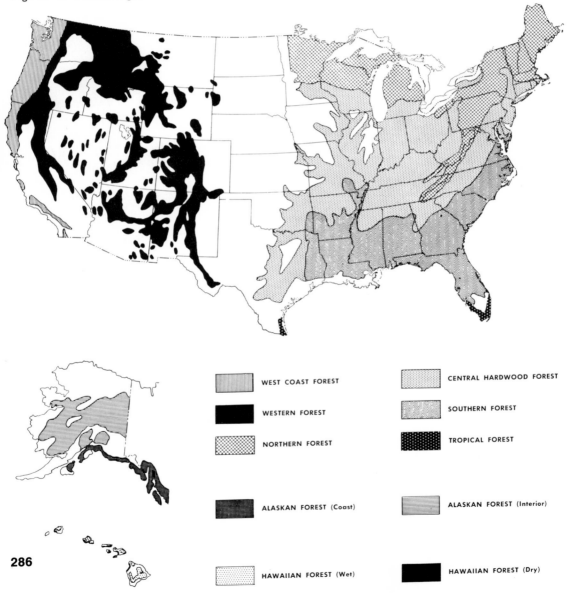

WEST COAST FOREST

WESTERN FOREST

NORTHERN FOREST

ALASKAN FOREST (Coast)

HAWAIIAN FOREST (Wet)

CENTRAL HARDWOOD FOREST

SOUTHERN FOREST

TROPICAL FOREST

ALASKAN FOREST (Interior)

HAWAIIAN FOREST (Dry)

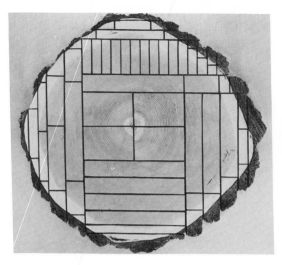

Fig. 63–9. How forest industries saw a round log into square boards. *(American Forest Products Industries.)*

Fig. 63–10. West Coast Forest. *(Western Wood Products Association.)*

exceeds 31 million acres and represents more than 550 billion board feet of timber. Less than 4 billion board feet are in hardwoods, including alder, maple, oak, and some others. This region produces about one-third of the lumber, about one-fifth of the plywood, and nearly all of the fir plywood in the United States.

The *Western Forest* (Fig. 63–11) includes the 12 western states, covering about 35 percent of the continental United States. Nearly 90 million acres are considered commercial forest land. From this land we get over 500 billion board feet of softwood timber, chiefly ponderosa, western white, and sugar pines, and some hardwoods. This area produces about one-fourth of our lumber supply.

The *Northern Forest* (Fig. 63–12) lies along the Great Lakes and in the eastern part of the United States. It contains northern white pine, red and white spruce, eastern hemlock, and other conifers, as well as hardwood trees. This region contains approximately 115 million acres of commercial forest land. It is estimated that there are

more than 62 billion board feet of softwoods, and over 108 billion board feet of hardwoods in this forest. Approximately one-tenth of our lumber supply, and about 20 percent of the pulpwood, grow here.

The *Central Hardwood Forest* (Fig. 63–13) extends roughly through the central-eastern section of the United States. Most of its trees are hardwoods, and it covers over 131 million acres. The yield is about one-twentieth of the lumber supply and 10 percent of the pulpwood.

The *Southern Forest* (Fig. 63–14) stretches from New Jersey through eastern Texas, and from Oklahoma to the Gulf of Mexico. Longleaf, shortleaf, loblolly, and slash pines predominate. Cypress grows in the southern lowlands, and a considerable amount of hardwood is found among the pines. This forest exceeds 123 million acres. We get nearly 194 billion board feet of hardwood, or one-third of the lumber supply, and more than 60 percent of the pulpwood from this region.

The *Tropical Forest* (Fig. 63–15) includes very small areas of the tips of south-

287

Fig. 63–11. Western Forest. *(American Forest Products Industries.)*

Fig. 63–13. Central Hardwood Forest. *(American Forest Products Industries.)*

Fig. 63–12. Northern Forest. *(American Forest Products Industries.)*

Fig. 63–14. Southern Forest. *(American Forest Products Industries.)*

Fig. 63–15. Tropical Forest. *(American Forest Products Industries.)*

ern Florida and Texas. Palm trees and some ebony trees grow in this section.

The *Alaskan Coastal Forest* (Fig. 63–16) contains about 5 million acres of commercial forest. It is almost all coniferous. The leading species in the production of lumber and pulpwood are Alaska yellow cedar, western red cedar, Sitka spruce, and western hemlock.

The *Alaskan Interior Forest* covers most of the heartland of this new state. Its 40 million acres of commercial forest land contain aspen, white birch, white and black spruce, and some poplar.

The *Hawaiian Dry Forest* is not considered commercially valuable. Algaroba, koa haole, and monkeypod are among the leading species.

Fig. 63–16. Alaskan Coastal Forest. *(American Forest Products Industries.)*

289

Fig. 63–17. Hawaiian Wet Forest. *(American Forest Products Industries.)*

Fig. 63–18. A forest fire presents a terrifying destructive spectacle. *(U. S. Forest Service.)*

The *Hawaiian Wet Forest* (Fig. 63–17) is comprised of about one million acres of commercial forest. Such species as koa, tree fern, kukui, mamani, eucalyptus, and tropical ash are used for lumber, furniture, and souvenirs.

The present forest area of the 50 states is 775 million acres. This is an area larger than all of the states east of the Mississippi River. Nearly 70 percent of today's forests, or 535 million acres, is capable of producing timber for commercial use.

The value of our American forests exceeds a billion dollars per year. Transportation of logs and forest products incurs the third largest annual freight bill in America.

With all this potential wealth in woodlands, however, there is tremendous waste caused by fire (Fig. 63–18). It is estimated that one forest fire starts every 4 minutes, for an average of approximately 120,000 fires each year. Were it not for the reforestation program (Fig. 63–19), our supply of timber would become exhausted. The many acres of forest land burned each year would produce enough timber to build 86,000 modern homes. This same amount of timber would make the paper which prints all the newspapers in the United States for one year. These figures show the disastrous waste caused by forest fires.

Insects are the greatest single cause of damage to live timber. One method of effective control is the aerial spraying of insecticides in the forest areas.

About two-thirds of the forest acreage is commercial. The remaining one-third is presently inaccessible, or has been withdrawn from commercial use to serve other purposes. The need for timber in the United States has grown so great that we can no longer depend entirely upon our forests to produce enough timber to satisfy all our needs. For example, we import 80 percent of our newsprint, a forest product, from Canada.

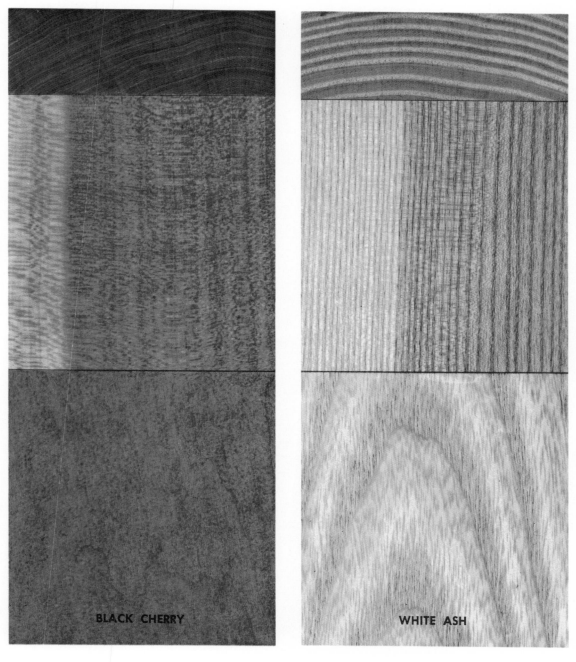

BLACK CHERRY

WHITE ASH

Stiff, strong, moderately hard and heavy. Hard to work by hand but machines well. Old sapwood narrow and nearly white. Heartwood: light to dark reddish-brown with distinctive luster. End-grain rays faint; appear as flakes on quarter-sawed surfaces. Average weight 35 lb to cu ft.

Strong, stiff. Holds nails well; easily worked, but splits easily. Heartwood: brown to dark brown, sometimes reddish. Sapwood: light, or nearly white. Large-pore area usually sharply defined. Small wood rays generally visible only on quarter-sawed surfaces. Average weight 42 lb to cu ft.

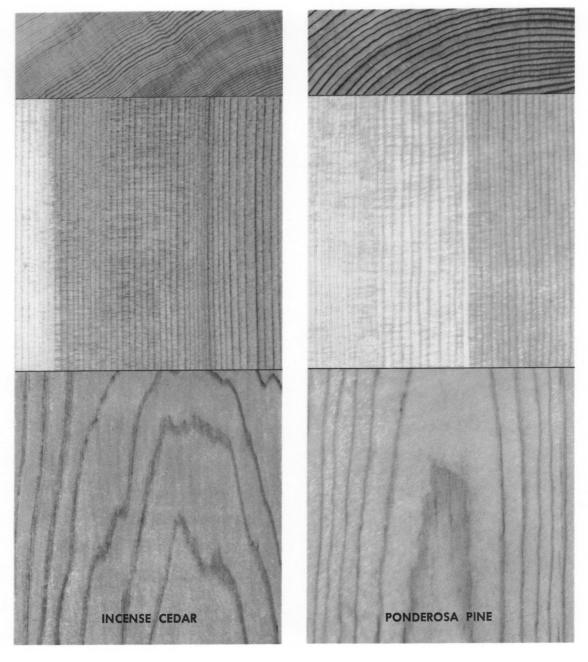

INCENSE CEDAR

PONDEROSA PINE

Among most decay-resistant woods. Splits and works easily. Is light in weight and holds paint exceedingly well. Sapwood is white or cream colored. The heartwood is light brown, often tinged with red; has a fine uniform texture and a strong, spicy odor. Average weight 26 lb to cu ft.

Outer wood fairly lightweight; strength low; soft, stiff. Texture uniform; straight-grained; not easily split. Heartwood: low to moderate in decay resistance; light reddish-brown. Springwood-summerwood change abrupt; summerwood bands narrow. Average weight 28 lb to cu ft.

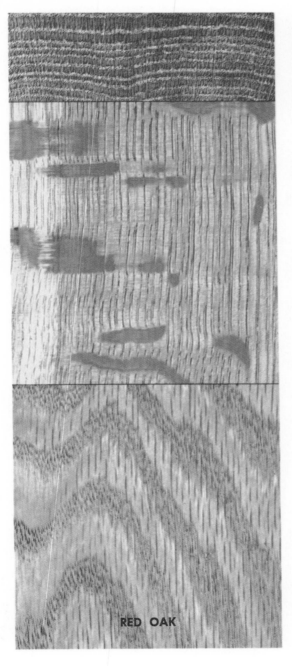

RED OAK

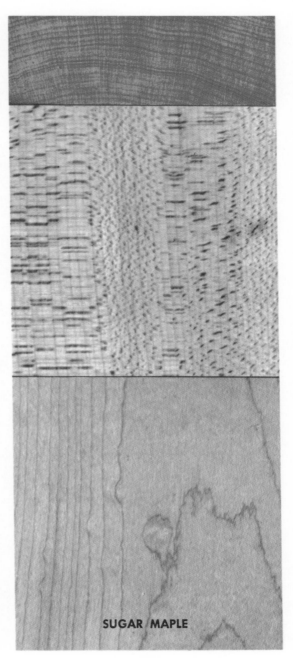

SUGAR MAPLE

Properties similar to white oak except it is extremely porous. Heartwood: grayish-brown with reddish tint. Larger pores distinct. Wood rays commonly ¼ to 1 in. high along grain. On end-grain surfaces, rays appear as lines crossing growth rings. Average weight 44 lb to cu ft.

Strong, stiff, moderately decay resistant. Holds nails well; markedly resistant to abrasive wear. Light reddish-brown, often with greenish-black streaks. Very small pores. Wood rays faint on end grain, very clear on quarter-sawed faces. Average weight 44 lb to cu ft.

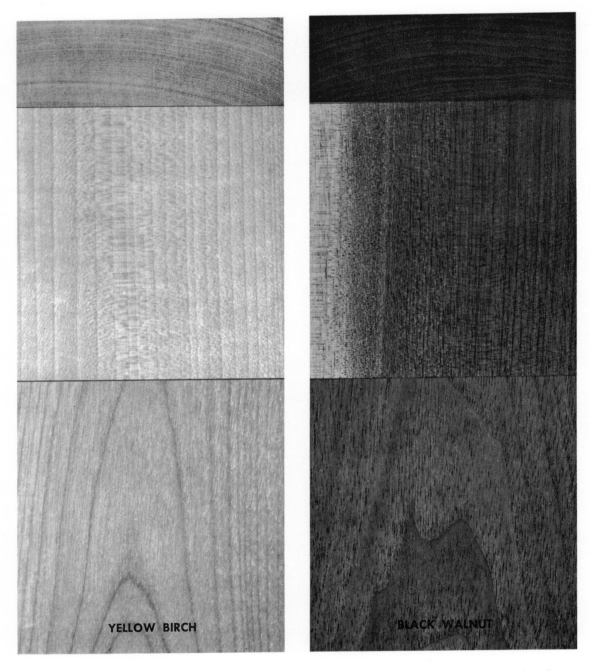

YELLOW BIRCH

BLACK WALNUT

Fine, close grained, uniform. Heavy, hard, stiff. Hard to work by hand, but machines well. Holds nails well; decays easily. Light reddish-brown; very small pores. Growth rings visible on plain-sawed surfaces; wood rays, on quarter-sawed surfaces. Average weight 43 lb to cu ft.

Strong, stiff, good shock resistance. Holds shape after seasoning; durable; easy to work. Handsome grain pattern. Light to dark chocolate-brown, often with purplish streaks. Pores faint on end grain, appear on longitudinal surfaces as darker grooves. Average weight 38 lb to cu ft.

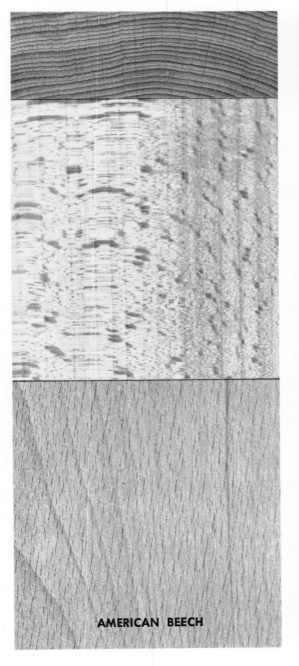

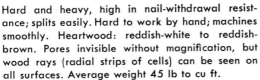

AMERICAN BEECH

YELLOW POPLAR

Hard and heavy, high in nail-withdrawal resistance; splits easily. Hard to work by hand; machines smoothly. Heartwood: reddish-white to reddish-brown. Pores invisible without magnification, but wood rays (radial strips of cells) can be seen on all surfaces. Average weight 45 lb to cu ft.

Moderately soft, moderately stiff. Intermediate in machining properties. Low nail-withdrawal resistance; little tendency to split when nailed. Holds paint well. Fairly decay resistant. Heartwood: brownish-yellow, usually with definite greenish tinge. Average weight 30 lb to cu ft.

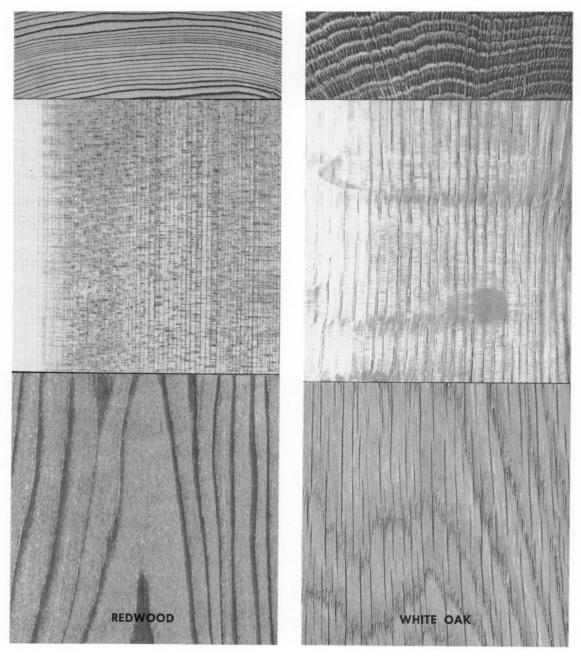

REDWOOD

WHITE OAK

One of most durable for outdoor use. Grain mild, straight, with smooth, silky sheen and thin, dark lines. Moderately hard, strong, and stiff. Holds nails fairly well, paint well; works easily by hand. Heartwood is usually uniform deep reddish-brown. Average weight 28 lb to cu ft.

Heavy, very hard, and strong. Machines very well. Heartwood: grayish-brown; resists decay. Heartwood pores indistinct and plugged with tyloses; wood is thus impervious to liquids. Rays lighter than background on end faces, darker on side faces. Average weight 47 lb to cu ft.

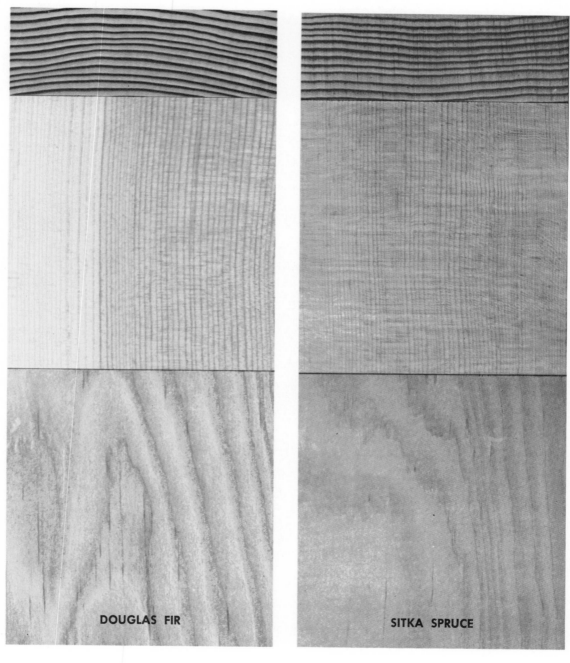

DOUGLAS FIR

SITKA SPRUCE

Varies widely in weight and strength. Most old-growth wood is moderately heavy, strong, hard, and shock resistant. Very stiff and difficult to work, but holds nails well. Moderate decay resistance. Heartwood: orange-red to red or yellowish. Distinctive odor. Average weight 33 lb to cu ft.

Grain straight; fine, uniform texture; fairly strong; works easily; holds nails well; decay resistance low; often produces fuzzy grain under planer knives. Heartwood: pinkish-yellow to pale brown. Springwood-summerwood change slow; flat-grain surface rings faint. Average weight 28 lb to cu ft.

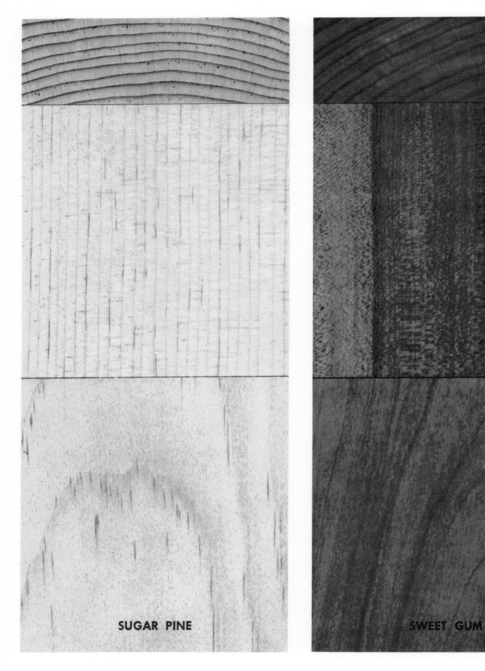

SUGAR PINE

SWEET GUM

Straight grain, fairly uniform texture; easy to work; holds nails well. Lightweight; strength moderately low; not stiff. Fairly decay resistant, soft. Heartwood: pale reddish-brown. Resin canals abundant and commonly stain the wood surface. Average weight 25 lb to cu ft.

Fairly hard, heavy, strong. Holds nails, resists splitting fairly well. Two classes of lumber: sap gum (light colored sapwood), and red gum (reddish-brown heartwood above). Pores invisible; growth rings usually faint; rays visible on quartersawed faces. Average weight 36 lb to cu ft.

Fig. 63–19. An aerial-seeding helicopter dropping millions of seeds in a West Coast reforestation project. Seed generally is scattered at the rate of one pound per acre. With over 40,000 seeds to the pound, an area one mile square will receive over 25 million seeds. *(Weyerhaeuser Company.)*

Discussion Topics

1. Name the three main parts of a tree.
2. Name and describe the growing parts of the tree.
3. What causes knots in lumber?
4. What do the annular rings of a tree indicate?
5. How does thinning forests affect the trees remaining?
6. Draw a cross section to show the methods of cutting a log to get plain-, quarter-, and rift-sawed lumber.
7. Name the principal forest regions in the United States. Give two characteristic types of trees for each region.
8. What is the greatest destructive agent of our forests?

unit
64
Common woods

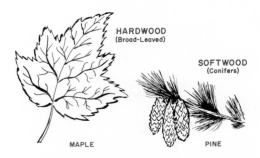

Fig. 64-1. Lumber is obtained from two groups of trees, hardwoods and softwoods.

Trees are one of the most valuable resources of America. Although there are more than 1000 species in American forests, only about 180 kinds are used for lumber or for making manufactured products. The two important types of trees in our forests are hardwoods and softwoods (Fig. 64–1).

HARDWOODS

Hardwoods usually have broad leaves that fall off in winter. Oak, maple, elm, poplar, hickory, gum, magnolia, and walnut are well known examples. Mahogany, imported from tropical America and Africa, is used extensively in furniture manufacture.

SOFTWOODS

Leaves of most softwood trees are needle-like. Because most of these trees remain green the year round, they are called ever-greens. Some of the more common types are pine, fir, hemlock, spruce, cedar, and red-wood. Figure 64–2 pictures five softwood species growing in a western woods region. Softwoods include valuable timber trees, as well as many ornamental evergreens. Most of them are durable and straight-grained.

CHARACTERISTICS, HABITAT, AND USES

Wood is used in more than 5,000 ways in our daily lives. Wood-using industries, public forestry agencies, and scientists work together constantly to improve the care and use of our forests. The importance of re-

Fig. 64-2. Softwood trees in the Western Forest region. Left to right: ponderosa pine, incense cedar, sugar pine, ponderosa pine, sugar pine, ponderosa pine, Douglas fir, and white fir. *(Western Wood Products Association.)*

search grows with the increasing usefulness of forest products. The government-owned Forest Products Laboratory in Wisconsin has accomplished important results in processing laminated wood, improved plywoods, wood- and paper-base plastics, and many other industrial products.

Some of the better-known species of trees used in woodworking are described in this unit. Included are the common and the botanical, Latin name; the general description and the characteristics of the wood; the illustration of the leaf or needle; the general shape of the tree, one side in summer foliage, the other in winter outline; the fruit or nut; the habitat (location); and the uses.

Ash, white (Fraxinus americana). Figure 64–3. Dark gray or gray-brown deeply furrowed bark. Hard, elastic, tough brown wood. Habitat: rich, moist, cool woods; fields and riverbanks; Nova Scotia to Minnesota; Florida to Texas. Agricultural implements, furniture, oars.

Basswood, or linden (Tilia americana). Figure 64–4. Deep brownish-gray bark. Soft, straight-grained, light brown, easily worked wood. Habitat: rich woods or fertile soil; Maine to Georgia, westward to Texas, northward to Lake Superior. General woodenware, furniture, wood pulp; inner bark used for mat fiber.

Beech (Fagus grandifolia). Figure 64–5. Light gray smooth bark. Close-grained, hard, pale brown or buff wood. Edible nuts. Habitat: rich uplands, moist rocky ground; throughout eastern United States from Maine to Lake Superior and south to Florida and Texas; most abundant in New England, New York, and Pennsylvania. Fuel, woodenware, chairs, shoe lasts.

Birch, yellow (Betula alleghaniensis). Figure 64–6. On young trees, thin, papery scales of silvery or yellow bark; on old trees, large, thin, dull plates of bark, gray-

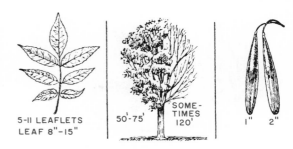

Fig. 64–3. White ash.

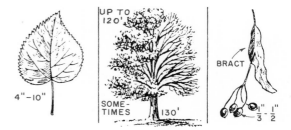

Fig. 64–4. Basswood, or linden.

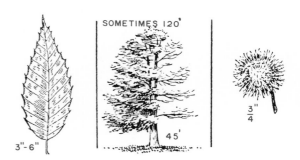

Fig. 64–5. Beech.

Fig. 64–6. Yellow birch.

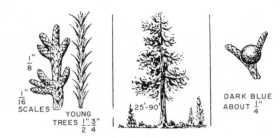

Fig. 64–7. Red cedar.

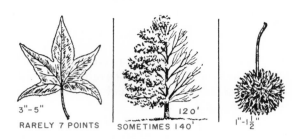

Fig. 64–11. Sweet, or red, gum.

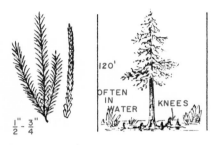

Fig. 64–8. Bald cypress.

Fig. 64–12. Black tupelo, or sour gum.

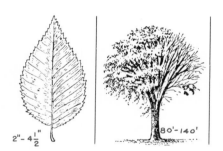

Fig. 64–9. American, or white, elm.

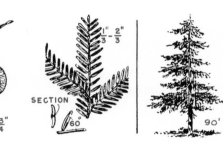

Fig. 64–13. Eastern hemlock.

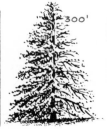

Fig. 64–10. Douglas fir.

Fig. 64–14. Western hemlock.

ish in color. Heavy, strong, hard, close-grained wood. Habitat: Rich uplands, swamps, stream banks; from Minnesota to Newfoundland, south to Pennsylvania, and along the mountains of North Carolina and Tennessee. Distinctive and pleasing grain figures in woodworking, furniture, flooring, and interior finishes.

Cedar, red (Juniperus virginiana). Figure 64–7. Light ruddy-brown bark. Light, soft, brittle, close-grained, fragrant, durable wood. Habitat: all soils, swamps to rocky ridges; Nova Scotia to South Dakota, south to Florida and Texas. Cedar-chests, closets, fence posts, lead pencils.

Cypress, bald (Taxodium distichum). Figure 64–8. Thick, pale ruddy-brown bark of long, thin scales. Straight-grained, easily worked, light brown wood. Habitat: southern swamps; Virginia to Florida; Gulf of Mexico to Texas. General construction, paneling, boats, railway ties.

Elm, American, or white (Ulmus americana). Figure 64–9. Brown-gray, short-furrowed bark. Heavy, tough, hard, coarse-grained, pale brown wood. Habitat: rich soil; from Newfoundland west to the Rocky Mountains; south to Florida and Texas. Wheel hubs, saddletrees, barrels, shipbuilding.

Fir, Douglas (Pseudotsuga menziesii). Figure 64–10. Dark gray-brown, rough bark. Light ruddy or tan-yellow wood. Habitat: Rocky Mountains to Pacific Coast; central British Columbia to northern Mexico. Construction purposes, railroad ties, piles, veneer for plywood.

Gum, sweet, or red (Liquidambar styraciflua). Figure 64–11. Gray-brown, deeply furrowed bark. Hard, heavy, close-grained, reddish-brown wood. Sap made into chewing gum and medicine. Habitat: rich wet lowlands, Connecticut to Florida and west to Kansas. Interior paneling, furniture, stained to resemble mahogany.

Gum, sour, or black; tupelo, black (Nyssa sylvatica). Figure 64–12. Gray-brown, smooth or rough bark. Pale buff, heavy, rather soft, tough, fine-grained wood. Habitat: watercourses, rich alluvial land, swamps; Maine to Florida and west to Michigan and Texas. Boxes, gunstocks.

Hemlock, eastern (Tsuga canadensis). Figure 64–13. Coarse, dull gray-brown bark. Light, tough, coarse-grained, easily splintered wood. Bark is used for tanning. Habitat: cold swamps, ravines, mountain slopes, rocky woods; Great Lakes states and mountains of eastern United States. Timber, joists, boxes, paper pulp.

Hemlock, western (Tsuga heterophylla). Figure 64–14. Reddish-brown, broad-scaled fissured bark. Tough, durable, light, strong, brown wood. Bark used for tanning. Habitat: moist valleys to uplands; tidewater to 6,000 feet; central region from southern Alaska to Oregon. Construction.

Hickory, shagbark (Carya ovata). Figure 64–15. Pale brown-gray, shaggy bark. Very hard, close-grained, flexible, pale brown, "tough as hickory" wood. Edible nuts. Habitat: rich uplands from Quebec to Minnesota and south to Florida and Texas. Agricultural implements, wagons, tool handles, baskets, fuel. Hickory is considered a very valuable hardwood.

Magnolia (Magnolia grandiflora). Figure 64–16. Brownish-gray, rough bark with short, thin scales. Moderately heavy, hard,

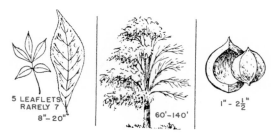

Fig. 64–15. Shagbark hickory.

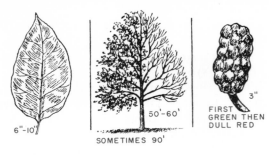

Fig. 64–16. Magnolia.

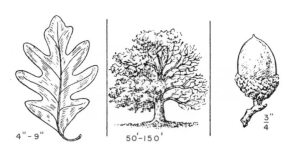

Fig. 64–19. White oak.

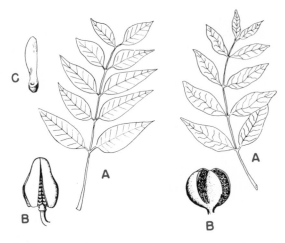

Fig. 64–17. Mahogany. *Left,* a tropical American mahogany, *Swietenia macrophylla:* (A) the compond leaf has leaflets like those of an ash; (B) the fruit pod is larger than an egg—when it splits open it liberates many seeds; (C) the flattened seed has most of its wing at one end. *Right,* African mahogany, *Khaya ivorensis:* (A) the compound leaf has leaflets like those of an ash; (B) the fruit is similar in structure to that of *Swietenia,* but shorter and more rounded. *(Mahogany Association, Inc.)*

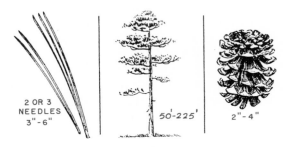

Fig. 64–20. Western yellow pine.

Fig. 64–21. Western white pine.

Fig. 64–18. Sugar maple.

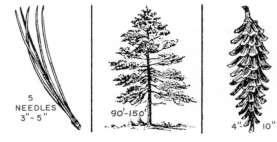

Fig. 64–22. White pine.

cream-colored, satin-lustered wood. Habitat: rich, moist soil; along the coast from North Carolina to Florida, westward to Texas; Mississippi to Arkansas. Planing-mill products, furniture, fixtures, Venetian blinds, finish, siding, boxes, crates.

Mahogany (Swietenia mahogoni, Swietenia macrophylla, and Khaya ivorensis). Figure 64–17. Ridged bark similar to that of the elm tree. Tough, strong, rich golden-brown, easily polished wood. Habitat: tropical American and African forests.

Maple, sugar (Acer saccharum). Figure 64–18. Light, brown-gray, deeply furrowed bark. Heavy, hard, strong, close-grained, easily polished wood. Sap makes maple sugar. Habitat: rich woods, rocky hillsides; every state east of the Mississippi River, but rare in the South. Interior finish, floors, turnery, shipbuilding, shoe lasts, fuel.

Oak, white (Quercus alba). Figure 64–19. Whitish-gray, firm, deeply furrowed bark. Strong, heavy, tough, hard, pale brown wood. Habitat: dry uplands, sandy plains, gravelly ridges; eastern half of the United States. Building, furniture, floors, beams, shipbuilding, veneer, railroad ties.

Pine, ponderosa, or western yellow (Pinus ponderosa). Figure 64–20. Light russet-red, scaly-surfaced bark. Hard, strong, light-colored wood. Habitat: open, park-like forests; dry or moist soils; from southern British Columbia south through the western Rocky Mountain region to northern Mexico. One of the most valuable lumber trees of the West, sometimes living five hundred years. Sash, doors, frames, siding, knotty paneling, interior finish, crates, boxes, wood novelties, toys, caskets.

Pine, western white (Pinus monticola). Figure 64–21. Lavender-gray, broken rough-squared bark. Light, soft, pale brown, commercially valuable wood. Habitat: west of the Rocky Mountains; abundant in Idaho, Montana, Washington. Cabinetwork, knotty

Fig. 64–23. Yellow poplar, or tulip tree.

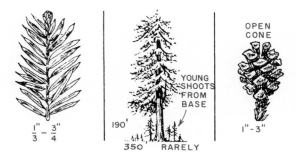

Fig. 64–24. Redwood.

paneling, millwork, exterior and interior finishes, siding, wooden matches.

Pine, white (Pinus strobus). Figure 64–22. Rough, gray-brown, small-segmented bark. Pale buff-yellow, soft, durable, easily worked wood. Habitat: light, sandy soil; throughout northwestern United States from Iowa and Minnesota eastward, southeastern Canada, Appalachian Mountains to northern Georgia. Building purposes.

Poplar, yellow, or tulip tree (Liriodendron tulipifera). Figure 64–23. Brownish-gray, confluent, round-ridged bark. Pale buff, close, straight-grained, light, soft, easily worked wood that does not readily split, warp, or shrink. Habitat: rich, moist soil; Rhode Island to Michigan, south to Georgia and Arkansas. Interior cabinetwork; excellent core for veneers; construction.

Redwood (Sequoia sempervirens). Figure 64–24. Deep cinnamon-brown, gray-tinted bark. Crimson-brown, soft, brittle, straight-grained, easily worked wood. Habitat: Pacific Coast, within the 20-mile-wide

297

Fig. 64–25. Black, or bog, spruce.

Fig. 64–27. Sycamore.

Fig. 64–26. Sitka spruce.

Fig. 64–28. Black walnut.

fog belt from southern Oregon to Monterey County, California. Tallest tree in the world, reaching 200 to 350 feet. Sometimes lives to be 1,200 to 1,400 years old. Great commercial importance; interior finish, woodwork, outdoor structures such as silos, barns, tanks, bridges, pipelines, flumes, mill roofs, cooling towers.

Spruce, black, or bog (Picea mariana). Figure 64–25. Thin, close-fitting, reddish-brown, small-scaled bark. Light, buff-yellow, soft, elastic, resonant, straight-grained wood. Spruce gum. Habitat: bogs, swamps, uplands, mountain slopes; Newfoundland west to Minnesota, south to New Jersey, Pennsylvania; along the Allegheny Mountains to Georgia. Paper pulp, light furniture, joists, sills, musical instruments, paddles, oars.

Spruce, Sitka (Picea sitchensis). Figure 64–26. Reddish-brown, thin, scaly bark. Light, soft, straight-grained, satiny, pale reddish-brown wood. Habitat: moist, sandy soil; swamps; Pacific Coast from Kodiak Islands in Alaska to Mendocino County,

California. Remarkable for rapid growth, great size, beauty as an evergreen, and great age. Boats, buildings, fencing, wooden utensils, boxes, barrels, paper pulp.

Sycamore (Platanus occidentalis). Figure 64–27. Greenish-gray bark which flakes off yearly in broad scales, exposing a greenish-white inner bark. Heavy, coarse-grained, hard, strong, light ruddy-brown wood. Habitat: rich bottom lands; moist woodlands; native from Maine to Minnesota, south to Florida and Texas. Cigar boxes, furniture, butchers' blocks.

Walnut, black (Juglans nigra). Figure 64–28. Thick, dark brown, deeply divided, broad round-ridged bark. Deep brown, hard, heavy, slightly brittle, nonwarping, even-textured, beautiful wood. Polishes well. Edible, tasty, nutritive nut. Habitat: rich woodlands; easily propagated; area of commercial importance: Missouri, Kansas, Illinois, Indiana, Ohio, Kentucky, and Tennessee. Fine furniture, woodwork, boat building, gunstocks, veneers.

1. Distinguish between hardwoods and softwoods.
2. From what places is mahogany imported?
3. Where is the government Forest Products Laboratory located?
4. Describe the bark of both the young yellow birch and the sycamore.
5. Name a fragrant wood and tell its outstanding use.
6. What wood can you stain readily to resemble mahogany?
7. Name a wood having a creamy color and a satiny luster.
8. What type of pine is one of the most valuable lumber trees of the West?
9. Give the sources of the wood most used for the following articles: (*a*) cigar boxes, (*b*) musical instruments, (*c*) wooden matches, (*d*) core for veneers, (*e*) barrels, (*f*) oars, (*g*) mat fiber, (*h*) agricultural implements, and (*i*) picture frames.
10. What two woods are used especially in the manufacture of fine furniture and veneer?
11. Name three woods particularly useful in shipbuilding.
12. What two trees grow to great size and age?
13. What types of trees are found most frequently along the Pacific Coast from Alaska to California?
14. What trees yield bases for maple sugar, chewing gum, and leather-tanning solution?
15. List the trees which grow in your area or region. Are they hard- or softwoods?
16. What are the characteristics and uses of the trees you listed in topic 15?

unit

65

Production of lumber

The lumber industry in America appears to have had its start about 1608 in Jamestown, Virginia. Since 1776 it has produced the staggering amount of approximately 3,000,000 million board feet of lumber (Fig. 65–1). This would be sufficient to build 300 million five-room frame houses. Management of for-

Fig. 65–1. Unlimited lumber resources are present in our forests. (*Weyerhaeuser Company.*)

299

Fig. 65-2. Planned block cutting in forest areas is the result of scientific management *(U. S. Forest Service.)*

Fig. 65-3. A large sawmill power plant and pulp mill. *(Weyerhaeuser Company.)*

est reserves ensures continuous production of timber crops (Fig. 65-2).

Thousands of sawmills, lumber wholesalers, commission salesmen, retailers, and transportation systems are involved in this gigantic industry. There are at least 32,000 sawmills (Fig. 65-3). Approximately 4,000 lumber wholesalers handle about 75 percent of the lumber produced. Thirty thousand retail lumber dealers account for its distribution to the American public.

The 508,845,000 acres of commercial forest land in the United States furnish more than 90 percent of the lumber needed. About 75 percent is harvested from the 366,977,000 acres of privately-owned commercial forest land. The remaining acreage is state- and nationally-owned (see Figs. 65-4 and 65-5).

There are over one thousand species of trees in commercial forests, of which only 180 have commercial value. Most of the lumber, however, comes from only 35 species.

Lumber production on a large scale in the United States began in Maine, where it was centered for almost 200 years. The heart of this industry is now on the West Coast. Oregon has led all states in the pro-

Fig. 65-4. Privately owned tree farms contribute greatly to lumber production. *(Western Pine Association.)*

Fig. 65–5. One hundred ninety-seven board feet of lumber were sawed out of a 14-inch diameter white pine, and laid on the ground. This was a dedication attraction for a tree farm in Massachusetts. *(American Forest Products Industries.)*

Fig. 65–7. A cruiser marks a redwood tree for selective cutting. *(U. S. Forest Service.)*

Fig. 65–6. A forester is making a scientific analysis of lumber availability. *(Western Wood Products Association.)*

Fig. 65–8. Two tractors work a logging operation. One machine pioneers a road while the other skids logs. (Caterpillar Tractor Company.)

301

Fig. 65-9. Felling a tree. *(Homelite Company.)*

Fig. 65-10. This is a logger using a power saw to "buck" (cut up) a large redwood tree into 20-foot lengths. *(U. S. Forest Service.)*

Fig. 65-11. Skidding (sliding) a huge redwood log to the loading site. *(Culname-Fattori Associates, Ltd.)*

Fig. 65-12. A tractor skids several pine logs on one trip during logging operations. *(U. S. Forest Service.)*

duction of lumber since 1938. The United States produces 27 percent of total world output of lumber.

Lumber mills have become highly mechanized. Machines do the work once performed by men and oxen in all phases of production, from the marking of the tree in the woods to the final stack of lumber in the lumberyard. Annual consumption of lumber in the United States is slightly over forty billion board feet. It is estimated that this figure will rise to around 45 billion by the year 1975.

Fig. 65–13. A load of logs on a carriage being moved by cable on a skyline crane to a loading site. *(U.S. Forest Service.)*

Fig. 65–15. Logs are being cable-lifted onto a truck. *(Weyerhaeuser Company.)*

Fig. 65–14. Air tongs are often used to load logs onto a truck. *(Western Wood Products Association.)*

Fig. 65–16. Sometimes a log is so huge that only one can be carried on a truck. This ponderosa pine log contains 4,710 board feet of lumber. *(Western Wood Products Association.)*

Fig. 65–17. A loaded log train rolls down out of the mountains on a western tree farm. Nearly half a mile of cars, loaded with logs, stretches behind this diesel locomotive. *(Weyerhaeuser Company.)*

Fig. 65–20. This log unloader can remove a load of logs from a truck, or from a railroad car, in one bite. *(American Forest Products Industries.)*

Fig. 65–18. Floating logs to a mill. *(Western Wood Products Association.)*

Fig. 65–19. Scaling (measuring) a redwood log on a logging truck at the scale house. This one is 72 inches in diameter, 20 feet long, and "scaled" at 4,930 board feet. *(U. S. Forest Service.)*

Fig. 65–21. Washing a yellow pine log as it enters the sawmill. *(American Forest Products Industries.)*

There are many processes involved in bringing wood from the forest to lumberyards and shops. Scientific studies determine the amount and suitability of timber in a forest (Fig. 65–6) and the methods of logging it. The amount, or volume, of timber in an area is estimated by men called cruisers (see Fig. 65–7). They make a sampling of the number of trees by species and size. On the basis of this information, commercial companies secure the maximum timber yield from their cutting. Cruisers also plan transportation routes.

If the timber stands in remote areas, it is often necessary to build a logging camp to house the workers. Logging roads must also be constructed in many instances in order to get men and equipment into the area (Fig. 65–8).

LOGGING

The first operations in logging are those of *felling* and *bucking*. Trees are felled, or cut down, as shown in Fig. 65–9, *bucked* or cut into suitable lengths (Fig. 65–10), and transported to the mills.

The cut logs must be skidded (Figs. 65–11 and 65–12) or moved by cable (Fig. 65–13) to loading sites. Logging trucks are used extensively in hauling logs to the mills (Figs. 65–14 through 65–16). In some parts of the country, logs are loaded on railroad cars for shipment (Fig. 65–17) or floated down rivers and streams to mills (Fig. 65–18).

PRODUCTION OF LUMBER

Sawmills have a cutting production of from 3,000 to 1,000,000 board feet of lumber per day. The larger mills (see Fig. 65–3) are usually steam- or electric-powered. Smaller ones often use gasoline or diesel engines.

Upon delivery to the sawmill, the logs are *scaled* (measured) for maximum square footage (Fig. 65–19). They are next un-

Fig. 65–22. Bark is blasted from logs by jets of water under 1,500 lbs. of pressure by a hydraulic barker. (*Weyerhaeuser Company.*)

Fig. 65–23. The head sawyer is a key man in the production of wood products. He saws each log into huge, rough slices, and he must know how to cut the log in a way to get the greatest value from it. (*Weyerhaeuser Company.*)

Fig. 65-24. Edge ripping a board to a standard width. *(Weyerhaeuser Company.)*

Fig. 65-25. A gang of trimmer saws for cutting boards to standard lengths. *(West Coast Lumbermen's Association.)*

Fig. 65-26. Lumber is sorted according to grade, size, and length. *(Weyerhaeuser Company.)*

Fig. 65-27. Stacking lumber for air drying. *(Clark Equipment Company.)*

Fig. 65-28. Stacked lumber ready to enter the kiln for drying. *(Weyerhaeuser Company.)*

306

Fig. 65–29. Stacking lumber for shipping. *(Clark Equipment Company.)*

Fig. 65–30. Packaged lumber being loaded onto a railroad car for shipment. *(Weyerhaeuser Company.)*

loaded (Fig. 65–20) and sorted according to species and grades. From here they are taken either to a pond for storage or the process of making lumber begins. They are then individually washed and cleaned in readiness for sawing (Fig. 65–21). Many companies debark logs before washing (Fig. 65–22). The bark is not wasted; it is used in the manufacture of by-products.

Logs are clamped on a movable carriage which works on a straight track. They are carried past a stationary band saw or a circular saw (Fig. 65–23). Larger mills generally use the band saw, smaller ones, the circular saw.

After the logs have been cut into boards, they fall on a set of rollers which takes them for further processing. In large mills, a machine called an edger (Fig. 65–24) rips rough edges off boards and cuts them into standard widths. They are then cut into standard lengths with trimmer saws (Fig. 65–25).

Fig. 65–31. Loading lumber aboard a ship. *(Towmotor Corporation.)*

The basic steps of making lumber are:

1. Cutting the log into boards
2. Ripping the boards into widths
3. Cutting the boards into lengths

The grading and sorting of lumber follow standardized rules (Fig. 65–26). Seasoning is accomplished either by air drying (Fig. 65–27) or in kilns (Fig. 65–28). The time required for air drying varies according to the kind of weather, the wood, the dimensions of the board, the arrangement of the yard, and the method of stacking. Kiln drying takes less time.

The lumber is now stacked in huge warehouses. It is then shipped to lumberyards or planing mills (Fig. 65–29). Other consumers of lumber from these warehouses are flooring mills, construction companies, furniture plants, and other wood-products industries. Shipments are made by railroads (Fig. 65–30), trucking firms, and maritime transportation (Fig. 65–31).

Discussion Topics

1. What is the oldest technical industry in America?
2. Approximately how many board feet of lumber have been produced since American independence?
3. What percentage of the lumber is produced from privately-owned forest lands?
4. Approximately how many species of trees are there in the United States?
5. How many of this number have commercial value?
6. In what part of the United States did lumber production begin?
7. What state is the greatest lumber producer?
8. Where is the nearest sawmill in your area?
9. What percentage of the total world production of lumber is produced in the United States?
10. Name two duties of a timber cruiser.
11. What are the two early operations in logging?
12. How are logs skidded?
13. Name three methods of getting logs to a sawmill.
14. How is power furnished in sawmills?
15. What are the three basic steps in the manufacture of lumber?
16. What is the purpose of the log pond at a mill?
17. What kinds of saws are used to saw a log in a mill?
18. What is the annual lumber consumption in the United States? What is it estimated to be by 1975?
19. What is an edger? A trimmer saw? Bucking?
20. Explain in detail the two methods of drying lumber and the advantages of each.

unit
66

The manufacture and use of veneer and plywood

Plywood is a crossbanded wood product made up of layers of veneer and/or lumber bonded with adhesives (glue). It is sometimes referred to as a wood "sandwich" consisting of an odd number of layers. The face grain is selected for its superior grain, markings, texture, and color.

The grain of each layer of wood is laid at right angles to the grain of the adjacent ply (wood sheet). The layers are permanently glued together. Because of this "layering" effect, modern plywood construction has added dimensional stability. Plywood is considered stronger for its weight than steel.

COMPOSITION OF PLYWOOD

Plywood differs from solid lumber because it is made up of *layers*, or *plies*, of lumber, as shown in Fig. 66-1. The outer two layers or sheets are called plies. One surface ply will usually be called the *face* veneer. The opposite one, the *back* veneer. The innermost ply is called the *core*. All other plies between the core and the face plies are termed *crossbands*. Figure 66-2 illustrates two general methods of plywood build-up.

There are three specific types of plywood construction. The *veneer core* type has all plies of wood veneer (Fig. 66-2). The *lumber core* type consists of strips of wood, edge-glued together to form the cen-

tral ply or core (Fig. 66-2). This core is covered on both sides with crossbands and face veneers. *Particle board core* uses particle board for the complete makeup except for the one or two surface plies of veneer.

VENEER

Veneer is a thin sheet or layer of wood sliced or peeled from the log, varying in thickness from $1/100$ to $1/4$ inch. Perfect specimens of veneered objects have been found in tombs of the Pharaohs of Egypt, dating from about 1500 B.C.

The veneer-cutting lathe and the veneer slicer were not developed until the middle of the 19th century. The piano manufactur-

FACE VENEER
CROSSBAND
LUMBER CORE
CROSSBAND
BACK VENEER

Fig. 66-1. Plywood is made up of an uneven number of wood layers, having the grain of each piece at right angles to the adjacent layers. *(Fine Hardwoods Association.)*

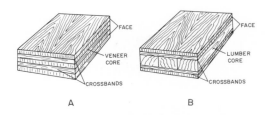

FACE
VENEER CORE
CROSSBANDS

FACE
LUMBER CORE
CROSSBANDS

A   B

Fig. 66-2. Two types of plywood construction: (A) crossbanded sheets of veneer, and (B) lumber core center. *(Paxton Lumber Company.)*

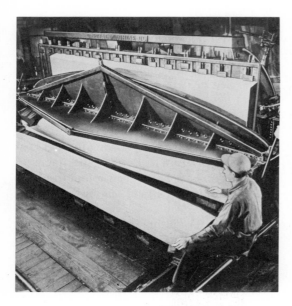

Fig. 66–3. Slicing veneer with a straight knife.

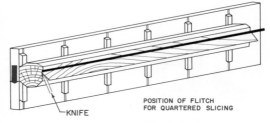

Fig. 66–6. (Fine Hardwoods Association.)

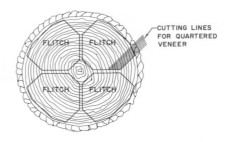

Fig. 66–7. (Fine Hardwoods Association.)

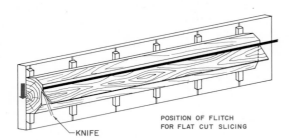

Fig. 66–4. (Fine Hardwoods Association.)

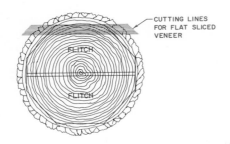

Fig. 66–5. (Fine Hardwoods Association.)

ing industry is credited with being the first to use plywood covered with exotic-grained veneers. It was not until the beginning of this century that plywood was a stock item for the consumer.

VENEER MANUFACTURE

Veneer is obtained from a log by *rotary cutting* (see Fig. 66–13) or *straight slicing* (Fig. 66–3). The rotary-cutting method is done by rotating the log against a stationary knife.

In *flat slicing*, the log is halved lengthwise and each half is placed on a slicer in such a manner that the veneer cut pieces will have a combination of straight grain (quarters) on each side of the sheet, with the flat-cut (heart) in the middle, as illustrated in Figs. 66–4 and 66–5.

The term *flitch*, as referred to in these figures, is used to designate a lengthwise section of a log. In veneer manufacturing, each log is sawed into flitches of no longer

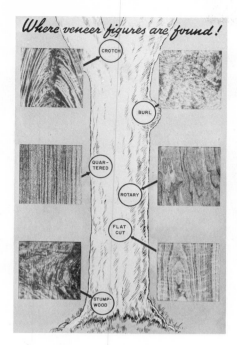

Fig. 66–8. Where veneer figures are found in a tree. *(Fine Hardwoods Association.)*

Fig. 66–9. Logs are stored in a pond for complete saturation with water. *(American Plywood Association.)*

Fig. 66–10. The log is being turned in a barker. *(American Plywood Association.)*

Fig. 66–11. Bark-free logs after sorting are being placed on a conveyor line for further processing. *(Weyerhaeuser Company.)*

than 17 feet. Each slice of veneer in a flitch is kept in consecutive order for grain matching. Manufacturers select their preferred grain in veneer by inspecting samples of these cuts which come from certain numbered flitches.

The difference between *quartered* and *flat-cut* veneer is in the preparation of the log, which is sawed into quarter-cut flitches. The veneer in each quarter is cut approximately at right angles to the growth rings, as shown in Figs. 66–6 and 66–7. This produces the straight and broken stripe figure common of quarter cutting.

Flat- and quarter-slicing methods are used generally on hardwood in order to obtain the maximum grain effect for final, clear finishing. Rotary cutting is almost always used on softwood to process plywood veneer. Figure 66–8 shows the areas of a tree where the various cuts of veneer may be obtained.

PLYWOOD MANUFACTURE

The process of plywood manufacture converts the natural resource, trees, into plywood by the unwinding or peeling of logs, or slicing of strips, into thin veneer. This is followed by the bonding of the thin sheets of wood into large panels. The manufacturing procedure for plywood is basically the same whether applied to softwoods or hardwoods; the construction of the cores or plies, as indicated in Figs. 66–1 and 66–2, does not affect the basic procedures.

Trees are first cut into 4- and 8-foot logs, and then are either *soaked* in ponds, or *sprayed* until they are saturated with water (Fig. 66–9). The log is next hoisted into a mill, where it is *debarked* (Fig. 66–10). The debarked logs are often then placed in a log-storage pond where they are *sorted* according to species, size, and grade (Fig. 66–11).

Logs next are placed in huge steaming vaults for *conditioning*. This softens knots and makes it easier to peel top-grade veneer from the log.

Following the log-selection process, the logs are moved, as shown in Fig. 66–12, to the veneering lathe. Figure 66–13 pictures both the veneer being *peeled*, and also the intricate machinery needed for *unwinding* the log into a continuous ribbon of veneer.

The continuous sheet of veneer is processed almost automatically as it enters the *clipping* machine (Fig. 66–14). This machine cuts (clips) the veneer into desired widths and grades, according to growth defects in the wood (Fig. 66–15).

Figure 66–16 pictures various veneer grades going through long dryers where the moisture content of the wood is reduced to approximately 5 percent. The dryers heat up to 280 to 300 degrees; the veneer remains in them from 5 to 10 minutes.

The veneer or core strips must be made into full-size sheets. This is generally done with an *electronic splicer* (Fig. 66–17).

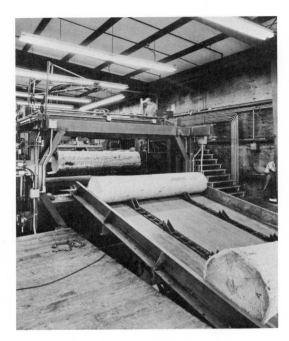

Fig. 66–12. Logs being moved up to a rotary cutting lathe. *(Georgia-Pacific Corporation.)*

Fig. 66–13. A continuous ribbon of veneer is being cut from the log. The photograph shows the intricate machinery necessary for peeling a log. *(Georgia-Pacific Corporation.)*

Fig. 66-14. A sheet of veneer leaving the lathe and entering a tray system en route to the clipping machine. *(Georgia-Pacific Corporation.)*

Fig. 66-16. Veneer sheets passing through a drying machine. *(American Plywood Association.)*

Fig. 66-15. Veneer being clipped or cut into desired widths and grades. *(American Plywood Association.)*

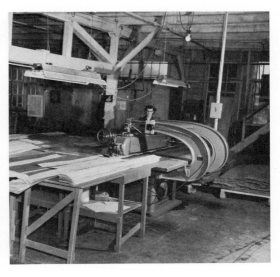

Fig. 66-17. An electronic splicer fastening narrow strips of veneer into required widths. *(U. S. Forest Service.)*

Fig. 66–18. Inspection of veneer sheets in a veneer storage area. *(U.S. Forest Service.)*

Fig. 66–20. Glue is rolled onto both sides of core veneer. *(American Plywood Association.)*

Fig. 66–19. Matching of African Kevazingo veneer used in the orchestra section of the Metropolitan Opera House in Lincoln Center, New York City. *(U.S. Plywood Corporation.)*

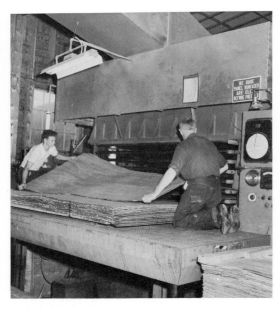

Fig. 66–21. Workers putting three-ply veneer into the pressing machine. *(U.S. Forest Service.)*

In the production of plywood, where one or both faces of veneer must have desirable surface-grain qualities for natural finishing, the veneer must be carefully selected (Fig. 66–18), and/or matched (Fig. 66–19), before final lamination.

Figure 66–20 shows core veneer having glue or adhesives applied to both sides as it is fed through the *spreader*. The panel is laid up or put together with grain of alternate plies running in opposite direction.

The wet-glued (sandwiched) panels are next hauled to the *hot press*. These panels are individually lifted into the hot press where heat of around 250 degrees Fahrenheit and pressure varying from 150 to 300 pounds per square inch are applied. These presses have 12 or more openings, each capable of making one thick panel or two thin ones (Figs. 66–21 and 66–22).

Glued plywood panels are sawed into standard widths and lengths, usually 4 × 8 feet. The one shown in Fig. 66–23, however, is a custom-made 16-foot long panel for the new Metropolitan Opera House in New York City.

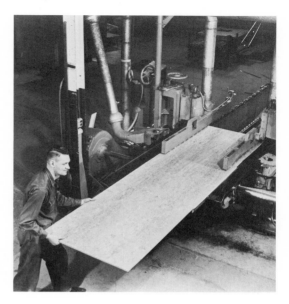

Fig. 66–23. Sizing (cutting to size) a plywood panel. *(U. S. Plywood Corporation.)*

Fig. 66–22. Giant hot presses bond the assembled veneers into a wood-and-glue plywood 'sandwich.' *(American Plywood Association.)*

Fig. 66–24. An inspector checks the panel after it has been machine-sanded to satin smoothness. *(American Plywood Association.)*

315

Fig. 66-25. Thin plywood is easy to bend. Note saw kerfs (cuts) on the backside, near where the craftsman is planing the edge. *(Georgia-Pacific Corporation.)*

Fig. 66-27. Veneers are pressed into a curved shape after 30 seconds in the electronic laminating press. *(Drexel Furniture Company.)*

Fig. 66-26. Veneer pieces are fitted into a mold for laminating into a curved form. *(Drexel Furniture Company.)*

Fig. 66-28. Brown, wormy chestnut plywood panels on the wall and ceiling make this an interesting den. *(U.S. Plywood Corporation.)*

Core voids (openings) on the edges of panels are filled with wood-flour mix. These openings might be caused by knot holes.

Sanding to a satin smoothness is done on double sanding drum machines (Fig. 66–24). Here is where inspection is needed to obtain quality.

Automatic *marking*, or labeling, and *strapping* machines prepare plywood for storage and subsequent delivery.

CHARACTERISTICS

Plywood has many structural advantages. Wood is stronger along the grain than it is across grain. By alternating the grain direction 90 degrees with each successive layer, the strength properties are equalized.

There is more efficient utilization of species of woods in the manufacture of plywood. Valuable woods can be used as face veneers, and less expensive ones used as solid cores or inner plies.

Plywood is more flexible. It is particularly adaptable to bending and forming processes (Figs. 66–25 through 66–27). Because of

Fig. 66–30. Plywood paneling expedites building construction. *(Georgia-Pacific Corporation.)*

Fig. 66–31. Fir plywood box girders being put in place for a new industrial plant. *(American Plywood Association.)*

Fig. 66–29. Walnut veneer makes these formed plywood chairs ultra-contemporary. *(Drexel Furniture Company.)*

Fig. 66–32. Water resistant plywood is a boon to the marine industry.

Fig. 66–33. Fir plywood, bonded to impregnated honeycomb core stock, forms the ceiling of a new school building. *(American Plywood Association.)*

Fig. 66–34. Resin-fiber-surface plywood panels form the basic construction material for a new space center launching complex. Architects describe this as the largest building in the world. *(Georgia-Pacific Corporation.)*

this, many plywood products are designed to make use of this particular characteristic, such as curved chair seats and backs, custom furniture parts, and boat hulls.

USES AND APPLICATIONS

Plywood products are used extensively in home building, for exterior siding, interior wall paneling, and flush doors. In the home there are chairs, tables, television sets, and all types of furniture constructed of hardwood plywood. In fact, it would be impossible to enumerate all the applications of this versatile material.

Wall paneling is shown in Fig. 66–28. Figure 66–29 pictures uses in furniture. Pine paneling of plywood is an application of softwood in building construction, as shown in Fig. 66–30. Figure 66–31 shows use of fir plywood box girders for a new industrial plant. The marine field has become a volume outlet for plywood manufacturers because of plywood's adaptability in forming and its capacity for being made water resistant (Fig. 66–32).

The forming characteristic of plywood makes it most suitable for industrial roof construction as shown in Fig. 66–33.

Fig. 66–35. Four successive steps in the preparation of a laminated golf club head. *(Wilson Sporting Goods Company.)*

Resin-fiber-surface panels made up the basic construction material for a new launching complex at the Kennedy Space Center (Fig. 66–34). An interesting application for small products is shown in the successive steps for the production of golf club heads (Fig. 66–35). These two radically different types of application stress the versatility and importance of plywood in modern technological activity.

Discussion Topics

1. Define and describe plywood.
2. Is plywood considered as strong as steel for its weight? Why?
3. How does plywood differ from solid lumber?
4. Name and illustrate two general methods of plywood construction.
5. What is veneer?
6. Trace the historical development of veneer.
7. Approximately when were the veneer-cutting lathe and the veneer slicer developed?
8. Describe the manufacturing procedure for plywood. List at least eight different steps in this process.
9. About when did plywood become a stock item for the consumer?
10. Name and describe the two general methods of cutting veneer.
11. What is a flitch?
12. What was the first industry credited with using plywood extensively?
13. List at least six characteristics of plywood which manufacturers claim make this product superior to solid wood.
14. Look around the school, business offices, and your home. List 20 specific items made from plywood.
15. Give five uses of plywood in building construction.

unit

67

The manufacture and use of hardboard

Hardboard is a descriptive term which is used to identify a wide range of processed wood products which are hard in composition. They are considered boards, since they are made of wood fibers shaped into a board or panel. Hardboard is the end result of much research and of market development.

Science, engineering, and technology are principally responsible for the manufactured product, which is shown in Fig. 67–1.

DEVELOPMENT

The history of hardboard illustrates how a company (Fig. 67–2) and an industry developed out of the initiative, imagination, resourcefulness, and know-how of one man. This industry began in 1924. The discoverer, William H. Mason, an engineer and inventor, came across this process somewhat by accident. He was trying to squeeze moisture out of a mat of wet fibers, using a steam-heated press (Fig. 67–3).

When he left his laboratory one day for a period of time, he turned off the steam. Upon his return he found that due to a faulty valve, the steam had kept on heating and the fiber mat had been pressed into a hot, dense, and dry board. This was the be-

Fig. 67-1. A few of the many patterns and surface textures available in hardboard. *(American Hardboard Association.)*

Fig. 67-2. An aerial view of the world's largest hardboard plant, Laurel, Mississippi. *(Masonite Corporation.)*

ginning of a product that does not split, splinter, or crack.

COMPOSITION

Hardboard differs from lumber or plywood in that the wood fibers have been rearranged during the manufacturing process to form hard panels.

Wood fibers are made of cellulose and lignin. Cellulose gives strength, while lignin is the binder which cements the fibers together. Hardboard consists entirely of fibers with a small amount of certain types of chemicals added to give the board special structural characteristics.

SOURCE OF RAW MATERIALS

Wood, in practically any form, was originally used for the raw material in the manufacture of hardboard. The demand for the raw base has become so great that timberlands are now developed especially for this industry. The thinning of forests, necessary to produce healthier woodlands, provides much wood for hardboard material. Extensive use is also made of wood residues from sawmills and plywood manufacturing plants. The fell-

Fig. 67-3. The steam-heated press which produced hardboard by accident. *(American Forest Products Industries.)*

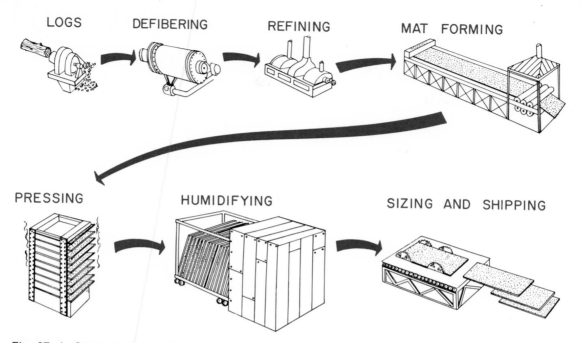

LOGS   DEFIBERING   REFINING   MAT FORMING

PRESSING   HUMIDIFYING   SIZING AND SHIPPING

Fig. 67–4. Steps in the manufacture of hardboard. *(American Hardboard Association.)*

ing and hauling of timber to make hardboard is very similar to the method employed in the production of lumber, explained in Unit 65, *Production of Lumber.*

MANUFACTURING HARDBOARD

The diagram in Fig. 67–4 shows the numerous steps in the manufacture of hardboard.

The logs, or raw material, must first go through a chipper. This is a revolving disk fitted with many sharp knives. The wood is cut into pieces approximately ⅝ inch wide and 1 inch long. The chips are stored in large silos (Fig. 67–5). They are loaded and unloaded from the silos on belt conveyors (Fig. 67–6). When the chips are needed, the conveyors carry them inside the plant where they are sorted for size on shaker screens.

The first actual step in the conversion of the wood chips into hardboard is the process of defibering, or tearing apart. The chips are torn apart by exploding them either by steam pressure (Fig. 67–7), or in defibering machines.

The fibers next go through a refining process. Soluble wood sugars and other undesirable elements of natural wood are washed away (Fig. 67–8). The water is removed from the fibers (now called wet-lap) by means of gravity suction and squeezing. This forms the mat (see Fig. 67–4). The wet-lap mat is now 4½ inches thick (Fig. 67–9). It will ultimately emerge as ⁵⁄₁₆-inch thick hardboard. While the 4- to 5-foot wide wet-lap is moving with the conveyor at a steady rate, it is cut by a traveling-knife slicer into 16- to 18-foot lengths (Fig. 67–10).

The cut sheets of wet-lap are conveyed into a giant hydraulic hot press to be compressed (Fig. 67–11). The intense heat drives out the moisture in the form of steam. The

Fig. 67–5. Large silos 34 feet in diameter and 80 feet high are used for the storage of wood chips. *(Masonite Corporation.)*

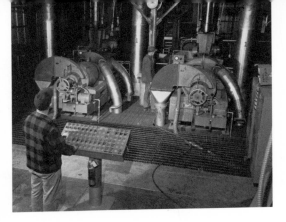

Fig. 67–7. Chips are defiberized (torn apart) by steam pressure, and are then further refined for final mat material. *(American Hardboard Association.)*

Fig. 67–8. Washing away wood sugar and other undesirable elements from wood fibers. *(Masonite Corporation.)*

Fig. 67–6. Conveyor belts carry wood chips from storage silos to the processing plant. *(Masonite Corporation.)*

lignin is reused to hold each fiber solidly in place in the hardboard panel.

The newly made hardboard sheets (Fig. 67–12), or panels, are sized (Fig. 67–13), edge-trimmed, graded, and stacked (Fig. 67–14). Hardboard at this stage is much drier than the air in which it will probably be used. Some moisture must therefore be added to the board. This is accomplished by placing the hardboard in a humidification chamber. This minimizes a tendency of the hardboard panel to warp, or twist.

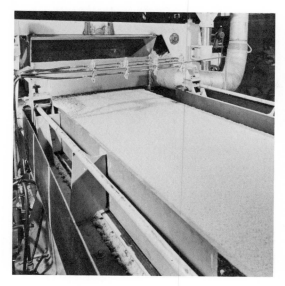

Fig. 67–9. Once chips are sized (graded), steamed, defiberized, and coated with a waterproof phenolic resin, the felter unit (upper left) discharges a continuous mat of wet fibrous pulp. The uniform thickness at this point is about 20 times the thickness of the final hardboard panel. *(Georgia-Pacific Corporation.)*

Fig. 67–11. A huge hydraulic press compresses many sheets of wet mats into hardboard. *(American Hardboard Association.)*

Fig. 67–10. Traveling saws cut hardboard into required lengths before the board is delivered to the dryer. *(American Hardboard Association.)*

Fig. 67–12. Hardboard panels emerging from the press unloader. From here they move to a humidifier in which they absorb moisture to give stability. *(Georgia-Pacific Corporation.)*

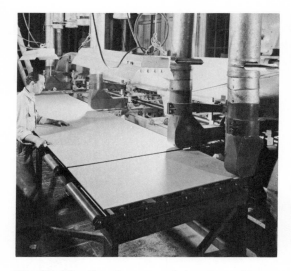

Fig. 67–13. Panels are cut to size with an easily adjusted gang rip saw. It is capable of 50-inch maximum width and minimum spacing between saws of 5 inches. There is also an automatic cut-off saw whereby strips can be stacked for volume precision crosscutting. *(Georgia-Pacific Corporation.)*

Many of the hardboard products will be given their final coating (Fig. 67–15) and simulated wood textures (Fig. 67–16).

ELECTRONIC CONTROL AND RESEARCH

The modern hardboard plant must maintain rigid specifications. Electronic panel instruments control the flow of electric current to machines, open and close valves, start and stop conveyors, and maintain quality standards of the product.

The quality of the raw materials and the finished hardboard product are continually checked and controlled by scientists and engineers. The physical properties of production samples are continually tested. Manufacturing plants of the hardboard industry, as those of other industries, must maintain research and development departments.

Fig. 67–14. Edge trimming, grading, and stacking pressed hardboard panels. *(Masonite Corporation.)*

Fig. 67–15. Hardboard panels receiving a finish coating through a precision roller-coater. The finish is cured by baking. *(Masonite Corporation.)*

Fig. 67–16. Wood graining applied to hardboard on an offset press. A protective coat is then applied and baked. *(Masonite Corporation.)*

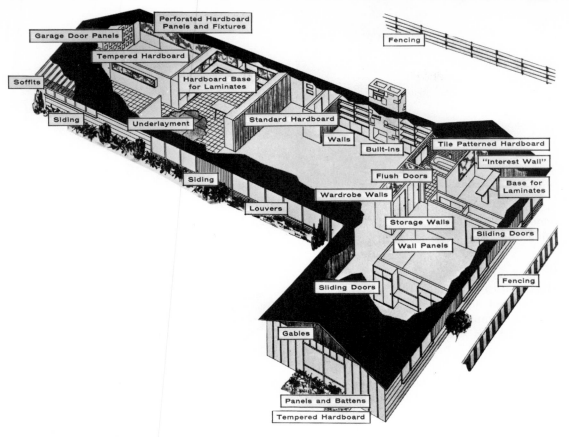

Fig. 67–17. Cutaway view of a typical home, showing some of the many uses of hardboard for home construction. *(American Hardboard Association.)*

Fig. 67–18. The hardboard exterior siding on this home is resistant to moisture, mildew, termites, grain raising, splitting, checking, and cracking. This siding can be worked with the usual woodworking and carpentry tools. *(American Hardboard Association.)*

Fig. 67–19. Patterns of filigree hardboard are excellent for decorative walls, room dividers, and screens. *(American Hardboard Association.)*

Fig. 67–20. Wood-grained hardboard wall panels and furniture fashion a most attractive living room.

Fig. 67–21. Peg-board provides utility and beauty for storage facilities. *(Georgia-Pacific Corporation.)*

USES

Hardboard is used in building construction, both indoor and outdoor. It is employed to make concrete forms, and is used as siding, ceilings, doors, wall panels, floors, and fences (see Figs. 67–17 through 67–21).

Hardboard is also suited to many types of farm structures. It is an important material in cabinetwork and in furniture. Large amounts of it are used in the manufacture of boats, toys, sporting goods, office equipment, automobile panels, trucks, mobile homes, displays, fixtures, packaging, aircraft, and railroad cars.

This industry is a multi-million dollar investment. Many millions of dollars are spent annually on research in the effort to produce better hardboard products to meet consumer demands (Fig. 67–22).

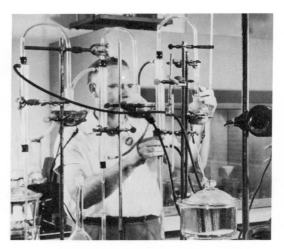

Fig. 67–22. Millions of dollars are spent annually in research by the hardboard industry to produce superior-quality products. *(Masonite Corporation.)*

Discussion Topics

1. What is the approximate number of wood products used in our everyday life?
2. List the raw ingredients for hardboard.
3. How would you describe hardboard?
4. How does hardboard differ from lumber and plywood?
5. In what year did the hardboard industry originate?
6. Who is credited with being the one to develop the hardboard industry?
7. Describe the original incident that led to the discovery of hardboard.

---

unit
68

The manufacture and use of particle board

Particle board, much like earlier-developed, currently available products such as plywood and hardboard, grew out of a need for greater utilization of trees, and the necessity for another type of manufactured wood product. Particle board, chip board, or flakeboard are terms often used to describe this new product. Technically, there are slight differences in each of these three compositions.

Particle board is made by combining wood particles (shavings and chips) with resin binders, then hot-pressing them into

Fig. 68–2. Pulp logs, such as used in the manufacture of paper, are also diverted into material for particle board. *(United States Forest Service.)*

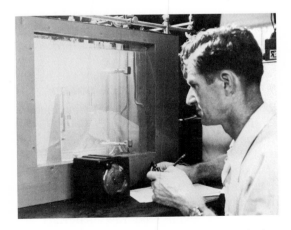

Fig. 68–1. Scientists are continually exploring the possibilities of new uses for wood products. *(United States Forest Service.)*

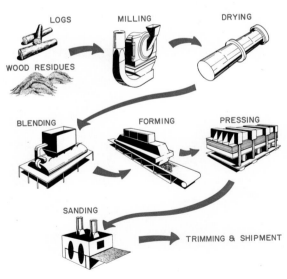

Fig. 68–3. Diagram of particle board manufacturing processes. *(National Particleboard Association.)*

Fig. 68-4. This milling equipment produces the desired types of tiny wood particles. *(National Particleboard Association.)*

Fig. 68-5. The dryer removes excess moisture from the wood particles, and controls moisture to the desired level. *(National Particleboard Association.)*

panels which result in carefully controlled physical properties. The scientifically designed panels use what was once considered a waste by-product of lumber.

DEVELOPMENT

Particle board was born of necessity in Europe immediately after World War II. It was devised because of the lack of available timber. Scientists and engineers in Germany, Switzerland, and Belgium were largely instrumental in perfecting the processing of this new product. American technicians and scientists (Fig. 68-1) have worked on the problem, and their ingenuity has developed new production systems having sophisticated forming, blending, and cutting equipment.

SOURCE OF RAW MATERIALS

Forest lands produce the basic material, *trees*, for the manufacture of all wood products. Thinning small trees in forests is one basic source of timber for use in the manufacture of particle board. Pulp logs, such as used in the manufacture of paper and hardboard, also furnish material (Fig. 68-2). Waste material consisting of culled lumber and ripping slabs is often ground into chips as another source of basic material for this new product. Dry shavings, once burned as waste, are now commonly processed into particle board.

MANUFACTURING PARTICLE BOARD

Particle board is a completely engineered product. From the basic ingredients to the finished panel, the process is expertly controlled; panels are developed by close tolerances to carefully tested composition. The diagram in Fig. 68-3 shows the basic steps in the manufacture of particle board.

In some plants the raw materials are stored in silos. At others, they are shipped from another location ready to process. In either case, the basic material must be milled by *flakers*, hammermills, or other types of milling equipment into wood particles.

The particles are then *screened* for size, thickness, width, and length (Fig. 68–4). Many particle boards have smaller sized particles on the surfaces and larger ones in the core. This gives the panel a smooth surface, and these boards are termed either "multi-layered" or "sandwich." These three-layered particle boards are preferred because the small fibers on the surfaces do not have a tendency to have the grain raise. The type having a uniform mixture of particle sizes is termed "homogeneous" board.

Usually after screening, the particles are *dried* in driers to a uniform moisture content (Fig. 68–5). The chips and shavings used as a source for particle board generally have around 15 percent moisture content. This must be reduced to 2 to 4 percent.

The next step, *blending*, is done on a highly automated production line where the particles are sprayed with a synthetic resin binder. These binding resins include urea-formaldehyde. From 8 to 10 percent of the final board weight is made up of binder which could account for 50 percent of the board cost.

The coated particles are next formed into *mats* (Fig. 68–6). Particle boards are dry-formed. That is, the particles are not deposited in a water solution as in the case of making paper. The mat-forming machine, shown in Fig. 68–6, lays a raw mat on a sheet of metal or plastic. The thickness of the mat is determined by the desired final thickness of the particle board. A finished ¾-inch-thickness board requires at least a 2½-inch thick mat.

Some companies process the mats immediately into a *hot press* where the mat is compressed to a given thickness. Others use a pre-press which decreases the thickness for clearance before being loaded into the main hot press.

Fig. 68–6. The forming machine deposits the treated wood particles onto belts, or metal or plastic plates, to form the mats. *(National Particleboard Association.)*

Fig. 68–7. Particle mats are pressed and the binders are cured in heated hydraulic presses. *(National Particleboard Association.)*

Fig. 68–8. Sanding in high-speed belt sanders produces the smooth surfaces and accurate thickness tolerances characteristic of particle boards. *(National Particleboard Association.)*

329

Fig. 68-9. Accuracy in thickness is checked periodically by an inspector who uses a micrometer. *(Weyerhaeuser Company.)*

Fig. 68-10. Particle boards trimmed and labeled, ready for stacking and shipping. *(Weyerhaeuser Company.)*

Fig. 68-11. Architectural woodwork in the Rayburn Congressional Office Building, Washington, D. C. has particle board cores. *(National Particleboard Association.)*

The main heated *hydraulic press* (Fig. 68-7) can consolidate and press many mats at the same time. Pressure is often as great as 1,000 pounds per square inch. Temperatures may range from 270 to 400 degrees Fahrenheit, depending on the type of resin used and the manufacturing process.

The mat is *cured* by steam heated platens. Some manufacturers use steam heated platens supplemented with high frequency electric heat.

After pressing, the boards are *cut* to width and length. They are then *sanded* on both sides (Fig. 68-8). Some manufacturers reverse this procedure and sand first, then trim. The sanding machines have several abrasive belts of different grit sizes, usually 30 and 80 grit. One thirty-second of an inch is required for sanding on each side.

Trimmings resulting from cutting the boards to size can be reused to make up approximately 30 percent of a new mixture. They can also be used for fuel.

Before boards are *labeled*, *stacked*, and *shipped*, they are carefully *selected for thickness* with a micrometer (Figs. 68-9 and 68-10).

PROPERTIES

Particle board has certain unique properties and features which have made this one of the fastest-expanding wood products industries. This product has no grain, because the axis of each wood particle is randomly oriented. This reduces the possibility of warping.

Particle board may be sawed, grooved, routed, drilled, or machined. The surface is smooth which makes it ideal for decorative finishes.

Another versatile characteristic of this product is that the physical properties can be varied and controlled in the manufacturing process, making it ideal for almost any use. The *control* consists of varying the amount of resin in the wood particles, or

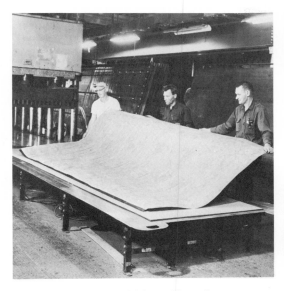

Fig. 68-12. Exotic African Kavazingo veneer being placed on fire-retardant particle board for lamination. *(United States Plywood Association.)*

Fig. 68-13. This functional and beautiful custom stereo cabinet is made with particle board core stock. *(National Particleboard Association.)*

Fig. 68-14. The playing surface of many pool and billiard tables is made from particle board because this product has less tendency to warp. *(National Particleboard Association.)*

Fig. 68-15. Particle board can be found beneath the floor covering, under the decorative plastic laminate counter top, and behind the wood veneers on cabinets in kitchens. *(National Particleboard Association.)*

Fig. 68-16. Grooved particle board makes excellent exterior siding for a home. *(National Particleboard Association.)*

331

altering the density of the board. Chemicals can be added during the manufacturing process to make this product fire-retardant, colored, or resistant to decay.

USES

The largest single use for particle board is as a core material for various types of furniture, case goods, and millwork. Figure 68–11 shows a meeting room in the Rayburn Office Building, Washington, D. C. Particle board was used as a core material throughout. More than 22 carloads of this core material were used for committee rostrums, doors, and architectural paneling in this building.

In Figure 68–12, workmen are laying a 16×5-$\frac{1}{2}$ foot sheet of African Kevazingo face veneer onto fire-retardant particle board for lamination in a giant hot press. Over 2,000 sheets of this exotic veneered paneling were used for interior decoration and acoustical treatment for the interior of the Lincoln Center new Metropolitan Opera House in New York.

Furniture designers and manufacturers use particle board increasingly as core stock for furniture parts (Fig. 68–13). Because this material offers resistance to warping, it is used for playing surfaces on pool and billiard tables (Fig. 68–14).

Utility-wise, the smooth surface characteristic has made it a very popular core material for sink and countertops. It may also be veneered with wood or with a plastic laminate to make it particularly useful in kitchen cabinet construction (Fig. 68–15).

The construction and home-building industry is making intensive use of particle board as a floor underlayment. It provides a smooth, sound base for tile or carpeting (see Fig. 68–15). Not to be outdone by other wood products, particle board is also produced for exterior siding on homes (Fig. 68–16).

Discussion Topics

1. What is the composition of particle board?
2. What historical event promoted the development of particle board? Why?
3. Name at least five basic forms of wood used in the manufacture of particle board.
4. Describe the difference between "multilayered" and "homogenous" particle board.
5. Name and describe at least six basic processes involved in the manufacture of particle board.
6. How does particle board differ from plywood and hardboard?
7. How thick must a raw mat be to obtain a finished $\frac{3}{4}$-inch-thickness particle board?
8. What percentage of the new mixture for particle board may be made from particle board trimmings?
9. List ten characteristics which make particle board outstanding.
10. How many square feet of particle board are being produced annually?
11. Cite at least eight uses of particle board.

unit

69

The manufacture and use of plastic laminates

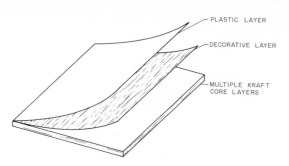

Fig. 69–1. Plastic laminates are made of layers of kraft paper, a decorative sheet, and a top protective layer.

Plastic laminates are made of layers of several types of paper which have been impregnated with synthetic resins to give the finished product the desired characteristics. Most of the decorative plastic laminate sheets are assembled from layers of kraft paper (filler stock) suitably treated with resin.

On top of this assembly is placed a piece of high quality paper on which the pattern has been printed. This print sheet (decorative layer), as it is called, has been treated with synthetic resin. On top of the print sheet goes a translucent paper, heavily impregnated with a melamine resin. The top layer becomes a transparent one during the curing process, and is the invisible surface which gives plastic laminate its enduring quality and beauty (Fig. 69–1). Other types of materials used for plies (layers) are asbestos, glass or fiberglass, cloth, matte, cotton, and different kinds of synthetic fabrics.

Laminated plastic sheets bonded (cemented) to plywood and particle board have become especially suited for many residential, institutional, and commercial uses.

PRODUCTION OF PLASTIC LAMINATES

The heavy kraft paper used to form the bulk of the decorative laminate sheets is called *filler stock*. It is processed and treated by passing it through an immersion tank filled

Fig. 69–2. Rolls of heavy kraft paper are used to make the several layers which form the core. *(Formica Corporation.)*

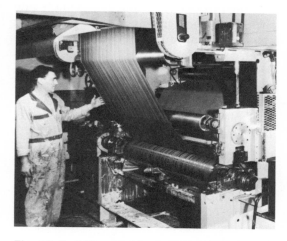

Fig. 69–3. Lithographic presses print the grain and colors to make up the texture of the decorative layer. *(Formica Corporation.)*

333

with resin (Fig. 69-2). The paper is saturated with a phenolic resin, such as phenol-formaldehyde. It is then dried by passing through a long oven. Filler stock makes up the *core*.

The *second layer*, making up the pattern or design, is produced on a *printing* or *graining press* (Fig. 69-3). A high-grade of specially prepared alpha cellulose paper is printed by rotogravure, lithography, or other graphic arts processes. Multicolors form the grain tone. After the paper is printed, it is re-rolled and stored for further processing.

The protective *top sheet* is a thin layer of translucent (semi-clear) material about 0.004 inch thick. It is heavily impregnated with melamine-formaldehyde resin, and becomes transparent during curing. This type of resin is used because of clarity, lack of color, hardness, and general resistance to damage from heat, water, and stains (see Fig. 69-1).

All of the processed layers which are used to form laminate sheets are temporarily stored until final assembly in dirt-free, humidity-, and temperature-controlled rooms. The final assembly is called "assembly into packs." A *pack* consists of the three basic units which make up the complete laminate sheet, as shown in Fig. 69-1. Giant presses (Fig. 69-4), used in curing and pressing, hold many packs. Each pack is protected from the other by a highly polished stainless steel plate placed above the top laminate. This produces a high gloss finish.

The platens (metal plates) in the huge hydraulic presses carry steam which produces the heat needed for starting the *curing* process (see Fig. 69-4). The presses exert pressure of about 1,500 pounds per square inch. They produce heat over 300 degrees Fahrenheit in beginning the curing.

The complete laminate sheets must be *edge-trimmed* to specified sizes. The *backs*

Fig. 69-4. Giant hydraulic presses cure laminated plastic sheets under heat and pressure. *(Formica Corporation.)*

Fig. 69-5. Laminated sheets are automatically edge-trimmed and back-sanded. *(Westinghouse Micarta.)*

334

Fig. 69–6. A famous lobby mosaic mural uses plastic laminate. This one is made up of red, white, and black units. *(Westinghouse Micarta.)*

Fig. 69–8. Plastic laminate covering on the doors, drawer fronts, and counter make this kitchen cabinet unit outstanding. It is also maintained easily. *(Westinghouse Micarta.)*

Fig. 69–7. Plastic laminate provides a lasting and beautiful material for the main bulkhead of this cruiser. *(Westinghouse Micarta.)*

must be *sanded* to a prescribed thickness (Fig. 69–5). The sanding operation is generally done with a medium grit abrasive to make the laminate easier to bond (fasten) to any surface.

The top (decorative) surface is further treated to produce extremely high-gloss, semigloss, or dull finishes.

CHARACTERISTICS

Plastic laminate sheet material can be cleaned easily. It is resistant to heat, denting, and scuffing, and it wears extremely well. It will also retain the original color and finish under normal use. It can be sawed, drilled, punched, filed, shaped, routed, sanded, and polished. The usual woodworking tools and

335

machines can be used to work with it, but it is desirable to have special blades and cutters.

Laminates are usually attached to flat surfaces, but they can be cold-formed around a radius as small as 10 to 12 inches. Special heated dies and fixtures are needed for producing radii of less than 8 to 10 inches. This process is often used in producing the cove or curved back section on kitchen drainboards.

USES

Finished, decorative, laminate sheets are very durable, colorful, and attractive. Uses include tops for pieces of furniture because the grain pattern can resemble any type of wood. This material is used extensively in the home, school, and commercial places (Figs. 69–6 through 69–8). Unit 23, *Applying Plastic Laminates* describes the procedure for fastening this product to wood or particle board panels and other flat surfaces.

Discussion Topics

1. Define plastic laminate.
2. Explain the three basic parts of a plastic laminate sheet.
3. Describe the manufacturing processes for making plastic laminate.
4. What makes plastic laminate so highly heat resistant, even though the basic material is paper?
5. What gives the face side of a plastic laminate sheet its extremely high gloss?
6. Why is the back side of laminate sanded and roughened?
7. Observe your home, neighborhood, school, and places of business. List 15 articles using plastic laminate. List where they are used.

---

unit

70

Other forest products

For centuries wood was used as a solid material. More recently, however, engineers, architects, designers, and scientists have learned how to bond layers of wood together to produce exceptional laminated beams and arches for construction purposes.

Fig. 70–1. Efficient use of raw material for numerous products. *(U. S. Forest Service.)*

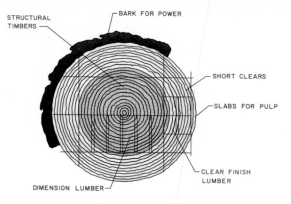

PRODUCTS FROM A TYPICAL SAWLOG

Fig. 70-2. Planned sawing results in effective use of a saw log. *(Weyerhaeuser Company.)*

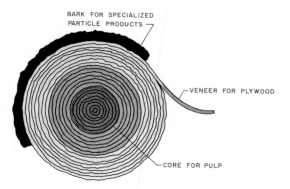

USING THE ENTIRE PLYWOOD LOG

Fig. 70-3. The entire log may be used in producing plywood veneer. *(Weyerhaeuser Company.)*

Fig. 70-4. The pulping industry can use all parts of a log. *(Weyerhaeuser Company.)*

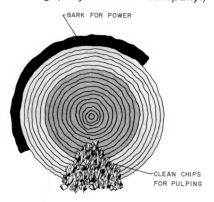

COMPLETE LOG CHIPPED FOR PULP

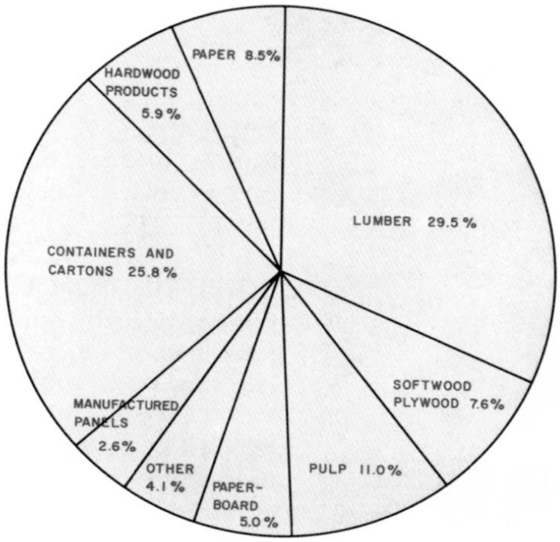

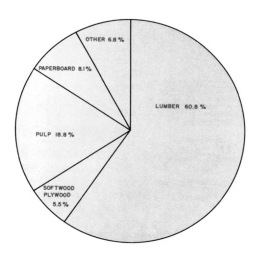

TODAY

Fig. 70-5. Product diversification in the lumber industry today. Study Fig. 70-6 and note the change in emphasis. *(Weyerhaeuser Company.)*

A DECADE AGO

Fig. 70-6. Product diversification in the lumber industry a decade ago. *(Weyerhaeuser Company.)*

Fig. 70–7.

SAWMILLS
SPECIALTY MILLS

SAWLOGS

PRODUCTS

USES

TIMBERS

Barges, bridges, building foundations, churches, dams, derricks, docks, factory and warehouse buildings, mine timbers, schools, ships, stringers, trailers, trucks, tugs

CONSTRUCTION LUMBER

Beams, boards, boat hulls and parts, dimensioned lumber, factory flooring, form lumber, heavy framing, joists, light framing, planks, posts, rafters, sheathing, sills, studs, subfloors, walls

FINISHED LUMBER

Baseboard, battens, casing, ceiling, flooring, lath, paneling, pickets, scaffolding, ship decking, siding, stepping

RE-MANUFACTURED LUMBER

Airplane parts, agricultural implements, athletic equipment (baseball bats, skis, tennis racquets, etc.), balusters, bowling alleys and pins, bobbins, boxes, burial boxes, butchers' blocks, cabinets (for radios, television, sewing machines, etc.), car construction and repair, caskets, clothespins, conduits, crates, cross-arms, displays, door jambs and frames, doors, dowels, floors, fixtures, furniture, glued laminated structural members, grain doors, gunstocks, gutters, handles, house trailers, ladders, lattice, laundry appliances, machinery, matches, medical supplies, millwork, moldings, musical instruments, novelties, pallets, panels, patterns, pencils, penholders, phonographs, playground equipment, plumbers' woodwork, professional instruments, printing material, pumps, radios, refrigerators, rollers for shades and maps, scientific instruments, ship and boat building (including aircraft carrier flight decks), shiplap, shoe heels and lasts, shuttles, signs, skewers, spools, sporting equipment, stage scenery, surgical supplies, tanks, toothpicks, toys, trim, trunks, valises, vehicles, venetian blinds, wedges, window frames, wood pipe, wooden shoes, woodenware

TIES

Railroad cross ties, mine ties, switch ties

COOPERAGE (STAVES)

Barrels, buckets, cooling towers, kegs, pipes, silos, tanks, tubs

MISCELLANEOUS

Acid washers, benches, corncribs, dunnage, elevators, fence pickets, grain bins, insulator pins, planks, reels, shingles, stakes, trestles, tunnel and mine props, wood chips for making wood pulp, wood turnings (for buttons, jewelry, etc.)

RESIDUES

Fuel, planer shavings for compressed fuel logs and briquettes, poultry litter, raw material for hardboard and particle board, and other bark, pulp, and sawdust products (such as sawdust soil conditioner)

(American Forest Products Industries.)

Fig. 70–8.

PLYWOOD MILLS
VENEER MILLS

PRODUCTS

USES

VENEER LOGS AND BOLTS

CONSTRUCTION PLYWOOD

Boxcar lining, boxes, cabinets, concrete forms, crates, door panels, finish, prefabricated houses, roofing, sheathing, siding, signboards, subflooring, truck floors and trailer panels, wainscoting, wall panels

MARINE PLYWOOD

Canoes, motorboats, naval craft, racing shells, sailboats

COMPREGNATED PLYWOOD

Airplane propellers, bearings, die stock, table tops, tubing, utensil handles, patterns

PACKAGE VENEER

Baskets, crates, hampers, matchboxes, wirebound boxes

FACE VENEER

Furniture, Pullman car lining, show windows, store fixtures, wainscoting, wall paneling, wallpaper

MISCELLANEOUS VENEERS

Applicators, balloon sticks, book covers, candy and ice cream sticks, cigar boxes and wrappers, floral sticks, ice cream spoons, luggage, mustard paddles, novelties, square stick matches, surgical items, toothpicks, tongue depressors

RESIDUES

Fuel, raw material for other bark and pulp products, paper roll plugs, particle board

(American Forest Products Industries.)

The location of much scientific experimentation with woods is the Forest Products Laboratory in Madison, Wisconsin. This is a research center, supported by the United States government, which aids in developing new products, improving old ones, and reducing wood waste. The research conducted at this laboratory benefits producers, processors, handlers, distributors, and consumers of many varied wood products and by-products. Since the establishment of this center in 1910, there have been over two million tests made to probe the fundamental and mechanical characteristics of wood and its many derivatives.

Many of the newer products are made from wood waste left over from other wood-manufacturing processes.

Conservation of woodlands and economy of production have resulted in improved

339

Fig. 70–9.

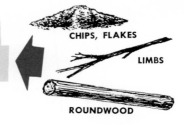

HARDBOARD PLANTS
PARTICLE BOARD PLANTS

PRODUCTS

USES

CHIPS, FLAKES

LIMBS

ROUNDWOOD

HARDBOARD

Battery separators, containers, decking, furniture and fixtures, paneling, sheathing, subflooring, signs, templates, toys

PARTICLE BOARD

Acoustical board, cabinet and wardrobe construction, door cores, molded furniture parts, paneling, patterns, sheathing, store fixtures, subflooring, window displays

(American Forest Products Industries.)

use of logs, eliminating in some instances all waste. This is illustrated in Figs. 70–1 through 70–4.

Wood-product diversification has developed and changed rapidly in the past decade. Compare Fig. 70–5, showing the utilization today, with Fig. 70–6, which illustrates use of wood ten years ago. Diversification not only helps use more of the log than ever before, but also results in greater sales market flexibility.

Forests provide the raw materials for over 5,000 products used in our daily lives. The broad scope of the many wood uses is illustrated in Figs. 70–7 through 70–13.

Furniture, books, magazines, radios, high fidelity sets, stereophonic loudspeakers, television cabinets, baseball bats, rolling pins, barrels, boxes, broom handles, turpentine for paint, resin for soap, sugar, plastics, rayon, and photographic film are just a few of the many products of our forests (Fig. 70–14).

Most homes are built of wood or at least have some wood in them. A more recent interesting development is chemically treated wood siding which does not need repainting for many years.

Over 70 percent of the entire tree — trunk, branches, top, and bark — goes into commercially useful products. Modern technology is constantly developing new uses for wood, therefore our need for timber will probably increase greatly in the future.

SPACE EXPLORATION

Balsa wood was selected to be used for a lunar capsule landing sphere. It has more impact-absorbing capacity than the other materials tested (Fig. 70–15).

The balsa segments surround and protect the sensitive instruments and absorb the shock of landing on the moon. In this particular scientific development, the various segments are glued together with epoxy glue around the instruments. After the landing impact, the crushed grain will swell and in a few hours the balsa will assume its original shape. Thus we see how balsa wood, long a favorite of model makers, was one of the first materials of earth's natural resources to be used in scientific exploration of the moon.

Wood was also used in the Polaris A-3 missile exploration. The nose cone of the Polaris missile is made of Sitka spruce ply-

Fig. 70-10.

PULP MILLS

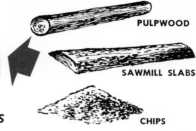

PULPWOOD

SAWMILL SLABS

CHIPS

PRODUCTS

USES

SULFITE PULP
Paper and paperboard for bags, blotters, printing papers, boxes, bristol board, envelopes, folding boxboard, fruit wrappers, greaseproof packaging, insulation, labels, paper napkins, patent coated boards, photo processing paper, sanitary tissues, stationery, stencils, tag board, wallpaper, waterproof packaging, wrapping
Dissolving pulps for cellophane, explosives, lacquers, plastics, photo film, rayon

SULFATE PULP
Paper and paperboard for bags, printing papers, bond paper, boxes, bristol board, chart paper, coating raw stock, condenser tissues, corrugated boxboard, envelopes, food containers, folding boxboard, insulation, ledger paper, liner board, offset paper, onionskin, parchment, sheathing paper, stationery, tag stock, towels, twisted cord and rope, waxed paper

SODA PULP
Paper and paperboard for blotters, printing papers, bristol board, corrugated paper, filters, insulating and wallboards, labels, liners for coated boards, stationery, testliners

SEMI-CHEMICAL PULP
Corrugated paper, egg cartons, insulating board, testliners, wallboard, printing papers, glassine paper

GROUNDWOOD PULP
Absorbent papers, bags, boards, building and insulating papers, newsprint, printing papers, wallboard, wood cement boards and blocks, wrapping paper, writing papers

RESIDUES (Liquor containing leftover cellulose and lignin not used in paper manufacture)
Sulfite liquors used in making adhesives, building briquettes, core binder, cymene, dyes, emulsifiers, ethyl alcohol, fatty acids, feeding yeast, fertilizers, fuel briquettes, linoleum cement, mordants, paint and varnish remover, plastics, road binder, tannins, vanillin
Sulfate liquors used in making acetic acid, acetone, dimethyl-sulfide, fatty acids, furfural, methyl alcohol, oxalic acid, pine oil, rosin soap, rosin acids, tall oil, turpentine, ore flotation, pharmaceutical chemicals
Soda liquors used in making acetic acid, acetone, calcium carbonate, methyl alcohol, oxalic acid, plastics

(American Forest Products Industries.)

Fig. 70–11.

  WOOD DISTILLATION PLANTS

BOLTS
LIMBS
SAWMILL
EDGINGS
STUMPS

HARDWOOD DISTILLATION PRODUCTS

PRODUCTS **USES**

ACETIC ACID
Acetate solvents, cellulose acetate for rayon, photo film, lacquers, and plastics; coagulant for latex, perfumes, and textile dyeing; manufacturing inorganic acetates, white lead pigments

ACETONE
Acetylene, explosives (cordite), solvent

CHARCOAL
Activated carbon, black powder explosives, chemical manufacture, fuel, livestock and poultry foods, manufacturing charcoal iron, medicines, metacase hardening compounds, producer gas, water purification

METHANOL
Antifreeze, dry-cleaning agents, formaldehyde, manufacturing chemical compounds, paints, pyroxylins, shellac, textile finishing agents, varnishes

PITCH
Insulation in electric transformers, rubber filler

TAR OIL
Flotation oils, gasoline (inhibitor oil), paints and stains, preservatives, solvent oils, wood creosote

SOFTWOOD DISTILLATION PRODUCTS

PRODUCTS **USES**

CEDAR OILS
Furniture polish

CHARCOAL
Activated carbon, black powder explosives, chemical manufacture, fuel, livestock and poultry foods, manufacturing charcoal iron, medicines, metacase hardening compounds, water filtration

CREOSOTE OILS
Cattle and sheep dips, disinfectants, medicines

DIPENTINE
Solvent for reclaiming old rubber

LACQUER SOLVENT
Lacquers, paints, varnish

PINE OIL
Disinfectants, fabric dyeing, flotation oil, paints

PINE TAR
Coating and binding materials, disinfectants, manufacturing cordage, medicines, oakum, soaps

ROSIN
Paper sizing, varnish, soap, greases, waterproofing, linoleum

TAR OIL SOLVENTS
Disinfectants, flotation oils, paints, soaps, stains

WOOD TURPENTINE
Paint and varnish manufacture, synthetic camphor for celluloid manufacture

(American Forest Products Industries.)

Fig. 70–12.

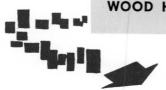

WOOD HYDROLYSIS PLANTS

SAWDUST

SLABS, EDGINGS, TRIMMINGS

PROCESS	PRODUCTS	USES
WOOD HYDROLYSIS	ACETIC ACID	Textile manufacture, white lead pigment, cellulose acetate, perfume
	BAKING YEAST	Bakery products
	BUTADIENE	Synthetic rubber
	CARBONIC ACID	Industrial chemicals
	ETHYL ALCOHOL	Solvents
	ANIMAL FOOD	Cattle feed, chicken feed
	FURFURAL	Resins, plastics
	GLYCERINE	Medicines, industrial chemicals
	LIGNIN POWDER	Plastic and laminates
	SUGARS	Stock feed, ethanol
WOOD CONDENSATION	FURFURAL	Resins, plastics
	SOIL CONDITIONER	To make soils more porous
ALKALINE FUSION	OXALIC ACID	Bleaching, industrial chemicals
	PYROGALLOL	Stains
	RESINS	Plastics

(American Forest Products Industries.)

Fig. 70–13.

MISCELLANEOUS PRODUCTS

PRODUCTS	USES
 **POLES, POSTS, PILINGS**	Antennae, arbors, bridges, channel markers, dams, docks, pole frame buildings, fence posts, flagpoles, foundations, guard rails, jetties, levees, revetments, signposts, tank traps, telephone poles, weirs, wharves
 **FUELWOOD**	Fireplace, stove, steam boilers
 **SAP AND GUM**	Balsam, birch beer, butternut syrup, gumthus, heptane, larch (Venetian turpentine), maple sugar, mesquite gum, rosin, spruce gum, storax, turpentine
 **BARK**	Adhesives, birch (flavoring) oil, cascara (drug), clothing (wood wool), drilling mud dispersants (oil industry), dye (osage orange and black oak), insulating wool, slippery elm (drug), soil building, tannins (hemlock, chestnut, and tanbark oak)
 **EDIBLE FRUITS**	Butternuts, chinquapins, hickory nuts, pawpaws, pecans, piñon nuts, serviceberries, walnuts, wild plums
 **NEEDLES**	Pine and cedar needle oil
 **SAWDUST**	Absorbent for explosives, artificial leather, artificial wood, body for paint, butcher shops, camouflage, clay products, composition flooring, curing concrete, filler for linoleum, filter for oil and gas, fireworks, glues, hand soaps, ice storage, insulating, insulating brick, livestock bedding, meat smoking, mild abrasives for cleaners, moth deterrent, nursery mulch, packing, plastics, soil conditioners, and wood flour for billiard balls, bowling balls, explosives, molded products
 **ROOFING FELTS**	Roll roofing, shingles
 **CHRISTMAS TREES**	Decorations

(American Forest Products Industries.)

Fig. 70–14. Forests provide raw materials for shelter, fuel, clothing, and scientific uses. (American Forest Products Industries.)

Fig. 70–16. Short boards being scarfed for making laminated timbers. Scarfing trims the end of a board at a bevel, like the edge of a chisel. Two boards so trimmed may be joined end-to-end to form a lapped joint in the laminating process. (Weyerhaeuser Company.)

Fig. 70–15. A balsa-covered lunar capsule has been tested for impact. This wood has a greater impact-absorbing capacity than any other material tested. (Ford Motor Company—Aeronutronic Division, Philco Corporation.)

wood. Research indicates that wood may also be a better performer than any other material undersea to depths up to 1,000 feet.

LAMINATED BEAMS AND ARCHES

An important consumer of lumber is the rapidly expanding glued-laminating and prefabricating industry. It produces laminated beams, trusses, arches, and other structural members for churches, schools, and civic and industrial buildings, as well as for ships and other marine uses. This industry has made great progress in manufacturing ready-cut wood buildings and pre-fabricated homes. Mobile homes are also an important segment of this industry.

Lamination has made possible the use of timbers in sizes and shapes never dreamed of formerly. Short boards (Fig. 70–16) are assembled, bent, and glued, resulting in clear-span arches in excess of 100 feet in

345

Fig. 70–17. Planing a large, glue-laminated arch for architectural construction. *(Weyerhaeuser Company.)*

Fig. 70–18. The largest glue-laminated beam ever made is being run through a sander. *(American Forest Products Industries.)*

Fig. 70–19. Reverse-curve glue-laminated beams. The striated grooved surface of the decking on top of the double-curved beams gives this bank lobby a distinctive appearance and improves acoustics. *(American Institute of Timber Construction.)*

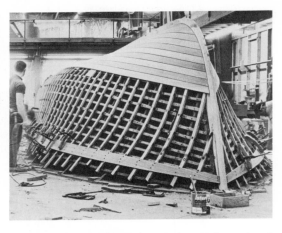

Fig. 70–20. Laminated wood members lend themselves to boat hull construction. *(Industrial Woodworking.)*

length (Figs. 70–17 and 70–18). These laminated members can be built with practically any properties desired (Figs. 70–19 and 70–20). Not only do they have strength, they also have aesthetic appeal as well. Properly treated, these timbers resist the ravages of weather and other deteriorating forces.

Because of the thermal properties of wood, specially treated timbers result in buildings which are now more fire safe than when built of other structural members.

IMPREGNATED PRODUCTS

Compreg is a product similar to plywood. It is made by soaking or impregnating sheets of wood with raw resin, piling one upon the other, then placing them under great pressure until the resin has set (Fig. 70–21). This product looks like wood because it has grain, but it has been changed by pressure and the resin which fills its cells to a harder, firmer, heavier substance of many uses (Figs. 70–22 and 70–23).

Researchers at the U. S. Forest Products Laboratory discovered that wood impregnated with polyethylene glycol no longer ex-

Fig. 70–21. *Compreg (right)* is wood which has been compressed to form a new, hard product. A block of natural wood is shown on the left. *(American Forest Products Industries.)*

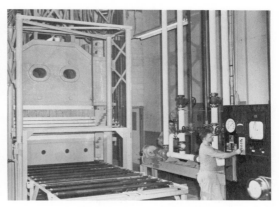

Fig. 70–22. This huge, 3,900-ton press produces *Compreg* by densifying stacks of impregnated veneer. This is done by application of pressure of about one ton per square inch at over 350 degrees Farhenheit. *(Permali, Incorporated.)*

hibits the undesirable unstable qualities it previously had. Even more dramatic is the development of the wood-plastic combinations wherein wood is impregnated with a liquid chemical and then polymerized (hardened) by exposure to gama radiation from a cobalt-60 source.

This treated wood is harder than natural wood by several hundred percent. It is stronger in shear and bending, yet retains the natural wood beauty. It can be worked with conventional tools, giving it a hard, satin-smooth finish.

Another fascinating discovery is that wood, impregnated with anhydrous ammonia, becomes so plastic that it can be bent by hand to any shape or form, including spirals, helices, and simple knots. When it is formed into a given shape and held or clamped for a few minutes, it hardens to retain the new shape. This process opens up vast opportunities for use of wood as a decorative material.

A pressure-impregnated model and pattern-carving wood, with unusual properties, is being used by many segments of

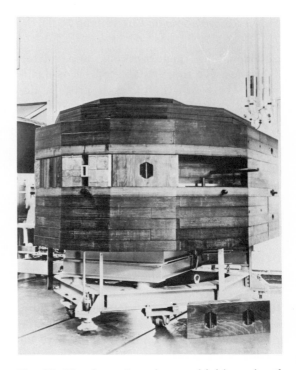

Fig. 70–23. A neutron beam shield made of *Compreg. (Permali, Incorporated.)*

347

Fig. 70–24. Impregnated Stabilite lends itself to machining for patternmaking. It is also used successfully for acid tanks and electronic equipment housings because of its resistance to heat, moisture, corrosion, and decay. *(Georgia-Pacific Corporation.)*

patternmaking, metalworking, and related industries. Termed "stabilite," it is laminated wood which utilizes a process developed recently by the U.S. Forest Products Laboratory. It is virtually unaffected by heat and heavy moisture. The carving blocks are made of hardwood veneers, pressure-impregnated before lamination with a phenolic-resin forming chemical. Unlike cross-laminated plywood, veneers are bonded with parallel grain to improve workability (Fig. 70–24).

OTHER ENGINEERED PRODUCTS

Some of the newer products are specially engineered for the building industry. Figure 70–25 illustrates a splined sheet deck. This was developed very recently to fill a need for a panelized decking product. This may be used for roof decking or subflooring, or other places where strong, durable panels of rigid material are needed.

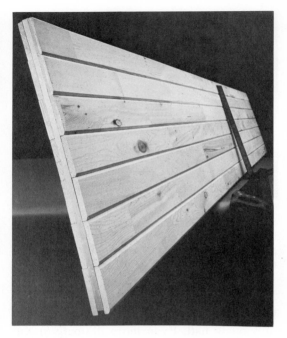

Fig. 70–25. A splined sheet deck panel for the building industry. Using sheets of this type saves on installation costs. *(Western Wood Products Association.)*

Fig. 70–26. A sheet-board panel. This is an especially-fine new product for more efficient building construction. *(Western Wood Products Association.)*

Fig. 70–27. A panel machine, cutting joints in a wood-product ceiling panel. This type of ceiling panel is fire resistant and acoustically treated. *(Western Wood Products Association.)*

Another ingenious research product is the sheet-board (Fig. 70–26). This is a labor- and cost-saving product in which several boards may be laid edge-to-edge then glued to wet-strength kraft paper on both sides with water-resistant adhesive. Pressure and heat permanently bond the paper and the wood. This makes it possible to install large panels of sheet-boards for roofs, floors, side-wall sheathing, and many other uses about the home and farm, and in industry.

Figure 70–27 shows the production of ceiling tile, a product being made from what formerly was wood waste. This type of material can be treated to be fire-resistant, and to possess acoustical qualities.

CREOSOTING

The process of creosoting impregnates logs, posts, railroad ties, and other timbers with creosote, a liquid preservative agent. It protects wood fiber from decay while subjected

Fig. 70–28. Peeled utility poles being hauled to the creosoting vats. *(Towmotor Corporation.)*

Fig. 70–29. Pine poles and hardwood rail ties ready to go into the pressure cylinders of the creosoting plant. *(U. S. Forest Service.)*

Fig. 70–30. Completion of the turning process on a novelty maple bowl. (*U.S. Forest Service.*)

Fig. 70–31. This man makes his living weaving oak splits into baskets in the doorway of his highway shop. This is an especially attractive item for tourists. (*U. S. Forest Service.*)

to water, insects, and other elements of deterioration. Figures 70–28 and 70–29 illustrate stacking posts, telephone poles, and hardwood railroad ties in preparation for submersion in creosote vats.

MANUFACTURING OF NOVELTY ITEMS

Wood has a warmth, as well as texture, which lends this material for use in novelty item production. Tourists are intrigued by roadside stands having products made from woods of a particular area. Figure 70–30 shows a homecraftsman producing bowls from wood native to his section of the country. These are made on a special shaper-lathe machine.

Another ingenious craftsman is shown in Fig. 70–31 weaving oak splits into baskets. His raw material comes from white oak logs from nearby farm forests.

PAPER AND PAPER PRODUCTS

This book would not be available if it were not for our forest crop. Eleven percent of the timber harvest is used for making pulp from which paper is manufactured (Fig. 70–32). Wood is converted into pulp by separating the cellulose fibers. It is chopped into fine chips, soaked in a chemical solution, and finally mixed with water. This pulp flows onto a continuous metal belt pierced with as many as 4,500 holes per square inch. As the belt moves—at from 40 to 60 miles per hour—the water drops through the holes, leaving a thin, damp film of fiber.

After further processing, the film of fibers passes onto an endless belt of felt, because it is not yet sufficiently strong to travel unsupported while being pressed. When the paper is dry enough to hold its own weight, it runs onto driers. Here all moisture is evaporated. The paper is then rolled so as to be ready for shipment (Fig. 70–33). A few of the many possible paper products are illustrated in Fig. 70–34.

Fig. 70–32. Pulpwood being unloaded from flat cars. These logs will be processed to provide pulp for paper and other cellulose products. (Caterpillar Tractor Company.)

Fig. 70–34. A few of the thousands of paper products which are made from pulp. (American Forest Products Industries.)

Fig. 70–35. Papreg, layers of compressed impregnated paper, has metal-like strength. (American Forest Products Industries.)

Fig. 70–36. Vinyl-laminated fiberboard panels beautify the ceiling and walls of a mobile home. (United States Plywood Corporation.)

Fig. 70–33. Flawless white paper from the machine that transformed it from pulp. (American Forest Products Industries.)

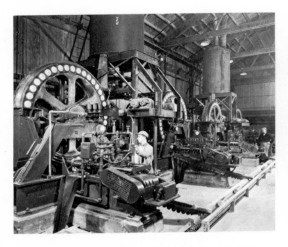

Fig. 70–37. Prest-O-Log machines compressing dry wood shavings and sawdust into hard, heat-rich fuel logs. (American Forest Products Industries.)

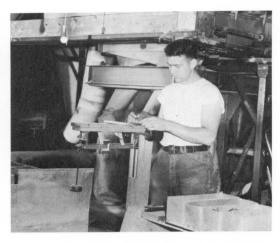

Fig. 70–39. Drying, grading, and bagging sawdust to be used by the furrier trade in cleaning furs. This is another use of an end product, formerly wasted. (U. S. Forest Service.)

Fig. 70–38. Excelsior is another by-product of wood waste. (Caterpillar Tractor Company.)

Fig. 70–40. The drapery material and bark-fiber blanket are wood products. (American Forest Products Industries.)

352

Papreg (Fig. 70–35) is produced by impregnating sheets of paper with resin. They are then heated and pressed. This material is lighter than, but not as strong as, metal. Papreg can be molded into a great variety of shapes.

INSULATION AND FUEL

Practically every bit of the tree serves some useful purpose. Sawmills have waste, such as slabs, shavings, sawdust, chips, and scrap wood. (Figs. 70–36 through 70–39). When the waste can serve no further purpose, it is burned as fuel in hopper-fed furnaces.

RAYON AND WOOD-WOOL FABRICS

Wood pulp is the source material for a high percentage of all rayons. Researchers discovered how to treat cellulose fiber to form one of the ingredients of rayon.

One important use of rayon is to weave these fibers into practically any serviceable cloth or fabric (Fig. 70–40). Some of the many other items it is possible to make from wood cellulose include draperies and blankets.

TREATMENT OF WOOD

About two-thirds of all wood is cellulose; the other third is lignin. *Cellulose* is the chief of the substances forming the cell walls of a tree. *Lignin* is a tough, durable substance which holds the cells of a tree together. These substances sometimes are called the "magic twins of the forest," for from them new products are made.

Processed by various chemical and mechanical means, cellulose is an important ingredient in gunpowder, imitation leather, felt, plastics, lacquers, glycerine, sugar, alcohol, molasses, yeast, and food proteins.

Scientists have found many uses for lignin. It serves, for example, as a tanning agent for leather, a binder for mixing concrete, a water softener and purifier, a base for

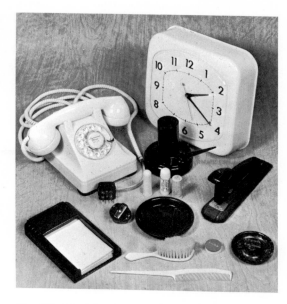

Fig. 70–41. Plastic articles using cellulose and lignin. *(American Forest Products Industries.)*

fertilizer, and a flavoring called vanillin. Lignin is also used to make plastics (Fig. 70–41).

Additional scientific yields from wood include buna rubber, which is made by chemical methods. Even the fuel burned in cars can be mixed with alcohol made from wood. In countries where petroleum supplies are inadequate, alcohol is used to a large extent for this purpose.

PRODUCTS EXTRACTED FROM TREES

Solvents, sugar, dyes, drying agents, and spirits necessary in manufacturing processes are extracted from trees. Southern pine trees yield oleoresin for the paint industry. Turpentines and resins are extracted from oleoresin and used as driers and solvents for paints, varnish products, and printing ink. They are also important in making soap, paper, and many other items. Turpentine and resin are obtained from a molasses-like substance, gum resin, which drips from the tree after the bark has been chipped.

Distillates, such as wood alcohol and acetone, and other important chemicals are by-products of wood. Dyes are extracted from hemlock bark and are used in leather tanning. Table delicacies from trees include maple sugar, maple syrup, and a wide variety of fruits and nuts.

Discussion Topics

1. Forests provide the raw materials for how many products used in our daily lives?
2. Approximately how many board feet of lumber are used in the average wood house?
3. List five features of a recently developed, chemically treated wood siding?
4. What percent of a tree goes into commercially useful products?
5. What wood was selected to be used for projected lunar capsules to absorb impact? What characteristic made this particular wood especially useful for this purpose?
6. Describe six buildings in which you have seen laminated arches used for architectural construction.
7. Explain the change in wood-products diversification which has occurred in the past ten years.
8. Name ten new wood products resulting from the more efficient use of end products of the lumber industry.
9. What kind of wood was used for the nose cone of the Polaris missile?
10. Describe the process involved in making laminated beams and arches.
11. Give three features of laminated beams and arches that make them desirable.
12. List 12 novelty items made of wood which you have observed in stores, or which are for sale at tourist centers.
13. What is *Compreg*? Where can it be used?
14. Describe briefly how paper is made.
15. What percent of our timber harvest is used to make pulp from which paper is manufactured?
16. What is papreg? How can it be used?
17. List eight products which are made from the waste of sawmills.
18. What happens to the sawmill waste which cannot be used in the making of some useful product?
19. Explain the differences between cellulose and lignin. Name five uses of each.
20. List ten products made for everyday use from wood.
21. Name and describe at least six products extracted from trees. Make a list of their uses.

unit

71

Numerical control and automation in the woods manufacturing industry

Numerical-control automated machines have been used for a number of years in American manufacturing industries. They are particularly important and profitable in performing certain operations in metals manufacturing. Numerical control is used in some of the most sophisticated functions in metalworking, such as multi-pattern drilling, milling, die-sinking, and many others which cannot be performed as accurately or rapidly by manual control.

It has been assumed for many years that tape control for woodworking was neither practical or economical. Part of this belief evolved from the economics concept that less costly materials and machines are involved in the woodworking industry than in metal manufacturing industries.

A recent, early adaptation of numerical control in woodworking was by applying the principle of numerical control from the vertical milling machine, commonly used in the metal industries, to the vertical router used in woods manufacturing. The potential for future expansion is being accepted and researched. Numerical control operation has recently been extended to efficient use on other woodworking machines.

TAPE CONTROL

A numerical-controlled machine utilizes a punched (perforated) tape which regulates motion through electronic circuitry. Tape control is a means for regulating the motion of a machine by a series of holes punched into the tape. The holes represent a numerical computation of coordinates which are read by photo-electric cells, amplified, and then fed to the proper servo-mechanism by an electronic circuit.

One can visualize the idea (concept) by considering that one combination of holes, and the impulses generated into the circuitry, will tell the machine to move "north." Another will say, "move east," "move south," or "move west." With combinations of different kinds of impulses, a machine can be told to move in any direction.

Another combination of impulses can be designed (programmed) to tell the machine to speed up, slow down or stop, or lift the operating mechanism to permit the operator to see what he wants to check. The instructions are limited only by the rows of holes in the tape and the sophistication of the electronic circuitry and the hydraulic actuating devices.

Numerical-control machinery receives instructions in the direction to go by designating the process through four different quadrants. There is no limitation in following either straight or very complex curves. Machines have been developed which will hold tolerances of 0.002 inch or less, in cutting wood. This is adequate for woodworking techniques. Numerical control in metalworking manufacturing sometimes requires tolerances of millionths of an inch.

HOW TAPES ARE CUT

Wood-product manufacturers who use tape-controlled machinery often send a prototype (sample part) of the product to be made, and drawings of it, to the manufacturer of the machine to be used. These product-drawings indicate all dimensions, radii, finish notes, and other information which would assist the machine builder to understand the wood parts to be produced. Tapes are then punched on a standard Flexowriter from manual calculations by a person known as a programmer.

PRODUCTION

When the tape is returned to the wood-products manufacturer, it comes as an endless roll which may be recycled continuously. The tape is dropped into a large plastic container known as a "tumble box" for later insertion into the control cabinet (Fig. 71–1).

After the plastic tumble box has been dropped down behind the front panel of the control cabinet, a section of the tape is fed into the photo-electric reader (Fig. 71–2).

The mechanism for operating the router is enclosed in a control cabinet connected by a cable to the router machine (see Figs. 71–3 and 71–5). This enclosed cabinet is dust-proof and is portable on casters to any location on the floor where desired. The circuitry in it is solid-state, which eliminates problems with high voltages, heat radiation, tube and relay replacement, and large-scale storage space.

The numerical-control operator starts the routing machines by using the controls on the tape cabinet (Fig. 71–3). Once the router has started the initial cut, the operator can make simple adjustments of the router head. He can regulate depth of cut on a sample part on which he experiments (Fig. 71–4).

During the routing process, the operator can move the portable control cabinet into any position on the floor near the router. This facilitates efficiency of operation and changing of blanks with finished parts so the machine can work continuously (Fig. 71–5). After the router has been set in accordance with the pre-punched tapes, it works automatically (Fig. 71–6), and the operator is free to remove completed pieces

Fig. 71–1. Control tape comes in endless rolls which may recycle continuously. The new tape is dropped into a large plastic tumble box for insertion into the control cabinet. *(Hitchcock Publishing Company.)*

Fig. 71–2. With the tumble box dropped down behind the front panel, a section of the tape is fed into the photo-electric reader which senses numbers and sequence of punched holes in the tape. *(Hitchcock Publishing Company.)*

Fig. 71–3. The operator uses two simple controls to start the machine along its pre-determined cutting pattern, and to stop it manually when necessary. *(Hitchcock Publishing Company.)*

Fig. 71–5. Everything is readily accessible to the operator, including the control cabinet which can be moved to any convenient position during to routing process. *(Hitchcock Publishing Company.)*

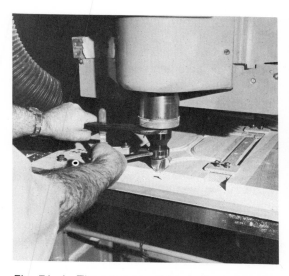

Fig. 71–4. The operator, if he desires, may use a sample pattern to locate exact depth of router cut for the new work. However, pre-set tooling is a more sophisticated procedure for this machine. *(Hitchcock Publishing Company.)*

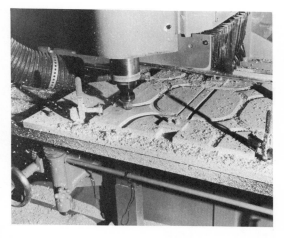

Fig. 71–6. After the cutting procedure is set, and in operation, the operator can remove finished pieces and insert new blanks for subsequent cutting. This process goes on until the required number of blanks has been routed. No pattern is too intricate for tape control. *(Hitchcock Publishing Company.)*

and insert new blanks for routing of the design.

NUMERICAL–CONTROL EFFICIENCY

While numerical control in the woods manufacturing industry has been in use only a few years, and has been limited to certain machine processes, it has already proved to be efficient and economical. The cuts produced on the numerical-controlled router have been extremely smooth and accurate.

The rate of production so far has been four times that of manual operation. Speed of production has been limited only by the time required to remove finished pieces and set up new blanks.

The technological potential for use of numerical control in the woods manufacturing industry is dependent upon the ingenuity of both the manufacturer of the equipment and the creativity and originality of those who manufacture wood products. Additional tape-controlled machines, performing other operations, are being developed and put into useful production. It is a new concept beyond automation furthering and revitalizing the field of wood-products manufacturing.

Discussion Topics

1. Define and explain numerical control.
2. Which woodworking machine seemed to lend itself most successfully to the principle of numerical control?
3. What is the advantage of using numerical control on woodworking machinery?
4. What is the name given to the operator who prepares the tape for a given sequence of operations?
5. How effective has the numerical-control concept made production in terms of the quantity of items?

unit

72

Careers in forest-products industries

Wood-products industries were among the first business and industrial activities to develop in America. Since the beginning they have become increasingly diversified, complex, and competitive. Woods industries are constantly expanding their scientific know-how in research to develop better and wider uses of the products of trees. Billions of dollars are invested in land, equipment, facilities, and the salaries of employees.

INDUSTRIAL AND ECONOMIC GROWTH

Because trees are products of soil, sun, and water, wood is constantly replenished through regrowth. This regrowth is aided by scientific forest management. Abundance of raw materials means added security for those who plan careers in the woods industries.

Forest-products industries rank fourth in the number of full-time employee salaries and wages paid, and add greatly to the value of manufacturing in the national economy. They provide annual jobs for more than 2 million persons, who are paid approximately $6 billion per year. The goods which they produce are worth over $22 billion annually. Thousands of people also have careers in industries concerned with the growing, handling, transporting, and processing of forest products. The natural resource of timber provides employment, either directly or indirectly, for approximately 14 million people in the United States.

About 750,000 people are employed full-time in the manufacture and distribution of lumber. Sawmills process logs into lumber and provide jobs for approximately 600,000 persons. About 70,000 people are engaged in woods and logging operations, and the remainder in manufacturing. In addition, there are thousands more who gain their livelihood in related industries which transport and handle wood products.

Distribution of lumber provides employment to many thousands of individuals. These include wholesalers, who have approximately 50,000 on their payroll, and retailers, who employ 188,000 more people.

The sawmilling industry employs two-thirds of the forest industries force, using about two-thirds of the industrial wood. It furnishes nearly half the gross value of all forest industries. The pulp and paper industry employs one-fourth of the forest industries labor force. It uses about one-fourth of the industrial wood, and furnishes more than two-fifths of the gross value of all forest industries.

Detailed statistics for woodworking occupations are available in a bulletin entitled, "Job Descriptions for the Lumber and Lumber Products Industries," U.S. Government Printing Office, Washington, D.C.

The woods industries spend over $1½ billion each year on upkeep and expansion of plants, equipment, and lands, all of which are valued at billions of dollars. More than

Fig. 72–1. Tomorrow's wood technoligists prepare for rewarding careers in the forest-products industries. *(National Lumber Manufacturers Association.)*

Fig. 72–2. A plant geneticist is supplying pollen to female strobili of 5-year old grafts. This young man has prepared himself as a professional forester. *(U. S. Forest Service.)*

Fig. 72–3. A forester examines the growth of natural longleaf reproduction in the third season of the grass stage. This area was seeded as the result of a prescribed burn for seed tests. *(U. S. Forest Service.)*

Fig. 72–5. In a fully equipped model sawmill, students are taught techniques and economics of cutting logs to lumber. *(National Lumber Manufacturers Association.)*

Fig. 72–4. The plant geneticist transfers cambium to another supply to keep the cambium cells growing. *(U. S. Forest Service.)*

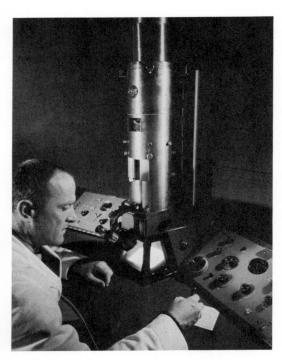

Fig. 72–6. A researcher works with an electron microscope at the Forest Products Laboratory to make further studies on the structure of wood. *(U. S. Forest Products Laboratory.)*

Fig. 72–7. Professional foresters microchip to determine the gum-yield potential of young slash pine. *(U. S. Forest Service.)*

Fig. 72–8. Students observe preservative treatment of wood poles at a commercial plant. Such visits are part of their technical training. *(National Lumber Manufacturers Association.)*

one-third of the lumber supply of the world, over half the plywood, two-fifths of the wood pulp, and half of the paper and paperboard are produced in the United States.

CAREER OPPORTUNITIES

High school graduates can find employment in woods industries; however, they must avail themselves of on-the-job training and other educational opportunities (Fig. 72–1). The progress of industry is very largely dependent upon those who have prepared themselves for professional careers. There are professional careers in the areas of general forestry, wood technology, wood products engineering, merchandising and construction, furniture manufacturing, pulp and paper technology, packaging technology, and tree-farm management.

In *professional forestry* (Fig. 72–2) young men prepare for careers in growing and harvesting timber crops, and in keeping the forest-products industries supplied with raw material. Their many interesting activities include planning (Fig. 72–3) and su-

Fig. 72–9. Architects, designers, and building contractors have developed many beautiful wood apartment housing units. *(National Lumber Manufacturers Association.)*

pervising logging operations, grading trees and logs, scaling and transporting logs, purchasing timber and logs, and procuring pulpwood.

Professional preparation in the areas of *wood technology and wood-products engineering* is very broad (Figs. 72–4 through 72–8). It requires a knowledge of timber harvesting, extending through the development of finished products and ending with distribution and sales. Career opportunities for people with such a background exist in industries which manufacture lumber, veneer, plywood, pulp and paper, fiberboard, hardboard, particle board, and flakeboard. Graduates with such training are sought by producers of flooring, furniture, millwork, shipping containers, and marine products.

Merchandising and *construction fields* include light and heavy building construction. Light construction deals with homes, farm structures, small churches and schools, and industrial buildings. Heavy construction is more concerned with shopping centers, apartment houses, churches, theaters, schools, factories, and bridges (Figs. 72–9 and 72–10). The construction industry consists of 485 thousand firms and 3½ million employees. They use about $25 billion worth of materials to produce $70 billion in structures. There are more than one million houses built annually. Four out of five of these are wood construction, with each averaging 10,000 board feet of lumber.

Distributors who supply this multi-million dollar industry include 12 thousand wholesale and over 25 thousand retail lumber dealers. It is evident from these figures that this highly competitive, advanced industry needs many technical specialists.

Furniture manufacturing requires technical persons with imagination and appreciation of the aesthetics of design. These professionally trained people are needed to design, produce, and sell distinctive wood

Fig. 72–10. The wood-products construction industry uses many cabinetmakers, carpenters, plumbers, and electricians. *(American Forest Products Industries.)*

Fig. 72–11. Handcraftsmanship produces intricate wood patterns for many molded castings. *(National Lumber Manufacturers Association.)*

362

furniture. More than 75 percent of home and office furniture is made of wood or wood products. Persons entering this field should have an excellent professional background in design, a thorough knowledge of the species of woods and of the capabilities and limitations of each of the species, the chemistry of finishing, and fabrication techniques.

Handcraftsmanship with woods is a highly respected vocation (Fig. 72–11). Skilled men make intricate wood patterns which are used as molds for castings.

The *paper* and *pulp industry* is one of the largest, fastest-growing, and most progressive segments, or parts, of the forest-products industries. Nearly half of the world's supply of pulp and paper is produced in the United States by over 800 paper or paperboard mills and approximately 300 pulp mills. Forty-two of our states are involved in this great industry. The fast growth of this field has been the result of skilled technologists and engineers who have developed the industry through research.

Packaging technology is a scientific development which has grown from simple boxes, bags, and barrels to complex engineered containers. Billions of feet of lumber, veneer, and plywood, and millions of tons of paperboard are used each year to produce containers. These range from small paper milk cartons to elaborate wooden crates for shipping trucks, aircraft, and heavy machinery. Packaging technology has opened interesting and challenging career opportunities for the forest-products engineer who is trained in this field.

Tree-farm management is a very important factor in producing timber. Income is obtained from the sale of woodland products directly as lumber. Woodlands occupy more acreage then any other crop on American farms (Fig. 72–12).

If you plan to prepare yourself for a career or a profession in the wood or wood-

Fig. 72–12. The number of tree farms is increasing annually. Such farms require well trained tree farm management. (*American Forest Products Industries.*)

Fig. 72–13. Study of basic drafting leads to an interesting career. The draftsman's pen translates ideas into visual patterns. (*National Association of Manufacturers.*)

products industries, you should have an excellent foundation in basic English, the sciences, mathematics, drafting (Fig. 72–13), and industrial shop work while you are in junior and senior high school. Further preparation in college or in the university should include specialization in any of the many professional career possibilities. Specific guidance is available to you through guidance advisors, teachers, college and university catalogues, and literature from industrial associations interested in wood products.

Discussion Topics

1. List the careers or occupations in your community which depend entirely upon wood.
2. How many cubic feet of wood are produced annually?
3. Why is wood a constantly replenished raw-resource material?
4. How much lumber has been produced since the United States received its independence?
5. How do the forest-products industries rank nationally in the number of full-time employee salaries and wages paid?
6. How many people in the United States have jobs affected by wood as a natural resource?
7. How much of the world's forest products does the United States supply in lumber, plywood, wood pulp, paper, and paperboard?
8. List eight broad professional career opportunities in the forest-products industries.
9. Describe the types of activities under each of the eight professional career classifications.
10. Visit a local industry which uses wood for its basic material. List the many types of jobs in this industry.
11. What school subjects should you study if you are interested in working in the wood or wood-products industries?

unit

73

Introduction to experimental research

Progressive and enterprising large industrial wood-products manufacturing industries maintain extensive and elaborate research facilities. They employ many scientists, engineers, and technicians whose interest is research in all phases of tree growth, lumber production, wood materials, manufacturing processes, and industrial and consumer products (Figs. 73–1 through 73–5).

Experimentation is essential to develop new and better products such as described in the several units of Section 7, concerning wood technology.

Students can enter into this exciting phase of experimentation, research, and development. This provides an opportunity to gain an understanding of the professional aspect of the wood-products industries.

Through proper forest management and conservation, and scientific data developed at the U. S. Forest Research Laboratories, wood has become an endless resource which

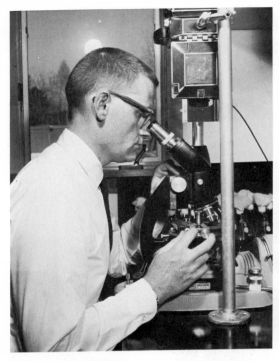

Fig. 73–1. A botanist, using a compound microscope, examines a finished slide of chlorophyll. *(U. S. Forest Service.)*

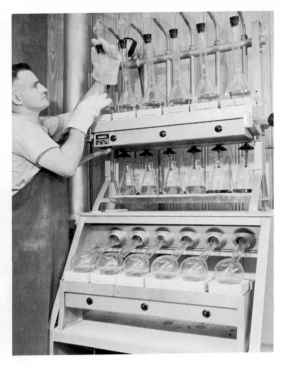

Fig. 73–2. This research forester is setting up a wood distillation machine to make a test. *(U. S. Forest Service.)*

supplies the needs of modern living and technology. Uses of it are limited only by the ingenuity, resourcefulness, and imagination of persons like you, the student.

Wood is a material that has warmth, workability, beauty, and many other desirable characteristics. These qualities make it one of the most popular basic construction and manufacturing materials.

You can learn much about woods and woodworking and the materials related to woodworking by performing the experiments in this section. A person working with wood usually has many questions, such as:

1. What kind of wood should be used for a project or activity?

2. What is the best kind of joint to use?

3. What is the best glue to use?

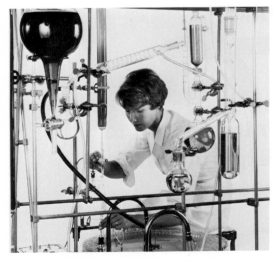

Fig. 73–3. This chemist is making an analysis of wood fiber. *(Weyerhaeuser Company.)*

Fig. 73–4. Radioactive isotopes are used by forest scientists as they seek to discover ways to grow better trees faster. Seedlings grown in chemical solutions containing radioactive materials are tested with a radiation counter as part of research on the movement of nutritional elements within the tree. *(Weyerhaeuser Company.)*

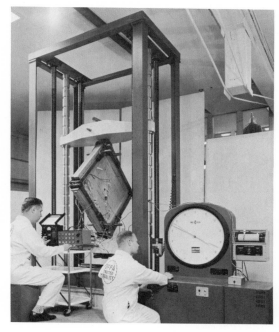

Fig. 73–5. Technicians run an experiment on the diagonal shearing power of plywood panels. *(American Plywood Association.)*

4. Is quartersawed or plain-sawed lumber best?

5. What is the difference between hardwoods and softwoods?

These, and many other questions, may be answered through experimentation. This activity is not only indicative of *what* is the best way to do something, it also tells *why* some procedure is the best method to follow. The experiments which follow are designed to assist you in answering some of the more common questions about wood.

Some of the experiments will require special equipment; others may be developed with that available in the school laboratory or shop. Often simple equipment can be designed to work almost as effectively as special types. For example, the load capacity of a wood beam may simply be tested by

suspending a sample of wood between two points with a bucket, or similar receptacle, tied in the center of the sample. This receptacle can be filled with water until the sample breaks. The load can be determined by weighing the receptacle and the water. Load capacity of columns may be tested with the force acting down on the vertical column.

Materials and special items, such as chemicals, Bunsen burners, ring stands, and others used for many of these experiments, may be borrowed from the science department.

The experiments which follow merely introduce a few of those which can be tested in the field of woods. Additional ones may be developed to determine other characteristics and uses. Activity such as this lends itself well to group and team action.

unit
74

Experiment: characteristics of hardwoods and softwoods

Fig. 74-1. Immersing wood samples in water.

Objectives:

To learn the structure of hardwoods and softwoods.

To learn how to distinguish hardwoods from softwoods.

References:

Groneman, Chris H., *General Woodworking,* Unit 64.

Wood Handbook, Handbook No. 72, U. S. Department of Agriculture, pp. 1–35.

Equipment and Material Needed:

Magnifying glass or microscope

Beaker of water

Samples of red oak and yellow pine, ¾ × ¾ × 3 inches

Procedure:

1. Fill a beaker about ⅔ full of water (see Fig. 74–1).

2. Immerse one end of a red oak sample in the water (Fig. 74–1).

3. Place your mouth over the dry end of the sample, and blow.

4. Repeat steps 2 and 3, using the sample of yellow pine.

5. Examine closely the dry end of each sample, using the magnifying glass (Fig. 74–2), or a microscope (Fig. 74–3).

Fig. 74-2. Examining the wood sample end grain with a magnifying glass.

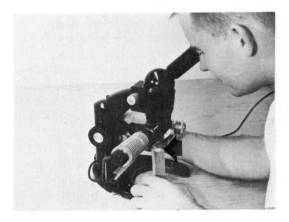

Fig. 74-3. Examining the wood sample with a microscope.

1. Describe what you observed through the magnifying glass or microscope. Compare this with Fig. 63–2 in this textbook.
2. Which sample permitted the greatest amount of air to flow through?
3. What part of the wood did the air flow through?
4. How can you identify hardwoods and softwoods?

unit

75

Experiment: characteristics of plain-sawed and quarter-sawed lumber

Fig. 75–1. Scratching across the grain on a wood sample.

Objective:

To determine the surface characteristics of plain- and quartersawed lumber.

References:

Groneman, Chris H., *General Woodworking*, Unit 64.
Wood Handbook, Handbook No. 72, U. S. Department of Agriculture, pp. 37–65.

Equipment and Material Needed:

One sample of plain-sawed yellow pine, ¼ × 4 × 4 inches
One sample of quartersawed yellow pine, ¼ × 4 × 4 inches
Sandpaper
Sharp instrument: knife or awl
Magnifying glass or microscope

Fig. 75–2. Sandpapering the surface of the wood sample with the grain.

Procedure:

1. Take a sample of plain-sawed lumber, and a sample of quartersawed lumber.

2. Scratch each sample across the grain, using a sharp instrument.

3. Observe the differences in the scratches (Fig. 75–1).

4. Sand one surface of each sample with medium sandpaper for one minute, sanding with the grain (Fig. 75–2).

5. Observe the differences in the sanded surfaces with, and without, the magnifying glass or microscope.

Questions:

1. What was the contrast (difference) in the scratches on the plain-sawed and quartersawed wood samples?

2. Which sample was flatter after being sanded?

3. Why was it flatter?

4. Would plain-sawed or quartersawed lumber make a more resistant floor?

5. Is plain-sawed or quartersawed lumber of the same species more expensive? Why?

---

unit

76

Experiment: the sawing and seasoning of lumber

Objectives:

To learn the procedures used in sawing logs into lumber.

To learn the difference between plain-sawed and quartersawed wood.

To learn why it is necessary to season wood, and how it is done.

References:

Groneman, Chris H., *General Woodworking,* Units 63 and 65.

Small Sawmill Operators Manual, Agriculture Handbook No. 27, U.S. Department of Agriculture.

Northeastern Loggers' Handbook, Handbook No. 6, U.S. Department of Agriculture

Wood Handbook, Handbook No. 72, U.S. Department of Agriculture, pp. 37–65.

Equipment and Material Needed:

Sample of a green log
Bandsaw
Rule
Balances
Brads
String
Hammer

Fig. 76–1. Sawing a wood sample from a section of green log.

Fig. 76–2. Making an accurate measurement of the green lumber sample.

Fig. 76–3. Weighing the green lumber sample.

Fig. 76–4. Green wood samples hanging to dry.

Fig. 76–5. A close view of two samples.

Procedure:

1. Cut one sample of plain-sawed and one of quartersawed wood from a section of a green log (Fig. 76–1). Each sample should be as uniform in shape as possible. The size of each should be 5 × 5 × ½ inches.

2. Number and letter each sample.

3. Measure each sample as accurately as possible (Fig. 76–2). To do this, measure each dimension in at least three places, and take the average of the readings.

4. Measure and record the weight of each sample (Fig. 76–3).

5. Note the exact shape of each wood sample.

6. Drive a brad in the end of each sample.

7. Secure a piece of string to the brad on each, and hang the samples in a suitable area to dry (Figs. 76–4 and 76–5).

8. Let the samples dry at least two weeks (until you receive instructions to continue the experiment).

9. Reweigh and remeasure the samples after the 2-week drying period. Also note the shape of each.

10. Calculate and record in table form the percentage of change in weight and size of each wood sample.

Questions:

1. What is the difference in plain-sawed and quartersawed wood?
2. What are some advantages and some disadvantages of each?
3. Account for the changes in the wood samples from the standpoint of size, shape, and weight.
4. What are advantages and disadvantages of kiln dried lumber over air dried lumber?
5. When is it desirable to use a band saw-mill, and when is it desirable to use a circular sawmill for sawing logs into lumber?
6. What are the advantages of a gang saw-mill over a band sawmill? What are the disadvantages?
7. Define the following:
   a. cant   d. headsaw
   b. edger   e. carriage
   c. trim saw   f. millpond
8. Why is lumber produced while a log is still green?
9. Compare the kiln drying time for a piece of yellow pine and a piece of oak with the air drying time for each.
10. Illustrate with a sketch two ways of stacking green lumber for drying.
11. Describe two kinds of lumber-drying kilns. Include in the description not only the physical appearance of the kiln, but also how the conditions of temperature and humidity vary within each kiln.
12. Why should lumber over 3 inches thick be air dried?
13. How can the exact moisture content of a piece of lumber be determined?
14. How can one determine whether or not a piece of wood has dried evenly throughout its thickness?
15. Wood loses moisture fastest from what surface?
16. About what should be the moisture content of furniture wood?
17. What should the moisture content be for construction wood?

unit

77

Experiment: making wood fire-resistant

Fig. 77-1. Placing wood samples in two chemical solutions.

Objective:

To become familiar with the two common chemical methods to protect wood from fire.

Reference:

Wood Handbook, Handbook No. 72, U. S. Department of Agriculture, pp. 399–428.

Equipment and Material Needed:

Four wood samples, all the same species, $1/16 \times 3/4 \times 2$ inches
Sodium silicate (water glass)
Zinc chloride solution
Bunsen burner
Two 250 milliliter (ml) beakers

Fig. 77-2. Testing two wood samples over a Bunsen (Fisher) burner flame.

Procedure:

1. Pour some zinc chloride into one beaker; pour some sodium silicate into the other (see Fig. 77-1).

2. Place a wood sample in each solution (Fig. 77-1).

3. Let one sample remain in the sodium silicate for five minutes, and one sample in the zinc chloride for 30 minutes.

4. Remove both samples after the time required.

5. Let each sample dry completely.

6. Hold both the dried with sodium-silicate-treated sample and an untreated sample over a flame. Note the results (Fig. 77-2).

Repeat Step 6 for the zinc-chloride-treated sample and an untreated sample (see Fig. 77-2).

373

1. How did the sample treated with sodium silicate and the untreated sample react when placed over the flame? What produced the difference?

2. How did the sample treated with zinc chloride and the untreated one react when placed over a flame? What produced this difference?

3. What are the common methods for applying sodium silicate and zinc chloride to lumber?

4. Which of the methods in question three is the more effective? The least effective?

5. What makes some methods of applying preservatives more effective than others?

unit

78

Experiment: creosoting wood by the hot-cold bath method

Objective:

To become familiar with a common method of preserving wood against decay and insect attack.

Reference:

Wood Handbook, Handbook No. 72, U.S. Department of Agriculture, pp. 399–428.

Equipment and Material Needed:

Hot plate
Two 1-gallon cans or containers
One gallon of creosote oil

Thermometer (Fahrenheit)
Set of balances
Samples of wood
Bandsaw
Cloth
Three or four paper towels

Procedure:

1. Pour ½ gallon of creosote oil into each of the cans or containers.

2. Heat one can over a hot plate to about 225 degrees Fahrenheit. Keep at this approximate temperature.

CAUTION: Creosote is inflammable.

3. Obtain from the instructor two samples each of yellow pine and white oak, $3/4 \times 3/4 \times 12$ inches.

4. Number and weigh each sample.

5. Place the four samples of wood in the hot creosote solution for 1 hour (Fig. 78–1).

6. After 1 hour, remove all the samples from the hot creosote. Immerse immediately one sample each of yellow pine and white oak in the container of cold creosote (Fig. 79–2).

7. Leave the two samples in the cold creosote for about 1 hour.

Fig. 78–1. Placing two wood samples in the hot creosote bath.

Fig. 78–3. Sawing the creosoted wood sample apart.

Fig. 78–2. Placing two wood samples in the cold creosote bath.

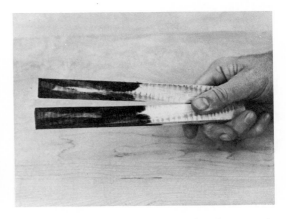

Fig. 78–4. Observing the depth of creosote penetration on the sawed sample.

8. Clean off the excess creosote from the hot creosoted samples.

9. Reweigh them.

10. Saw each of the hot creosoted samples down the middle on a bandsaw (Fig. 78–3).

11. Observe the depth of penetration of the hot creosote liquid (Fig. 78–4).

12. Remove the samples from the cold creosote oil; reweigh them; and saw each sample down the middle for a penetration check.

1. Account for the changes in weight of each sample.
2. Why did some samples change more than others?
3. Is creosoting by the hot bath, or the hot-cold bath, superior for penetration? Why?
4. Why is creosoted lumber not desirable for use in a home?
5. Does creosote make wood more or less flammable?
6. What method of creosoting is superior to either of the methods used in this experiment?
7. What are two methods of creosoting that are not as good as either method used in the experiment?

unit

79

Experiment: creosoting wood with pressure

Objective:

To become familiar with a common method of preserving wood products with creosote.

Reference:

Wood Handbook, Handbook No. 72, U.S. Department of Agriculture, pp. 399–428.

Equipment and Material Needed:

Pressure creosoting unit (Fig. 79–1).
Creosote
One sample of yellow pine; one of white oak; each ¾ × ¾ × 8 inches
Air pressure supply
Pressure regulator
Adjustable end wrench
Bandsaw or handsaw
Set of balances

Procedure:

1. Weigh each sample and record the weights.
2. Remove the end cap from the creosoting pressure tank.
3. Place one sample each of yellow pine and white oak on the rack in the tank (Fig. 79–2).
4. Replace the gasket and the end cap on the pressure tank. Tighten the end cap nuts with a wrench.
5. Place the pressure regulator on the creosote storage tank. Open the pressure tank valve (Fig. 79–3).
6. Open the line valve from the storage tank to the creosoting pressure tank (Fig. 79–4).
7. Apply about 2 pounds of pressure to the storage tank to force the creosote into the pressure tank (Fig. 79–5).
8. Close the line valve when all the creosote has entered the pressure tank (see Fig. 79–4).

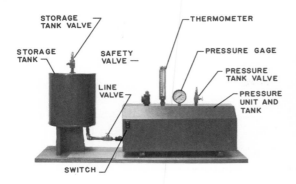

Fig. 79-1. A pressure-creosoting apparatus.

Fig. 79-2. Placing two wood samples in the creosoting pressure tank.

Fig. 79-3. Opening the valve of the pressure tank.

Fig. 79-4. Opening the line valve from the storage tank to the creosoting pressure tank.

Fig. 79-5. Adjusting the pressure for the storage tank.

9. Apply 40 pounds of air pressure to the pressure tank containing the creosote.

10. Turn on the switch that operates the heating coil (see Fig. 79-1).

11. Heat the creosote to about 120 degrees Fahrenheit. Adjust the thermostat to maintain this temperature.

12. Keep the temperature at 120 degrees Fahrenheit for 1 hour. (If pressure exceeds 75 pounds, reduce the temperature.)

13. After 1 hour, open the storage tank valve first (see Figs. 79-1 and 79-4).

14. Next open the line valve. This causes the creosote to be forced from the pressure tank back into the storage tank.

15. Close the line valve when all of the creosote has entered the storage tank.

16. Open the pressure tank valve to relieve the remaining pressure (see Fig. 79–3).

17. Remove the samples.

18. Remove the excess creosote from the samples.

19. Reweigh them.

20. Record the weights.

21. Split the samples with the bandsaw or handsaw.

22. Note the depth of creosote penetration.

Questions:

1. Which sample indicated the greatest depth of creosote penetration, the hardwood or the softwood? Why is this so?

2. What are some disadvantages of preserving woods using the pressure method?

3. Describe a technique added to the pressure method that increases the depth of penetration.

4. How does the method you have just described increase penetration?

5. How does the pressure method compare in depth of penetration to the hot-cold bath process? The hot-bath process?

6. Name some items that are usually preserved by the pressure-creosote method.

---

unit

80

Experiment: testing the load capacity of hardwood, softwood, and plywood beams

Objectives:

To compare the load that can be placed on a hardwood, a softwood, and a plywood beam.

To compare the deflection of hardwood, softwood, and plywood before fracture.

To compare the loads on quartersawed and plain-sawed lumber.

References:

Groneman, Chris H., *General Woodworking*, Units 22 and 66.

Wood Handbook, Handbook No. 72, U.S. Department of Agriculture, pp. 203–216; 275–289.

Equipment and Material Needed:

Testing machine

Six samples of wood, $3/4 \times 3/4 \times 12$ inches. Two of pine (one quartersawed, one plain-sawed), two of oak (one quartersawed, one plain-sawed), two of plywood

378

Fig. 80–1. A wood sample beam in the testing machine, ready for testing.

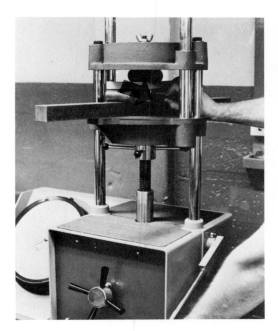

Fig. 80–2. Measuring the amount of deflection, using a depth micrometer, as pressure is applied.

Fig. 80–3. Failure of a beam sample.

Fig. 80–4. Reading the maximum load on the gage.

Procedure:

1. Raise the bottom platen until the round steel test fixture rests on top of the sample (Fig. 80–1).

2. Measure the distance from the bottom platen to the sample (Fig. 80–2).

3. Slowly apply pressure to the testing machine. When the first fracture is heard, measure the distance from the bottom platen to the sample, using the depth micrometer, or rule and dividers (Figs. 80–2 and 80–3).

4. Record the measurement.

5. Apply pressure to the sample until it completely breaks.

6. Record the maximum breaking strength of the sample (Fig. 80–4).

7. In the same manner described above, test the quartersawed pine, the plain-sawed oak, and the quartersawed oak samples.

8. Record all results.

9. Test one plywood sample with the face up.

10. Record all results.

11. Test the other plywood sample with the edge up.

12. Record all results.

Questions:

1. Is hardwood or softwood normally more flexible? Why?
2. How did the plywood samples compare in flexibility with the hardwood and softwood? Why?
3. Is quartersawed or plain-sawed wood more flexible? Why?
4. What part of a piece of wood is most resistant to bending?
5. Explain how the grain of the individual layers or plys of plywood are arranged.
6. Did the plywood samples test the same, or differently, when tested on the face and on the edge? Why?

unit

81

Experiment: testing the load capacity of hardwood and softwood columns

Objective:

To compare the load that can be placed on hardwood and softwood columns of different sizes.

Reference:

Wood Handbook, Handbook No. 72, U.S. Department of Agriculture, pp. 216–226.

Equipment and Material Needed:

Testing machine

Four wood samples: one of yellow pine, one of white oak, sizes ¾ × ¾ × 8 inches; one yellow pine, one white oak, sizes ¾ × ¾ × 4 inches

Try square

Procedure:

1. Place a sample of yellow pine, ¾ × ¾ × 8 inches, in the testing machine in a vertical position (see Fig. 81–1).

2. Raise the lower platen until both platen plates touch the sample. Check the sample for squareness, using a try square.

Fig. 81–1. An 8-inch sample wood column before failure.

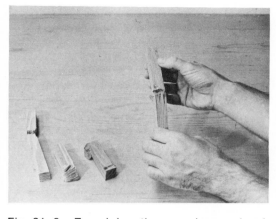

Fig. 81–3. Examining the sample wood columns after failure.

Fig. 81–2. Failure of a sample 4-inch wood column.

3. Apply pressure slowly with the testing machine until the sample breaks (or until the highest reading is obtained) (Fig. 81–1).

4. Record the maximum load.

5. Test the $\frac{3}{4} \times \frac{3}{4} \times 8$ inch white oak sample, following the same procedure as outlined above.

6. Test the two smaller samples ($\frac{3}{4} \times \frac{3}{4} \times 4$ inches) of yellow pine and white oak, following the above procedure (Fig. 81–2).

7. Examine the pieces; record the results (Fig. 81–3).

Questions:

1. Define a column in your own words.
2. Give four uses for columns.
3. What was the difference in the way the longer and shorter column of the same type of wood failed?

4. Which was stronger, the longer or the shorter columns? Why?
5. Which was stronger, the softwood or the hardwood columns? Why?

unit
82

Experiment: testing the strength of glues and adhesives

Fig. 82–1. Glued wood block samples ready for testing.

Objective:

To compare the strength of some common types of glues and adhesives.

References:

Groneman, Chris H., *General Woodworking*, Unit 25.
Wood Handbook, Handbook No. 72, U.S. Department of Agriculture, pp. 233–240.

Equipment and Material Needed:

Testing machine
Polyvinyl-resin glue, plastic-resin glue, resorcinol-resin glue
Handscrew or C clamps
Three cans, or glue containers
Six pieces of wood, ¾ × 2 × 3 inches (all the same species)
Bandsaw

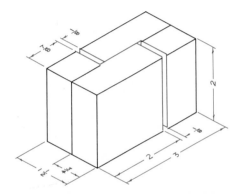

Fig. 82–2. A drawing showing measurements for the wood block samples.

Procedure:

1. Glue two pieces of wood face-to-face, using polyvinyl-resin glue; two with plastic-resin; two with resorcinol-resin. Use adequate clamp pressure. Let the glue dry thoroughly (Fig. 82–1).

2. Cut a kerf on the opposite ends, and on the opposite faces of each block (see Figs. 82–1 and 82–2).

Fig. 82–3. Failure of a glued-block sample.

Fig. 82–4. Examining the failure of the glued sample.

3. Place one sample in the tester, and slowly apply pressure to the platen.

4. Observe the sample as pressure is applied (Fig. 82–3).

5. When the sample breaks, remove it from the tester.

6. Record the maximum load.

7. Examine the broken sample. Determine if failure occurred at the glue joint, or in the wood (Fig. 82–4).

8. Test the two remaining samples, using the procedure described above.

Questions:

1. Give the characteristics of the glues used in this experiment.

2. What are the advantages and disadvantages of each of the three kinds of glues used in this experiment?

3. What causes the glue to hold the two pieces of wood together?

4. Describe how each sample failed when pressure was applied. Which glue seemed to be the strongest?

unit

83

Experiment: a strength comparison of two common wood joints

Objective:

To learn about the strength characteristics of dowel joints and mortise-and-tenon joints.

References:

Groneman, Chris H., *General Woodworking*, Unit 21.

Wood Handbook, Handbook No. 72, U.S. Department of Agriculture, pp. 240–245.

Equipment and Material Needed:

Testing machine

Dowel joint sample; mortise-and-tenon joint sample (Fig. 83–1). Also see working drawings in Figs. 83–2 and 83–3.

Procedure:

1. Place the dowel joint sample in the testing machine (see Fig. 83–1).

2. Raise the bottom platen until both platen plates rest against the sample.

383

Fig. 83–1. Mortise-and-tenon, and dowel joint samples.

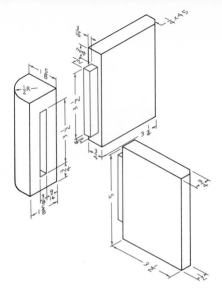

Fig. 83–3. The working drawing for a mortise-and-tenon joint sample.

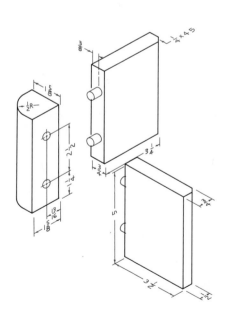

Fig. 83–2. The working drawing for a dowel-joint sample.

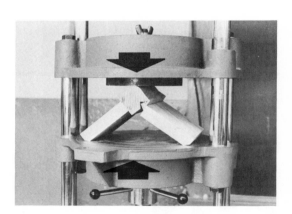

Fig. 83–4. Failure of a sample joint.

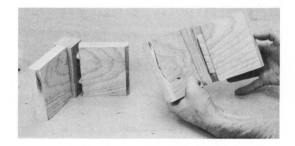

Fig. 83–5. Examining the joint failure.

384

3. Slowly apply pressure to the testing machine until the sample breaks (Fig. 83–4).

4. Observe the sample as it fails. Record the maximum load.

5. Test the mortise-and-tenon joint.

6. Observe the broken sample as it fails. Record the maximum load.

7. Observe both broken samples. Record the characteristics of the performance of each (Fig. 83–5).

Questions:

1. Name the various kinds of mortise-and-tenon joints. Where would they be used?
2. Where are dowel joints of the type tested generally used?
3. Which joint was easier to make, the dowel or the mortise-and-tenon?
4. Which type of joint was strongest? Why?
5. How could strength of the mortise-and-tenon joint be increased? Of the dowel joint?
6. If you were constructing a piece of furniture, which joint would you select to use?

---

unit

84

Experiment: wood distillation

Objectives:

To learn what the process of wood distillation is, and how it is done in industry. To become familiar with the products of both softwood and hardwood distillation.

References:

Groneman, Chris H., *General Woodworking*, Unit 70.

Brown, Nelson C., *Forest Products*, John Wiley & Sons, Inc., N.Y., 1950, Chapter 24.

Equipment and Material Needed:

Ring stand
Test tube clamp
Test tube holder
Two large, hard-glass test tubes
Bunsen burner
Water
Glass and rubber tubing
Glass jet
Wood chips, about ¼ inch across each dimension: yellow pine, oak, and cedar

Procedure:

1. Make enough wood chips of each of the three species to fill separate test tubes about one-fourth full.

2. Place the chips of one species in the tube. Turn the tube horizontally in the ring-stand clamp (see Fig. 84–1).

3. Insert a one-hole stopper (with glass delivery tube) into the test tube. The delivery tube should extend down through a two-hole stopper into another test tube about

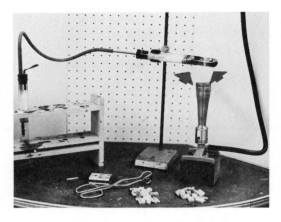

Fig. 84–1. Heating one species of the wood chips.

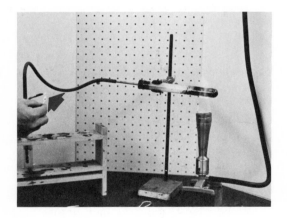

Fig. 84–2. Testing to determine if a combustible gas is being produced.

Fig. 84–3. Examining the contents of the test tube.

$\frac{1}{4}$ full of water. The other hole in the stopper should contain a glass jet (see Fig. 84–1).

4. Heat the chips for about $\frac{1}{2}$ hour (Fig. 84–1).

5. Note the changes which take place during the heating process, and the resulting products.

⬡ CAUTION: Use goggles to look closely at the apparatus while it is heating. Do not let water back up into the delivery tube.

6. Check the jet periodically with a flame to see if a combustible gas is being produced (Fig. 84–2).

7. After the major flow of gas ceases, inspect the contents of the test tube (Fig. 84–3).

8. Try to identify the product.

9. Repeat the above procedure with each of the two other species of chips.

Questions:

1. Make a table listing each product obtained from each of the three kinds of wood chips distilled.
2. Give a use for each product, and another source of the product if there is one.
3. What are two species of trees which yield a superior grade of charcoal?
4. Describe the production and processing of gum naval stores.

unit
85

Experiment: making paper

Objectives:

To become familiar with the various methods used to make paper.

To make paper, using a semi-chemical process.

References:

Groneman, Chris H., *General Woodworking*, Unit 70.

Groneman, Chris H., and Glazener, E. R., *Technical Woodworking*, McGraw-Hill Book Company, New York, N.Y., 1966, Unit 12.

Equipment and Material Needed:

2000 milliliter (ml) flask
1000 ml beaker
Wood shavings (yellow pine)
Hot plate or Bunsen burner
Lye
Bleach
Mechanical mixer (kitchen type)
Strainer
Large, shallow container
Screen
Two felt pads
Electric iron
Vacuum cleaner
Can or receptacle for mixing fibers

Procedure:

1. Break the shavings into fine pieces.
2. Put them in the flask (Fig. 85–1).

Fig. 85–1. Pine shavings in a flask.

Fig. 85–2. Cooking the shavings in the lye solution.

Fig. 85–3. Straining the liquid from the wood fiber.

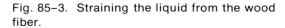

Fig. 85-4. Mixing the fibers with clean water.

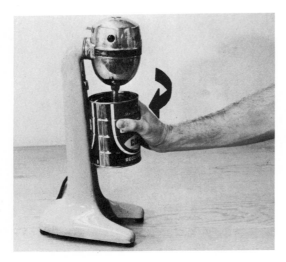

Fig. 85-5. Beating the water-and-fiber mixture, using a mixer.

Fig. 85-6. Breaking the fibers apart by hand.

3. Cover the wood shavings with a solution of 25 percent lye and 75 percent water.

CAUTION: Do not breathe the lye fumes or get the solution on your hands (see Fig. 85-2).

4. Place the flask over a Bunsen burner, or a hot plate.

5. Cook the chips until they separate (Fig. 85-2).

CAUTION: Do not allow the solution to boil over.

Cooking the wood chips may take from 4 to 6 hours, and may have to be done prior to class time.

6. Strain the liquid from the wood fibers (Fig. 85-3).

7. Add clean water to the fibers, and stir the contents (Fig. 85-4).

8. Strain the water from the fibers.

9. Repeat Steps 7 and 8 until all the lye has been removed from the fibers.

10. Put the cleaned fibers in a can; add water.

11. Beat this mixture for about 10 minutes, using the electric mixer (Fig. 85-5).

12. Strain the water from the fibers.

13. Break the fibers apart further by hand (Fig. 85-6).

14. Put the fibers in a 1000 ml beaker; cover them with bleach (Fig. 85-7).

15. Mix the contents thoroughly, then strain.

16. Repeat Steps 14 and 15 until the fibers become light in color.

17. Pour sufficient water in the pan to allow the screen to be submerged completely (see Fig. 85-8).

18. Add wood fibers to form a mixture 90 percent water and 10 percent fibers. Stir.

19. Submerge the screen, then lift it slowly from the mixture (Fig. 85-8). A layer of fibers will be on the top of the screen after the water drains through.

Fig. 85–7. Bleaching the fibers.

Fig. 85–10. Removing the damp paper from the screen.

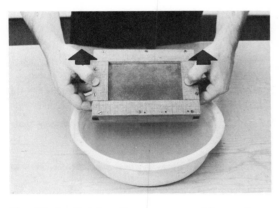

Fig. 85–8. Raising the screen and frame from the solution of fibers and water.

Fig. 85–11. Drying the damp paper between felt pads.

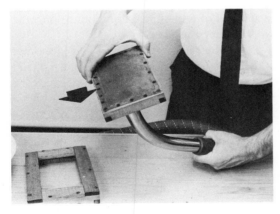

Fig. 85–9. Removing the excess water with vacuum suction.

Fig. 85–12. The finished piece of hand-made paper.

20. Draw the excess water from the underside of the screen (Fig. 85–9).

21. Remove the outer frame of the screen.

22. Place a felt pad on top of the paper (Fig. 85–10).

23. The damp paper should adhere to the felt pad when it is removed (see Fig. 85–10). If it does not, remove an edge from the screen to the pad, using a knife.

24. Place another felt pad on the opposite side of the paper after it is removed from the screen. The sheet of paper is now between two felt pads (as shown in Fig. 85–11).

25. Iron the felt pads to evaporate the remaining moisture (Fig. 85–11).

26. Remove the completed sheet of paper when the moisture has been ironed out (Fig. 85–12).

Questions

1. What are the three basic methods of making paper mechanically?
2. What are the advantages and disadvantages of each?
3. Explain the operation of the Fourdrinier.
4. After you cooked the wood chips, what was contained in the liquid solution that was drained from the fibers?
5. What determines the thickness of paper?
6. What was the purpose of the lye in the solution?
7. How does paper made from hardwood chips differ from that made from softwood chips?
8. What can be added to make paper less absorbent? More opaque?
9. What was the name of the process you used for making paper?

---

unit
86

Experiment: the characteristics of wood-plastic combinations

A new development in the use of wood that may greatly influence the woodworking industries in the future is called wood-plastic combinations (WPC). These are developed by, first, treating the wood in a vacuum to draw out air and moisture, and second, forcing a liquid monomer (a simple unpolymerized form of a chemical compound) into the wood under pressure.

The combination of wood and monomer is then irradiated with gamma rays, which act as a catalyst. The catalytic action causes the monomer molecules inside the wood to form into chains, becoming a plastic.

Wood-plastic combinations have many advantages over natural wood, and should be considered for certain wood products. Some suggested uses are for golf-club heads, furniture, cutlery handles, flooring, paneling, gun stocks, and tool handles. Research shows that wood-plastic combinations are superior to natural wood in terms of hard-

Fig. 86–1. Wood-plastic combination samples.

ness, weather resistance, mar and abrasive resistance, and many other factors.

The American Novawood Corporation has done much research with wood-plastic combinations, and has developed a sample educational kit at nominal cost. It contains various kinds of woods treated with plastics (Fig. 86–1).

Objectives:

To learn the characteristics of wood-plastic combinations.

To compare wood-plastic combinations with natural wood.

References:

The American Novawood Corporation, 2432 Lakeside Drive, Lynchburg, Virginia 24501.

Western New York Nuclear Research Center, Inc., Power Drive, Buffalo, New York.

Commercialization of the Process of Manufacturing Radiation-Produced Plastic Impregnated Wood in the Southern Region, The Clearinghouse of Federal Scientific and Technical Information, National Bureau of Standards, U.S. Department of Commerce, Springfield, Virginia 22151.

Equipment and Material Needed:

Wood-plastic combination samples: two maple-plastic combination, $3 \times 3 \times 1$ inches and $1 \times 3 \times \frac{1}{8}$ inches; one yellow-pine plastic combination, $2 \times 4 \times 12$ inches (see Fig. 86–1)

Natural wood samples: two maple, $3 \times 3 \times 1$ inches and $1 \times 3 \times \frac{1}{8}$ inches one yellow pine sample, $2 \times 4 \times 12$ inches (to be made from available supply)

Rockwell Hardness Tester

1000 milliliter (ml) beaker

Hot plate

Balance

Bunsen burner

Hammer and nails

Jointer

Buffer

Procedure:

1. Set up the Rockwell Hardness Tester with the $\frac{1}{8}$-inch ball.

2. Using the $3 \times 3 \times 1$ inch maple-plastic combination:

    a. place it on the plate of the tester

    b. adjust the needle

    c. apply the weight force to the sample (Fig. 86–2).

    d. after the needle has stopped, release the weight force

    e. record the reading

3. Using the $3 \times 3 \times 1$ inch natural maple sample, follow steps a, b, c, d, and e.

4. Use an accurate balance and weigh the $3 \times 3 \times 1$ inch maple-plastic combination. Record the weight.

5. Use an accurate balance and weigh the $3 \times 3 \times 1$ inch natural maple sample. Record the weight.

6. Fill the 1000 ml beaker $\frac{3}{4}$ full of water.

7. Place both samples in the beaker of water; place the beaker on the hot plate. Boil for about 15 minutes (Fig. 86–3).

Fig. 86–2. Testing a wood-plastic combination sample on the hardness tester.

Fig. 86–3. Boiling the maple-plastic combination sample and the natural maple sample.

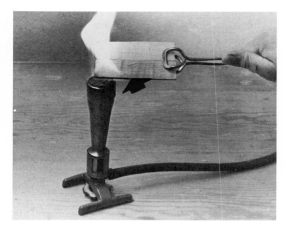

Fig. 86–4. Burning the maple-plastic combination sample and the natural maple sample.

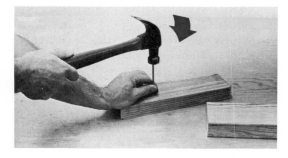

Fig. 86–5. Testing the yellow-pine-plastic combination sample and the natural yellow pine sample for resistance to nailing.

8. Remove the samples from the beaker after 15 minutes of boiling.

9. Reweigh both. Record the results.

10. Using the $1 \times 3 \times \frac{1}{8}$ inch maple-plastic combination sample, and also the natural maple sample:

    a. hold the two samples over an open flame for 30 seconds (Fig. 86–4)

    b. observe the two and record the results

    c. hold the two samples again over the flame, but for one minute this time

    d. observe the flame and the charred samples

    e. record your observation

Fig. 86–6. Buffing the yellow-pine-plastic combination sample.

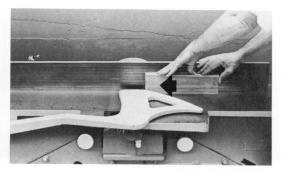

Fig. 86–7. Jointing (planing) an edge of the yellow-pine-plastic combination sample.

11. Using the 2 × 4 × 12 inch natural yellow pine sample:
    a. drive a nail into this sample (Fig. 86–5)
    b. record your observation

12. Using the 2 × 4 × 12 inch yellow-pine-plastic combination:
    a. attempt to drive a nail into this sample (Fig. 86–5)
    b. record your observation

13. Using a buffing wheel, buff a section of the yellow-pine-plastic combination (Fig. 86–6). Compare the buffed section with an unbuffed one.

14. Joint (plane) the yellow-pine-plastic combination on one edge (Fig. 86–7).

15. Joint the natural yellow pine sample on an edge.

16. Observe the differences when jointing, and also the results.

Questions:

1. Describe how wood-plastic combinations are produced.
2. How do wood-plastic combinations and natural wood compare in hardness?
3. Give three uses where wood-plastic combinations may be preferred over natural wood because of hardness.
4. How do wood-plastic combinations compare with natural wood in terms of weight? Is this an advantage or a disadvantage?
5. Which sample weighed more after boiling in water? Why?
6. Give an example where wood-plastic combinations may be preferred over natural wood because of their resistance to moisture.
7. Which sample burned more, the wood-plastic combination or the natural wood? Why?
8. How can you drive a nail into a wood-plastic combination? Is this an advantage or a disadvantage?
9. Should wood-plastic combinations be finished like natural wood? Why?
10. Are wood-plastic combinations as easy to work with machines as natural wood?
11. What could be done to the machine to aid in cutting a wood-plastic combination?

SECTION 9

PROJECT 1
SHADOW BOX

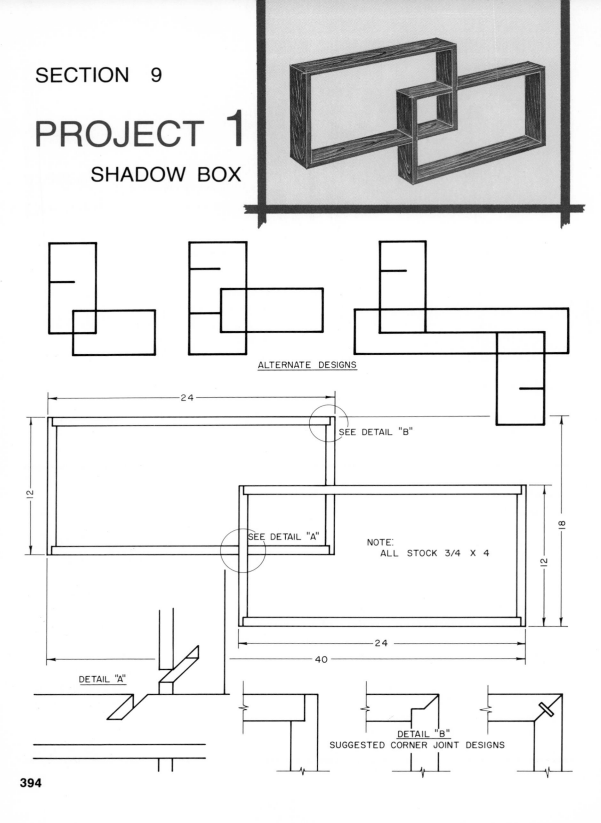

ALTERNATE DESIGNS

24

12

SEE DETAIL "B"

SEE DETAIL "A"

18

12

40

24

NOTE:
ALL STOCK 3/4 X 4

DETAIL "A"

DETAIL "B"
SUGGESTED CORNER JOINT DESIGNS

PROJECT 2
SERVING TRAY

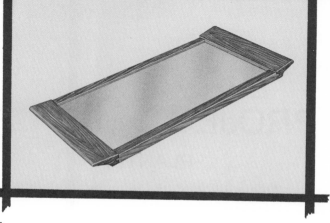

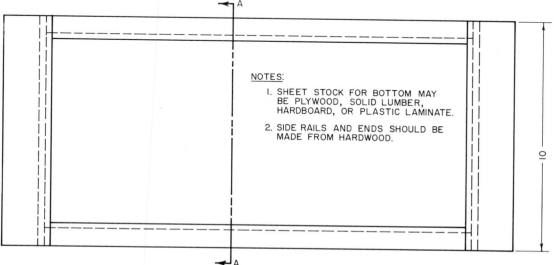

NOTES:

1. SHEET STOCK FOR BOTTOM MAY BE PLYWOOD, SOLID LUMBER, HARDBOARD, OR PLASTIC LAMINATE.

2. SIDE RAILS AND ENDS SHOULD BE MADE FROM HARDWOOD.

10

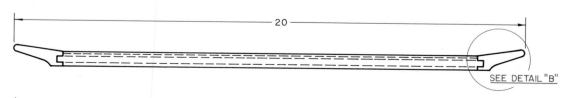

20

SEE DETAIL "B"

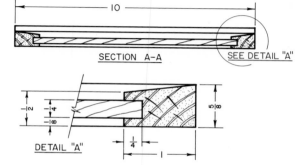

10

SECTION A-A

SEE DETAIL "A"

DETAIL "A"

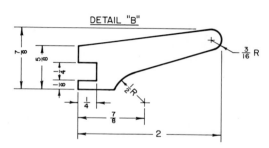

DETAIL "B"

$\frac{3}{16}$ R

$\frac{7}{8}$ $\frac{5}{8}$ $\frac{1}{4}$ $\frac{1}{8}$

$\frac{1}{4}$

$\frac{1}{2}$R

$\frac{7}{8}$

2

PROJECT 3
PLANTER

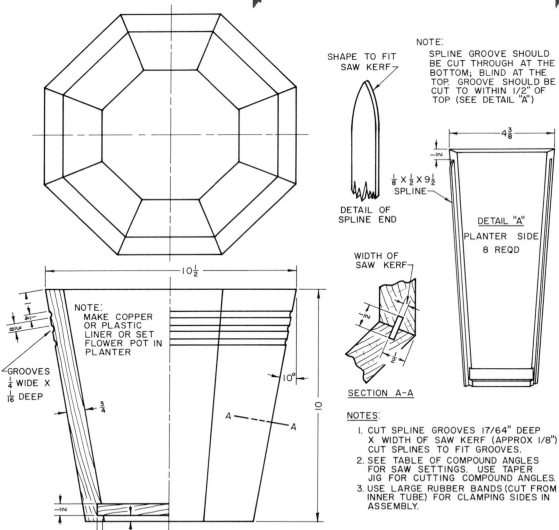

SHAPE TO FIT
SAW KERF

DETAIL OF
SPLINE END

NOTE:
SPLINE GROOVE SHOULD
BE CUT THROUGH AT THE
BOTTOM; BLIND AT THE
TOP. GROOVE SHOULD BE
CUT TO WITHIN 1/2" OF
TOP (SEE DETAIL "A")

$\frac{1}{8}$ X $\frac{1}{2}$ X $9\frac{1}{2}$
SPLINE

$4\frac{3}{8}$

DETAIL "A"
PLANTER SIDE
8 REQD

WIDTH OF
SAW KERF

SECTION A-A

$10\frac{1}{2}$

NOTE:
MAKE COPPER
OR PLASTIC
LINER OR SET
FLOWER POT IN
PLANTER

GROOVES
$\frac{1}{4}$ WIDE X
$\frac{1}{16}$ DEEP

$\frac{3}{4}$

10°

10

A —— A

$\frac{1}{4}$

NOTES:

1. CUT SPLINE GROOVES 17/64" DEEP
   X WIDTH OF SAW KERF (APPROX 1/8")
   CUT SPLINES TO FIT GROOVES.
2. SEE TABLE OF COMPOUND ANGLES
   FOR SAW SETTINGS. USE TAPER
   JIG FOR CUTTING COMPOUND ANGLES.
3. USE LARGE RUBBER BANDS (CUT FROM
   INNER TUBE) FOR CLAMPING SIDES IN
   ASSEMBLY.

396

PROJECT 4
DRESSER VALET

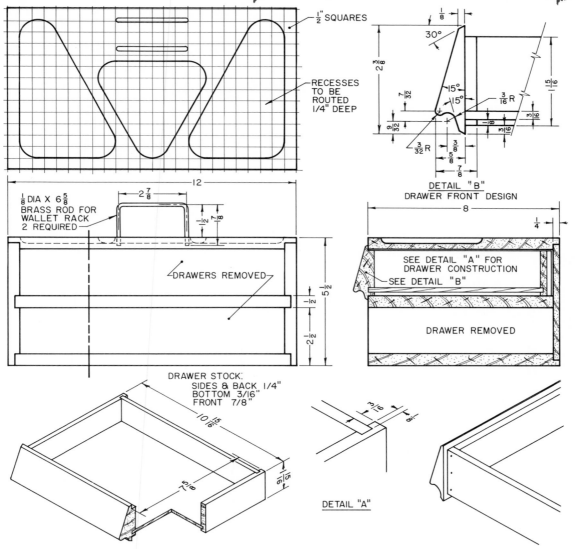

$\frac{1}{2}$" SQUARES

RECESSES TO BE ROUTED 1/4" DEEP

DETAIL "B"
DRAWER FRONT DESIGN

$\frac{1}{8}$ DIA X 6$\frac{5}{8}$ BRASS ROD FOR WALLET RACK 2 REQUIRED

DRAWERS REMOVED

SEE DETAIL "A" FOR DRAWER CONSTRUCTION
SEE DETAIL "B"

DRAWER REMOVED

DRAWER STOCK:
SIDES & BACK 1/4"
BOTTOM 3/16"
FRONT 7/8"

DETAIL "A"

PROJECT 5

BIRD FEEDER

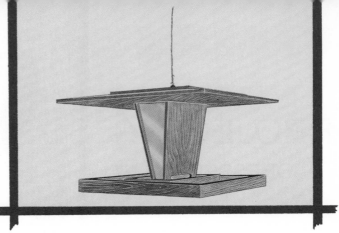

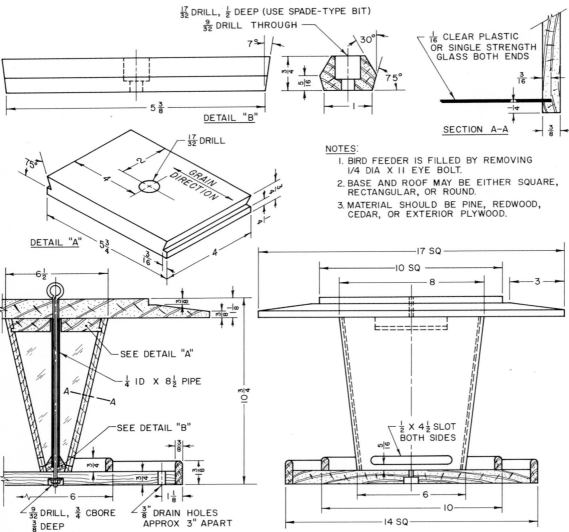

$\frac{17}{32}$ DRILL, $\frac{1}{2}$ DEEP (USE SPADE-TYPE BIT)
$\frac{9}{32}$ DRILL THROUGH

7°

30°

$\frac{3}{4}$

$\frac{5}{16}$

75°

1

$\frac{1}{16}$ CLEAR PLASTIC
OR SINGLE STRENGTH
GLASS BOTH ENDS

$\frac{3}{16}$

$\frac{1}{4}$

$\frac{3}{8}$

SECTION A–A

5 $\frac{3}{8}$

DETAIL "B"

$\frac{17}{32}$ DRILL

75°

2

4

GRAIN DIRECTION

$\frac{1}{4}$

$\frac{1}{4}$

DETAIL "A"

5 $\frac{3}{4}$

$\frac{3}{16}$

4

NOTES:

1. BIRD FEEDER IS FILLED BY REMOVING
   1/4 DIA X 11 EYE BOLT.

2. BASE AND ROOF MAY BE EITHER SQUARE,
   RECTANGULAR, OR ROUND.

3. MATERIAL SHOULD BE PINE, REDWOOD,
   CEDAR, OR EXTERIOR PLYWOOD.

6 $\frac{1}{2}$

$\frac{3}{8}$

$\frac{1}{8}$

SEE DETAIL "A"

$\frac{1}{4}$ ID X 8 $\frac{1}{2}$ PIPE

A

A

SEE DETAIL "B"

$\frac{3}{8}$

$\frac{3}{4}$

$\frac{3}{4}$

$\frac{3}{8}$

10 $\frac{3}{4}$

1 $\frac{1}{8}$

6

$\frac{9}{32}$ DRILL, $\frac{3}{4}$ CBORE
$\frac{3}{8}$ DEEP

$\frac{3}{8}$" DRAIN HOLES
APPROX 3" APART

17 SQ

10 SQ

8

3

$\frac{1}{2}$ X 4 $\frac{1}{2}$ SLOT
BOTH SIDES

$\frac{5}{16}$

6

10

14 SQ

PROJECT 6
HANGING LAMP

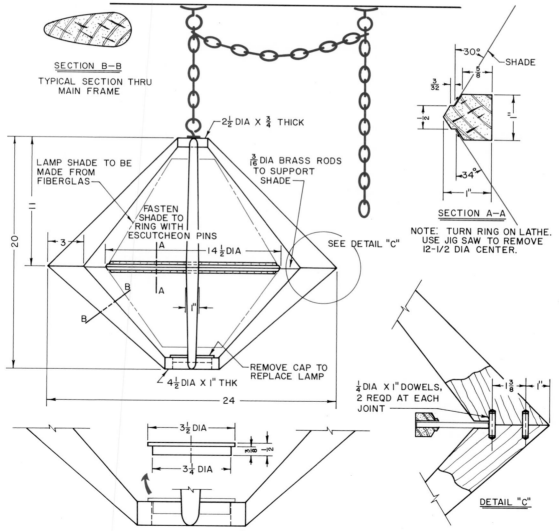

SECTION B–B

TYPICAL SECTION THRU
MAIN FRAME

2½ DIA X ¾ THICK

LAMP SHADE TO BE
MADE FROM
FIBERGLAS

$\frac{3}{16}$ DIA BRASS RODS
TO SUPPORT
SHADE

FASTEN
SHADE TO
RING WITH
ESCUTCHEON PINS

14½ DIA

SEE DETAIL "C"

20

11

3

1"

B

B

A

A

REMOVE CAP TO
REPLACE LAMP

4½ DIA X 1" THK

24

—30°

SHADE

$\frac{5}{8}$

$\frac{3}{32}$

½

1"

—34°

1"

SECTION A–A

NOTE: TURN RING ON LATHE.
USE JIG SAW TO REMOVE
12-1/2 DIA CENTER.

3½ DIA

3¾ DIA

$\frac{3}{8}$ ½

¼ DIA X 1" DOWELS,
2 REQD AT EACH
JOINT

1$\frac{3}{8}$ 1"

DETAIL "C"

PROJECT 7

TABLE

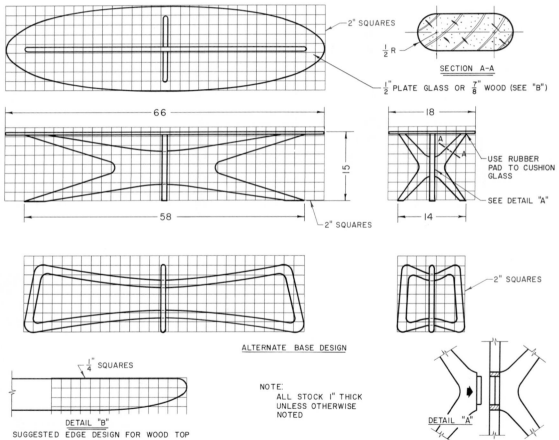

2" SQUARES

$\frac{1}{2}$ R

SECTION A-A

$\frac{1}{2}$" PLATE GLASS OR $\frac{7}{8}$" WOOD (SEE "B")

66

15

58

2" SQUARES

18

USE RUBBER PAD TO CUSHION GLASS

SEE DETAIL "A"

14

2" SQUARES

ALTERNATE BASE DESIGN

$\frac{1}{4}$" SQUARES

DETAIL "B"

SUGGESTED EDGE DESIGN FOR WOOD TOP

NOTE:
ALL STOCK 1" THICK UNLESS OTHERWISE NOTED

DETAIL "A"

PROJECT 8
COFFEE TABLE

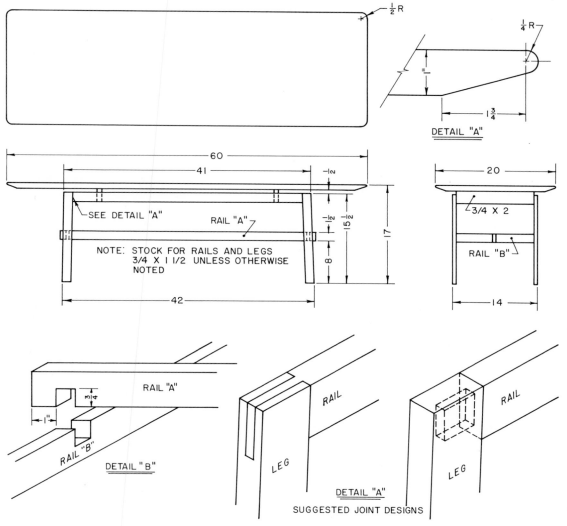

$\frac{1}{2}$ R

$\frac{1}{4}$ R

1"

1 $\frac{3}{4}$

DETAIL "A"

60

41

$\frac{1}{2}$

SEE DETAIL "A"

RAIL "A"

NOTE: STOCK FOR RAILS AND LEGS
3/4 X 1 1/2 UNLESS OTHERWISE
NOTED

42

$\frac{1}{2}$

15 $\frac{1}{2}$

17

8

20

3/4 X 2

RAIL "B"

14

RAIL "A"

$\frac{3}{4}$

1"

RAIL "B"

DETAIL "B"

RAIL

LEG

DETAIL "A"

SUGGESTED JOINT DESIGNS

RAIL

LEG

PROJECT 9

KNOCK-DOWN TRAY TABLE

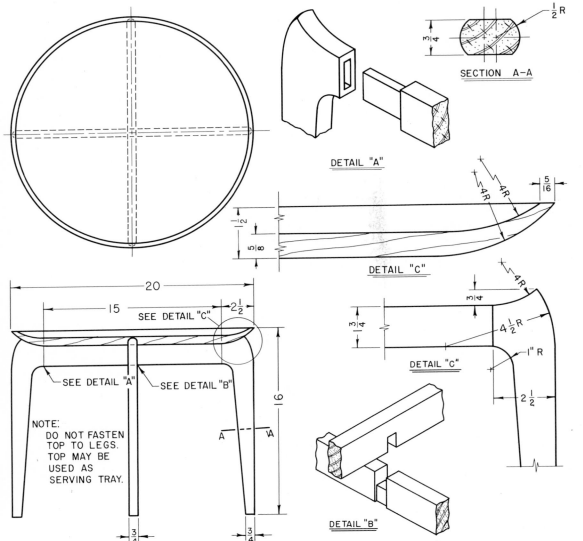

SECTION A-A

$\frac{1}{2}$ R

$\frac{3}{4}$

DETAIL "A"

DETAIL "C"

$\frac{5}{16}$

4R

4R

$1\frac{1}{2}$

$\frac{5}{8}$

DETAIL "C"

4R

$\frac{3}{4}$

$4\frac{1}{2}$ R

1" R

$2\frac{1}{2}$

20

15

SEE DETAIL "C"

$2\frac{1}{2}$

16

SEE DETAIL "A"

SEE DETAIL "B"

A   A

NOTE:
DO NOT FASTEN
TOP TO LEGS.
TOP MAY BE
USED AS
SERVING TRAY.

$\frac{3}{4}$

$\frac{3}{4}$

DETAIL "B"

402

PROJECT 10
END TABLE

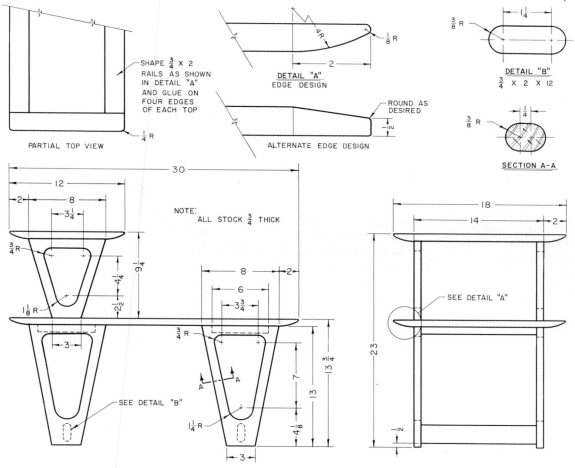

SHAPE $\frac{3}{4}$ X 2 RAILS AS SHOWN IN DETAIL "A" AND GLUE ON FOUR EDGES OF EACH TOP

$\frac{1}{4}$ R

PARTIAL TOP VIEW

DETAIL "A"
EDGE DESIGN

$\frac{4}{4}$R

$\frac{1}{8}$ R

2

ROUND AS DESIRED

$\frac{1}{2}$

ALTERNATE EDGE DESIGN

$\frac{3}{8}$ R

$1\frac{1}{4}$

DETAIL "B"
$\frac{3}{4}$ X 2 X 12

$\frac{3}{8}$ R

$\frac{1}{4}$

SECTION A-A

NOTE:
ALL STOCK $\frac{3}{4}$ THICK

30

12

2

8

$3\frac{1}{4}$

$\frac{3}{4}$R

$9\frac{1}{4}$

$4\frac{1}{4}$

$2\frac{1}{2}$

$1\frac{1}{8}$ R

3

SEE DETAIL "B"

8

2

6

$3\frac{3}{4}$

$\frac{3}{4}$ R

A

A

$1\frac{1}{4}$R

7

13

$13\frac{3}{4}$

$4\frac{1}{8}$

3

18

14

2

SEE DETAIL "A"

23

$\frac{1}{2}$

403

PROJECT 11

PEN HOLDER

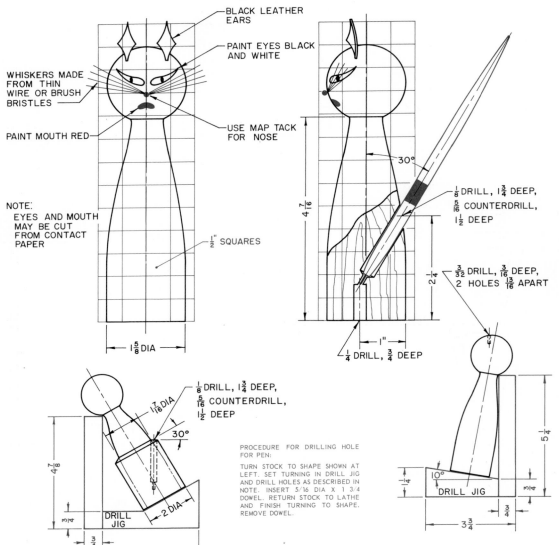

BLACK LEATHER EARS

PAINT EYES BLACK AND WHITE

WHISKERS MADE FROM THIN WIRE OR BRUSH BRISTLES

USE MAP TACK FOR NOSE

PAINT MOUTH RED

NOTE:
EYES AND MOUTH MAY BE CUT FROM CONTACT PAPER

$\frac{1}{2}$" SQUARES

$1\frac{5}{8}$ DIA

$30°$

$4\frac{7}{16}$

$\frac{1}{8}$ DRILL, $1\frac{3}{4}$ DEEP, $\frac{5}{16}$ COUNTERDRILL, $1\frac{1}{2}$ DEEP

$\frac{3}{32}$ DRILL, $\frac{3}{16}$ DEEP, 2 HOLES $\frac{13}{16}$ APART

$2\frac{1}{4}$

1"

$\frac{1}{4}$ DRILL, $\frac{3}{4}$ DEEP

$1\frac{7}{16}$ DIA

$\frac{1}{8}$ DRILL, $1\frac{3}{4}$ DEEP, $\frac{5}{16}$ COUNTERDRILL, $1\frac{1}{2}$ DEEP

$30°$

$4\frac{7}{8}$

$\frac{3}{4}$

DRILL JIG

2 DIA

$\frac{3}{4}$

$4\frac{3}{4}$

PROCEDURE FOR DRILLING HOLE FOR PEN:

TURN STOCK TO SHAPE SHOWN AT LEFT. SET TURNING IN DRILL JIG AND DRILL HOLES AS DESCRIBED IN NOTE. INSERT 5/16 DIA X 1 3/4 DOWEL. RETURN STOCK TO LATHE AND FINISH TURNING TO SHAPE. REMOVE DOWEL.

$5\frac{1}{4}$

$10°$

$\frac{1}{4}$

DRILL JIG

$\frac{3}{4}$

$3\frac{3}{4}$

PROJECT 12

BASKETBALL BACKBOARD

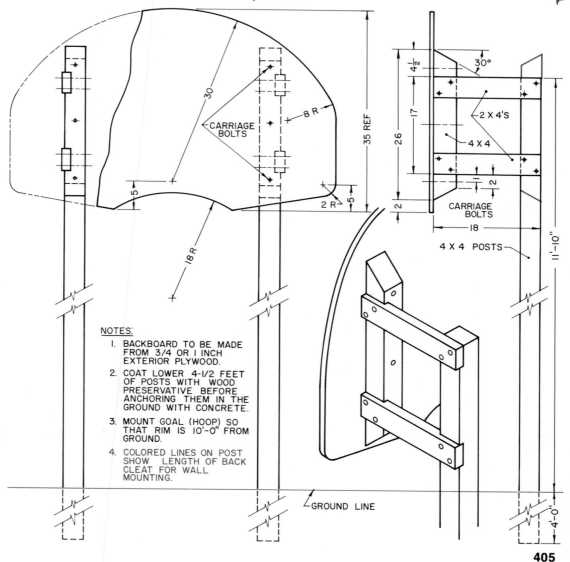

CARRIAGE BOLTS

30

8 R

35 REF

5

2 R

5

18 R

30°

4 1/2

17

26

2 X 4'S

4 X 4

2

2

CARRIAGE BOLTS

18

4 X 4 POSTS

11'-10"

NOTES:

1. BACKBOARD TO BE MADE FROM 3/4 OR 1 INCH EXTERIOR PLYWOOD.

2. COAT LOWER 4-1/2 FEET OF POSTS WITH WOOD PRESERVATIVE BEFORE ANCHORING THEM IN THE GROUND WITH CONCRETE.

3. MOUNT GOAL (HOOP) SO THAT RIM IS 10'-0" FROM GROUND.

4. COLORED LINES ON POST SHOW LENGTH OF BACK CLEAT FOR WALL MOUNTING.

GROUND LINE

4'-0"

405

PROJECT 13

BOOK CASE

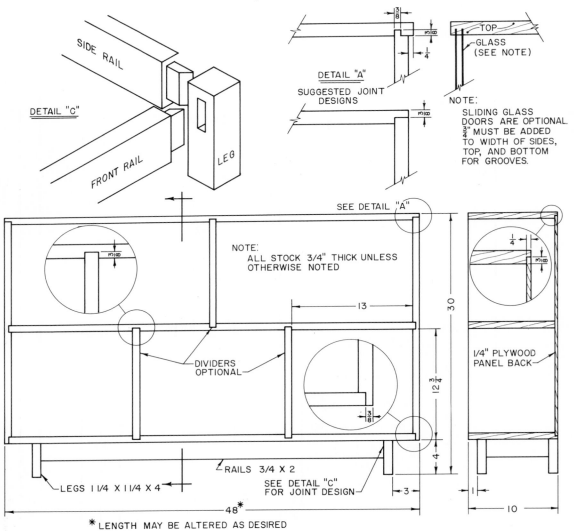

SIDE RAIL

DETAIL "C"

FRONT RAIL

LEG

DETAIL "A"
SUGGESTED JOINT DESIGNS

3/8

3/8

1/4

TOP

GLASS
(SEE NOTE)

3/8

NOTE:
SLIDING GLASS DOORS ARE OPTIONAL. 3/4" MUST BE ADDED TO WIDTH OF SIDES, TOP, AND BOTTOM FOR GROOVES.

SEE DETAIL "A"

3/8

1/4

3/8

NOTE:
ALL STOCK 3/4" THICK UNLESS OTHERWISE NOTED

13

30

12 3/4

4

3/8

DIVIDERS OPTIONAL

1/4" PLYWOOD PANEL BACK

RAILS 3/4 X 2

SEE DETAIL "C" FOR JOINT DESIGN

LEGS 1 1/4 X 1 1/4 X 4

3

1

48*

10

* LENGTH MAY BE ALTERED AS DESIRED

406

PROJECT 14

BED HEADBOARD

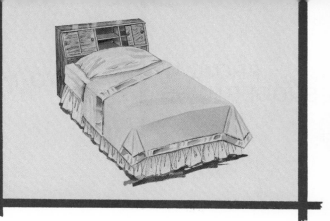

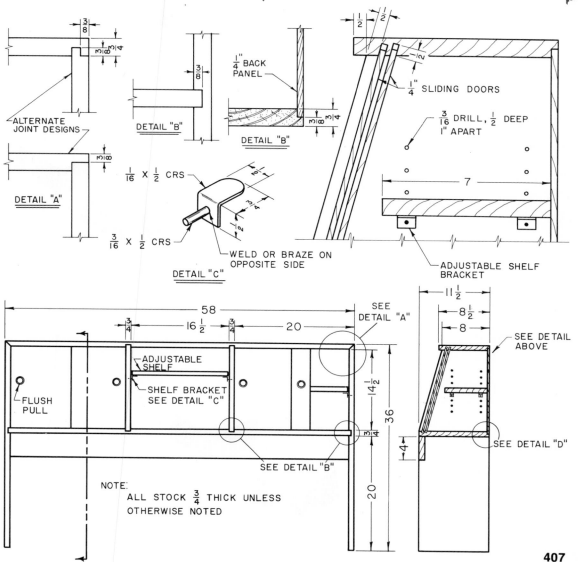

ALTERNATE JOINT DESIGNS

DETAIL "A"

$\frac{3}{8}$

$\frac{3}{8}$ $\frac{3}{4}$

DETAIL "B"

$\frac{3}{8}$

$\frac{1}{4}$" BACK PANEL

DETAIL "B"

$\frac{3}{8}$ $\frac{3}{4}$

$\frac{1}{16}$ X $\frac{1}{2}$ CRS

$\frac{3}{16}$ X $\frac{1}{2}$ CRS

WELD OR BRAZE ON OPPOSITE SIDE

DETAIL "C"

$\frac{1}{2}$ $\frac{1}{2}$

$\frac{1}{2}$

$\frac{1}{4}$" SLIDING DOORS

$\frac{3}{16}$ DRILL, $\frac{1}{2}$ DEEP 1" APART

7

ADJUSTABLE SHELF BRACKET

58

SEE DETAIL "A"

$\frac{3}{4}$ 16$\frac{1}{2}$ $\frac{3}{4}$ 20

ADJUSTABLE SHELF

SHELF BRACKET SEE DETAIL "C"

FLUSH PULL

SEE DETAIL "B"

14$\frac{1}{2}$

$\frac{3}{4}$

36

20

11$\frac{1}{2}$

8$\frac{1}{2}$

8

SEE DETAIL ABOVE

SEE DETAIL "D"

4

NOTE:
ALL STOCK $\frac{3}{4}$ THICK UNLESS OTHERWISE NOTED

407

PROJECT SUGGESTIONS

EASY TO MAKE

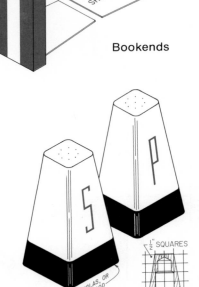

USE CONTRASTING HARDWOODS FOR UPRIGHTS

BASE 18 GAGE SHEETMETAL

Bookends

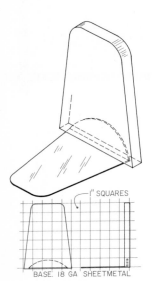

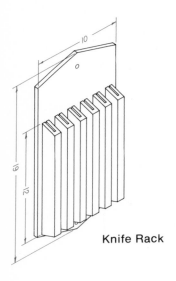

1" SQUARES

BASE 18 GA SHEETMETAL

Bookends

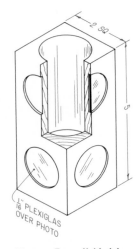

2 SQ

5

1/16" PLEXIGLAS OVER PHOTO

Photo-Pencil Holder

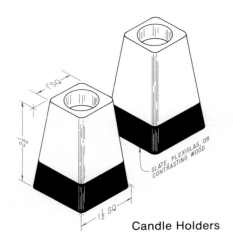

S

P

SLATE, PLEXIGLAS, OR CONTRASTING WOOD

1/2" SQUARES

Salt and Pepper Set

10

O

19

12

Knife Rack

1" SQ

2 1/2"

SLATE, PLEXIGLAS, OR CONTRASTING WOOD

1 1/2 SQ

Candle Holders

TURNING

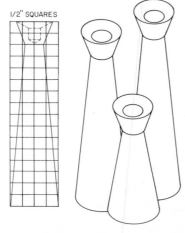

Candlesticks

1/2" SQUARES

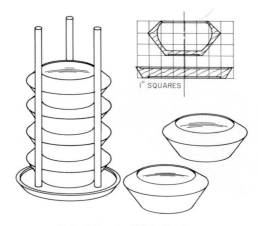

Salad Set

1" SQUARES

1" SQUARES

Salad Bowls With Rack

S P

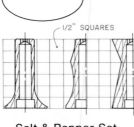

1/2" SQUARES

Salt & Pepper Set

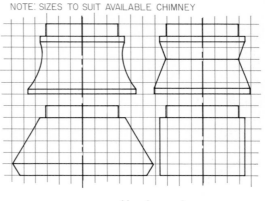

NOTE: SIZES TO SUIT AVAILABLE CHIMNEY

Hurricane Lamp

PROJECT SUGGESTIONS | SERVING

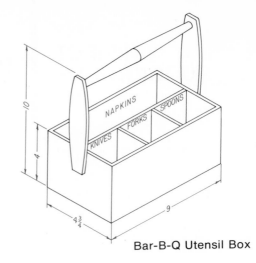

Bar-B-Q Utensil Box

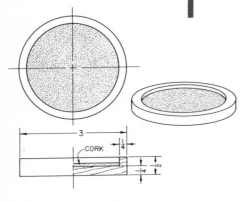

Turned Coaster

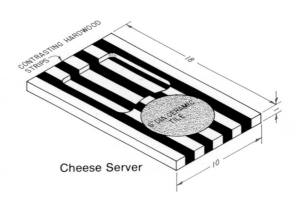

Cheese Server

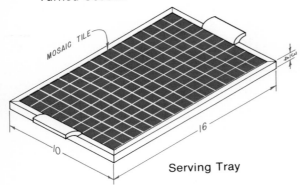

Serving Tray

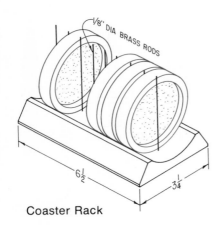

Coaster Rack

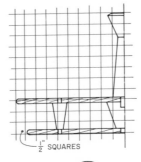
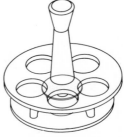

Paper Cup Serving Rack

PROJECT SUGGESTIONS | FOR THE OUTDOORS

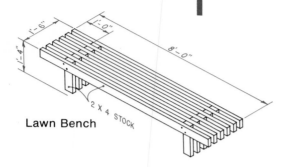

1'-6"
1'-0"
1'-4"
8'-0"
2 X 4 STOCK

Lawn Bench

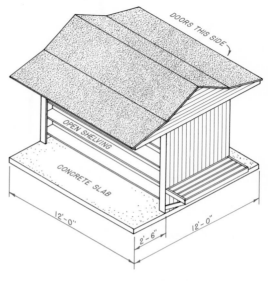

DOORS THIS SIDE
OPEN SHELVING
CONCRETE SLAB
12'-0"
12'-0"
2'-6"

Lawn & Garden Shed

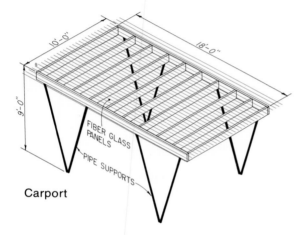

10'-0"
18'-0"
9'-0"
FIBER GLASS PANELS
PIPE SUPPORTS

Carport

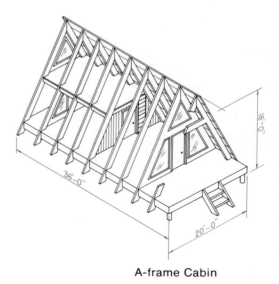

18'-0"
36'-0"
20'-0"

A-frame Cabin

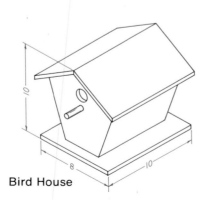

10
8
10

Bird House

CARVING AND LAMINATION

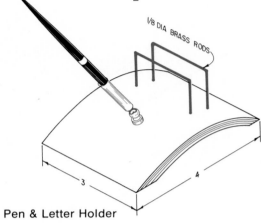

1/8 DIA BRASS RODS

3

4

Pen & Letter Holder

1" SQUARES

Ping-Pong Paddle

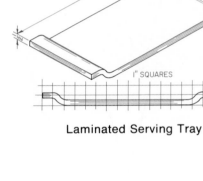

9

16

1" SQUARES

Laminated Serving Tray

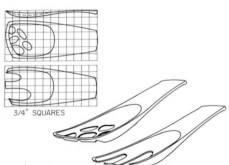

3/4" SQUARES

Carved Salad Fork & Spoon

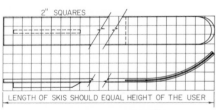

2" SQUARES

LENGTH OF SKIS SHOULD EQUAL HEIGHT OF THE USER

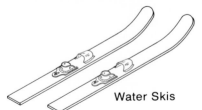

Water Skis

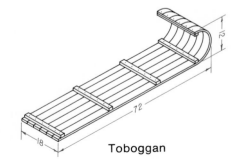

12

72

18

Toboggan

412

IDEAS FOR THE DESK TOP

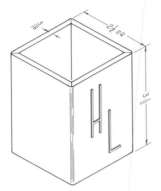

Pencil Holder

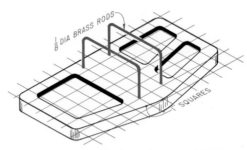

Desk or Dresser Caddy

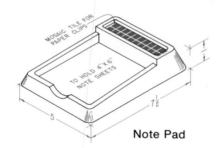

Note Pad

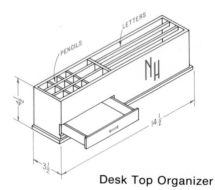

Desk Top Organizer

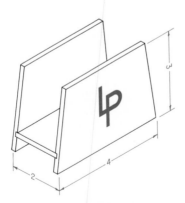

Letter or Napkin Holder

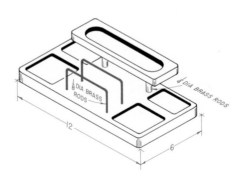

Desk or Dresser Caddy

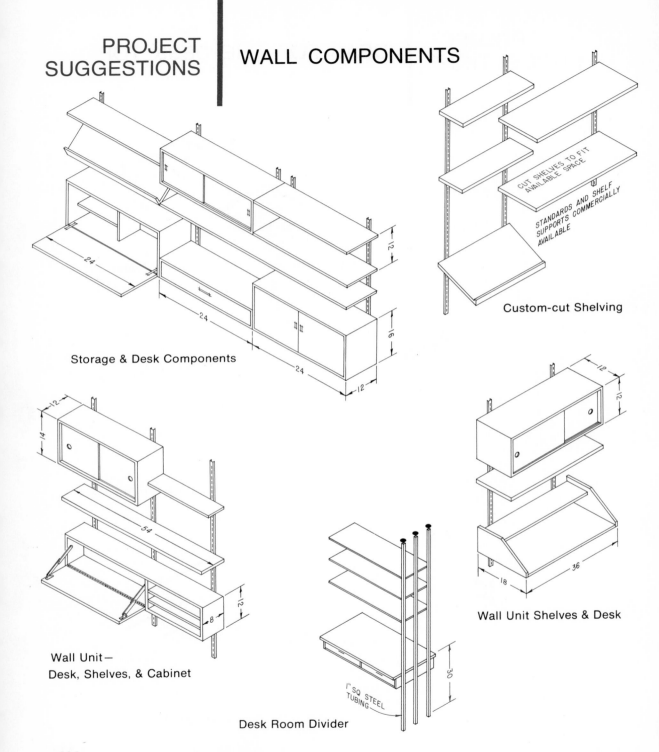

Custom-cut Shelving

CUT SHELVES TO FIT AVAILABLE SPACE

STANDARDS AND SHELF SUPPORTS COMMERCIALLY AVAILABLE

Storage & Desk Components

Wall Unit—
Desk, Shelves, & Cabinet

Desk Room Divider

1" SQ STEEL TUBING

Wall Unit Shelves & Desk

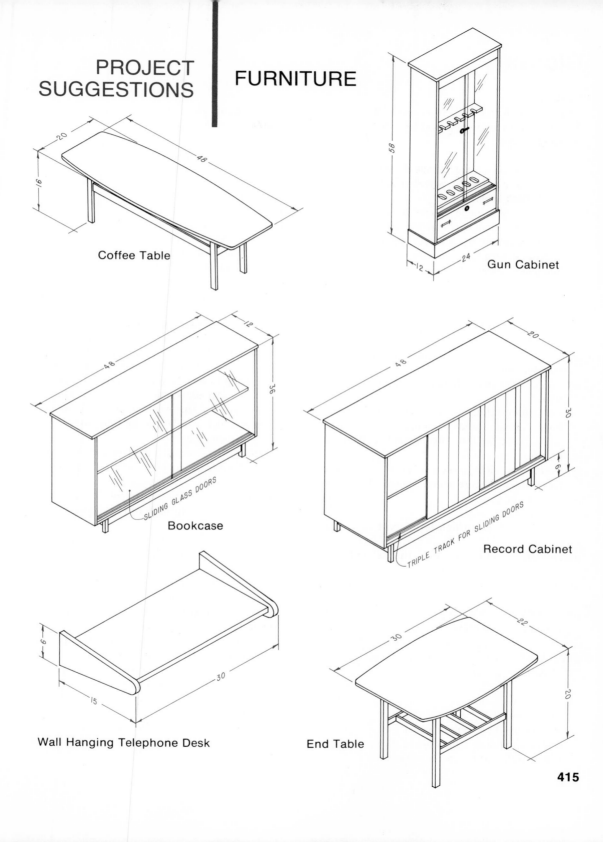

PROJECT SUGGESTIONS

FURNITURE

Coffee Table

Gun Cabinet

Bookcase

SLIDING GLASS DOORS

Record Cabinet

TRIPLE TRACK FOR SLIDING DOORS

Wall Hanging Telephone Desk

End Table

415

Glossary

Many of the terms used in *General Woodworking,* and listed in this glossary, have several meanings. The definitions given here will help you understand the technical application of these terms to the field of woodworking.

abrasive　A substance or agent, such as sandpaper or a grinding wheel; used to smooth or sharpen tools.

acute angle　An angle of less than 90 degrees.

adhesive　A substance capable of holding materials together by surface attachment. It is a general term and includes cements, glue, mucilage, paste, and resins.

adjust　To bring about the proper relationship of parts for fitting and cutting.

air-dried lumber　Lumber which has been seasoned by drying in the open air; abbreviated *AD.*

alcohol　A shellac thinner made from ethyl and wood alcohol.

alignment　Precise adjustment or correct position.

animal glue　Glue made from animal hides, bones, hoofs, and trimmings; available in liquid form, in thin sheets, and in flakes or powder.

annular rings　Rings seen in cross sections of trees which indicate yearly growth. Also called *growth rings.*

apron　See *rail.*

arc　A curved line which forms part of a curve or circle.

assembling　Putting together the related parts which comprise any tool, object, or project.

auger bit　The cutting edge of a compound tool used to bore holes in wood.

auger-bit file　A file designed for sharpening the nibs and cutting lips of auger bits.

automatic drill　See *push drill.*

awl　A pointed tool; used for marking locations of nails or screws

backsaw　A reinforced or stiffened handsaw blade.

back veneer　The veneer sheet on the back of a plywood panel. The grain of the back veneer runs parallel to the grain of the core.

band saw　An endless saw blade running on revolving wheels; the power saw incorporating this blade.

bar clamp　See *cabinet clamp.*

bark　The tough protective external covering of a tree.

bayonet saw　The name sometimes given the portable electric jig saw.

belt sander　An electric motor-driven portable machine equipped with an endless sanding belt.

bench hook　A board with cleats on each end; used for holding boards stationary on the workbench during certain processes.

bench rule　A rigid measuring strip of wood graduated in inches and fractions of inches.

bench stop　An adjustable metal device recessed in the top of the workbench; used to hold boards which are flat on the table top.

bevel　A sloping edge.

bevel (tool)　For measuring or laying off bevels, or for testing the angle of a bevel. Sometimes called T-bevel.

binder　The adhesive used to bind wood particles together to form hardboard and particle boards.

bleaching　Lightening the surface color of wood by the use of oxalic acid and/or other similar chemicals.

block plane　A small hand plane; generally used for planing end grains.

blueprint　A photographic print of a drawing; white lines on blue paper.

board foot　A unit of measurement for lumber. One foot square and one inch thick.

bolt　A metal rod fastener with a head and a body threaded to take a nut.

bonding agent　An adhesive used to fasten plies of wood together.

border line　A line enclosing a drawing.

boring　The process of cutting a cylindrical hole in wood.

box nail A slender metal fastener with a point on one end and a flattened head on the other; originally used for nailing boxes together.

brace A crank-shaped tool for holding and turning auger bits; constructed so that turning leverage may be obtained.

bracket A part which projects from a wall or surface to support other objects.

brad A small finishing nail, varying in length from ¼ inch to 1¼ inches.

buck To saw felled trees into shorter cuts, or logs.

buckling Jamming of a board between a circular saw blade and the fence guide.

bullnose plane A small plane for dressing joints or other places which other planes cannot reach; a type of rabbet plane.

burl A swirl in the grain of a board caused by an abnormal growth of the tree.

burlap A coarse material woven from jute or hemp; used in upholstering.

burnisher A tool of hardened and polished steel; used for finishing the edges of scraper blades.

burr A ragged or wiry edge on a piece of metal usually caused by grinding.

butt hinge A door hinge which butts against a closed door edge.

butt joint A joint made by fastening together the ends or edges of two pieces of wood; this is a perpendicular joint.

C clamp A clamp formed like the letter *C*.

cabinet clamp A clamp with a long bar and two adjustable clamping jaws; also called a *bar clamp*.

cabinet hinges General term for a variety of hinges used in cabinet construction.

caliper A tool used to measure the diameter of cylindrical or circular work.

cambium A thin layer which lies between the xylem and the phloem in most woody plants.

cambric A rather stiff cotton fabric with a slightly glazed surface; often used on the underside of upholstered furniture.

cant See *flitch*.

carbide-tip circular saw blade A circular saw blade with a carbide tip on each tooth.

carbohydrate Any of a group of compounds (sugars and starches) made of carbon, hydrogen, and oxygen; a tree food.

carriage A piece of sawmill machinery. It is mounted on wheels and rolls on a metal track carrying a log back and forth past the head-saw as the log is cut into rough lumber.

casein glue Glue made from the curd of milk; available in powdered from (to be mixed with water).

casing nail A slender metal fastener with a point on one end and a shaped head on the other; similar to a finishing nail.

cauls Metal sheets used in making particle board which support the mat of particles before pressing.

cellulose The chief substance in the cell walls of a tree.

center lines Vertical and/or horizontal lines which represent the center of a symmetrical object. They are made up of light long and short dashes.

chamfer A beveled edge or corner.

check A split or defect on the end of a board resulting from a separation of wood fibers.

chest hinge A hinge especially adapted for use on cedar or cedar-lined chests.

chipper Machine with revolving knives used to reduce large wood pieces to chips.

chips Uniform pieces of thin wood, about five eighths inch wide and an inch long.

chisel A woodworking tool with a wedge-shaped cutting edge.

chlorophyll The green coloring matter of plants.

circle A closed curved line in a plane, all points of which are a given distance from a fixed point called the center.

circular saw See *table saw*.

claw hammer A woodworking hammer with a flat driving surface and a pulling claw.

clinching Bending over the pointed ends of nails extending through a board; clinching makes nails hold more securely.

combination blade A circular saw blade with a combination of ripsaw and crosscut-saw teeth; operates on a power-driven saw frame.

combination hinge A combination hinge and lid-support built especially for cedar or cedar-lined chests.

common nail A slender metal fastener with a point on one end and a flattened head on the other; slightly larger in diameter than a box nail.

compass An instrument for scribing circles and curves and for marking distances; also called *dividers*, *compasses*, and *pair of compasses*.

compass saw A handsaw with a small, straight, tapered blade.

concave Hollow; curved inward. Compare *convex*.

coniferous Cone-bearing.

construction The act or art of building; that which is built or the type of building.

container Something used for holding goods or materials.

convex Curved like the outer surface of a sphere or ball. Compare *concave*.

coping saw A narrow saw blade about 6½ inches long, held in a steel bow frame with pins; used for cutting curves.

cordwood Four- to eight-foot logs of small diameter; one of the major sources of raw material for hardboard and particle board plants. Much of these short lengths is cut from *thinnings*.

core The center layer or layers of a piece of plywood. There are two general types of plywood core: the veneer core and the lumber core. Thin sheets of plywood usually have veneer cores, while thick sheets often have lumber cores. A panel which has a lumber core is called *lumber-core plywood*.

corrugated fasteners Small pieces of sheet iron formed with ridges and depressions; used to reinforce certain edge joints.

countersink To enlarge the surface end of a hole for a flat- or oval-head screw so that the screwhead can be recessed.

countersink bit A tool for countersinking.

crack A split in wood which needs repair.

crossband The veneer sheet, or sheets, between the core and the faces of a piece of plywood.

crosscut saw A saw for cutting across the grain.

cruiser A timber estimator; a lumbering occupation.

cubic inch A unit of cubic measurement; a cube one inch long, one inch wide, and one inch high.

curved line A line of which no part is straight.

dado joint A joint made by fitting the end of one board into a groove in another board.

decay The decomposition of wood.

deciduous trees Trees which shed their leaves in the autumn. Most deciduous trees are hardwoods and have broad leaves.

defibering The process by which chips are reduced into fibers or fiber bundles.

density A measure of the weight of a material for a specific volume of the material. Usually expressed as pounds per cubic foot.

dent A groove or blemish in the surface or edge of a board.

depth gage A gage which allows for boring to a desired depth when attached to an auger bit.

diagonal A straight oblique line between the non-adjacent angles of a polygon (a closed figure with straight sides); such a line would divide a rectangle into equal parts.

diameter A straight line from a point on the circumference of a figure or object which passes through the center of the figure or object and extends to another point on the circumference.

diamond-point chisel A narrow-bladed wood-turning chisel with a point shaped for cutting sharp bottom grooves.

die Metal tool with top and bottom which converge toward outfeed end of die, thereby exerting pressure against material being forced through die.

dimension A measurement with respect to length, width, or thickness.

dimension lines The lines on drawings which show the size of an object or some part of the object. They are usually placed between *extension lines*.

dividers A pair of compasses for setting off distances.

double-cut file A file with a double series of teeth crossing each other at an oblique angle.

dowel joint A joint fastened with dowel pins.

dowel pin A cylindrical wooden pin often used as a fastener for reinforcing joints or for aligning boards.

dowel pointer A small tool with a flared end; used to round the ends of dowel pins.

drawknife A two-handled wood-cutting tool with the handles at right angles to the cutting plane.

drilling The process of cutting holes in wood with a drill bit.

dry formed   Process in the making of particle board in which particles are formed into a mat in a dry state rather than from a water slurry.

dry kiln   A heated chamber in which lumber is dried under controlled conditions of temperature, relative himidity, and velocity of air in contact with the lumber.

durability   As applied to wood, durability refers to its lasting qualities or permanence in service with particular reference to decay. Durability may be related directly to an exposure condition.

edger   A machine consisting of several circular saws; used in sawmills to rip lumber, to square it, and to edge it by cutting away the wane.

efficient   Productive without waste.

ellipse   A closed oval curve in a plane.

embossed hardboard   A variety of hardboard that has a decorative pattern imprinted or pressed into its surface.

emery cloth   Cloth to which powdered emery has been glued; usually used for polishing metal.

enamel   An oil paint used as a finishing material; dries with a hard, glossy finish because it contains varnish.

end checking   Small splits which develop in the ends of logs if dried too fast after logging. It also occurs in boards if dried too fast after manufacture.

engineer   A technical specialist in design, construction, and planning in many industrial fields.

expansive bit   A wood-boring bit with an adjustable cutter for drilling holes of different diameters. This bit is designed to cut holes larger than one inch in diameter.

explosion process   Separation of wood fibers by the sudden release of high-pressure steam.

extension lines   The lines in a drawing which extend from the corners of an object to indicate to what part of the drawing the dimension refers. See *dimension lines.*

exterior   A term frequently applied to plywood, bonded with highly resistant adhesives, that is capable of withstanding prolonged exposure to severe service conditions without failure in the glue bonds.

external   On an outer edge; for example, an external cut made by a jig saw on the outer edge of a workpiece.

extruded particle board   A particle board manufactured by forcing a mass of particles coated with a binder through a heated die with the applied pressure parallel to the faces and in the direction of extruding.

face veneer   The veneer sheet on the front side of a plywood panel. It is usually of finer quality than the other layers of the panel. The grain of the face veneer runs at right angles to the grain of the crossband. Compare *back veneer.*

fell   To cut down a tree.

fence   An adjustable metal guide bar. For example, a fence is mounted on the top of a circular-saw table as a guide for ripping.

ferrule   A short metal bushing, usually brass, designed to fit over the end of a chair or table leg.

fiber   Tiny thread-like parts of which wood is made; fibers are composed of lignin and cellulose; they are from one twenty-fifth to one third of an inch long.

figure   The natural design or pattern seen on the surface of wood.

file   A hard steel blade with cutting ridges. Files come in various shapes, sizes, and cuts. They are used to shape and smooth wood or metal.

file cleaner   A brush fitted with short fine wires; used to clean files. Also called *file card.*

filled particle boards   Particle boards having a factory applied coating of filler on one or both faces to prepare the surface for further finishing by printing, lacquering, painting, etc.

fines   Small particles of wood, generally of such a size they will pass through a 20-mesh screen.

finishing orbital sander   See *orbital sander.*

finish nail   A slender nail with a small round head on the unpointed end.

fish glue   A high-quality liquid glue made from the skins of fish.

flakeboard   A composition board consisting essentially of flat, shaving-like flakes of wood bonded together with synthetic resins.

flakes   Specially generated thin flat particles with grain of the wood essentially parallel to the flat surface and with dimensions usually long and wide with respect to the thickness.

flat-head screw A wood-holding screw with a flat head; used in counter surfaces.

flat-platen pressed A method of consolidating and hot pressing a panel product in which the applied pressure is perpendicular to the faces.

flexible steel rule A flexible measuring strip of steel, graduated in inches and fractions of an inch.

flitch A log with two or four slabs cut off so that it is no longer round but flat on two or four sides. It is ready to cut into boards. Also called a *cant*.

floor underlayment A grade of particle board made to close thickness tolerances for use as a leveling layer and to provide a smooth surface under flooring materials.

flute A concave cut, or channel, in a leg or column or other cylindrical object; usually cut on a shaper or a router.

foam rubber A commercial rubber padding widely used in upholstering.

Foerstner bit A wood-boring tool without a feed screw; used to bore holes to any depth without breaking through the wood.

folding rule A collapsible rule used for measuring; usually two feet long.

forest management The application of sound business methods and technical forestry principles to the growing of timber as a crop.

forming machine Equipment used in the wet-process production of hardwood that forms the fibers into a mat.

forming tool A tool which has corrugated cutting edges on a flat surface; resembles a file or a plane.

framing The skeleton of a structure; the act or art of building a frame.

framing square A large, ordinary steel square used by carpenters; it contains guides and scales for determining angles on rafters and other carpentry processes; used to measure, to square lines, and to test large surfaces for wind.

friction catch A metal fastening used on small doors or cabinets to keep them closed.

front view That part of a drawing which shows the front of an object or project.

gain A notch cut out of a piece of wood into which a hinge is fitted.

gang saw A set of evenly-spaced vertical saws which cut *flitches* into several boards of uniform thickness in one operation.

garnet paper An abrasive paper coated with sharp crushed garnet.

gimlet A wood-boring tool composed of a grooved shank with a screw point, and a wooden cross handle.

gimp Cord or braid used for edge-trimming in upholstery.

gimp tack An ornamental tack used for holding upholstery gimp in place.

glide Usually a metal dome which is fastened on the bottom of the leg of a chair or table to enable the piece of furniture to slide easily on the floor.

glue A substance capable of holding materials together by surface attachment. In woodworking it often means a substance capable of forming a strong bond with wood.

gouge A wood-cutting chisel which has a concave cutting edge with either an inside or an outside bevel. Gouges are used for grooving, for shaping edges, and for making models.

grade To sort lumber or logs and classify them according to grade, or quality.

grading rules Quality specifications used in the classification of lumber.

grain The size and arrangement of the cells and pores of the tree. The three principal types of wood (by grain) are fine, medium, and coarse.

graining The process of printing a natural wood grain pattern onto a surface.

graph paper Paper ruled into small squares for drawing, for plotting graphs, and for making diagrams.

green lumber Lumber which has been sawed from timber but has not been seasoned.

grinder A machine used for sharpening and grinding tools or cutting away metal.

gross A quantity: 144, or twelve dozen.

growth rings See *annular rings*.

half-lap joint A lap joint used to connect two pieces end to end in a straight line.

half-surface hinge A hinge in which only one plate is exposed when the door to which it is fastened is closed.

hammer milling A form of grinding in which pieces of material are reduced in size by the action of hammers or knives mounted on a rapidly rotating shaft in the machine.

hand drill A tool designed to hold a drill bit; operated with a crank on a handle.

handsaw A flat crosscut or ripsaw blade with a handle on one end.

hand-screw clamp A clamp made of two parallel jaws and two screws.

hanger bolt A bolt with a thread on one end for a nut, and a screw thread on the other end.

hardboard Panels manufactured from interfelted woody fibers, consolidated under heat and pressure in a hot press to a density of 31 pounds per cubic foot or greater.

hardwoods Porous, close-grained, dense, heavy woods from deciduous trees; oak, hickory, and ash, for example.

hasp A metal strap fastening for a lid or a door which is usually secured by a staple and a pin or padlock.

heartwood The dense, hard, central part of the trunk of a tree. Compare *sapwood*.

heat treat To treat metal, usually steel, by carefully controlled heating and cooling.

heel The end of the saw blade which is directly under the handle.

hemp A tough Asiatic plant fiber used for making cloth, rope, and very sturdy twine.

hexagon A plane figure with six sides and six angles; all sides and angles of a regular hexagon are equal.

hidden line A line on a drawing consisting of short dashes; used to represent a hidden part.

hobby A pastime engaged in for pleasure.

homogeneous boards Particle boards having a uniform mixture of particle sizes throughout.

hone A special stone used for whetting tools. To whet a tool edge.

horizontal Parallel to the horizon, or perpendicular to a vertical line.

hot press Giant, multiple-opening, heated hydraulic press that compacts the wood fiber mat into hardboard or particle board by exerting hundreds of pounds of pressure per square inch at temperatures up to 500 degrees Fahrenheit.

internal On an internal edge; for example, an internal cut made with a jig saw in the center of a workpiece.

intersect To pierce or divide by cutting through or across.

intersection The point at which two or more things meet.

invisible hinge A hinge which is mortised into the adjoining boards of a lid so that the hinge will not be seen when the lid is closed; for example, the hinge on the lid of a writing desk.

invisible line See *hidden line*.

irregular Out of the usual form.

jack plane A general utility plane; used for roughing a board to approximate size.

jig A special device which holds or guides a tool.

jig saw A power-driven, open-throat frame which holds a narrow, thin, short saw blade which operates with an up-and-down cutting motion.

jointer plane A long-bed plane; used to true edges.

kerf The cut made by a saw.

kiln-drying The process of seasoning lumber in a drying room or kiln; faster than air-drying. Abbreviated *KD*.

knot A defect in lumber caused by a branch or limb when the tree was growing.

kraft paper A brownish paper made of sulfate pulp; used for wrapping paper, bags, containers, and various other products where strength is more important than color.

lacquer A spirit varnish, especially that obtained from the sap of an Asiatic sumac; used for finishing.

laminate To bond or glue wood in layers, as in the construction of plywood. The laminated unit is stronger than the original wood itself.

lap joint A joint made by overlapping two boards; dadoes are cut in each, usually half the thickness of the board, so that the joint will fit smoothly.

lateral adjustment The side or crosswise adjustment of a plane iron.

lathe A power-driven machine used for spindle and faceplate turning.

leather Dressed hides of animals.

leftovers Slabs, bark, small pieces of wood, and sawdust which remain after a manufacturing process.

lignin   A substance which, with cellulose, makes up the cell walls of trees; it is the bonding agent between cells.

linear   Pertaining to line measurement; for example, a linear foot.

line symbol   A type of line used in drawings to designate a special meaning.

linseed oil   Oil from flaxseed; used in paints and varnishes.

lubricant   Oil, grease, or other substance used to reduce friction and heat.

lumber   Sawn wood.

lumbering   The business of cutting and getting timber or logs from the forest for lumber.

machinery   Machines in general, or the working parts of a machine.

mallet   A wooden or fiber hammer; used to drive wood chisels.

marking gage   A device for marking lines parallel to the edge of a board.

marking knife   A handle attached to a blade with a cutting edge.

matching   The placing of sheets of veneer to obtain a particular pattern.

mat-formed particle board   A particle board in which the coated particles are formed first into a mat having substantially the same length and width as the finished board before being flat-platen pressed.

medullary rays   See *vascular rays*.

mill file   A single-cut file.

millwork   Generally all building materials made of finished wood in millwork plants or planing mills, including sashes, doors, frames, and other items of exterior and interior trim.

miter box   A device used to hold the saw at the proper angle in cutting edges for miter joints.

miter joint   A joint made by fastening together two pieces of wood whose ends have been cut at an angle; usually a perpendicular joint.

mohair   An upholstery covering fabric made of Angora goat hair.

mortise   A space, usually rectangular, cut into a piece of wood to receive another piece.

mortise-and-tenon joint   A joint made by fitting a tenon, or projecting tongue, of one piece into a mortise, or cavity, in another piece.

moss   Stuffing material used in upholstery.

multi-layered boards   Particle boards having particles of different sizes or shapes in different areas of their cross section. Commonly fine particles or very thin flakes are used on the surfaces of the boards to provide a high degree of smoothness.

multiple sawing   Making the same cut in a number of boards simultaneously. Also called *gang cutting* or *gang sawing*.

multiview drawing   Graphic presentation of an object in several views, such as front, top, and right end; sometimes called *orthographic drawing*.

muslin   A coarse cotton cloth used for holding down layers of upholstering materials.

nail   A slender metal fastener; usually one end is pointed and the other has a head.

nail set   A short steel rod with one end tapered and slightly cupped to fit a nailhead; used to set the nailhead below the surface of the wood.

nibs   The cutting points of an auger bit.

nick   A depression or a break made in cutting an edge.

object lines   Fairly heavy lines which show the visible portion of an object on a drawing.

obtuse angle   An angle greater than 90 degrees and less than 180 degrees.

octagon   A plane figure with eight sides and eight angles; all sides and angles of a regular octagon are equal.

oil stain   An oil-base stain; used to color wood surfaces.

oilstone   A smooth abrasive stone; used for sharpening tools.

open defect   Any irregularity such as checks, splits, open joints, cracks, knot holes, or loose knots that interrupts the smooth continuity of the veneer.

orbital sander   A power-driven portable sanding machine equipped with an abrasive pad. The name *orbital* comes from the circular, or orbital, motion of the base pad.

orthographic drawing   See *multiview drawing*.

oval-head screw   A wood-holding screw with a slightly oval head; the wood should be countersunk to take the screwhead.

overlaid particle boards Particle boards having factory applied overlays which may be resin treated papers, high or low pressure decorative plastic laminates, plastic films, hardboard, hardwood veneers, etc.

paint A pigment or color mixed with oil and other ingredients; used for coating wood.

panel A sheet or strip of molded wood, such as a plywood panel.

parallel lines Lines extending in the same direction which are equidistant at all points.

pare To trim a surface or an edge by cutting or shaving off; compare *scrape*.

particle board A generic term for a panel manufactured from lignocellulosic materials (usually wood) primarily in the form of discrete pieces or particles, as distinguished from fibers, combined with a synthetic resin or other suitable binder and bonded together under heat and pressure in a hot-press by a process in which the entire inter-particle bond is created by the added binder.

particle board corestock Common name given to a particle board manufactured for use as a core for overlaying.

particles The aggregate component of particle board; manufactured by mechanical means from wood, including all small subdivisions of wood. Particle size may be measured by the screen mesh that permits passage of the particles and another screen upon which they are retained, or by the measured dimensions, as for flakes.

parting tool A wood-turning tool with a narrow blade; used for cutting grooves and recesses and for cutting away surplus wood.

penny A term used to indicate nail size, as: a 10-penny nail. Abbreviated *d*.

Phillips-head screw A wood-holding screw with a cross-shaped slot; may have a flat, round, or oval head.

phloem Complex tissue which, together with xylem, forms part of the vascular, or conducting, tissue of trees. The phloem carries the food (sugars and protein) manufactured by the tree.

pictorial Illustrated as a picture.

pierce To perforate or cut into.

pilot hole A hole drilled in a piece of wood as a guide for a screw. The diameter of the hole is smaller than the body of the screw so the screw may cut its own threads as it is driven into the wood.

pith The loose, spongy tissue occupying the center of a tree.

plain-sawing Cutting parallel to the squared side of a log.

plane A hand tool for smoothing or shaping boards.

plane forming tool A forming tool which resembles a plane.

plane iron The cutting blade of a plane.

planer A power-driven machine for dressing or planing the surfaces of boards.

planer mill shavings Shavings produced in lumber planing mills.

plastic resin Urea formaldehyde powder mixed with water to make glue; used mostly for exterior or weather-exposed surfaces.

platens Any flat plates, especially the flat plates in the hot-press which compress the mats into particle boards.

ply A layer, or thickness, of plywood; see *veneer*.

plywood A wood material made of three or more plies, or layers, joined with glue. Usually each ply is laid with its grain at rights angles to the grain of the adjoining plies.

polyvinyl resin A fast-setting liquid glue.

production The act or process of making something. That which is made; a product.

project A task or problem engaged in by the student or hobbyist; the object constructed.

protractor A tool for measuring and laying off angles; used in drawing.

pry To raise, move, or pull apart with a pry, or lever.

pulley A small wheel used with a rope, chain, or belt to increase applied force and to change the direction and point of application of the force.

pulp Wood fiber ground up and mixed with water for making paper and rayon.

pumice Light volcanic glass; generally used for rubbing down or polishing finished surfaces.

push drill A ratchet tool which holds wood-drilling bits.

push stick A wooden safety device; used to push and guide a narrow board through a woodworking machine.

quartersawing Sawing a log into quarters by cuts made parallel with the vascular rays of the log.

rabbet A groove cut on the edge or face of a board; especially as part of rabbet joint.

rabbet To cut a rabbet in a board; to join two edges in a rabbet joint.

rabbet joint A joint made by fastening two rabbeted pieces together.

rabbet plane A plane designed for cutting grooves in wood, or for trimming places which are too small for most planes.

radius The given distance from the center of a circle to its circumference. A straight line drawn from the center of a circle to a point on its circumference.

rafters Parallel ribs or beams which support a roof; the rafters extend from the ridgepole to the tops of the walls. See *ridgepole.*

rail The top horizontal member between the legs of a bench or table; also referred to as the *apron.*

regulator A straight steel tool, ranging from six to twelve inches in length; one end is flattened for easy handling and the other end is tapered to a point; used to adjust upholstery stuffing.

relief cuts Preliminary band-saw cuts made on a piece of stock to enable the saw to cut a sharper curve.

resaw To reduce the thickness of boards, planks, slabs, and other material by cutting into two or more thinner pieces.

resin Synthetic binder material used to bond wood particles together to form particle boards.

resin canal A tube-like space between tree cells, which contains resin secreted by the surrounding cells.

resin-coated nail A nail to which a chemical coating has been added for greater holding power.

resorcinal resin Glue made by mixing liquid resin with a catalyst; the ingredients are packaged in a double container to be mixed just before use.

revolutions per minute The unit of measure for the rate of speed of machines; abbreviated *rpm.*

ridgepole The horizontal beam at the highest part of a roof; it supports one end of each rafter.

right angle An angle of 90 degrees formed by the intersection of two perpendicular lines.

ring, annual The annual growth layer as viewed on a cross-section of a stem, branch, or root.

rip To saw or split lumber with the grain.

ripsaw A saw for cutting wood with the grain.

rotary cut Veneer obtained by rotating a log against a cutting knife in such a way that a continuous sheet of veneer is unrolled spirally from the log.

rottenstone Decomposed limestone in powder form. Rottenstone is used for polishing finished surfaces.

rough Not smooth; irregularities or ridges on the surface.

round-head screw A wood-holding screw with a round head.

roundnose chisel A wood-turning tool; used for rough turning and for cutting grooves and coves.

router A portable electric tool which uses numerous types of cutters to produce intricate joints, decorative cuts, and cuts for inlays.

rubbing oil A lubricant with a petroleum or a paraffin base; used with pumice or rottenstone to make a rubbing paste.

rub collar A metal disk fitted on a shaper spindle to control the depth of the cut.

saber saw The name sometimes given the portable power-driven jig saw.

sandpaper Paper coated on one side with sharp grated flint or quartz crystals.

sapwood The younger wood beneath the bark, which carries sap from the roots to the leaves of trees. Compare *heartwood.*

saw clamp A vise or clamp made especially for holding the saw blade stationary while the teeth are being set and sharpened.

sawhorse A flat trestle used by carpenters and cabinetmakers as a support for sawing lumber.

sawlogs Logs large enough to be made into lumber.

sawmill A plant at which logs are sawed into salable products. The sawmill includes all the machinery and buildings necessary for the operation of the plant.

saw set A tool used to give the proper set to saw teeth.

sawtimber Trees large enough to be harvested for sawlogs.

saw tooth The cutting edge of a saw blade.

scale A wooden straightedge with graduated and numbered spaces; used by draftsmen for measuring and laying off distances.

scale In drawing, the proportional relationship between two sets of dimensions. For example, one foot in the dimensions of an object may be represented by one inch in the dimensions on a drawing of that object.

scarfing The beveled cutting of the ends of plywood panels preparatory to forming a glued joint (scarf joint) between two panels.

scrape To smooth wood by rubbing the surface with a sharp-bladed tool. Compare *pare*.

scraper A flat blade for smoothing wood surfaces.

screw A tapered, round metal shaft with a point on one end, a slotted head on the other, and a continuous spiral rib.

screwdriver A rod of steel flattened on one end to fit a screwhead slot.

scribe To mark a line with the point of an awl or knife.

scroll saw See *coping saw* and *jig saw*.

season To dry lumber, either in the open air or in a kiln.

seasoned lumber Boards which have been sawed from timber and seasoned in the air or in a kiln.

set To bend; especially to bend the teeth of a saw in order to produce a saw cut, or kerf, which is wider than the thickness of the saw blade.

shank hole A drilled hole large enough to accommodate the shank of a screw.

shaving A thin slice or strip or wood pared off with a knife, or other cutting instrument, in which the cut may be either across, parallel to or at an angle to the axis of the fibers.

shearing Cutting or slicing obliquely. Compare *pare*.

shellac A mixture of lac resin and alcohol; used as a wood filler and finish.

silex Powdered silica; used as a filler for wood and paints.

single-cut file A file with parallel lines of teeth running diagonally across the face in one direction only.

skew chisel A wood-turning tool with a cutting edge which is not at right angles to its sides; used to make shearing cuts.

skidding Refers to the process of moving logs from where they are cut to a central loading spot where they are collected and transported to the mill. Skidding is usually done by dragging the log by mechanical or animal power.

slabbed Refers to the process of sawing off the outer surfaces of the log, including the bark if it has not been removed.

slicing cut A sliding cut used in producing thin pieces of veneer.

sliding bevel See *bevel*.

slim taper file A long slender file, usually triangular in shape; used often for sharpening saw teeth.

slip seat An upholstered seat with a removable frame.

slip stone A small wedge-shaped oilstone; used principally for whetting turning tools and gouges.

sloyd knife A cutting knife similar to that used in the Swedish sloyd system of woodworking.

smoothing plane A short-bed plane, usually not over eight or nine inches long. This plane is used for final smoothing of boards.

socket chisel A woodworker's chisel with a handle driven into a socket at the upper end of the shank.

soffit The underside of a building member. Usually used to describe the covering of the underside of roof overhangs.

softwood Long-fibered, nonporous wood from coniferous trees; spruce, pine, and redwood, for example.

Sound 1 Side A grade of plywood panel; such a panel has one surface free of defects.

Sound 2 Sides A grade of plywood panel; such a panel has both surfaces free of defects.

spar varnish A waterproof, heat-resistant finish; used on boats and exterior wood surfaces.

species A distinct sort or kind of tree. A class of trees having qualities in common.

spindle The vertical steel rod on a shaper, to which is fastened a cutter head.

spirit stain An aniline dye mixed with alcohol; used to color wood.

splinter Particles of nearly square or rectangular cross section with a length (parallel to the grain of the wood) at least four times the thickness of the particle.

spokeshave A double-handled plane used for dressing concave and convex edges on wood.

springwood That part of the yearly growth of the wood of a tree which appears in the first part of the growing season. Compare *summerwood*.

square A plane figure with four equal sides and four right angles; the opposite sides of a square are parallel.

square To plane all faces and edges of a board to make them flat, smooth, and at right angles to each other.

square See *framing square*; *try square*.

square foot An area equivalent to 144 square inches. A unit of measurement for surfaces; generally applied to plywood.

stairs The complete set of steps between two floors of a building.

standard lumber grades Systems of classifications of lumber based on quality. A considerable degree of uniformity between the different standards of various grading associations is maintained through the use of American Lumber Standards as a recognized guide.

steel square See *framing square*.

steel wool Fine threads of steel matted together; used as an abrasive.

stick shellac Shellac in stick form; the sticks can be heated to fill cracks and scratches.

straight-shank drill A drill for cutting holes to a specific diameter. It has a straight shank and no handle.

student's plan sheet A paper showing plans and estimates for a student project. It may include a dimensioned working drawing, a bill of materials, and an order of procedure for the project the student plans to make.

summerwood The part of the annular ring which appears in the second part of the growing season. Compare *springwood*.

surface A face of a board; the exterior of an object.

Surfaced 4 Sides The term applied to a board which has been planed or surfaced on two faces, or surfaces, and two edges. Usually applied to legs or square stock and abbreviated *S4S*.

Surfaced 2 Sides The term applied to a board which has been planed or surfaced on both faces, or surfaces. Abbreviated *S2S*.

surface hinge Two plates of metal connected by a pin. The parts of a surface hinge are fully exposed when the door to which it is attached is closed.

sustained yield Management of a forest so that the growth in the sense of economic increment over any given period will be equivalent to the volume removed in the harvest for that period.

table saw A power-driven saw built into a table or frame. Also called a *circular saw*.

tacks Small, short, sharp-pointed nails with broad, flat heads; used in upholstering.

tang chisel A wood chisel, the end of which is driven into the handle.

taper To narrow gradually toward one end.

tapestry A heavy ornamental upholstery fabric; used as the final covering.

temper The degree of hardness or toughness of steel. A special temper is required to produce a desirable edge for cutting and scraping.

tempered hardboard Hardboard made by adding small quantities of special oils or resins to standard hardboard, which is then heat-treated — or "tempered" — to increase stiffness, strength, moisture resistance, and abrasion resistance and to enhance other properties.

template A pattern or guide.

tenon A tongue extending from the end of a board; this projection is usually cut and trimmed to fit a rectangular hole called a *mortise*.

thinnings Smaller trees removed from a stand of growing timber in order to provide better growth conditions for the other trees which remain for a later harvest.

timber Trees suitable for cutting and use as construction materials. Also, wood cut into logs or into large pieces of five inches or more in the least dimension.

toenailing Driving nails so that they cross each other in a slanting direction.

tongue A projecting rib cut on the edge of a board which fits a corresponding groove on the edge of another board.

tongue The narrow or short side of a steel square.

tool An instrument for doing work.

top view The view on a drawing which shows an object as seen from a viewpoint directly above it.

tracing A copy of an original drawing made on transparent material for reproduction in quantity.

trammel points The heads of a beam compass. The trammel points slide along a straight bar. The beam compass is used to scribe arcs and circles too large to be made by an ordinary compass.

transpiration The process of evaporation of water through leaf pores.

tree farm An area of privately owned, taxpaying forest land which is producing repeated crops of wood under the standards of the American Tree Farm System. It is usually marked by a green and white sign, "Member American Tree Farm System."

trestle A sawhorse with a wide top and a stuffed roll around the edges; used in upholstering.

triangle A plane figure with three sides and three angles.

trim Something which ornaments the final appearance of an object.

true Fitted or formed accurately.

try square A measuring device used to test squareness and to lay off right angles.

turpentine A paint, enamel, and varnish thinner. The main sources of turpentine are the slash and longleaf pines.

twine A thread or string made of flax fiber or hemp; used in upholstering.

twist drill A drill with two spiral grooves extending along its usable length.

tyloses Growths of certain cells in trees which fill and block nearby vascular canals.

upholstery Fabric covering for furniture.

upholstery springs The metal supports in certain types of furniture seats. Two types are coil and no-sag springs.

utilization The process of manufacturing trees into useful products.

varnish A mixture of certain resins in oil or alcohol; used for producing a hard-finish surface on wood.

vascular rays Ribbon-like, radial bands of conducting tissue in trees which pass from the xylem through the cambium and the phloem.

velour An upholstery covering fabric with a velvet-like finish.

veneer A thin layer of fine wood glued to an inferior wood to produce a superior grain effect. Also, any layer of plywood.

vertical Perpendicular to the horizon; upright.

vise A clamp with two jaws and a tightening device; used to hold boards stationary while they are being worked on.

vise dog A small adjustable piece of metal in the movable part of a bench vise; used as an aid in holding boards flat on the bench.

wane A lumber defect, characterized by the bark or the rounded surface of the tree remaining on the lumber.

water glass Sodium silicate; an ingredient used to make wood fire resistant.

water resistant A term frequently applied to plywood which has been bonded with moderately resistant adhesives; such plywood is capable of withstanding limited exposure to water, or to severe conditions, without failure in the glue bonds.

water stain A coloring for wood surfaces made of aniline dye powder mixed with hot water.

wax Any of a class of substances of plant or animal origin made into a liquid or paste and used as a preservative and protection for finished surfaces.

webbing A jute fiber made into a close-woven tape; used as an upholstery support on frames.

webbing stretcher A wooden tool with sharp steel teeth on one end and a pad on the other; used for stretching webbing across upholstery frames.

427

wetlap In making hardboard, the formed fiber board, with most of the moisture removed, prior to its entry into the hot press.

wet process Manufacture of hardboard using the principle of water suspension in the forming of the fibers into a mat.

whet To sharpen the cutting edge of a tool by rubbing it on an oilstone.

whittle To pare or cut off pieces of wood with a knife.

wind A twisting warp in a board.

wipe-on finish A popular protective finish for wood surfaces, wiped on with a cloth or sponge.

wooden button A plug used to fill a hole where a screw is recessed.

wood fiber A long, slender, thick-walled cell in wood.

wood filler A mixture of ground silex and linseed oil, japan drier, or turpentine; used for filling pores of open-grained wood.

wood rays See *xylem ray*.

wood residue Slabs, edgings, trimmings, and small pieces of wood left over from the saw-milling or veneer-manufacturing operation.

working drawing A drawing which contains all views, dimensions, and instructions needed for completing an object or a project.

working face The flat surface of a board which has been planed smooth, squared, and then used as a basis for squaring the other surfaces.

xylem Complex tissue which, together with phloem, forms part of the vascular, or conducting, tissue of trees. The xylem carries mainly water and dissolved inorganic substances. It also serves as support tissue.

xylem ray The part of a vascular ray located in the xylem.

zigzag rule A folding rule made in short sections; zigzag rules vary in length from two to eight feet. The name indicates the manner in which the rule opens and closes.

Index